ALSO BY WARREN G. HARRIS

SOPHIA LOREN

&

A BIOGRAPHY

WARREN G. HARRIS

SIMON & SCHUSTER

SIMON & SCHUSTER
Rockefeller Center
1230 Avenue of the Americas
New York, NY 10020

Copyright © 1998 by Warren G. Harris

All rights reserved,
including the right of reproduction
in whole or in part in any form.

SIMON & SCHUSTER and colophon are registered trademarks
of Simon & Schuster Inc.

Designed by Karolina Harris
Photo section designed by Liney Li
Manufactured in the United States of America

10 9 8 7 6 5 4 3 2 1

Library of Congress Cataloging-in-Publication Data
Harris, Warren G.
Sophia Loren : a biography / Warren G. Harris.
p. cm.
Filmography: p.
Includes bibliographical references and index.
1. Loren, Sophia, 1934– . 2. Motion picture actors and actresses—Italy—Biography. I. Title.
PN2688.L65H37   1998   97–36255   CIP
791.43'028'092—dc21 [B]
ISBN 0-684-80273-2

Unless otherwise credited, photographs provided by Archive Photos™.

FOR KYLE RUSSELL WRAGE,

"THE BEST IS YET TO COME"

CONTENTS

BABY No. 19

S H E was an illegitimate child, born in the charity ward of the Queen Margherita Clinic in Rome, on September 20, 1934, the twelfth year of Italy's fascist statehood. Her naming was delayed. The nursery listed her as No. 19 in its current inventory of bastards. If her unmarried mother couldn't provide a decent home for her, she would be put up for adoption or sent to be raised in an orphanage. Italians were expected to observe the strict moral principles of Roman Catholicism, the official state religion. In the Catholic view, any woman giving birth out of wedlock had no legal rights over her child.

The mother of No. 19 was Romilda Villani. The father, who had yet to identify himself as such, was Riccardo Scicolone. They were involved in a frenzied affair that lasted about six weeks, no longer than it took for two total strangers to meet and become lovers, conceive a child, and then split over differences about their future.

Born in Rome in 1907, Riccardo belonged to a comfortable bourgeois family with ancestral ties to the noble Scicolones of Murillo in medieval Sicily. As a boy, he dreamed of becoming an engineer and building magnificent *palazzi,* but while attending college during the reckless 1920s, he got caught up in Rome's *dolce vita* and never earned enough credits for a degree. When his father died in 1929, Riccardo also lost his family allowance and had to get a job, winding up as an engineering assistant in one of the state railway's many new construction projects.

He wasn't earning much, but enough to support his favorite pastime—pursuing women. He had an excellent record of success, due more to his charm and persuasive powers than to his looks. Tall and slenderly built, he was not handsome, with a roundish face, beaked nose, and full lips. But he dressed well and seemed the perfect gentleman that many women fancy.

Riccardo was especially attracted to younger women with curvaceous figures, long legs, and sultry looks. Seven years his junior, Romilda Villani more than filled those requirements. She bore a striking resemblance to cinema goddess Greta Garbo. Though she was nine years younger than Garbo and had darker, reddish-brown hair, people often stopped her on the street and asked for an autograph.

Romilda came from Pozzuoli, a small coastal town near Naples in the south, the most impoverished and backward region of Italy. Both sides of her family tree, the Villanis and the Pertegnazzas, were never more than humble laboring class, but Romilda early showed musical talent and seemed destined for a better future. She learned to play the piano in school, won a scholarship to the Naples Conservatory of Music, and at sixteen received certification to give private lessons.

She hoped ultimately to perform on the concert stage, but as those Garbo looks ripened, her ambition swerved in another direction. So many people told her that she could be a movie star that she started to believe it. At seventeen, she decided to enter a beauty contest being held in Naples. The Italian affiliate of Metro-Goldwyn-Mayer was conducting a countrywide search for "Garbo's Double," to hype the star's first talkie, *Anna Christie*. The grand prize was a free trip to Hollywood, plus an MGM screen test that could lead to a studio contract.

Romilda won easily in Naples and qualified for the national finals when the contests in other cities were over. Whether she would have won the grand prize and gone on to Hollywood stardom is anybody's guess, but her strict Catholic mother was horrified by the prospect and insisted that she withdraw.

Luisa Villani would never permit her daughter to travel abroad without coming along as chaperone, which was impossible for a woman with a husband and other children to take care of. Furthermore, like most Italians, Luisa lived in terror of the Sicilian Mafia, the Neapolitan Camorra, and other secret societies that reached all over the world. She believed that if Romilda became a big star in America, a jealous rival might arrange for a branch of the Mafia to murder her. That supposedly was the fate of Italy's very own Rudolph Valentino, although the official medical reports attributed his sudden death in New York in 1926 to complications from an emergency operation for a perforated ulcer.

None of Romilda's pleading could change her mother's mind. "It was such a blow that I left home, in anger and disappointment," she recalled. "I went to Rome intending to have a career. Instead, I met Riccardo Scicolone and had a baby."

Romilda actually arrived in Rome a full year before meeting Riccardo. She apparently did make the rounds of the Rome studios. A photo exists of Romilda, wearing a Garboish beret and raincoat, waiting to be screentested for a 1932 low-budget effort entitled *Giovinezza eroica* (*Heroic Youth*). But she didn't get the job, and the movie itself turned out so badly that it never received distribution. Whether she supported herself by teaching piano or by other means is unknown, but her activities during this year would later be the subject of rumors.

It wasn't until a chilly evening in November 1933 that Romilda Villani and Riccardo Scicolone first met. He spotted her walking on the Via Cola di Rienzo, on the Vatican side of the Tiber, and followed her into town as far as the Piazza del Popolo before making a pass.

Romilda agreed to join him for an espresso at a bar on the corner. When they got to talking, Riccardo claimed to know several movie producers at the Rome studios who might be able to give her work. Not the most original of pickup lines, but it worked rapidly, if not instantly, on Romilda. "We met a few times after that, and then we went to bed together," she remembered.

They were soon shacked up in a cheap *pensione* on the Piazza di Spagna. Years later, in a memoir, Scicolone wrote: "To our enamored eyes, our tiny room seemed a palace. Then, in the midst of winter, our days of carefree, romantic love ended when Romilda realized she was pregnant. We were shocked into reality and forced to confront the precariousness of our situation. I was about to start a new job as a sales representative for a publishing house, working on a commission basis. My first earnings would be modest and irregular, hardly enough to support a family."

But that wasn't the whole truth. Riccardo really had no desire to marry anyone. He was a chaser, not a nester. As soon as Romilda started making demands, he fell out of love very quickly. When she rejected his suggestion of an abortion, he fled. She didn't see him again until he turned up at the Queen Margherita Clinic the day after their daughter's birth.

What drove him there was Luisa Villani, who since learning of her daughter's pregnancy had been bombarding him with threats of legal action and ecclesiastical intervention. Scicolone wasn't hard to locate, having moved back to his family's apartment in the old quarter of Rome near the Piazza Venezia. In Italy, single adults traditionally resided at home; even after marrying, many stayed on with their spouses and children.

Riccardo hadn't changed his mind about marrying Romilda, but her mother shamed him into taking some responsibility. He started by declaring himself the father of No. 19 and signing papers that gave her the right to use his name. From now on, she would also carry his mother's Christian name and be known as Sofia Scicolone. Devoted Italian sons always named their firstborn child for one of their parents.

Romilda couldn't have been happier. With "father unknown" on the birth certificate, her daughter would have been a social outcast, deprived even of an education in the state-financed, Catholic school system.

Riccardo's action also raised Romilda's hopes of eventually becoming Mrs. Scicolone. He planned on their moving in with the rest of the Scicolones—his widowed mother and his four unmarried brothers—but the matriarch ruled otherwise. She would never permit his whore and her bastard to cross the threshold. Rejected by Mrs. Scicolone, Riccardo and Romilda moved back to their former love nest in the *pensione* in Piazza di Spagna.

As future beauties sometimes are, Sofia Scicolone was an ugly baby. The ingredients were there, but not yet in the right proportions. Her eyes were too big for her head, and she seemed to have inherited her father's large nose and fleshy lips. There was nothing to suggest, either, that her mother might have been Greta Garbo.

Since Riccardo had deserted Romilda when she became pregnant, it seemed unlikely that he would hang around long once his guilty conscience eased. He wanted neither a wife nor a family. He did need a sex partner, but Romilda had postnatal resistance to everything but breast-feeding Sofia and trying to regain her own strength. They spent most of their time quarreling. Romilda wouldn't give up on the marriage issue or complaining about Riccardo's low wages, which barely covered their room and board.

Riccardo's favorite excuse for not marrying Romilda was that he'd never been confirmed, a sacrament required for marriage in the Roman Catholic faith. One day, when he couldn't take any more of her ranting and raving, he finally agreed to apply at St. Peter's in Vatican City. Years later he told a wild story of being assigned to a priest who was newly posted to the Vatican from South America and did not speak Italian.

"He expressed himself in Latin and I tried to understand him," Scicolone recalled. "Not only did we not understand each other, but he became more and more unfriendly toward me. When I started my confession, he became angry to a point where he finally left me in the lurch, uttering incomprehensible words and glaring at me with disgust before disappearing into the sacristy."

If Riccardo confessed everything about Romilda and the baby, the priest's reaction suggests a much better comprehension than he thought. Why Riccardo didn't go to another priest is anybody's guess, but he just gave up and went home with his excuse for not marrying Romilda still intact.

Riccardo worked for a publisher of fascist propaganda. Unfortunately, there wasn't much demand for such books and pamphlets, which meant that his commissions were near zero. The failure of the Mussolini government to keep Italy out of the world economic depression had everybody grumbling.

In her dissatisfaction with their situation, Romilda was pushing Riccardo to the breaking point, he claimed. "She had a rotten disposition. She insulted me with foul language and compared me to a rat from the sewer. As a wife, she would have been my scold. I became convinced that marriage would have been a mistake that we would have paid for all our lives," he recalled.

Meanwhile, baby Sofia seemed to be suffering from malnutrition. Romilda had developed a tendency to constipation and was using a homemade remedy that Riccardo obtained from his mother. In view of Mrs. Scicolone's hostility toward Romilda and Sofia, it's possible that she took advantage of Romilda. In any case, the purgative also affected the nursing mother's milk supply and eventually dried it up completely. At six weeks old, Sofia looked like skin wrapped around bones.

Riccardo couldn't bear hanging around any longer. Without telling Romilda, he arranged a job transfer to the publisher's office in Milan, 350 miles to the north of Rome, and deserted again.

Romilda had to decide whether to remain in Rome or to return to Pozzuoli, where she expected a hostile reception. While Luisa Villani had tried her best to persuade Riccardo to marry Romilda, she was also terribly disapproving of her daughter's indiscretions and had yet to show any signs of acceptance or forgiveness.

Baby or not, Romilda still dreamed of a career, so Rome seemed preferable for the moment. But she had no money and would have to find a job, until she could pay the back rent and get a bit ahead. She persuaded the landlady to extend her credit and also to take care of Sofia while she was out looking for work.

Unluckily, the well-meaning landlady tried to fatten up Sofia by feeding her a puree of lentils and stewed tomatoes, which led to a severe attack of gastroenteritis. When Romilda came home and found Sofia screaming and feverish, she wrapped her in a blanket and rushed her to the clinic where she had been born. The doctor on duty said there wasn't anything that could be done medically, but that the baby should recover if she was restricted to frequent feedings of mother's milk. If she became too dehydrated, she could suffer brain damage or even die. Romilda, however, was still unable to nurse Sofia.

Abandoned by her lover and rejected by his family, Romilda had no one in Rome to help her. As an unmarried mother, she knew she had no chance of getting state or Church assistance. Her only hope was to take Sofia home to Pozzuoli and pray that her family wouldn't turn them away.

In Pozzuoli, Romilda headed straight for the Villani apartment on the Via Solfatara. The family was too poor to own a telephone, so they weren't expecting her. When Romilda walked in carrying the sick baby in her arms, her parents were too stunned to order her to leave. Mama Luisa rushed over to embrace them. Papa Domenico, who'd been sipping a glass of wine, raised it and proposed a toast to his first grandchild.

When Romilda sobbed out the story of her dried-up milk supply, Luisa wondered why she hadn't resorted to a deficient mother's best friend—a wet nurse? There was one in the district named Zaranella, whose breasts must have suckled a veritable army of babies over the years.

Luisa hurried off to make arrangements, which proved more expensive than she anticipated. Besides a fee of fifty lire per month (equivalent to about two dollars then), Zaranella demanded meat—and lots of it—to fuel her milk factory. The Villanis were forced to go on a vegetarian diet. After providing for Zaranella, they couldn't afford meat for their own table.

Many years later, after her suckling had grown into an Oscar-winning movie star, the long-retired Zaranella emerged to speak to a reporter about her experience: "Sofia was the ugliest child I ever saw in my life. She was so ugly that I'm sure that no one else would have wanted to give her milk. It was my milk that made Sofia beautiful and talented, but she's never acknowledged me. I gave milk to hundreds of children, but none of them drank as much as Sofia. Her mother gave me fifty lire a month, but Sofia drank at least a hundred lire worth of milk. *Madonna mia!*"

Her former charge scoffed at Zaranella's claims: "Okay, she took me to her breast, and I'm grateful to her. But she used to tell everybody I looked like a rat. Well, it shows even rats have a chance in life! I wouldn't have cared if she said she saved my life, which is true. But to say that because of her milk she gave me my looks, my body, and my abilities is ridiculous. Everything, I promise, came from my parents."

SOFIA TOOTHPICK

✍

W H I L E Rome was Sofia Scicolone's birthplace, Pozzuoli very early became her true home and shaped her character. Living in the outskirts of Naples, the capital of the region known as Campania, she grew up in a culture radically different from the rest of Italy. Neapolitans spoke a pungent dialect that baffled outsiders. Though the majority were poor slum-dwellers, they survived on cunning or shady dealings, enjoyed life to the hilt, and believed absolutely in the supernatural world.

Sophia Loren would be a typical Neapolitan in that respect. "I always wear something red—even if it's sometimes out of sight—and carry a small red cloth packet containing rock salt. Broken mirrors, spilled salt, black cats—all these things are bad," she once said. "I am more than superstitious. I am a witch." Perhaps she is, although nothing happened in her youth to suggest it.

As a tot, she had slight contact with Naples itself, but Pozzuoli was close enough and had the same heartbeat. The townspeople also spoke a dialect that was even rougher than the Neapolitan. It could be a severe handicap to social acceptance if one wanted a life beyond the region, but it was the language that Sofia learned, and all that she spoke until she became aware, much later, that it caused a social problem.

Situated slightly to the northwest of Naples, Pozzuoli is the nearest mainland port to the island of Ischia and also part of the Burning Fields (Campi Flegrei), a volcanic area of ancient history and classical mythology. The Romans established a trading port there in 194 B.C., but the Greeks had been there before them, frequently dropping anchor in the area for rest and relaxation when they were masters of the Mediterranean.

Two of the most fiendish of the Roman emperors, Nero and Caligula, built seaside villas in the vicinity. Pozzuoli has one of the finest ruins of ancient architecture in all of Italy, the Anfiteatro Flavio, built at the end of the first century A.D. to accommodate 40,000 spectators. The amphitheater's wing portions, where animals were caged, gladiators made ready, and Christian martyrs were jailed, survived the centuries in good condition. In A.D. 305, Gennaro, the patron saint of Naples, was thrown to the lions in the arena. When they rejected him, he was beheaded. Nineteen centuries later, a relic of his dried blood is said to liquefy during the twice yearly Festival of San Gennaro in Naples.

A tourist attraction today, Pozzuoli was then just another drowsy coastal town of sea-washed pink buildings with green shutters on the windows. The men were fishermen or factory workers. The best-known product was "Pozzuolana," a cement made from volcanic ash.

The Villani apartment at 5 Via Solfatara was on the second and top floor, above a vinegar distillery. Luisa Villani always had something simmering on the stove that would mask the vinegar fumes that seeped through the floorboards. But when the windows were open, nothing could keep out the stench of the volcano that loomed over the town. While Solfatara hadn't erupted since 1198, the bubbling hot mud from its springs was a constant reminder that it still could.

Baby Sofia became the seventh member of the household, but under a new name. Grandma Luisa dubbed her "Lella," so that nobody would have to be reminded of the child's hated Scicolone namesake. For the rest of her life, she was never called anything but Lella by her closest kin, though the name's origin remained a mystery to her. But her grandmother might have simply made it up from *ella,* the Italian pronoun for "she."

Also living in the apartment were Romilda's three siblings, Dora, Guido, and Mario. The apartment had two bedrooms, living room, dining room, and kitchen. The two brothers shared one bedroom, the rest of the family bunked in the second. Dora shared an enormous four-poster with her parents. Romilda had a much smaller bed for herself and Sofia. Such arrangements were normal for poor families in those days.

Until bedtime, daily life revolved around the kitchen and dining room. The living room, which Neapolitans traditionally reserved for entertaining company, was rarely used. Domenico Villani and his two sons worked in the Ansaldo munitions factory, but came home for lunch and the afternoon siesta.

Mama Luisa started cooking at five in the morning. A huge pot of bread-and-bean soup would serve for both breakfast and midday. In the evening, she prepared a more substantial soup of pasta and vegetables, with fish added on Fridays. Meat, when it was no longer requisitioned by Sofia's wet nurse, was saved for Sunday's "sacred stew," doled out when the family returned from Mass at the Church of the Madonna del Carmine.

By the time of her first birthday in September 1935, Sofia's health had improved but not enough for her mother to be overly optimistic. "She was such a skinny child," Romilda Villani recalled. "I'd cry at night from looking at her thin little arms. I thought she'd surely die before she was thirteen, the age of confirmation."

Meanwhile, things were happening around Sofia that were beyond an infant's comprehension but would cause trauma and suffering in a few years' time. Determined to expand Italy's colonies in Africa, Mussolini had dispatched almost a million troops to Italian Somaliland and was about to invade neighboring Ethiopia. Although Italy was victorious, it became one of the worst cases of bloodshed in the history of warfare, with over 500,000 Ethiopian soldiers and civilians killed. Fascist Italy, which up to then had been accepted in the world community, was immediately condemned by the League of Nations and driven closer to its only supporter, Nazi Germany. In 1936 Mussolini and Hitler banded together to supply military aid to Franco's Fascist rebellion in Spain. In November of that year, Italy and Germany formed what Mussolini called the "Rome-Berlin Axis," boasting that it would eventually control the destiny of Europe.

In Pozzuoli, the most immediate repercussion from those events was an increase in production at the munitions plant where Sofia's grandfather and uncles worked. They were putting in longer hours and earning more money, enough to buy a crystal chandelier and a radio for the living room. If things kept up, the family might be able to afford a bathroom. They now had only a toilet and were dependent on the kitchen sink and the municipal *bagni* when they needed to wash.

All over Italy, and especially in the smaller towns where there were few options, women stayed home but worked just as hard if not harder than the men. In the Villani household, Luisa ran everything, but her daughters were expected to pitch in and earn their keep. Romilda and Dora helped with the cooking, cleaned the house, did the shopping and laundry. In spare moments, they mended clothes and made dresses, blouses, and skirts for themselves and Sofia.

Though Romilda's dreams of a career in music or the movies had been thwarted, she seemed unlikely to forget them or to settle for a life of drudgery in her parents' home. She knew that no man would marry a single mother, not in Pozzuoli, so as soon as she felt secure about leaving Sofia with the other women of the household, Romilda started spending more and more time in Naples, or so she claimed. She was often gone for weeks, returning with stories of attending drama school and supporting herself by playing the piano in restaurants and bars. Neighbors aware of her past believed otherwise.

But it finally became certain that she'd been spending some of the time pursuing Riccardo Scicolone. She was still obsessed with marrying him. It seemed the only way of making life right again. They could move someplace where nobody knew them and make a fresh start.

It might have made sense to Romilda, but not to Riccardo. He was, however, still strongly attracted to her. "She was at the height of her physical splendor," he recalled. "It was inevitable that there should be new outbursts of passion between us."

In August 1937, a month before Sofia's third birthday, Romilda turned out to be pregnant again. Riccardo still saw no reason to marry her, claiming this time that he might not even be the father. Romilda had no choice but to return to Pozzuoli and hope that her family would be as understanding as before. They were, but as soon as Romilda's condition became obvious, the people of the neighborhood turned vicious. To escape their taunts and curses, she seldom left the house.

During the time of Romilda's confinement, Italy suffered an economic setback as a result of Mussolini's overspending on aid to the Franco Fascists in the Spanish Civil War. Il Duce's popularity plummeted and hit an all-time low as rumors began circulating about a new mistress young enough to be his daughter.

To cement his alliance with Nazi Germany, Mussolini made his first official visit to Hitler. The Fuehrer reciprocated with a trip to Rome in May of 1938.

Romilda's final month of pregnancy coincided with Hitler's visit. Although Hitler never traveled beyond Rome, Mussolini's propaganda machine whipped the whole country into pro-Nazi demonstrations and parades. The excitement was still very much in the air when Romilda Villani gave birth to her second illegitimate child on May 14.

Since Sofia had been named after her father's mother, Romilda decided that the new arrival should honor Riccardo Scicolone's eldest sister, Maria. Romilda wouldn't give up on being accepted into the Scicolone clan, but her ploy didn't work. When she sent Riccardo a telegram with the news, his reply said that she could name the baby anything she liked, but not with Scicolone at the end of it. He denied being the father and refused to sign any documents certifying her as Maria Scicolone. The baby would have to carry her mother's maiden name and be known as Maria Villani.

Rather than put up a fight, Romilda realized it didn't really matter for now. Everybody in Pozzuoli knew her circumstances.

Meanwhile, Sofia had a jumbled comprehension of her parentage. Having joined the Villani household at the age of three months, she believed that grandfather Domenico was her father, and called him Papa. Since her true father never visited, no one discouraged her. She also called her grandmother Mamma and her mother Mammina, or "little mother."

Maria's arrival caused some immediate changes in domestic sleeping arrangements. Sofia could no longer share her mother's bed and moved into the big one with her grandparents and Aunt Dora. To manage that, Domenico slept on the right side of the mattress, Luisa in the center, Dora on the left. Sofia slept across the bottom.

Thanks to Luisa making sure that the expectant mother got proper nourishment, Romilda this time had no nursing problems. Maria seemed a much happier and healthier baby than Sofia had been. Indeed, going on four, she still hadn't fleshed out substantially. Her mother made billowy dresses for her and put big bows in her hair to detract from her spindly limbs and dark little face. She was very shy and introverted. Her big eyes were lively and inquisitive, but she spoke very little.

As before, Romilda intended to resume her "career" as soon as Maria was weaned. Back to playing piano in cafés and giving private lessons on the side, she also had a trial run as an actress with a repertory theater group in Naples. She made several more attempts to land Riccardo Scicolone, none of them successful, but at least she didn't get pregnant again. Meanwhile, Romilda's mother cared for the children.

Then in her early fifties, Luisa Villani took her family responsibilities very seriously, but always tried to make life fun for her two granddaughters. Her kitchen became their playroom. While she prepared the meals, she told them fairy tales or sang nursery rhymes and Neapolitan evergreens. She had a vivid imagination and often made up stories about Sofia and Maria marrying rich men who would give them mansions, diamonds, and fur coats, the ultimate peasant dream in those days.

Then 1939 came along. In April, after Franco's victory in Spain freed Italy from providing military and financial support, Mussolini pumped all of Italy's might into annexing Albania. In May, Italy and Germany formalized their alliance by signing the "Pact of Steel," which stipulated that if one country became involved in a military conflict, the other would immediately assist with its full strength. Although Italy's war machine was woefully antiquated and deficient, Mussolini misrepresented its power to Hitler and boasted that he was ready to support Germany immediately in its planned invasion of Poland.

But when the time came on September 1, Germany alone attacked Poland. War clouds spread quickly over Europe, but for the time being Italy was under an umbrella. Though he still yearned to be Hitler's partner, Mussolini took a neutral position. While he bargained with Germany for raw materials and equipment that were needed to build up his forces, Italy could continue commercial trading with England and France.

On September 20, Sofia Scicolone celebrated her fifth birthday. Her mother thought it was high time that Sofia met her father. If war came, she might never have another chance.

Getting Riccardo Scicolone to come to Pozzuoli required drastic measures. Romilda sent him a telegram that Sofia was dying. Suspecting another of Romilda's ruses to force him into marriage, he didn't rush, arriving several days later. He brought a present for Sofia but nothing for her younger sister, whom he still refused to acknowledge as his child.

As Riccardo guessed, Sofia's health was fine, but her homeliness came as a shock. Romilda had dolled her up as best she could, but the girl would obviously never be a beauty. "This is your father," Romilda said, as she escorted her into the Villanis' seldom-used living room.

"A man stood there, he was tall, seemed like a giant to me then," Sophia Loren remembered. "He smiled at me and shook my hand. I ran from the room sobbing, 'He's not my father! I already have a father. Let him go away. I don't want him!' I was hurt. But my father must have been very hurt, too. He left the blue pedal car he'd brought me in the hall and went away. It was an unhappy day."

Romilda tried to explain the situation to Sofia, but the child was unable to understand. Sofia would learn the truth when she started school. Up to now, she'd lived within the confines of the family, which made sure that she was well shielded from the scorn of the locals.

Like all the other kids in Pozzuoli with certified parentage, Sofia was entitled to twelve years of state-funded education, the first five at the *scuola elementare,* the rest at the *scuola magistrale.* The curriculum was set by the government but included religious training in the Roman Catholic faith. Most of the personnel were Catholic clergy. While there were some lay teachers, the majority were nuns, with priests usually in the supervisory jobs.

Unfortunately, Italy got caught up in the European war just as Sofia was getting ready to start the first grade, so her education would be under constant threat. As Mussolini watched Germany's swift conquests of Norway, Denmark, Belgium, and Holland, he became not only convinced that Hitler would win the war, but also petrified that he would eventually invade Italy if it tried to back out of their alliance. As either ally or captured territory, Germany needed Italy as a conduit to the Mediterranean, the Balkans, and North Africa.

On June 10, 1940, while German forces were advancing on Paris, Italy declared war against France and England. Mussolini predicted it would all end in a few weeks, and that soon happened in France, where a new government signed an armistice with Germany and Italy.

For the time being, war would be a distant event for the civilian population of Italy. While Hitler concentrated on the invasion of England, Mussolini engaged the British in North Africa and started wars with Yugoslavia and Greece in the Balkan Peninsula.

Sofia's first days at school traumatized her and left permanent scars. Whether it was the fault of the nuns in the registration office or children from Via Solfatara who already knew about her illegitimate birth, she quickly became an object of scorn and ridicule. "You know how cruel children can sometimes be," Sophia recalled. "They used to talk among themselves, point at me, and laugh. I hated it, so I would go to school either at five minutes to nine when almost everybody was in, or at eight o'clock because nobody would be there yet."

She found comfort sitting among the orphans, who were always assigned to the back rows of the classroom. She felt sorry for them because they had no parents at all. They never taunted her about her dubious pedigree.

At six, Sofia had no conception of what "illegitimate" meant. In her very limited experience, she noticed that most children had two parents, a mother and a father. She thought that she was being picked on because she had no father. She knew nothing of the disgrace that went with being born out of wedlock. She became obsessed with the idea that if she only had a father, everybody would be nice to her.

As Sofia grew a bit older and wiser, it dawned on her that it wasn't simply a father that she needed. He had to behave like a father and take an active interest in her life. When she finally accepted the fact that Riccardo Scicolone was her father, she began to hate him for never being there and totally ignoring her.

Sofia had a simultaneous problem to contend with. Taller and considerably thinner than most girls her age, she was dubbed "Sofia Stuzzicadente" (Sofia Toothpick) by a punster in the class. The nickname stuck and spread to the neighborhood where she lived. One day she found it chalked on the Villanis' front door.

Sister Maria, no longer a baby, became her best and only friend. Their mother, meanwhile, worked sporadically in Naples. She told her daughters that she was an actress in the theater. They wanted to be actresses, too, and she encouraged them.

The sisters loved to climb on top of the sturdy old kitchen table to perform. Sofia dreamed up plays for them, and they also sang and danced. Romilda taught them how to make costumes from tissue paper, and loaned them lipstick and rouge to make up with.

By the beginning of 1941, the war was getting dangerously close to Pozzuoli. After the clobbering of Italian forces in North Africa and the Balkans, Mussolini had to appeal to Hitler for assistance. With dazzling speed, Germany conquered Greece and Yugoslavia and made a good start on expelling the British from North Africa. In exchange, Hitler demanded that Italy send thousands of workers to Germany to man its depleted factories and farms. He also wanted Italian battalions to assist in his planned invasion of the Soviet Union. And since Hitler didn't have much faith in Italy's home defenses, he insisted on dispatching German troops to shore up its bases and antiaircraft installations.

Mussolini was notified a few days before the December 7, 1941, bombing of Pearl Harbor and gave it his delighted approval. But when he announced that Italy was at war with the United States, most Italians were shocked and dismayed. They wanted an early end to the war, not an extension of it. Many, especially in the impoverished south, also revered the United States and had relatives or friends who'd emigrated there for a better life.

Four months later, in the spring of 1942, Italy already showed signs of defeat, even though no actual combat was going on there. Mussolini had sent 200,000 troops to the Russian front, at least half of which were killed. His African forces as well as his navy were in ruin. His contributions of manpower, food, and raw materials to Germany had caused desperate shortages at home, and antifascist strikes and demonstrations were breaking out.

It seemed inevitable that once the Allies had the air and naval strength to reach Italy, Naples and the whole surrounding coastal area, including Pozzuoli, would be among the main targets. The Germans understood that better than the Italians and rushed units there to bolster the existing defenses and to build new ones.

The arrival of the Germans with tanks and cannons in Pozzuoli was Sofia's introduction to the war. From the perspective of a seven-year-old, the young, predominantly blond and blue-eyed soldiers in snazzy uniforms were magical. "It was exciting to stand in front of our house and watch the troops march by," she recalled. "They were our allies, and friendly. The war became our plaything."

Not for long. In December, Allied planes began bombing Italian cities. On short-wave radio, Winston Churchill promised "prolonged, scientific, and shattering air attack," but offered the Italian people the choice "to say whether they want this terrible thing to happen to their country or not."

Since the Allied command needed Naples as a base and could not risk destroying its port facilities, bombings were directed away from the city toward the surrounding area. Pozzuoli became a favorite target because of its munitions factory and German garrisons.

With Sofia's grandfather and uncles working at the factory, the family was in double jeopardy. If the men weren't blown up at work, they would be left jobless with no money to pay the rent or to buy even the meager quantities of food that were available under rationing.

Late at night, when bombings were heaviest, people rushed for shelter in a long railway tunnel near the Pozzuoli station, often staying until the commuter service to Naples resumed in the morning. "All of us used to go, carrying our mattresses and whatever food we had, lying there in the dim light of candles, often freezing. People would be sleeping, arguing, laughing, making love," Sophia remembered.

The packed interior stank and had a resident population of fleas, cockroaches, and rats. Staying there night after night, Sofia developed a lasting fear of the dark and being trapped in enclosed places. Even as an adult, she couldn't go to sleep without the lights being on.

One night the town sirens failed to sound. The family was still home in bed when bombing vibrations started to crack walls and break windows. Though her mother told her to get dressed fast, Sofia was so confused that she only got as far as stripping off her nightgown. When her mother came to fetch her, she was standing naked and quaking with fear.

Romilda dressed Sofia and her sister as best she could, and they all headed for the railway tunnel. En route, some flying shrapnel sliced into Sofia's chin, leaving a bloody wound and eventual scar. Maria lost a shoe and cut her foot on broken glass. When they returned the next morning, they found the house half destroyed, which meant that the eight occupants would have to share even closer quarters than before. Still, it was preferable to having no home at all. Many in Pozzuoli weren't that lucky.

Meanwhile, the Germans were rounding up what men they could find to dispatch to the fatherland for "patriotic service," which really amounted to slave labor. Sofia's grandfather was considered too old, but her two uncles opted to quit their jobs and go into hiding to avoid being sent away and possibly never coming back.

In another part of the country, Riccardo Scicolone was also on the run, not only from the German stalkers, but from another reckless love affair as well. While hiding out in Foligno, a town near Assisi in central Italy, he became involved with a girl named Nella Rivolta, who soon turned out to be pregnant. He tried everything to squirm out of marrying her, including appealing to Romilda Villani for help!

Crazy though it may seem, Riccardo sent Romilda a telegram stating that unless he heard from her immediately, he was going to marry another woman. What he expected to accomplish is uncertain, but possibly he was counting on Romilda to claim that she had a prior right to become his wife. Presumably, Nella Rivolta would have to go along with it, and he could then find some new excuse for not marrying Romilda, either.

But Romilda's passion for Riccardo had turned to disgust over his total disregard for her and their daughters. She informed him that she no longer wanted him and that he could marry anyone. Nella Rivolta's family all but held a gun to his head and forced the marriage, just in time for Giuliano Scicolone to be born legitimate. They later had a second son, Giuseppe. It would be years before Sofia and Maria discovered that they had two half-brothers.

By the spring of 1943, the Allied bombing raids were so frequent and devastating that the mayor of Pozzuoli ordered all residents to evacuate the town. In typical government fashion, no provision had been made for helping people to relocate, so the Villani household had some fast thinking to do. Grandma Luisa fixed on a married cousin who lived in an apartment in Naples. She was a cold, mean-spirited woman, but they would all pray to Saint Gennaro to melt her heart enough to take them in.

WARTIME NAPLES

SOFIA Scicolone had never been away from Pozzuoli in the eight years since her mother brought her there at the age of three months. Because it was the only home she'd ever known, she threw a tantrum when told they were moving to Naples. Romilda tried to explain that it would only be for a short time. From the meager amount of clothes and belongings that they were able to carry with them, it certainly appeared that way.

Sofia's two uncles, still trying to avoid forced labor service in Germany, emerged from hiding to make it a group of eight. They were counting on the train to Naples being so crowded that the German guards would skip the usual identity check, but that didn't happen. Luckily, two nuns sitting side by side in the same compartment noticed the men's panic and came to the rescue.

When they heard the Germans approaching, the nuns beckoned to Mario and Guido to crawl under the seat, then rearranged their long black skirts to conceal them. It worked. When the Germans spotted the nuns, they just moved on to the next compartment.

The Villanis' relatives, the Mattias, resided on Via d'Arsia, which is up in the hills of Naples and reachable by one of the funicular railways. Fortunately, the cars were running that day, or the eight evacuees would have collapsed from exhaustion by the end of their long climb up the alternate route of twisting roads.

As expected, Signora Mattia didn't jump for joy when cousin Luisa and family turned up at the front door of her apartment, but she didn't turn them away. She agreed to provide lodging but little more. Food had become so scarce that the Mattias claimed they had none to share. The Villanis could use the kitchen, but they would have to buy their own groceries—if they could find any—and observe mealtimes that didn't inconvenience their hosts.

Sofia, Maria, and their mother would share a tiny bedroom, which at least had a balconied window overlooking the street. Luisa, Domenico, and daughter Dora moved into the only other spare room. Mario and Guido would bunk on the living room floor until they could find a safer place to hide from the Germans.

In 1943 Naples had over a million inhabitants, sharply divided among a small wealthy class; a substantial number of poor professionals, clerks, and civil servants; and a vast majority of paupers and beggars. In the ancient belly of the city, 250,000 people lived in decaying tenements, many in ground-floor or basement rooms with cobblestone floors and no windows or sanitary facilities.

Faced with such overwhelming numbers of destitute and desperate people, Sofia's family spent most of their waking hours foraging for food, or at least the adults did. Grandma Luisa suspected that her cousin might have a sudden change of heart and lock them all out. To guard against that, Sofia and Maria were always left behind while the others went out. For the duration of their stay, the sisters' experience of Naples would be limited to what they could observe from the little balcony of their room.

If they were lucky, their mother or one of the other relatives would come home with a sack of rice or potatoes that could be stretched into a week's meals. As soon as Guido and Mario arranged for a hiding place, there were only six people to feed. They often had to be content with just the glutinous black bread that could still be found in some shops if one arrived well before opening time and got a good place in the queue.

Making matters worse, the Villanis knew by the kitchen aromas and from peeking through keyholes that the Mattias were never short of food and probably had been hoarding it for years. Grandma Luisa bided her time, hoping that her cousin would feel a little compassion and offer them some. Finally she confronted Signora Mattia and begged for anything, even scraps from the table, but was refused. Screaming matches between the two women became a daily occurrence. Sofia would cover her ears because she couldn't bear the sound of people being angry with each other.

Sofia's education had ended for the moment. Schools were operating on limited schedules, if at all. The family also had no residency papers for Naples, so trying to enroll Sofia would cause more trouble than it was worth.

By the summer of 1943, the winds of war were shifting directly toward Italy and developing hurricane force. An Allied victory in North Africa paved the way for the invasion of Sicily and the Italian mainland. Meanwhile, Hitler ordered more divisions to Italy and persuaded Mussolini to give Germany sole command of joint military operations. Fearing that Hitler intended to incorporate Italy into the German empire, the Fascist Grand Council lost all confidence in Mussolini's leadership and appealed to King Victor Emmanuel to remove him and to restore the constitutional monarchy. The king promptly appointed as prime minister Marshal Pietro Badoglio, who then forced Mussolini's resignation and sent him into detention on the island of Ponza. On the radio that night, Badoglio announced that the new regime would continue fighting against the Allies, but he was only trying to appease Hitler, to prevent him from taking revenge for Mussolini's ouster.

Then on September 3, after some secret negotiations between the Allies and the Badoglio government, Italy officially signed the armistice and the Allied invasion began. The Axis defense of Italy now became the sole responsibility of Germany, and its Fuehrer vowed to be victorious.

While the Allies were crossing from Sicily into Calabria and preparing to attempt another landing farther north on the coastline at Salerno, Hitler launched "Operation Axis," the German occupation of Italy, which would start with the removal of the new government and the capture and incarceration of all members of the Italian military. On the night of September 8, German forces entered Rome, but the prime minister and the royal family managed to escape to Brindisi, on the Adriatic, which became the temporary headquarters of the new government.

The next day the Allies established a beachhead near Salerno, the first step toward capturing Naples, which was only thirty-four miles away. Meanwhile, the Germans had taken total control of Naples and were starting to treat the Italian citizenry ruthlessly. Men and youths were snatched off the streets by the truckload and forced into hard labor to free German troops from having to do it. Those who resisted were often shot and left to die in the gutter. Jews and officials of the new government were packed off to concentration camps in Germany.

On September 12, the situation took a startling turn when a unit of Nazi daredevils using gliders and a small plane landed on the 9,000-foot high mountain where Mussolini was being held captive by supporters of the new government and succeeded in abducting him back to Germany for rehabilitation at Hitler's headquarters at Rastenburg. Three days later, in a radio broadcast beamed to Italy, Il Duce announced that he had resumed supreme power over Italy and that the deposed officials of the Fascist government should return to their posts and help him form a new regime that would be untainted by monarchy. He also ordered all members of the Fascist militia to reassemble and to fight side by side with the Germans in expelling the Allied invaders.

On September 20, Sofia Scicolone turned nine years old, knowing nothing about the war except for what she saw from the window or heard in the way of gunfire and exploding bombs. Luckily for her and others in the upper reaches of Naples, Allied planes were concentrating on naval installations near the harbor. Several thousand people were killed, and it was later established that 200,000 were left homeless.

The bombings ruined Naples' water supply and sewage system. Often the only water was whatever could be collected in pots and pans during a rainstorm. Typhoid was a constant menace. Sofia never caught it, but Maria did. When her sister was burning up with fever, their mother could find no water for her to drink, so she finally ran out into the street and drained some from the radiator of a German army truck parked a few doors away.

By September 28 the Allies had reached the outskirts of Naples and the Germans started evacuating northward, destroying whatever stood in their path and planting time bombs and land mines to greet their pursuers. So many Neapolitans were needlessly and viciously killed that the people finally rebelled and began attacking anyone in German uniform. Without plan or organized leadership, they took guns out of hiding, sharpened knives and axes, built catapults and gasoline bombs, erected barriers in the streets, and installed snipers on rooftops.

For four days the Neapolitans hunted Germans, cornering and massacring them in the alleys, crushing them in an avalanche of rocks, tiles, lead pipes, washtubs, whatever heavy materials they could find. German corpses were left to rot in the streets. Many had been disfigured after death. Some skulls had long nails hammered into them.

Hundreds of *scugnizzi,* the ragged street youths of Naples, were the most courageous fighters. Some had stolen hand grenades from the Germans. Others made kerosene bombs or fashioned torches from bundles of straw. Banding together in groups, the boys blew up tanks and trucks or climbed onto them and tried to incinerate the Germans inside. Many succeeded, but some ended up being killed in the process.

Sofia was the same age as some of the boys, but only a spectator. From her balcony, she saw a boy being chased down the street by two German soldiers who had just climbed out of a burning tank. Although their hair and uniforms were ablaze, the soldiers seemed determined to kill their attacker and were shooting at him with pistols. After the trio disappeared from Sofia's view, she could still hear gunshots, but she never did find out whether the boy escaped or not.

On October 1, the Germans packed up and headed north toward Rome. Later that day, the Anglo-American Fifth Army marched in to "liberate" a city that had already been liberated by its own people. For the first time since she arrived in Naples, Sofia was permitted to go outside to watch the parades and festivities.

American soldiers driving by in trucks and jeeps threw candy and other goodies to the crowds. Sofia managed to catch a chocolate bar and a small can of concentrated coffee. She and her family quickly gobbled up the chocolate, but it took them a while to figure out how to prepare the coffee. It had the aroma of coffee, but they needed ground beans for their *caffettiera*. Finally Grandma Luisa thought of mixing it with hot water. The end product was hardly up to espresso standards, but it had been so long since they'd tasted the real thing that nobody complained.

By the time of the German withdrawal, half a million or more Neapolitans were homeless, unemployed, and starving. For lack of water and proper sanitation, there were epidemics of typhus, scabies, lice, and fleas. Venereal disease also flared to epidemic proportions as the Allied occupiers began patronizing the bordellos and streetwalkers.

For Sofia Scicolone, as well as for all Italians now living under AMGOT (the Allied Military Government of Occupied Territory), the war was over but not over. The northern half of Italy, including Rome, was still under German control, as was most of Europe. Although the Allies had finally started to show signs of being victorious, it was far from a sure thing. Meanwhile, the people of liberated Italy were not exactly prisoners of the Allies, but in their custody and subject to their rules and regulations until fate dealt the next hand.

By this time, Sofia and her family had been staying with their relatives in Naples for over five months. With the exodus of the Germans, the two Villani brothers emerged from hiding and rejoined the group, so there were now six adults and two children testing the patience of their grudging hosts. How much longer was anybody's guess, but Grandma Luisa didn't want to leave until things calmed down a bit and they could make sure that they still had a home in Pozzuoli to return to.

Naples was in total chaos. There were occasional thundering explosions, with whole buildings blown up by delayed-action devices that the Germans had left behind. Hundreds of people were killed or maimed each time. Many who escaped were forced to camp out in the streets. Thousands more became afraid to go home at all when a rumor spread that the Germans had planted five thousand bombs to go off when one of the city's damaged electrical power lines was repaired and switched on again. Happily, that didn't happen.

Both the Villanis and the Mattias were suddenly forced to move when the Allied command requisitioned the entire apartment building to use as an officers' residence. Before there could be any discussion of their cousins coming to stay with *them* in Pozzuoli, the Villanis sneaked out very early the next morning and headed back home. Unfortunately, all public transportation had been suspended due to bombed-out roads and railroad tracks, so eight of the nine walked the entire fifteen miles. Uncle Mario had to carry the still convalescent Maria on his shoulders.

"The road to Pozzuoli was choked with refugees, lugging their possessions on their backs, and in carts and wagons and all manner of wheeled contrivances," Sophia recalled. "The road itself was in terrible condition, covered with bomb craters. People got in each other's way, carts broke down and blocked the road, some people tumbled into the craters, there was yelling and screaming and joyful reunions and fistfights and exhausted people sitting on the roadside, but nevertheless, I felt elated because we were going home."

By nightfall, they reached the outskirts of Pozzuoli. As they marched ever faster through streets of wrecked buildings, they became petrified of finding their own premises reduced to rubble. Fortunately, 5 Via Solfatara was still standing, but with the roof sagging, all the window panes broken, and the interior a mess of fallen ceilings, cracked walls, and damaged furniture. For the duration of the war at least, repair materials would be scarcer than food. The family would just have to rough it, mask the windows with whatever they could find, and be thankful for not being forced to camp out under the stars.

All nine came back from Naples infested with lice that no amount of washing and scrubbing with boiling water and disinfectant could permanently remove from scalp, body, or clothing. Sofia suffered such intolerable itching that in later years just remembering it would cause her to start scratching.

Sofia had somehow contracted scabies in Naples. The U.S. Army was providing free DDT treatments to local Italians to kill the parasites, but in Sofia's case the DDT proved only partially effective. An army doctor had to prescribe a sulfa drug to rid her of scabies. When she was finally pronounced cured, she felt like the war itself had finally ended, but in actual fact it still had a long way to go. There were still nights when the Villanis had to run to the railroad tunnel for shelter.

On March 19, the world suddenly seemed to be coming to an end, but not due to the war. In Pompeii Mount Vesuvius erupted, and by nightfall the smoke had built into a mammoth cloud that rose 35,000 feet into the sky and covered the entire Bay of Naples area. By the next day, Naples, Pozzuoli and the islands of Capri and Ischia were covered with several inches of volcanic ash. Portions of San Sebastiano, a town close to Vesuvius, were buried under thirty feet of lava.

Panic swept Pozzuoli from fear that the eruption would start a chain reaction and that Solfatara, the volcano just up the road from Sofia and her family, would begin spewing its deadly sulfuric vapors on the town. Everyone prayed to Saint Gennaro, and perhaps he worked a miracle. Vesuvius began to cool down after five days.

The black market was seizing the food supplies, leaving the bombed-out and decaying Naples region a seething cesspool of poor, hungry, and homeless people who would do anything just to stay alive. Many women became prostitutes, serving the thousands of Allied troops now stationed in the area.

In September 1944, Sofia turned ten years old. She'd grown too tall to be called a *bambina,* but it would be another two or three years before she was physically a *ragazza.* Her soul, however, was aging faster. "When we returned to Pozzuoli from Naples, the experience had changed her. Her childhood had gone," her aunt Dora recalled.

After Sofia became world famous as Sophia Loren, rumors began circulating that she had been a prostitute during the war. She has always denied it. When writer Rex Reed brought it up during a 1976 interview, Sophia's eyes flashed with anger as she said, "That is typical of the things they've said about me. In 1944, when the Americans arrived, I was ten years old. I was a rather mature child, but I wasn't *that* mature."

The rumors about Sophia always claimed her mother was also a prostitute. By then in her early thirties, Romilda Villani still had that Greta Garbo allure. Romilda had allegedly been hustling in Naples since the war started, shifting from a German to an Allied clientele when the command changed. Thousands of Italian women found this the only way to feed their children in war-torn Italy. The truth about Romilda Villani may never be known, but even if she did as alleged, who is to blame her?

According to Sophia Loren, her mother *did* entertain Allied servicemen, but in conventional ways. Pozzuoli had lots of U.S. Army and Navy personnel, but few places for social relaxation. When Romilda became the pianist in a small café-bar and started to acquire a following, Grandma Luisa had the bright idea of turning the family's unused living room into a club. Six-year-old Maria, who had a good singing voice and loved to perform, would augment her mother's piano playing. Sofia, who was too shy to take part, assisted her grandmother and aunt in serving liquor and cleaning up afterward.

The family staked whatever money they had on buying pure alcohol, cherry brandy, and sugar on the black market. Grandma Luisa turned it into a house cocktail that contained about 75 percent water and was highly sweetened to please American and British palates. Luisa also made a fifty-fifty deal with a farmer for some of his homemade *vino,* which they also sold.

Although the GIs had an early curfew and Club Villani closed up tight at 6:00 P.M., business thrived. Other families in the neighborhood opened similar premises. Fortunately, the Villanis had the edge because of Romilda and Maria's musical contributions. The Americans often brought records to play on the family's old wind-up Victrola to teach Romilda and Maria the latest hits back home. Since neither spoke nor understood English, their renditions of songs like "Don't Fence Me In" and "Acc-cent-tchu-ate the Positive" must have been hilarious but delightful.

Besides paying cash, many servicemen left a tip in the form of cigarettes, candy bars, or chewing gum. Repeat customers sometimes brought gifts of canned foods, flour, and coffee from the PX. Many had become smitten with Romilda, and she encouraged their attention for its bonus values.

One day, Romilda showed an American admirer the shrapnel scar on Sofia's chin and asked him whether he could do anything to help. He took Sofia to his battalion's doctor, who performed some minor surgery that over time made the scar close to invisible.

The sufferings of wartime were still not over. The winter of 1944–45 was Europe's most frigid in decades. In regions like southern Italy, where winters were usually mild and most dwellings lacked heating or insulation, hundreds died from exposure to the cold and a related epidemic of tuberculosis.

The Villanis were forced to suspend operation of their little drinking club while they struggled to save themselves from freezing to death. Food became scarce again. Without the patronage of the GIs or the gifts they brought from the PX, the family couldn't afford to buy on the black market, where supplies had shriveled anyway.

The arrival of winter also forced a halt to the combat in northern Italy. By that time, the Allies had liberated Rome and advanced as far north as Bologna. But fully expelling the Germans from Italy across the snow-bound Alps would risk too many Allied lives. Mussolini, meanwhile, took advantage of the situation. His puppet government at Salo had become notorious for its brutality and the sadistic torture of its opponents. Guerrilla partisans loyal to the Communists, Socialists, and other parties vying to govern Italy after the war were determined to eradicate Il Duce, but he was well protected by the Germans and the freezing weather. Then, on April 9, Allied forces in Italy advanced into the Po River valley, within close reach of Mussolini, who panicked and moved his headquarters to Milan.

On April 25, as the Allies neared Milan, Mussolini, together with mistress Clara Petacci and some of his cabinet officers, fled toward neutral Switzerland, from where they intended flying to sanctuary in fascist Spain. Traveling in several cars, they were all captured by partisans, taken to a hideaway near Lake Como, and, on April 28, savagely executed by machine gun. The next day, after the fifteen corpses had been dumped in one of Milan's main squares, partisans took the bodies of Il Duce, Petacci, and three others and hung them upside down by their ankles from the roof girders of a bombed-out gas station. By evening, the corpses of Mussolini and his lover had been spat on, stabbed, and shot at so many times that Allied soldiers took them down.

In southern Italy, the celebration of V-E Day on May 8 was less jubilant than in the north, more like an anticlimax. "Liberated" for almost a year, the people of the south were starting to discover that postwar life wasn't going to be easy.

For Sofia and family, the most immediate consequence of V-E Day was a sharp decline in business at their little club. The Allied command had all but moved to Rome. Combat troops were being shipped out in huge numbers to the Pacific region for a planned invasion of mainland Japan in November, which proved unnecessary after the U.S. dropped two atomic bombs on Japan.

Romilda and Sofia had been living with the Villanis for over a decade now, Maria for a few years less. How much longer the arrangement would continue depended entirely on Romilda. With the war over, she had more options but was still burdened by the demands of motherhood. Her prewar income from playing piano and giving lessons had never amounted to much. She couldn't support two children on that, and knew that she could never count on their father for help. Riccardo Scicolone had contacted her from time to time during the war. He was living in Rome with his wife and two sons, but showed slight interest in his Villani family.

While the drinking club was in full swing, Romilda had received several marriage proposals from GIs who wanted to take her back to America after the war. The Naples region was in the grip of "war bride fever." Scores of women and teenagers had married and were waiting to be shipped out as soon as their husbands got back to the United States and could arrange transportation for them.

Romilda had some relatives in the United States—her father's brother, Vincenzo, and family had emigrated there before the war. The prospect of making a fresh start in life, in a rich country like America, appealed to her very much, but unfortunately, none of her GI suitors were willing to accept her two daughters, and Romilda would not think of leaving them behind.

Sofia resumed her schooling. Though now seven years old, sister Maria could not attend school because of her bastard status. Romilda intended suing Riccardo Scicolone to get that changed, but that would have to wait until she could save enough money to hire a lawyer.

4

⟨𝒢⟩

B Y the time of Sofia Scicolone's eleventh birthday in September 1945, World War II had officially ended, and Italy was in chaos. Most of its infrastructure had been destroyed or severely damaged, and millions of people were homeless. Unemployment, which had been bad enough before the war, was made worse by the hordes returning from military service or POW and slave labor camps.

It was an atmosphere for revolution. Free spirits who had suffered through the Fascist regime feared that the Communists or Socialists would install a new totalitarian government.

Although the monarchial government that ousted Mussolini was granted the status of a cobelligerent in the last year of the war, the Allies treated Italy like a defeated power in the peace settlement. They stripped Italy of all its colonial possessions, ordered it to pay $400 million in reparations to Greece, Yugoslavia, the Soviet Union, and other nations it had wronged, and severely restricted the rebuilding of its military forces.

During the peace negotiations, Winston Churchill had envisioned Great Britain taking charge of Italy's rehabilitation, but Britain was bankrupt and nearly overwhelmed by its own postwar adjustment, so the United States became the main Allied arbiter. A general election for a new government was to be held in June 1946. In the meantime, the government of Victor Emmanuel III would continue. The elderly king, who'd been on the throne for forty-five years, was expected to abdicate in favor of his son, Umberto, if Italians voted to retain the monarchy.

At age eleven, Sofia Scicolone wasn't much concerned about the future of Italy, if she even thought about it. But the quality of her life was unlikely to improve for a long time to come.

She'd returned to the *Scuola Elementare,* and had also started taking piano lessons under her mother's tutelage. Romilda Villani was showing signs of turning into a prime example of that show business phenomenon known as the stage mother, or *madre ambiziosa di teatro,* as they're called in Italian.

While Maria seemed more musically talented, Sofia was older and nearer to an age when she would be eligible to work. The family's piano, originally purchased for Romilda when she was a child and more recently used in their servicemen's club, was now Sofia's to master. Trying to make up for lost time, Romilda pushed too hard and expected too much.

It was the first time that Sofia ever rebelled against her mother. "She was terribly impatient with me. Every time I made a mistake she banged me on the head," Sophia Loren recalled. "I finally gave up. I loved everything about the piano, even practicing, but my headaches from being knocked on the head became so severe that I had to stop. Parents rarely make good teachers for their own children, and my mother was certainly no exception."

Sofia wanted to be a nun, a common dream among schoolgirls who were taught by them. That began to change, however, as she became addicted to Hollywood movies, which had been absent from Italian screens since before the war. By the end of 1938, Mussolini's nationalization of the film industry had made it impossible for American companies to do business there. Now American films were starting to trickle in under the supervision of the U.S. Army's Department of Psychological Warfare, which chose them mainly for their propaganda value. Chaplin's antifascist *The Great Dictator,* the inspirational *Song of Bernadette,* and the rousing *Yankee Doodle Dandy* were among the first to be released.

Since the eight major Hollywood studios produced about 2,500 films between 1939 and 1946, Italian moviegoers would be put through a veritable bombardment as soon as new trade agreements were worked out. Not all of that backlog, of course, would be of interest or have appeal to Italian audiences, but those movies deemed marketable would be dubbed into Italian. Back when talkies started, the Mussolini government had insisted that all foreign-made releases be dubbed into Italian, and audiences grew accustomed to the practice. To save time and money, the first postwar American releases were shown with Italian subtitles. Purists were delighted to hear the real voices of the

actors, but the mass public complained and boycotted, causing dubbing to become mandatory again.

Sofia Scicolone reached movie-going age just as the war started, so she
never saw many films, although, despite the disappearance of American
films, there had been plenty of others to choose from. Up until 1944, the
Italian studios maintained a steady output of about forty features per year,
and there were also many imports from Germany and Nazi-occupied France.
Actually getting to *see* those movies was the real problem. In wartime, theaters were potential mass deathtraps. Many operated on very limited schedules, if at all. Pozzuoli's only cinema was closed throughout the war, but a
few in Naples staggered on as best they could. Sofia's Aunt Dora took her
there several times. Sofia would later remember what she saw there only as
"drab Italian films."

And drab they probably were in comparison to the first Hollywood movies
that Sofia saw. Some were in vivid Technicolor, introducing her to such gorgeous creatures as Tyrone Power, Rita Hayworth, Betty Grable, Robert Taylor,
Maria Montez, and Maureen O'Hara. But she was equally dazzled by the mono-
chromatic Clark Gable, Lana Turner, Cary Grant, Gary Cooper, Hedy Lamarr,
and Alan Ladd.

In the very first American movie that she saw, *The Picture of Dorian Gray,*
Sofia fell instantly in love with the lead actor, Hurd Hatfield. Judging by his
handsomeness, she guessed Hatfield to be the greatest star in Hollywood, but
when she couldn't find him in any more films, she shifted her ardor to Tyrone
Power after twelve viewings of *Blood and Sand*.

Tyrone Power, with his scrumptious dark looks and gentle manner, became
the god of her adolescent years. "I would return to see his pictures over and
over again. I would go the first thing in the morning and stay through the last
showing at night," Sophia recalled. "There was always something magic to me
about movies. I couldn't get over the way it was—on the wall, persons suddenly started to live. For years, I always used to look where the projector was,
to see where the people came from."

Pozzuoli's only cinema, Teatro Sacchino, built long ago for plays and variety
shows, got battered in the war, but enough of its baroque decor remained to
make Sofia feel like she was in a little palace. Too young to attend by herself,
she had to ask someone in the family to take her, usually Aunt Dora, who also
loved movies but wouldn't sit through them more than once. When Tyrone
Power's *The Black Swan* docked at Teatro Sacchino, Aunt Dora accompanied

Sofia to the first showing and other relatives came to relieve her in shifts so that Sofia could remain until closing time.

The flood of Hollywood movies would subside as Italy returned to self-government and the United States gradually lost its influence over internal affairs. In that 1946–48 period, Italy turned into a political battlefield as the parties fought to win the majority voice in the new government. Mass demonstrations and labor strikes fostered more unemployment and inflation. Simultaneously, Italy became a pawn in the so-called Cold War between the Soviet Union and the democratic bloc led by the United States. In 1947, the U.S. made Italy one of the main beneficiaries of the $29 billion European Recovery Program (better known as the Marshall Plan), then threatened to withdraw all aid if the Communists got into power in the 1948 election.

Meanwhile, in September 1947, Sofia Scicolone entered her teens, and had not only outlived her mother's expectations of an early death from starvation, but was actually flourishing. "At thirteen—like a miracle from God, who wants to help you—she began to bloom slowly and naturally, like a flower, and became beautiful," her mother recalled.

That process took eighteen months according to the girl herself, who later claimed she was fourteen and a half when she reached full-bodied womanhood. Whatever the exact age, Sofia was no longer an ugly duckling. She still had thick lips and a big nose, but male admirers were too likely to be fascinated by her chest to notice. As Grandpa Domenico told her, "You've stopped growing up, you're now growing out."

The boys at school, as well as some of the instructors, were suddenly entranced. After weeks of watching Sofia doing calisthenics while dressed in shorts and a snug-fitting top, a young gym teacher detained her after class one day, confessed that he was madly in love with her, and proposed marriage. "He had blond hair and marvelous blue eyes," she remembered. "I laughed and sent him off to see my mother. She told him to go home and take a cold bath."

Sophia Loren would later claim that she was a slow starter and had few, if any, romantic experiences in her girlhood. One boy that she liked very much was a seventeen-year-old named Manilo. "One day we took a walk along the highway to Bagnoli," she remembered. "All of a sudden, he took my hand, and I realized he was breathing hard and that his eyes were all bloodshot. Then he kissed me on the mouth. I was terrified. I left him in the lurch and ran off like some crazy thing, and I never saw him again."

Rosetta d'Isanto, a school friend who shared the same desk for five years, recalled that girls who'd shunned Sofia in the past were now awed by her. "She demonstrated, and we all copied," d'Isanto said. "No matter what she wore she always made it seem as if it had come from a boutique. She always wore very full skirts and tight blouses. She had marvelous long, straight legs, and she was always glad to lift up her skirts to show them to the girls. We were all captivated by the way she walked, the hips moving, but never the head. We used to run into the cloakroom after class and beg her to demonstrate. We would then practice it, but it was never the same."

No precise explanation can be given for Sofia's magical transformation. Rumor has it that her mother was teaching her, and rumor further says that Romilda was a prostitute. Supposedly Romilda supported herself and her daughters by teaching piano, but in Italy's depressed economy, how many pupils could she have had?

By the summer of 1948, just over three years after the end of the war in Europe, living conditions in Italy were finally starting to improve. With fervent campaign support from the Vatican and the U.S. government, the Christian Democrats scored an overwhelming victory over the Communists and Socialists in the May election and gained an absolute majority in the seating of the new government. The parliament went on to elect Luigi Einaudi, an economist and university professor, as the Republic's first president. Italy was now guaranteed the hundreds of millions of dollars it needed in Marshall Plan funds to revitalize industry and create more jobs.

Already showing signs of recovery was Italy's motion picture industry. Since the end of the war some of the new Italian films, especially those in the neorealistic style of Roberto Rossellini's *Rome: Open City* and Vittorio De Sica's *Shoeshine,* had been winning acclaim abroad and earning top money. If it continued, Italy stood to benefit not only from the foreign revenues, but also from the prestige and the favorable image that its films created for the country. Perhaps foreign producers would also want to come to work there. One of the Mussolini regime's better accomplishments was Cinecittà, built in Rome's outskirts in 1936, which rivaled the giant studios of Hollywood and could easily be restored to its prewar efficiency.

By 1948, Hollywood films were flooding the cinemas of Italy, but Italian producers and distributors were receiving more screen time and pressuring the government to impose quotas limiting the number of foreign-made releases. Though Sofia remained loyal to Tyrone Power and had started to identify with sultry Hollywood beauties like Rita Hayworth, Linda Darnell, and Yvonne De

Carlo, she was also acquiring favorites among the Italian stars. The volcanic Anna Magnani and elegant Isa Miranda were too mature for Sofia to appreciate at age fourteen, but she adored Alida Valli and Valentina Cortese, both now working part time in Hollywood, as well as Lucia Bosé, Alba Arnova, Lea Padovani, and Silvana Pampanini. Gossipy magazines, which had disappeared during the war years, were also making Sofia aware for the first time of Italy's lesser celebrities, the starlets and beauty contest queens, among them Pier Angeli, Silvana Mangano, Gina Lollobrigida, Marina Berti, and Gianna Maria Canale.

Although seventeen years had passed since Romilda Villani's brief moment of triumph in the Greta Garbo lookalike contest, her heart still ached whenever she thought about her missed opportunities. Romilda believed that if she'd taken that trip to Hollywood, she could have become its queen when Garbo took her early retirement.

Sofia's budding beauty started Romilda to daydreaming again. If she couldn't make a pianist of her daughter, perhaps she would have better luck capitalizing on Sofia's physical allure.

One day in the spring of 1949, Romilda found her launching pad when a Naples newspaper announced a contest for "Queen of the Sea," with many prizes topped off by a screen test at Titanus Film in Rome. Although Sofia was half a year younger than the minimum age of fifteen, her mother entered her anyway, guessing rightly that no one would ask for a birth certificate when they saw her daughter's buxom development.

Panic ensued over the dress rules. Sofia had a fancy Sunday dress that Grandma Luisa had recently made for her, but she lacked the evening gown required for the second of two promenades before the contest judges. Grandma solved that problem with one of the pink living room drapes, which she quickly transformed into a floor-length gown. Sofia's only dress shoes looked shabby, so her mother painted them with two coats of whitewash. Now all they had to do was pray that it didn't rain.

The judging was held at a posh club overlooking the Bay of Naples. Wearing makeup for the first time ever, and with her hair upswept like Rita Hayworth in *My Gal Sal,* Sofia must have been quite a sight as she arrived straight off the train from Pozzuoli. She wore an old school coat over her pink gown. Her mother led the way, carrying Sofia's second dress in a paper bag.

When Sofia noticed that many contestants were wearing expensive, store-bought outfits, she felt like bolting, but her mother held her in an iron grip until her name was called. "I had been scared to death, but when my turn came, I found, to my astonishment, that my nervousness seemed to fly off me. I walked back and forth before the fourteen judges and answered their questions with composure," she later remembered.

Over two hundred contestants had turned out, so it was a very long judging and the results weren't revealed until well after midnight. There was no fairy-tale finish. Sofia Scicolone did not become Queen of the Sea, but she was over-joyed when she heard her name announced as one of the twelve princesses.

The grand prize winner was not a popular selection. "The audience didn't like the girl who was chosen to be queen, and when they don't like something in Naples, they get really excited. They threw things at her and shouted insults," Sophia recalled.

An official handed Sofia a bouquet of red roses and took her to join the other winners in a group photograph. When it was published in the next day's *Il Mattino,* the accompanying story misspelled Scicolone, but that didn't spoil the thrill of that afternoon, when Sofia and the rest of the royal group were piled into a horse-drawn carriage and paraded through the streets of Naples. Accompanied by a marching band, they drew cheers from the onlookers and were pelted by flowers, which made a happy change from the deadly violence that Sofia had witnessed in Naples five years before.

A princess for only a day, Sofia returned to Pozzuoli with several more durable prizes. The most valuable were 23,000 lire in cash (which may seem a considerable sum but was equivalent to about $35 then) and a round-trip train ticket to Rome. Courtesy of some of *Il Mattino's* advertisers, she also received a white linen tablecloth with twelve matching napkins, and eight rolls of wallpaper with a pattern of large green leaves against a white background.

By the weekend, the wallpaper was covering the Villani living room, con-cealing the scars of World War II. Decades later, the paper was still hanging, with her aged relatives proudly pointing it out to visitors as the first evidence of Sophia Loren's success.

Romilda put the prize money and train ticket in safekeeping until they were ready to take another shot at launching Sofia in the world. Sofia was, of course, still attending school, with a teaching career at the end of the rainbow when she earned her diploma. Her father, in one of his rare communications with Romilda, had expressed the hope that Sofia would, one day, become a teacher, which is perhaps the reason why neither mother nor daughter were enthusias-tic about the idea.

Classmate Rosetta d'Isanto, who did become a teacher, recalled: "All that Sofia talked about in those days was getting a husband! And success. It didn't matter at what, she just couldn't bear not being successful. I have never known an ambition like it."

Romilda Villani was the driving force. Sofia's designation as a Princess of the Sea was all the proof she needed that her daughter could be a star. Without stopping to consult Sofia she enrolled her in an acting school in Naples. It was more of a studio workshop, with its owner, retired actor Carlo Maria Rossini, as the only teacher, but it had flexible hours and Sofia could continue in school in Pozzuoli at the same time.

Professor Rossini used a method with beginners that he called "shaping an actor out of stone." Learning how to express herself with her face alone, without relying on words or hand gestures, was Sofia's first assignment. She and her classmates were given a master list of emotions, which Rossini proceeded to teach them at the rate of one per session. The professor made faces at the students, and then they made faces back at him and at each other until quitting time.

"We never read a line of anything, or acted anything, we just made faces," Sophia Loren remembered. "Joy was both eyebrows up; surprise, both eyebrows up with the mouth formed in an O; skepticism, one eyebrow up; horror, big eyes; pain, little eyes; and so on."

Sofia Scicolone may have been wasting her time *and* her mother's money. Italians seem to be born with the ability to speak with their faces. As Orson Welles once observed, "Italy is full of actors, fifty million of them, in fact, and they are almost all good; there are only a few bad ones, and they are on the stage and screen."

During drama class one day, Professor Rossini announced that a spectacular American film based on *Quo Vadis* was going to be produced at Cinecittà. There would be jobs for thousands of extras and bit players.

Sofia rushed home and told her mother, who instantly recognized a golden opportunity for both of them and began making plans. Sofia's beauty contest winnings would help them get to Rome, but they couldn't afford to take Maria along. She would be left temporarily with the Villanis. Romilda's parents were strongly opposed to the two leaving, but she couldn't be talked out of it.

To facilitate the trip, Romilda had to go to Sofia's school and sign the release papers required by law. Sofia Scicolone was fourteen at the time. It marked the end of her formal education.

As Sophia Loren, she later remembered the train trip to Rome: "I wore a pale blue dress, white shoes with high heels. When my mother and I got in the compartment we sat opposite each other, both of us knowing what a gamble we were taking. I felt an enormous admiration for her. We had very little money, few clothes, and no prospects beyond joining the queue at Cinecittà. It took a lot of courage."

When they arrived in Rome, Romilda rushed to a public telephone in the station and placed a call to Riccardo Scicolone. Although she'd mentioned nothing about it to Sofia, the trip to Rome provided Romilda with another chance at trying to set things right with Scicolone. Needless to say, he was outraged when she phoned and caught him in the midst of having lunch with his wife and two sons.

Scicolone turned even testier when Romilda demanded to see him immediately. But when she started sobbing that Sofia was very sick and needed an operation, he agreed to meet them at his mother's apartment near the Piazza Venezia. Sofia finally met her grandmother and namesake, whose only civility was to offer her a glass of milk, after which she left the visitors alone to await Riccardo's arrival.

The audience with Riccardo Scicolone lasted less than five minutes. Since Sofia hardly looked seriously ill, he knew instantly that Romilda was up to her usual tricks. When she told him of her plans for Sofia as a movie actress, he just laughed and refused to help. Times were tough, he had no money to spare, and no place for them to stay. His mother wouldn't put them up for even one night, so it was "*Arrivederci*" and "*Buona fortuna*" as he escorted them to the door.

According to Sophia Loren, her mother had a woman cousin who agreed to lodge them temporarily. How Romilda suddenly produced a relative in a city where she had none when she lived there prior to the war is unknown, but the cousin turned out to be no more hospitable than the Mattias in Naples. Sofia and her mother were permitted to share a folding bed in the living room, but they were ordered to be up and out of the house by early morning so that the family could use the room. The two women had to rush into the bathroom and get dressed for the day before the relatives awoke.

Romilda introduced Sofia to Rome, and both tried to learn everything they could about employment opportunities in movies, stage productions, nightclubs, and modeling. Television, which was then revolutionizing show business in America, had yet to arrive in Italy, so attendance at cinemas and "live" forms of entertainment was high and promised to get even better as the economy improved.

By 1950, to encourage the growth of its own industry, the Italian government was severely restricting the release of Hollywood films. Also, after being deluged by Hollywood movies in the four years since the war, Italian moviegoers were tired of seeing life portrayed from an American viewpoint. Their demands for more films about their own country, featuring Italian talent, had created a boom in native production.

Quo Vadis, the movie that Sofia and her mother hoped to find work in, was a cross-breed production, the result of Italy's restrictions on the export of monies earned by foreign-owned companies. Metro-Goldwyn-Mayer, one of the Hollywood giants, had accumulated billions of lire since 1946, but could only get the funds out indirectly, by spending it on production in Italy. That made everybody happy because it pumped money back into the Italian economy, while MGM got a ready-made film that would earn dollars when released in the United States.

Quo Vadis would use up about 4 billion of MGM's blocked lire (equivalent to $6.4 million), the studio's highest expenditure since its prewar investment in David O. Selznick's *Gone With the Wind*. In addition, $1 million was spent by MGM in the United States for cameras and equipment that were needed to bring Cinecittà up to current Hollywood standards. MGM's investment turned Cinecittà into probably the finest studio in Europe.

Sofia was too young to remember that *Quo Vadis* had been filmed in Italy once before, way back in 1913, but her mother had seen it as a child. Directed by Enrico Guazzoni, the drama of Christian martyrdom during Nero's reign was the most expensive and spectacular movie produced anywhere up to that time. It became a huge hit all over the world and influenced every biblical or Roman epic made after that, including those of D. W. Griffith and Cecil B. DeMille in the United States. It is still considered one of the masterpieces of the silent cinema.

How do you improve on a masterpiece? MGM intended a colossal Technicolor blend of gore, catastrophe, sex, sadism, and spiritual uplift, with bigger sets and more people than the eye could take in.

For some scenes, MGM would be hiring as many as 30,000 extras, so Sofia and her mother stood a chance of being hired if they arrived at the "cattle call" at daybreak when Cinecittà opened. "Extras" in Italy were not unionized as they were in the United States, which made it easier to get work but for much lower pay than in Hollywood. The salary was 4,000 lire (about $6) per twelve-hour day, plus whatever food you could grab from buffet tables provided at lunch and *ora del tè*.

At Cinecittà that morning, the sexes were being processed separately. Sofia and her mother landed in a waiting area with hundreds of other women. When an assistant director called the names "Scicolone" and "Villani," Sofia and Romilda weren't the only ones to step forward. Joining them was Nella Scicolone, wife of Riccardo, who'd apparently seen an opportunity for herself when her husband told her that Romilda and Sofia were going to try to get work as extras. In any case, Nella pointed at Sofia and yelled, "She's no Scicolone, that's my name! She's Scicolone nothing."

Sofia, of course, did have the legal right to her father's name. Romilda Villani was seething, but an assistant director intervened and sent Nella to calm down until her name could be called again.

All three women were hired as extras, but *Quo Vadis* was a big movie, and they never worked in the same scenes. Sophia Loren would later claim that she never met Nella Scicolone ever again after that one brief moment, but it left an indelible impression. "It was an extraordinary way to meet your stepmother," she said. "I knew about her, of course, because my mother had told me about the marriage. But there in the studio, in front of hundreds of women, having someone dispute your right to your name, and to discover who your accuser actually was, was quite a shock."

Before being assigned to scenes, Sofia and Romilda were asked if they could speak English, which would qualify them for slightly higher pay as bit players. Without hesitating, Romilda said yes, which gained them access to a mass audition in front of the film's American director, Mervyn LeRoy. As they were lining up with about thirty other girls and women, Romilda told Sofia to answer "Yes" to any questions.

When they passed Mervyn LeRoy's table, he showed no interest in Romilda but stopped Sofia to ask if she spoke English and had any previous acting experience. She said "Yes" to both, but when he shifted to "What's your name?" and "How old are you?" and she also answered "Yes," he knew she was faking. More amused than angry, he told an assistant to send her back to the pool of mute extras.

As luck would have it, one of Sofia's idols, Robert Taylor, was the top star of *Quo Vadis,* but she wasn't scheduled for any of his scenes and never even caught a glimpse of him at Cinecittà. Taylor did become involved with two other young actresses working in the film. His escapades with Marina Berti and Lia de Leo hit all the gossip columns and finally caused his wife, actress Barbara Stanwyck, to fly over from California to discredit rumors that their long and supposedly happy marriage was over. Unluckily for Stanwyck, Taylor decided it was. They were divorced the following year.

The filming of *Quo Vadis* at Cinecittà took a full seven months, but unfortunately for Sofia and her mother, MGM tried to be fair in the hiring of extras. There were so many applicants that few worked more than four or five days. Sofia and Romilda earned a grand total of 50,000 lire (about $76) from *Quo Vadis,* which didn't leave them with much to live on while they waited for more such work to materialize. They took a small furnished room on Via Cosenza in the northeastern part of Rome near the garden park of Villa Torlonia.

"The room was part of an apartment that belonged to our landlady, a witch really. She was about sixty and had a lover, a real country bumpkin. This woman became jealous of me. One day she attacked me—grabbed me by the hair and tried to hit me," Sophia Loren remembered.

Romilda intervened, and while holding the woman at bay, she told Sofia to phone Riccardo Scicolone for help. Her father's only response was "You two wanted to stay in Rome, didn't you? You're on your own."

But it didn't end there. After Sofia and her mother packed up and found lodging elsewhere, Romilda advised Scicolone of their new address and he promptly reported them to the police for living in Rome illegally. Scicolone may have claimed that they were working as prostitutes. In any case, they were summoned to the local police station and asked to bring proof of how they were supporting themselves. They showed pay stubs from *Quo Vadis* and a newspaper clipping reporting Sofia's winnings in the Queen of the Sea contest. The officer in charge seemed satisfied and released them.

"I have never in my life felt so degraded as I did that day, in the presence of the police, having to face my own father's insinuations," Sophia Loren remembered. "It seemed he would try anything to send us back to Pozzuoli. His wife was behind it. She didn't want us in Rome because she was afraid we would take him away from her."

Then, at some point in 1950, Sofia's sister, Maria, became seriously ill and Romilda returned to Pozzuoli to take care of her. Sofia, who was no more than sixteen at the time, remained in Rome to pursue her "career." She began to model for *fotoromanzi,* which are similar to comic books but use black-and-white photographs instead of color drawings to illustrate the stories. To some readers, the balloons of dialogue emerging from the mouths of the characters in the *fotoromanzi* looked like puffs of smoke, or *fumetti,* which became the more popular name for the magazines in Italy.

Aimed at an unsophisticated adult readership, *fumetti* were romantic, melodramatic printed versions of the soap operas heard on the radio. They were immensely popular. The public's obsession with the heroes and heroines of *fumetti* had been examined by Michelangelo Antonioni in a 1948 documentary film, *L'amorosa menzogna* (*The Loving Lie*). In 1951, Federico Fellini would get around to spoofing them in his first solely directed feature, *Lo sceicco bianco* (*The White Sheik*).

Working for *fumetti* finally enabled Sofia to call on the dramatic training she had received from Professor Rossini in Naples. Registering emotion was the only acting required in a still photograph that reduced to a mere square inch or so on the printed page. Like comics, the pictures ran in strips; each panel rarely had more than two or three people in it, and props and backdrops were minimal. The advantage of that for Sofia was frequent closeups or medium shots. Her face, if not her name, gradually became known to readers, and not only in Italy. With translated puffs of dialogue, the *fumetti* were often syndicated in other European countries, the United Kingdom, and South America.

With her dark looks, Sofia started out portraying villains and temptresses of gypsy or Arabic extraction. In a story entitled "Man of Her Dreams," she graduated to the role of heroine, a Maltese barmaid in love with a British naval lieutenant who turns out to be heir to a vast fortune.

The scripts, such as they were, took six days to photograph. There were usually about sixty stills per story, but twice that number had to be shot to give the editor a choice. Models rarely appeared in every picture, but were required to be in the studio in case of a sudden change in the schedule. At the conclusion, Sofia would be paid 20,000 lire (about $32), which was no improvement over what she'd earned as an extra on *Quo Vadis,* but at least gave her some public recognition.

After several of Sofia's *fumetti* were published, readers started sending in requests for the name of the anonymous model. Before answering, her editor politely suggested to Sofia that if she had any intention of becoming somebody, she should use a different name than Scicolone, which was easily misspelled and a tongue twister when spoken.

Since Sofia had never been happy with the name or the father it came from, she quickly agreed to the editor's suggestion of Lazzaro, a solid middle-class name that had a nice zing to it as it bridged the opposite ends of the alphabet in a single leap.

A drawback to modeling for *fumetti* was that editors could not use the same faces too often. Sofia was lucky to get one assignment per month, which meant finding additional means of income. One route was the beauty contest, which amounted to a national fixation in those days.

Italians loved watching women compete with their bodies. Contests were always being held somewhere for Miss Rome, Miss Tuscany, Miss Fiat, Miss Extra Virgin Olive Oil, and so on. Prizes of cash or merchandise that could be traded for credit were a lure for Sofia. Movie talent scouts often attended and offered screen tests. At the very least, Italians would see more photographs of her in the newspapers and magazines.

Since Rome was the center of the national railway system, Sofia could get to most parts of Italy quickly and inexpensively. One weekend she traveled to the coastal resort town of Cervia to compete for the title of Queen of the Adriatic Sirens. Entrants were required to wear traditional native costumes provided by the sponsors of the contest. Sofia drew a two-piece peasant dress with ankle-length skirt and a matching bodice, and a white headdress with a long train at the back. She looked so dowdy that she failed to win even an honorable mention.

She had better luck in a "Miss Elegance" contest held at Salsomaggiore, a health resort near Parma. Dressed only in high-heeled shoes and a strapless one-piece bathing suit that her mother made for her, she wasn't quite elegant enough to win, but took home the second prize of 25,000 lire.

Although she possessed the beauty, Sofia would have a hard time convincing anyone that she could be a movie star. She had a Neapolitan accent and the dialect that went with it, both of which were out of favor in Rome.

Making the rounds of casting offices with a scrapbook of her *fumetti* clippings, Sofia was hired as an extra in *Hearts at Sea,*[*] a B-quality melodrama with France's Jacques Sernas, Italy's Milly Vitale, and the American Doris Dowling in the leads. Sofia worked only one day, as a silent onlooker in a restaurant scene, but she gained a credit that enabled her to secure similar jobs. Before 1950 was over, she had decorated the backgrounds of three more films, only one of which, *Bluebeard's Seven Wives* with the beloved comic star Toto, drew crowds.

Somewhere around that time, Sofia met the man who would bring her to the world's attention. So many conflicting stories have been told about when and

---

[*]This title and others that follow are English translations of Italian titles.

how that happened that we may never know the truth. Sophia has claimed to have been anywhere from fourteen and a half to sixteen, which could place the date as early as the spring of 1949. Since *Quo Vadis* did not start filming until a full year later, in May of 1950, it's possible that Sofia and her mother left Pozzuoli for Rome much earlier than is believed.

The official version of what happened is a chance meeting at an open-air nightclub in Oppian Park, near the ancient Colosseum. Sofia happened to be dining there with a few friends from the *fumetti* studios and discovered that a beauty contest was about to begin. When an official came over to ask her if she'd like to participate, she said she wasn't prepared and declined.

A few minutes later the man returned, offering the compliments of one of the judges, movie producer Carlo Ponti, who'd seen her in the crowd and thought she should enter the competition. Needless to say, she did, though Ponti apparently didn't have enough power to sway the jury. Sofia won second place.

"It didn't bother me too much," Sophia Loren recalled. "I hadn't gone there to participate, so I didn't care. But Carlo came over to my table afterwards. He started to talk exactly like a producer. 'Listen,' he said. 'I've launched a great many stars like Lollobrigida, Alida Valli, Rossi Drago, Lucia Bosé. It was for me that they made their first films, I can do the same for you.' But I was skeptical. It was too much like the cliché situation. I just sat there listening with a smile on my face. But he had very kind eyes. He just didn't look at me the way most men did."

Ponti handed Sofia his business card and told her that if she came to his office the next day, he would arrange a screen test. *If?* Nothing could keep her away.

INTRODUCING

SOPHIA LOREN

B y the time of Sofia Scicolone's birth in 1934, Carlo Fortunato Pietro Ponti was nearly twenty-four years old and a rising executive in the Italian film industry. Born in Magenta, a town near Milan, he originally wanted to be an architect, but switched to law because it took less time to get a degree and he wanted to be able to earn good money quickly. While studying at the University of Milan, he paid for his tuition by working part-time in his father's music printing shop. Following graduation, he practiced law privately until a client who was emigrating to America recommended him as his replacement in a film company. Ponti's expertise at writing and negotiating contracts quickly earned him a vice-presidency.

In 1939, Ponti produced his first movie, *Piccolo mondo antico* (*Old-fashioned World*), which was directed by Mario Soldati. It made an overnight star of its leading lady, Alida Valli, and was a box-office smash.

"The success was so big," Ponti later recalled, "that I lost my mind. Women, women, women."

Mussolini's censors interpreted *Piccolo mondo antico*—which was about Italian unification and independence from the Austro-Hungarian Empire—as anti-German propaganda, and Ponti was briefly jailed as a warning to the film industry to be more careful in the future. For the rest of the war, he switched to producing safer romantic dramas and light comedies. Movies were considered essential to public morale during that period; Italian production rose from seventy-seven features in 1939 to ninety-six by 1942, then started to decline and had dropped to thirty-seven in 1944, the last year of the Fascist regime. Ponti produced two or three pictures per year during that period, often working with master directors like Alberto Lattuada, Mario Camerini, and Luigi Zampa.

With all his contacts and experience, Ponti became one of the leaders in the postwar rehabilitation of the Italian film industry. He joined Lux Film and produced some of the first so-called neorealist movies that would restore Italy to its former eminence in the world industry. Box-office hits like Zampa's award-winning *To Live in Peace* and Lattuada's *Without Pity* and *The Mill on the Po* also helped to make Ponti's name familiar to moviegoers outside Italy.

As a star maker, Ponti's most conspicuous achievement was Gina Lollobrigida, whose *busto provocante* had earned her the pet name of "La Lollo" from her countrymen. Ponti produced some of her first hits, including *The Bride Can't Wait* and *Miss Italy,* and launched her on her way to becoming Europe's first postwar sex goddess.

"I don't like actors," Ponti once said. "I prefer women." He has often claimed to have "discovered" the majority of Italy's leading actresses of the early postwar era. Gossip had it that he was personally involved with some of them, as well as many "starlets" who never became more than that.

In 1946, after a marital engagement prolonged by the war, Ponti finally wed his college sweetheart, Giuliana Fiastri, who was also a lawyer. They had two children, Guendolina, born in 1948, and Alexander, who followed two years later.

A tall, willowy brunette, Mrs. Ponti was a shy homebody totally devoted to her husband and family. Ponti was the direct opposite, a night owl who prowled restaurants and night clubs until the wee hours and had a reputation as a skirt chaser. His power in the film industry seemed the main reason for his success with women since he was short, potbellied, and balding. He had no clothes sense and favored drab suits and brightly colored socks.

In 1949, Ponti formed a partnership with another of Lux's producers, Dino De Laurentiis. Although they received financing and Italian distribution from Lux, they planned eventually to become international producers by forging an alliance with one of the major Hollywood studios.

Lux was Italy's equivalent of MGM and operated in the Hollywood manner. Ponti and De Laurentiis adopted the brash style of moguls, with several telephones on their desks and a squad of secretaries and gofers assisting them.

Nine years younger than Ponti, De Laurentiis started working at fourteen in his Neapolitan family's pasta business, but at sixteen he left home to study at the Centro Sperimentale di Cinematografia (National Film School) in Rome. At twenty he started a small production company, but at the outbreak of the war he went into hiding to escape serving in the Italian forces or being conscripted by the Germans.

In 1946, De Laurentiis became a producer at Lux in Rome and went on to a spectacular world success with the 1948 *Riso amaro* (*Bitter Rice*), a sexy melodrama directed by Giuseppe De Santis with Silvana Mangano, Vittorio Gassman, and Raf Vallone in the leading roles. It became the first Italian movie since the silent era to receive wide commercial distribution in the United States and Great Britain.

Standing knee deep in dirty water and dressed only in crotch-hugging shorts and a skintight sweater, eighteen-year-old Silvana Mangano became an instant icon of the Italian cinema with her portrayal of an exploited rice-picker in the Po River paddies. A former dancer and Miss Italy contest winner, Mangano was bachelor De Laurentiis's "protégée" and played small parts in several Lux films before he decided she was ready for bigger things. That included making her his wife in 1949, after she'd confirmed her right to stardom with another box-office hit, *Il lupo della Sila* (*The Wolf of Sila*).

By the time the renamed Sofia Lazzaro met Carlo Ponti that night of the beauty contest in Oppian Park, De Laurentiis and Mangano were the golden couple of the Italian movie world. Sofia surely must have realized that Ponti could be her own Svengali if she played her cards right.

For her visit to Ponti's office the next day, Sofia found herself sans a knock-out dress to wear, so she borrowed a red one with white polka dots from a friend. In her rush, she misread the address that Ponti gave her and arrived at a police station instead. For a moment, she thought she'd been conned, but when she showed Ponti's card to a *carabiniere,* he directed her to the building next door.

"I walked up the stairs, into a large office, and there was Carlo, surrounded by some of his people. He smiled, and I felt guilty for not trusting him," she remembered. Making a deeper impression was the fact that everybody called him "Dr. Ponti," the traditional show of respect for that small minority of Italians who had earned college degrees.

Ponti and De Laurentiis were shooting some scenes for their next movie on the stage of a theater near the office. Ponti took Sofia there to make a screen test during one of the breaks. The wardrobe lady gave her a bathing suit to change into. An assistant director handed her a cigarette and matches to use as props. The test would consist of her lighting up and parading back and forth in front of the camera. Sofia had never smoked in her life, but she pretended to be Bette Davis and got through without a call for a retake.

After Sofia left, the cameraman warned Ponti to expect the worst when the film came back from processing: "She is quite impossible to photograph! Too tall, too big-boned, too heavy all around. The face is too short, the mouth is too wide, the nose too long!"

When he screened the test, Ponti had to agree. He invited Sofia to his office the next day and broke the news as gently as he knew how. He blamed most of the failure on the lighting and the makeup, which she'd applied herself just before the test. A skilled cosmetician could work wonders, but would need a little help, Ponti said. The camera added ten pounds to even the gauntest face, so she could stand to lose some weight and should also do something about her nose. Maybe, just maybe, she should go to a plastic surgeon, as several legendary stars had when they were just starting out.

Sofia got very upset. She admitted that she was probably larger and taller than the average woman, but doubted that dieting would make a difference. Nor would she ever permit an operation on her face. Nothing that Ponti said could change her mind.

Ponti thought that Sofia was nuts, but chalked it off to her being a stubborn teenager trying to get her own way. With so many other aspiring actresses to choose from, he wished Sofia luck with her career, and that seemed to be the end of it.

Of course it wasn't. But how quickly Sofia and Ponti became personally involved, and under what circumstances, is known only to them. Sofia may not have discovered it yet, but Ponti was currently having a passionate affair with a gorgeous twenty-one-year-old blue-eyed blonde from Sweden named Majbritt Wilkens, whom he'd "discovered" on a business trip to Stockholm and brought back to Rome as a Ponti–De Laurentiis contractee. Rechristened May Britt, she made her acting debut in the title role of *Yolanda, Daughter of the Black Pirate* and became an overnight star in Italy.

By the time the three-hour *Quo Vadis* was finally released in November 1951, the "extra" girl Sofia Lazzaro was still a nonentity. She continued modeling for *fumetti* and grabbing whatever film work she could find.

Though she would later deny that Ponti arranged it, Sofia played a bit part in the Ponti–De Laurentiis production *Anna,* another sexy showcase for Silvana Mangano, this time as a nursing nun with a sordid past as a nightclub entertainer and gangster's moll. Costarred were Vittorio Gassman and Raf Vallone, her leads from *Bitter Rice*. Directed by Alberto Lattuada, the melodrama had flashbacks that enabled Mangano to trade her nun's robes for slinky, skintight outfits and perform songs composed for her by Nino Rota. A rhumba called "Baion," also known as "Anna's Song," became a worldwide hit when the movie was released.

Sofia Lazzaro also danced in the movie, but with a male partner as one of many couples in an outdoor party scene. "She looked so good that I decided to give her a line," director Lattuada recalled. "Vittorio Gassman makes a pass at her and says, 'Well, my beauty, when?,' and she replies, 'Never!' ".

Though her appearance amounted to only a few seconds of screen time, Sofia was recognizable to those who knew her, and she received the added satisfaction of being in a box-office smash seen by millions of people. *Anna* was the first Italian movie to gross 1 billion lire in Italy; it went on to earn an additional $3 million in the foreign release.

Sofia didn't need anyone's help in securing a few days' work in *It's Him— Yes, Yes!*, a screwball comedy with Walter Chiari, Italy's equivalent of Danny Kaye. Sofia's awesome breastwork and her willingness to work nude to the waist assured her a front-row place in the corps of harem girls recruited for a scene depicting one of Chiari's erotic dreams.

In those days, Italy had ultrastrict film censorship, and full or partial nudity would never get by, but France, Germany, and Scandinavia were different. The producers wanted to spice up the movie for those markets. The scenes that Sofia worked in for the usual extra's fee of 30,000 lire per day were shot twice. She wore her scanty harem girl's skirt and brassiere the first time, then stripped off the top for the scene that would replace it in the "foreign" version.

Rumor has it that Carlo Ponti saw the rushes of Sofia's breast-baring and discovered hidden talents that were worthy of another screen test. There may have been as many as ten, not all in the presence of cameras or technicians, resulting in an unwritten agreement between them. Sophia Loren would later admit that "I did not ever sign a contract with Carlo. He told me: 'I, personally, am going to give you a certain amount of money each month and I am going to take care of you in the film business.' So we had this agreement, but it was always outside of the Ponti–De Laurentiis production company."

For starters, Ponti enrolled Sofia at the National Film School to study acting and to lose her Neapolitan accent. A fleet of blue trolley cars connected downtown Rome to the school's front doors, which were nine miles into the suburbs and directly opposite the sprawling Cinecittà studios. Classes were scheduled with working students in mind, which meant that Sofia wouldn't have to pass up any job opportunities that came along.

Presumably, Ponti's "taking care" of Sofia also included a cash subsidy for her rent and other expenses. By this time, Sofia's mother and sister had moved up permanently from Pozzuoli to live with her. Sofia's sporadic earnings as a model and film extra were hardly enough to support one person, let alone three.

Due to her sufferings with Riccardo Scicolone, Romilda Villani was very suspicious of Carlo Ponti's interest in Sofia. She feared that Ponti was just another philandering married man who would dump Sofia as soon as he found someone more attractive. Even if he were in love with Sofia, he could never marry her because of Italy's divorce laws. Romilda wanted to spare her daughter the shame and humiliation that she'd gone through as Scicolone's discarded mistress.

Romilda may also have been jealous of Ponti's becoming the maestro of Sofia's career. Up to now, Romilda had been the guiding force. Whenever Sofia was working or interviewing for jobs, Romilda usually went with her and did any negotiating that was necessary. Around magazine offices and film studios, Romilda was known as *il maresciallo* (the major), a role she reveled in but would lose if Ponti took over.

Romilda always claimed credit for landing Sofia her first movie role of any consequence, but it was Ponti who was responsible. Through the grapevine, Ponti heard of some work that might suit Sofia over at Titanus Film, so he phoned his friend, studio head Geoffredo Lombardo, and arranged an audition for her.

The movie in preparation, *Africa sotto i mari* (*Africa Under the Seas*), started out as a documentary, photographed in glorious Italian Ferraniacolor in the depths of the Red Sea off the coast of Ethiopia. But Titanus decided the footage wasn't exciting enough on its own and intended turning it into a ninety-minute feature, with a fictional story about a documentary film crew linking the undersea scenes. Sofia auditioned for the role of a spoiled rich girl who falls in love with the skipper of a yacht chartered by the filmmakers.

Fortunately, Sofia brought both a bathing suit and her mother to the interview. The director liked Sofia's looks, but when he asked if she could swim, she had to look to Romilda for advice before she lied yes. Sofia got the job, which included a week of filming in the sea beyond Rome's coastal resorts. On the first day, the director ordered her to jump from the boat into the water and bob up in front of the cameras. Looking into the murky depths, she lost her nerve and confessed she couldn't swim. Couldn't they just hire another girl and let her go home?

The director refused, claiming it would cost a fortune in delays. He said there were several professional swimmers working as lifeguards who could probably teach her enough to get by, but in the meantime she must do the shot. There would be someone in the water to make sure she didn't drown. Before she had time to argue, he pushed her in.

To get the best available light, the director had positioned the cameras at the rear of the boat. Sofia went down within a few feet of the propellers, and might have been chopped to pieces if a lifeguard hadn't immediately grabbed her and pulled her away.

In a few days Sofia had learned to swim well enough to do some underwater scenes wearing an Aqualung and fins. What she had yet to master, however, was how to speak intelligibly for the dramatic scenes. Her voice later had to be dubbed by another actress, which, by Italian standards, was nothing shameful. Because of the diversity of dialects and to save on costly retakes due to noise or other disturbances on the set, most Italian films were "postsynchronized," which means that the spoken dialogue was rerecorded and matched as closely as possible to lip movements. If the original actor wasn't available or had voice problems, he or she would be replaced. As a classic example of that, Italian moviegoers never heard Gina Lollobrigida's real voice coming from the screen until well after she became a major star.

While *Africa Under the Seas* was being edited, Geoffredo Lombardo decided that a leading lady named Sofia Lazzaro wasn't likely to help Titanus get foreign distribution for the movie. Antonio Cifariello, the Italian actor playing opposite Sofia, had already been rechristened Steve Barclay. Lombardo summoned Sofia to his office to discuss changing her name.

Glancing around the room for inspiration, Lombardo focused on a poster for an upcoming Titanus film starring Marta Toren, a Swedish actress who'd resumed working in Europe after failing to click in Hollywood. Lombardo removed the "T," took the "L" from his own name, and came up with "Loren," not a name known in Italy. "Sofia Loren" struck a nice balance with five letters each, but Lombardo suggested that "Sofia" be changed to "Sophia," which would make it more pronounceable to the Americans and British. Unfortunately, the sound of "ph" as "f" doesn't exist in the Italian language, so Sofia would have to contend with being called "Sopia" in her own country.

Sofia went along with Lombardo's suggestions, but it took many years for Italians to finally accept them. Italian purists often turned "Sophia" back into "Sofia" in the news media and in the advertising for her movies, and there wasn't much that she could do about it.

Her first movie under the name of Sophia Loren flopped in Italy and received distribution elsewhere only years later, after she had become an international star. Dubbed into English in 1957, *Africa Under the Seas* was retitled *Woman of the Red Sea* and ran on the exploitation circuits in the United States and England with a mammary-driven advertising campaign copied from Jane Russell's *Underwater.* It quickly sank to the same watery grave.

The film's release in Italy in 1952 at least gave Sophia Loren entry into the media world beyond *fumetti.* Gossip magazines and tabloids gobbled up every sexy publicity still that Titanus distributed and demanded more of the same. Carlo Ponti hired a press agent named Mario Natale to make sure that no photo opportunities were missed. In her eagerness to be a success, Sophia tried to keep the photographers happy, even if it meant swirling her skirt waist high to expose her scanty lingerie. A magazine cover showing Sophia wrapped only in a towel incited the censors to ban the issue from sale and to sue the publisher for indecency.

With her publicist's help, Sophia's breastwork became the sensation of Italy. One day in Rome, Natale let it be known that she was going shopping for brassieres in a shop on the Via Condotti. Three fire brigades had to be summoned to break up a mob of men who stormed into the place and trapped Sophia in one of the try-on cubicles.

As a cover for Sophia's very private relationship with Ponti, Natale matched her up with another of his clients, a handsome young singer named Achille Togliani. When Sophia and Togliani started turning up together at all the movie premieres and nightclub openings, the press labeled them lovers and soon had them engaged to be married. *Oggi* reported Sophia ordering a wedding dress from Count Ledio Galateri, a famed Neapolitan designer. It was all nonsense, but kept her name in the headlines.

Though Sophia Loren was fast becoming famous, producers weren't showering her with film offers, which caused Carlo Ponti to take up the slack by handing her a small role in the next Ponti–De Laurentiis effort, *La tratta delle bianche* (*The White Slave Trade*). It was another steamy melodrama in the tradition of *Bitter Rice* and *Anna,* but a bit too trashy now for Silvana Mangano, whose husband had insisted on more prestigious films.

The script focused on a Genoa vice ring that recruits chorus girls and stripteasers for nightclub jobs in South America, where the women end up working in bordellos instead. Two of Italy's reigning sexpots, Silvana Pampanini and Eleanora Rossi Drago, portrayed the major victims. Vittorio Gassman had the romantic lead, with Marc Lawrence, the scar-faced veteran of countless Hollywood gangster movies, enacting the sadistic ring leader (his voice would be dubbed by an Italian actor).

Director Luigi Comencini had a knack for working with women, so Ponti felt comfortable putting Sophia in his charge. Besides a learning experience for Sophia, it also gave Ponti a chance to experiment with lighting and makeup to overcome her large nose and other physical flaws. He may have gone too far. When the movie was released in Italy, several critics said that newcomer Sophia Loren was difficult to keep track of because she looked so different in each of her several scenes.

Sophia portrayed a starstruck girl who enters one of the dance contests that the white slavers use to find "talent" for foreign export. Though she had the smallest of fourteen speaking roles, she received a salary of 250,000 lire per week (about $400), one of the perks of being the producer's protégée. Still, it was only a week's work, and not likely to spoil her. Sophia's "big" scene, if it could be called that, lasted all of ninety seconds, but she shared it with Silvana Pampanini, a former Miss Italy and Italy's equivalent of Marilyn Monroe. While dancing in the contest, Sophia collapses and is carried into singer Pampanini's dressing room to recuperate. As Sophia regains consciousness, she confesses to Pampanini that she's pregnant.

When the rushes of Sophia's bit were screened the next day, someone in the darkened projection room babbled excitedly, "*Mamma mia,* she eats up Pampanini. The girl is terrific!" No doubt Ponti had more than just yes-men working for him.

Sophia's voice was again dubbed for *The White Slave Trade.* That didn't matter for an actress in a minor role, but if Sophia was going to advance to playing leads, she would have to use her own voice. The critics in Italy detested stars who relied on the voices of others; it was considered cheating, giving half a performance at best.

Carlo Ponti hesitated about hiring Sophia for another of his own films; if she turned up in too many, the press might become suspicious and a scandal could erupt. Professionally, the most that Ponti could do was to badger other producers into giving her work. Unfortunately for her, starlets would never be in short supply. Until Sophia Loren proved that she had that extra ingredient that made a star, nobody was much interested.

Ponti finally made a breakthrough when Gina Lollobrigida rejected an offer of the title role in *Aida,* a condensed version of Verdi's opera that would retain all the principal arias and ballets. To overcome the incongruity of stout opera singers portraying svelte and sexy roles, the producers intended to dub the best voices of La Scala and the Rome Opera into the throats of the most attractive actors they could find. Lollobrigida considered it an insult to be a mere stand-in for Renata Tebaldi, but it seemed a made-in-heaven opportunity for Sophia Loren. It was the big star part she needed to start her on her way, and all it required of her was to look beautiful and to pretend to be singing.

Although his name would not be attached to *Aida,* Ponti reportedly invested 50 million lire (about $80,000) of his personal funds in the production to make certain that Sophia got the part instead of Silvana Pampanini, Rossana Podesta, or several other established stars who were being considered to replace Lollobrigida. Renzo Rossellini, brother of Ponti's director-friend Roberto, was the musical supervisor of *Aida* and allegedly served as Ponti's go-between with producers Ferrucio de Martino and Federico Teti.

Before filming began, Sophia spent two weeks with Renzo Rossellini listening to the recordings that Renata Tebaldi had already made for the soundtrack. Sophia needed to learn all the lyrics and be able to sing along so that her lip movements synchronized with Tebaldi's voice. Sophia stood in front of a mirror for hours every day, trying to match every word and at the same time working on the facial expressions and hand gestures that went with acting the role.

Aida is an Ethiopian princess who has been captured by the Egyptian army and brought back to serve as personal slave to the pharaoh's daughter, Amneris. The role of Aida was usually performed according to the theory that she had dark skin, achieved with makeup. (Prior to 1960, no singer of African heritage had been given a chance at the role.) Since Sophia's complexion already had an olive quality, the makeup department decided to use a shade known as "Egyptian #24." In Sophia's case, her entire body had to be painted. The costumes designed by Maria de Matteis revealed more flesh than any worn by previous Aidas on stage or screen. To save hairdressing time, Sophia wore frizzy black wigs that would have been described as "Afro" if the word had been in use then.

In silent days, *Aida* had been filmed several times in various countries—nonsinging dramatizations, of course, but with theater orchestras, pianists, or organists playing Verdi's music for background. There was at least one sound version (in Italy before the war), but Sophia's was the first *Aida* to be photographed in color and may also have been, as the producers claimed, the very first opera film in color (research suggests that the Russians beat them to it with a version of *Boris Godunov*). It was certainly the first in Ferraniacolor, a single-negative process with fidelity claimed equal to Hollywood's more expensive three-negative Technicolor.

Director Clemente Fracassi wanted to make a real movie rather than a photographic copy of an opera house production, so filming took three months on colossal sets that covered every sound stage at Rome's Scalera Studios. The scenes in which Sophia appeared amounted to about a month's work in early 1953.

"I nearly froze to death," she recalled. "The scenes were supposed to be in sultry Egypt, but the filming took place in winter in an unheated studio. To dispel the clouds of steam coming from my mouth whenever I opened it, a makeup man kept a hair dryer pointed at my lips."

Aida made a star of Sophia Loren, but not overnight. It would be six months before the movie was released in Italy and another year or more before it reached other countries. The foreign distribution was entrusted to a governmental agency, Italian Films Export (IFE), which dealt with the major markets. In the United States, IFE also had a company called IFE Films, which distributed movies that American firms were reluctant to handle for reasons of limited appeal or censorship problems.

But meanwhile, the advance publicity for *Aida* created more interest in Sophia Loren and landed her lots more film work. In 1953 she made a total of ten movies, bobbing back and forth between leads and supporting roles.

"I will be a big star," she told an interviewer at the time. "I want everything that big stars have, and I will work very hard for it. I am not going to be poor any more."

About half of those ten 1953 films carried the imprint of Carlo Ponti, who also used his influence to get Sophia the other roles. By then, Ponti and De Laurentiis had made a foreign distribution deal with Paramount Pictures and were getting ready to produce a spectacular version of Homer's *Odyssey* with Kirk Douglas as Ulysses (Odysseus). The project seemed an ideal one for Sophia, but De Laurentiis got there first with his wife, Silvana Mangano, who wound up enacting all three of the main female characters (Penelope, Circe, and Calypso)!

After *Aida,* Sophia portrayed an aspiring music hall entertainer who supports herself by posing for naughty postcards in *Carosello napoletano* (*Neapolitan Carousel*). The episodic color musical was based on a popular stage extravaganza and traced the history of Neapolitan song and dance from the Middle Ages to the present.

During the making of *Tempi nostri* (*Our Times*), a collection of comedy sketches with a large cast of prominent Italian and French players, Sophia met Vittorio De Sica and Marcello Mastroianni for the first time, but they didn't actually work together in the film. Sophia landed in the shortest episode, as stooge to the lantern-jawed comedian Toto, who portrayed an amateur photographer using her as his model.

Director Alessandro Blasetti recalled: "Sophia was then very untried, to say the least, and I was apprehensive about a couple of scenes that she had to do with Toto, who was notorious for improvising dialogue and adding his own little flights of fancy not in the script. Suddenly we're shooting one of these scenes, and he's doing exactly what I was afraid of. But there was Sophia, giving as good as she got, daring Toto to go along even further. There was an instinctive Neapolitan rapport between the two of them."

Sophia darkened her complexion again for *Due notti con Cleopatra* (*Two Nights with Cleopatra*), in which she played both the Egyptian queen and a slave girl impostor. Comedian Alberto Sordi, who would later become one of Italy's foremost stars, had the task of trying to bed both Sophias. For the foreign release version, she again agreed to bare her breasts, which were brushed with "Egyptian 24" to match the rest of her.

Though she missed out on *Ulysses,* Sophia got a leading part in another Ponti–De Laurentiis epic, *Attila, flagello di Dio* (*Attila, Scourge of God*). The title role went to Anthony Quinn, who had a three-picture deal with Ponti–De Laurentiis that also included *Ulysses* and Federico Fellini's upcoming *La Strada.*

For the first time Sophia played a villain, the deceitful sister of a Roman emperor who is under attack by Attila, king of the Huns, and his barbaric tribesmen. After disposing of her brother, the new Empress Honoria offers herself to Attila, in hopes of co-ruling the world as his queen. But Attila is only interested in bedding Honoria, and afterwards he orders her killed. Attila is finally defeated when Pope Leo, with help from God, summons up a devastating windstorm just as the Huns are about to pillage Rome.

Anthony Quinn was the first Hollywood star of any importance that Sophia had ever worked with. He'd recently won an Oscar for his supporting performance opposite Marlon Brando in *Viva Zapata!,* but he was regarded by many colleagues as an egomaniac.

Quinn had caused so much trouble during the filming of *Ulysses* that Carlo Ponti warned Pietro Francisci, the director of *Attila,* to make sure that the actor treated Sophia decently and didn't get out of line. Quinn, who'd yet to learn of Sophia's affair with Ponti, got a shock when he was getting ready for their first love scene. As he later recalled:

"This guy who was one of the English-Italian interpreters on the set comes up to me and says, 'Please, take it easy with Sophia in this scene.' I said, 'Why do you want me to take it easy?' And he repeats, 'Just take it easy, that's all.'

"I said, 'Come on—what kind of shit is this? What do you mean? I play a love scene, so I play a love scene! Okay?' But I notice nobody is saying anything. As it was, it was going to be a terrible scene because I'm eating lamb chops at the time. I'm this barbarian Hun and suddenly, when I see Sophia, I have to grab her, kiss her, and start making love to her with a half-eaten lamb chop in my mouth."

Quinn sent the interpreter over to Sophia to ask her if she had made the request. "Sophia denied knowing anything about it, so I spoke to the director and there was a big, big hassle. He took me aside and said, 'Listen, she's a friend of the producer.' I said, 'Fuck you. Nobody's going to tell me how to play a love scene with this girl.' When the time came, I grabbed her and kissed her the way a barbarian is supposed to kiss, except I've still got this lamb chop in my mouth. And it was a hell of a kiss. But I must say, Sophia took it very sweetly. She knew that what I did was out of defiance, and she pulled back, started to laugh, and said, 'You don't have to take it out on me because they told you to take it easy!' And that was that."

Sophia later described it as "my most unpleasant experience as an actress." Fortunately, her character is murdered halfway through *Attila,* so she didn't have to put up with Quinn's misbehavior beyond the two weeks it took to film all of their scenes together.

Like many of Sophia's early films, *Attila* had a peculiar distribution history. Released in Europe and England in 1954, it was such a critical and box-office disaster that Ponti–De Laurentiis couldn't find a buyer for the American rights until 1958, when an obscure Boston distributor named Joseph E. Levine would acquire them for $75,000.

When Carlo Ponti viewed the rushes of Sophia's work in *Attila,* he was appalled by her hammy histrionics and realized that she needed help from a master if she was ever to become an accomplished actress. Who better than his close friend Vittorio De Sica, who had directed nonprofessionals to astonishing heights in *Shoeshine* and *The Bicycle Thief,* and was himself one of Italy's greatest actors?

De Sica and his script-writing partner, Cesare Zavattini, were preparing a multi-episode comedy-drama for Ponti–De Laurentiis based on Giuseppe Marotta's popular book *L'oro di Napoli* (*Gold of Naples*). Silvana Mangano had already been cast in one of the six stories. Surely there was also room for Ponti's protégée in another.

To spare Sophia distress if De Sica decided not to use her in the film, Ponti arranged a casual meeting between the two just to get acquainted. They'd seen each other around the studios but had never really talked. While not actually born in Naples, De Sica had grown up there, so they had an instant rapport. As they chatted about their past experiences, he became enchanted.

"It was a revelation," De Sica remembered. "Sophia was created differently, behaved differently, affected me differently, from any other woman I have known. I looked at that face, those unbelievable eyes, and saw it all as a miracle. . . . The outstanding quality was her impulsiveness. Neapolitans are extroverts. All her gestures and statements were always outgoing. Nothing is held inside. No internal reflection. I don't say this only of Sophia, all we Neapolitans are the same. We improvise. We speak first, think later. We go by instinct."

Sophia, of course, got the part, and also found a father figure who would be second only to Carlo Ponti in her professional life. The silver-haired De Sica was then fifty-two years old. Before World War II, he had been Italy's leading romantic actor, often compared to Cary Grant and Ronald Colman. He was still in great demand for starring roles, which filled the gaps between his directorial assignments and helped to support a double private life that included a wife and daughter, a mistress and illegitimate sons.

In *Gold of Naples,* De Sica assigned Sophia to a vignette with actors Giacomo Furia and Alberto Farnes entitled "Pizza on Credit," in which she played the philandering wife of the owner of a pizza bakery. When her husband notices that she's not wearing her wedding ring, she suddenly remembers that she left it on a table in her lover's bedroom during their last tryst. To save herself, she claims that the ring must have slipped off her finger while she was making the pizza dough. She then sneaks a phone call to her lover and tells him to order a pizza and pretend that he found the ring inside. Her husband, however, turns out to be not as dumb or unsuspecting as she assumes.

The location filming took Sophia back to Naples and the streets she knew from her youth. "From the first day, De Sica became my school, my teacher, my mentor, my everything," she recalled. "Every day he would arrive on the set and say, 'Ah, *Sophia cara,* it's so beautiful to see you first thing in the morning, you make my day.' I couldn't have found anyone better to be with in the beginning of my career.

"The thing I always remember most is De Sica saying, 'When the camera comes close up, *do* something, so you won't be frightened by it. So many actors I see are frightened by the camera.' Acting is so personal, to be able to portray what's inside you. The treasure inside nobody can give you, but with De Sica I learned how to bring out whatever I had within me. I was like a child when I started. How could I show it? Nobody knew what was inside of me— least of all I myself."

The twenty-minute episode would be memorable for a scene of Sophia strutting through the neighborhood during a rainstorm, with her drenched dress clinging to her body, her bosoms bouncing and her eyes flashing at every man she passes. "De Sica made it so easy for me," she remembered. "Whatever a scene required, he always did it first and showed me what he wanted. All I had to do was imitate him. You should have seen him with one hand on his hip, doing the walk for me. Then, while you are working, he stands close to the camera and acts along with you. His face lights, his eyes dance, his mouth, his shoulders, his arms, his whole body acts with you, almost as if he carries you along with him. And it becomes contagious—like he spills his emotion into you and through you back into the camera."

Sophia's return to Naples to work in a De Sica movie caused rejoicing among her family in Pozzuoli. The little stick had become the town heroine. Grandpa Domenico gave copies of her glossy publicity stills to shopkeepers to display in their windows. Sadly, Grandma Luisa had cancer and was too ill to visit the filming. She died six months later, aware that her dreams for her granddaughter were starting to come true.

Carlo Ponti adored Sophia's performance in *Gold of Naples* and decided to risk a full-length starring vehicle similar to the lurid melodramas that launched Gina Lollobrigida and Silvana Mangano into sexpot heaven. The result was *Woman of the River,* a blend of Lollo's *The Wayward Wife* and Mangano's *Bitter Rice* that required the services of eight writers, including novelist Alberto Moravia for the original idea and young Pier Paolo Pasolini for some of the dialogue. Ponti assigned the direction to Mario Soldati, a much-revered filmmaker and novelist whose work was noted for its spontaneity and vitality and who'd guided Alida Valli to a star-making performance in Ponti's first success, *Piccolo mondo antico.*

Since Ponti couldn't be at the studio or on location every day, he selected his longtime associate, Basilio Franchina, to be the film's associate producer. The Sicilian-born writer had been Ponti's troubleshooter, doctoring scripts when they needed it, pacifying difficult stars and directors, and so forth, but from now on he would be associated with all of Sophia's films, and not always with his name in the credits. Franchina spent so much time around Sophia that many believed him to be her bodyguard and under orders from Ponti to make sure she didn't get romantically involved with any of her male associates.

Like Silvana Mangano in the black-and-white *Bitter Rice,* Sophia would wear brief shorts and tight sweaters or blouses through most of *Woman of the River,* but Ponti splurged on Technicolor photography to heighten her voluptuousness. The story was again set among the peasants of the Po River valley, where the hip-booted Sophia cuts sugar cane and struggles to raise an illegitimate two-year-old son whose father is a villainous boat captain currently in jail for smuggling. Sophia had tipped off the police after he refused to marry her, so when he breaks out of jail, she'd better watch out.

In *Bitter Rice,* Mangano had Vittorio Gassman and Raf Vallone fighting over her. Both actors had advanced to high-salaried stardom by this time, so Ponti hired sexy Italian newcomer Rik Battaglia and the dapper Frenchman Gerard Oury to costar with Sophia. By casting Oury in one of the leads, Ponti qualified the movie as an international coproduction and could collect subsidies from both the French and Italian governments, which was becoming a necessity as filming costs soared and the raising of financial backing became more difficult.

Sophia's portrayal of sultry Nives Mongolini ran the dramatic gamut, from passionate lovemaking in bedroom scenes to an emotional breakdown when her little boy drowns in the river. When Sophia first read the script, she felt she wasn't experienced enough to do the role justice. By the third day of filming she had developed a wheezing condition that her doctor diagnosed as asthma. It came only at night, but was accompanied by fever and prevented her from sleeping.

Basilio Franchina suspected it was psychosomatic, since it miraculously disappeared every day when she arrived on the set and became engrossed in her work. To ease her insecurities, he began coaching her on the more difficult scenes; with the completion of each one, her breathing problems gradually eased. After the final scene, which she did in one take, her "asthma" vanished and never returned.

The last filming day of *Woman of the River* happened to be Sophia's twentieth birthday, which called for a double celebration. But she wasn't quite prepared for the surprise that Carlo Ponti sprang when he came over to the corner of the set where she was sitting and placed a little box in her hand. When she opened it and found a diamond ring inside, she looked at Ponti in stunned amazement, but he just smiled back and then walked away.

"It was a marvelous yet frightening moment," she remembered. "It was the first time I sensed I meant more to him than just an actress under contract. Every moment of my day, all my thoughts and feelings were concentrated on him. I realized he was married with two children. Yet at that age you don't try and rationalize passion. I loved him deeply, and he had given me a ring. He hadn't kissed me. He didn't say, 'I love you and want to marry you.' Nothing. But it was a ring just the same. I went back into my dressing room and wept."

If Ponti intended it as an engagement ring, theirs promised to be a long engagement, since his wife was in excellent health. In Italy, divorce was next to impossible, except under extreme circumstances that had to be approved by the Vatican.

When Sophia showed the ring to her mother, Romilda looked at it disgustedly and said it would bring nothing but heartbreak. Ponti was too old for Sophia, a married man with two children. If he was a good father, he would never leave them. If Sophia wanted to go through the same suffering that she had with Riccardo Scicolone, she was welcome to it.

6

CHEESECAKE AND
ENGLISH MUTTON

⁂

W HATEVER the future of Sophia Loren's relationship with Carlo Ponti, it was certainly doing her career no harm. Nor her jewelry box or wardrobe closet. Ponti was the most generous of protectors. Starting a custom that continued over the years, he surprised her with something dazzling in diamonds, rubies, or emeralds whenever she completed another movie. He gave her charge accounts at all the top fashion houses and boutiques in Rome and Milan, and took her to Paris several times a year to buy whatever she wanted at her adored Christian Dior. Of course, Ponti could find ways of writing most of it off as a business expense, aimed at making Sophia Loren one of the most glamorous movie stars in the world, but it was still his thoughtfulness that counted and endeared him even more to her.

The year 1954 proved to be Sophia's first big season. The steady barrage of publicity stemming from *Aida, Gold of Naples,* and *Woman of the River* made her famous in Italy and started to establish her in Europe and the rest of the world even before the films were released.

Naturally, most of the attention was focused on Sophia's anatomy, which made her a serious contender in the news media's seemingly never-ending search for the world's best-endowed beauty. In Italy, at least, she already seemed to be number one. In a survey conducted by IFE as part of its efforts to popularize Italian movies abroad, Sophia scored highest among twenty actresses who symbolized the best (and the most) that Italy had to offer.

The results, published in an illustrated brochure entitled "*Bella, Bella!:* A Glossary of Italian Film Beauties," cited Sophia's bust, waist, and hip measurements as an hourglass-shaped 38-24-37, and her height as 5'9". A full inch smaller in every way were Silvana Pampanini and Gianna Maria Canale. Italy's current glamour queen, Gina Lollobrigida, was only 36-22-35 and 5'6".

Six years older than Sophia, La Lollo had been the first of the postwar European sex-bombs, creating as much excitement worldwide as Hollywood's Marilyn Monroe, Rita Hayworth, and Ava Gardner. Critics described her acting ability as minimal, but from age eighteen, her beauty had gained her stardom in Italian and French movies. In 1949, Howard Hughes, owner of RKO, signed her to a seven-year Hollywood contract, but when he tried some sexual hanky-panky, Lollobrigida fled back to Italy. She was legally barred from working in the United States for the balance of her RKO deal. However, she was in great demand in Europe, and three of many films that she made gained her international fame: the Italian sex romp, *Bread, Love, and Dreams,* with Vittorio De Sica; the French swashbuckler *Fanfan la Tulipe,* opposite Gérard Philipe; and John Huston's British-made *Beat the Devil,* where she costarred with Humphrey Bogart and Jennifer Jones.

Sophia's press agent, Mario Natale, saw an opportunity to capitalize on Lollobrigida's great popularity and started a "battle of the bosoms." The two women had never met, but Lollobrigida had often worked for Carlo Ponti in the past and was a close friend of his wife. Any animosity that Lollobrigida expressed toward Sophia was motivated more by Sophia's husband-stealing than by professional rivalry.

Their paths finally crossed at the 1954 Berlin Film Festival. It was Sophia's first trip abroad, another confirmation of her rising status. She was part of a contingent of celebrities that IFE flew over for the opening gala. Included in the group was Yvonne De Carlo, one of the Hollywood idols of Sophia's youth, who'd just finished a film in Rome. Sophia went a bit gaga when she recognized De Carlo. She threw her arms around her and asked if she noticed any similarities. De Carlo's distinctive eye makeup, with a thin line drawn close to the lashes in the style of ancient Egyptians, had made such an impression on Sophia that she'd been copying it ever since.

Later, at a cocktail party where all the celebrities were scattered about the room, a photographer asked De Carlo if she'd pose with Sophia and Gina Lollobrigida. De Carlo agreed, but insisted upon checking with the others to make sure that they were willing. De Carlo walked over to Lollobrigida first and received a frigid "With *that* woman?" response at the mention of Sophia's name. But De Carlo finally persuaded her, and the three lined up, with the American in the middle to make sure that no Italian *sangue* was spilled. All three were wearing low-cut dresses and the short "Italian cut" hairstyle that was all the rage then. When the photo was sent out over the wire services, the accompanying caption was headlined "Need They Look So Much Alike?" But apart from the haircuts, their differences were obvious.

Several months later, the "feud" accelerated when Sophia and Lollobrigida were part of a group flown to London for Italian Film Week, a cultural event sponsored by IFE to showcase movies that had yet to be released in England. Lollobrigida stormed out of a press reception at the Savoy Hotel when photographers tried to talk her into joining Sophia for a chest measuring contest. Sophia, garbed in a skintight woolen knit dress, made the most of the situation. She told a reporter: "Why is Gina mad at me? I want to be friendly with her, why not? It's true that my measurements excel hers, but is that a reason to be furious with me?"

Queen Elizabeth and the Duke of Edinburgh attended the opening night festivities at the Tivoli Theatre. Before Sophia left Rome, Carlo Ponti had bought her a stunning white strapless evening gown, with a matching fur-trimmed cape, to wear for the occasion. To top it off, she chose a rhinestone tiara for her hair.

When Sophia joined the royal reception line that night, an official told her it was improper to wear a tiara in the presence of the queen, but Sophia didn't want to disturb her coiffure and kept it on. Queen Elizabeth looked a bit perturbed when Sophia curtsied before her, but she said nothing as photographers' cameras flashed. The next day the news tabloids had a field day, reporting sarcastically that England now had two queens, Queen Elizabeth and Queen Sophia, and implying that Sophia had done it deliberately to win publicity for herself. If she did, she certainly succeeded.

By this time *Aida* had been released in Italy, where opera is a sacred national pastime. Critics blasted the movie's abridged music and libretto. Reviewers also weren't impressed by Sophia's performance, with comments like "She registers every emotion with her bosom" and "She has a minimum of talent and a maximum of everything else."

In the United States, opera had a devoted but minuscule following, so IFE could not get a distributor for *Aida* and finally had to release the movie itself, making a deal with impresario Sol Hurok to front for it. The hallmark "S. Hurok presents" had been attached to classical music events and ballet for forty-five years, but never before to a movie. For a percentage of the gross, the Russian-born Hurok agreed to promote *Aida* through his nationwide subscription list. He had such a prestigious reputation that his sponsorship was crucial.

Aida had its American premiere in November 1954 at New York's Little Carnegie Playhouse, a 600-seat "art" cinema a few doors east of Carnegie Hall. Carlo Ponti wanted to fly Sophia over from Rome to publicize the opening, but Hurok nixed it. Since she didn't speak fluent English and would not be able to do interviews without the aid of an interpreter, Hurok was afraid that she'd wind up getting the sort of tawdry photo coverage that might offend the dignified audience of opera lovers that he needed to reach.

With help from a favorable review by *New York Times*'s Bosley Crowther, who was the most influential American film critic, especially for foreign-made releases, *Aida* broke the box-office record in its first week and went on to run for several months. Crowther wrote of the star performance:

> Sophia Loren, the handsome girl who plays the dark-skinned and regal Aida, might just as well be singing the glorious airs that actually come from the throat of Renata Tebaldi and have been synchronised to her lip movements. The advantage is that a fine voice is set to a stunning form and face, which is most gratifying (and unusual) in the operatic realm.

According to IFE, *Aida* eventually played 250 engagements throughout the United States, earning about $300,000 in rentals. Though *Aida* was actually seen by a scattered few, the corresponding advertising and publicity for the movie at least introduced Sophia Loren to the mass American public and made her a recognizable name and face. Amusingly, it also encouraged IFE to raise her to star billing in *The White Slave Trade,* which was dubbed into English and retitled *Girls Marked Danger* for release to Main Street "exploitation" theaters that specialized in sexy foreign fare.

Back in Italy, Sophia had just finished *Woman of the River* when Alessandro Blasetti, director of her episode with Toto in *Tempi nostri,* decided she was ready for a full-length leading role and arranged through Carlo Ponti to hire her for a comedy entitled *Peccato che sia una canaglia* (freely translated as *Too Bad She's Bad*). Blasetti, whose reputation had survived several pro-fascist masterworks made during the Mussolini regime, had the bright idea of teaming Sophia with two of his favorite actors, Vittorio De Sica and Marcello Mastroianni.

Sophia agreed to tint her hair blondish for the title role, a change that suited her face very well and tempted her to keep it that way. She portrayed De Sica's daughter, following in his footsteps as a pickpocket and thief. In fact, their whole family are crooks, but Marcello Mastroianni, as a Rome taxi driver, is a victim who turns Sophia honest when they fall in love.

Blasetti was the first to discover that for Sophia, just acting opposite De Sica brought the same results as being directed by him. Their Neapolitan souls merged, and while Mastroianni came from a bit farther north in the region, he had the same temperament and meshed perfectly with them.

"As soon as we met on the set, there was a spark between us," Sophia remembered. "The three of us were united in a kind of complicity that the Neapolitans always have among themselves. The same sense of humor, the same rhythms, the same philosophies of life, the same natural cynicism. All three of us did our roles instinctively."

The combination worked so well that Carlo Ponti wanted some of it for the Ponti–De Laurentiis company and commissioned director Mario Camerini to prepare a remake of his *The Three-Cornered Hat,* which had been a prewar smash hit. Meanwhile, Sophia filled time by acting with De Sica again in director Dino Risi's droll comedy, *The Sign of Venus,* in which she had a showy supporting role as the wanton cousin of a desperate spinster (played by rising star Franca Valeri). In the modern adaptation of a story by Anton Chekhov, Sophia had flings with De Sica, Raf Vallone, and Alberto Sordi before the fade-out.

With Sophia, De Sica, and Mastroianni in the leads, *The Three-Cornered Hat* became *The Miller's Beautiful Wife* in the latest version of the classic play by Pedro de Alarcón. Director Camerini's earlier (1934) filming had starred his actress-wife, Assia Noris, one of the great beauties of the Italian cinema. To erase memories of that black-and-white studio-made film, Ponti chose to shoot his protégée's version on historic locations in color and the new wide-screen process known as CinemaScope.

Set in seventeenth-century Naples during the time of the Spanish occupation, the plot found De Sica as a lecherous Spanish governor who overtaxes the peasant proprietors and chases after their wives. To conquer Sophia, he sends hubby Mastroianni to jail on false charges, then offers to trade a pardon for a night in her bed. But the crafty Sophia makes sure that De Sica signs the pardon first, then slips him a mickey and rushes to get Mastroianni released. But alas, her husband has already escaped. Returning home and finding De Sica asleep in *his* bed, Mastroianni leaps to the wrong conclusion and vows to take revenge by raping the governor's wife.

By the time *The Miller's Beautiful Wife* started filming, *Too Bad She's Bad* had opened in Italy and was proving so popular that Ponti instructed Camerini to copy its farcical style and to play down the romanticism of his earlier version. Since Camerini wasn't adept at slapstick, he relied on De Sica for guidance, and the latter ended up in control. Proving that De Sica should never direct his own performances, critics panned his hammy acting when the film came out in Italy in 1955. But they liked the work of Sophia and Mastroianni. When the box-office flop was finally released in the United States two years later, Bosley Crowther wrote that "Miss Loren is a monument to her sex and the mere opportunity to observe her is a privilege not to be missed."

When Sophia finished *The Miller's Beautiful Wife,* Carlo Ponti persuaded producer-friend Marcello Girosi to hire her as De Sica's costar in the third in a series of saucy comedies with similar-sounding titles. Once again, Sophia would be replacing Gina Lollobrigida, who'd starred with De Sica in *Bread, Love, and Dreams* and *Bread, Love, and Jealousy.* Since then, Lollobrigida had become the highest-paid star in Europe at the equivalent of $100,000 per picture, but Girosi decided that was too rich for his $750,000 budget.

Since Vittorio De Sica's role of an amorous police chief who dotes on frisky young peasant types was the main link to the first two *Pane, amore e* films (Lollobrigida dumped him, possibly forever, in the ambiguous ending to the second), Girosi figured he could get away with a new leading lady in the open-titled *Bread, Love, and . . .* The script had De Sica reassigned to his hometown of Sorrento, where he falls for a voluptuous fishmonger who turns out to be using the middle-aged roué only to arouse the jealousy of a lover nearer to her own age.

At Ponti's suggestion, Girosi replaced Luigi Comencini, director of the first two movies, with Dino Risi, who'd handled Sophia and De Sica so effectively in *The Sign of Venus.* While the previous *Bread, Love . . .* films had been shot in black-and-white, color and CinemaScope were added to glorify the Sorrento locations and Sophia's beauty. One of the key scenes found her squeezed into a low-cut, flaming red dress as she danced a hot mambo with De Sica and drove him wild.

By this time, technicians had found a way to deal with Sophia's large nose. Special lighting and makeup were part of it, but the most essential thing was to avoid camera setups showing her in full profile. She looked her best if photographed straight on or turned just enough to save the nose from casting a shadow on her face.

Sophia's spoken Italian had improved enough that she could now dub her own voice, at least for the Italian release versions of her films. But abroad, unless the film was shown with subtitles, Sophia's voice would be dubbed by an actress who sounded nothing like her. To end that problem, Sophia began studying the other Romance languages and taking lessons in English. Ponti told her she would need to know them all, and especially English, if she wanted to have an international career like Lollobrigida's.

Sophia's next film was a step in that direction, an Italian-French coproduction made possible by teaming her and Marcello Mastroianni with the great romantic idol Charles Boyer, who'd recently moved back to France after a long career in Hollywood. *La fortuna di essere donna* (*Lucky to Be a Woman*) copied the style of *Too Bad She's Bad,* with the same director, Alessandro Blasetti. Though Vittorio De Sica had costarred with Sophia and Mastroianni in the first film, the producers decided that Charles Boyer would be a bigger box-office attraction abroad.

Sophia turned blond again for her role as a nobody who's suddenly launched toward fame and fortune when newspapers publish some sexy photographs taken by a candid photographer when she stopped in the street to adjust her stockings. Lenser Mastroianni receives so many inquiries about Sophia that he promises to help her to become an actress and model. Naturally, they fall in love, but when Mastroianni introduces Sophia to Charles Boyer, a wealthy impresario who offers to take over her career in exchange for the usual favors, it becomes a guessing game as to which man she'll end up with.

Lucky to Be a Woman was the seventeenth film that Sophia had worked in during the past three years, probably more than any Hollywood star did in the heyday of the studio factory system. Many of the films had yet to be released outside Italy (and some never would), but combined with the coverage she received in the popular press and "girlie magazines," they had placed Sophia Loren on the brink of becoming a name and body recognized throughout the world.

Sophia was now often selected to represent Italy at film festivals and galas throughout Europe. One of those occasions was the basis for her belief that she had the extrasensory power of a witch. The day before she was supposed to attend a ball in Brussels, she had an overwhelming feeling of imminent disaster, so she canceled. Another young actress, Marcella Mariani, a former Miss Italy winner, took her place, with the same hotel and plane reservations. On the return flight to Rome, the plane crashed and Mariani, along with everyone else on board, was killed. And while Sophia would go on having accurate premonitions of danger throughout her life—including several robberies and a house fire—

she always kept those premonitions to herself. "To talk about them—to tell any-one else—that's a jinx!" she once said.

In January 1955 the Italian Newspaper Guild voted Sophia outstanding screen personality of 1954. The award placed her in the "big four" of Italian cin-ema, along with last year's winner, Gina Lollobrigida, and the longer-established Anna Magnani and Silvana Mangano.

In the first six months of 1955, Sophia appeared on covers of most of Italy's and Europe's top magazines. In August, America's most-read weekly magazine, *Life,* finally took notice with a cover and feature story pegged to the release of *Scandal in Sorrento,* which IFE chose as the English title for *Pane, amore e . . .*

Sophia received so much press coverage because she loved posing and would agree to almost anything that photographers suggested so long as it didn't exceed the limits of decency. For *Life,* she did a bit of striptease for a Pinocchio doll, raising her skirt and exposing some of her black stockings and garter belt. She also got down on the floor on her hands and knees to display her pendulous cleavage. Dressed in a sheer black nightgown, she bounced on a sofa bed and kicked one leg in the air. Her press agent recruited several Native Americans from a traveling Wild West show to join in some joke shots of Sophia being taken captive.

In the process of making herself so accessible to the press, Sophia was often hassled by packs of photojournalists who usually worked for gossip tabloids and magazines and came to be known as *paparazzi,* a word concocted from the plu-rals of *papataceo* and *bacarozzo,* or killer mosquitoes and cockroaches. By this time, Sophia had revealed enough of her squalid past in interviews for the pa-parazzi to torment her with questions designed to get an explosive reaction and a good picture. They would ask her how it felt to be a bastard, what she charged for sexual services, or where she had her nose fixed.

Nothing yet had been published specifically naming Carlo Ponti as Sophia's lover and impresario. The press in Italy was restricted by tough libel laws. *Life* said she was "the protégée of an Italian movie magnate" and left it at that.

Ponti and Dino De Laurentiis were in the midst of filming their latest attempt at an international superproduction, based on Leo Tolstoy's *War and Peace* and cofinanced to the tune of $6 million by Lux Film, Paramount Pictures, and Associated British Pictures. To keep peace in the office, the producers refrained from casting Sophia and Silvana Mangano in the movie, which had Paramount contractee Audrey Hepburn costarring with her actor-husband, Mel Ferrer, and Henry Fonda.

Carlo Ponti's other "protégée," May Britt, did land in the cast of *War and Peace,* but it marked the end of her contract with the producers. She'd signed a new one with 20th Century–Fox and would soon leave for Hollywood. Her American career never took off, however, and more or less ended when she married black entertainer Sammy Davis Jr., with whom she had two children. Interracial marriage was considered taboo in the mainstream America of the 1950s.

British director Michael Powell, who traveled to Rome during the filming of *War and Peace* to discuss a future project with Audrey Hepburn and Mel Ferrer, attended a dinner party that the Ferrers held for Ponti, De Laurentiis, and their ladies. In his diary recollections of the evening, Powell referred to the latter as "wives," but that was true of only one of them. He remembered the two producers' "awesome magnitude and unimaginable wickedness" and the "sultry splendour" of the women. He recalled that Silvana Mangano, dressed in an outfit that looked like "a heap of black and silver tissue," sat smoldering all evening, saying almost nothing.

"The other woman," Powell said, "was a very large girl with gaps between her front teeth and a red dress gathered in a sash on one splendid hip. Standing with Audrey, who was tall and slender as a boy, they looked two different species, and both of them collector's items. With everybody trying their best in three languages, the evening never really got going.

"The only bright spot," Powell continued, "was dinner, which was roast venison plus a statement by the mountainous red girl that she and her husband lived in a tomb. With thoughts of Romeo and Juliet in our minds, we encouraged her to explain. It really was an historic monument, and millions of lire had passed from hand to hand to make it comfortable to live in. She got quite animated about it. It was obviously chic to live in a tomb."

Powell had stumbled upon one of Rome's best-kept secrets (or at least one that had not leaked out to the general public). Ponti had bought a huge twelve-room apartment in the grandiose Palazzo Colonna, which overlooked the Michelangelo-designed Piazza del Campidoglio on what was once the Capitoline hill of ancient Rome. Ponti had a business office on the first floor. Adjoining it were two big rooms packed from floor to ceiling with Ponti's art collection, some of it hanging on the walls but much of it in portfolios or storage cabinets. There were several hundred paintings and drawings by his favorite Italian modernists, Giorgio Morandi, Giuseppe Guerreschi, Renzo Vespignani, Ennio Morlotti, and Sergio Vachi.

On prominent display in the apartment upstairs were works by some of the more famous painters that Ponti had been collecting since he first struck it rich as a film producer, including Pablo Picasso, Graham Sutherland, Salvador Dali, and Francis Bacon.

For the sake of appearances, the residential apartment was supposed to be the home of Sophia and her family. But she and Ponti occupied most of the space, and Romilda and Maria shared a small flat of their own.

Ponti spent a fortune renovating the decaying interior, which retained a period look with antique Venetian and Chinese furnishings. But he also installed modern bathrooms and a so-called American kitchen, where everything was concealed in cabinets and not out in the open as in the traditional Italian style.

Sophia's mother was equivalent to head housekeeper. She always had relatives or friends from Pozzuoli staying there to do the cooking and housework, which saved hiring strangers who might snitch to the press about Sophia and Ponti's relationship.

Sophia was already embroiled in scandal because of the long-running battle with her father over Maria's paternity. The previous year, Sophia had used some of her earnings from *Aida* to literally buy the Scicolone name for her sixteen-year-old sister. Riccardo Scicolone had demanded 1 million lire (about $1,500) to sign the necessary documents acknowledging Maria as his daughter. Romilda Villani became so enraged that she threatened to murder Scicolone, but Sophia wanted an end to Maria's suffering and paid.

The deal, however, infuriated Scicolone's wife, Nella, who had two sons by him and didn't want another stepdaughter who might jeopardize their rights. In the summer of 1955, Nella finally persuaded Riccardo to take legal action that would invalidate Maria's right to the family name. A Rome court ruled in Maria's favor, but the case made headlines and embarrassed everybody concerned, including Mrs. Scicolone, who was discovered to be working part-time as an usher at a cinema where some of Sophia's films had premiered.

Life magazine had predicted that before 1955 was over, Sophia Loren would be snapped up for her first Hollywood movie. It didn't happen quite that way. The American independent producer Stanley Kramer made a deal with United Artists for an epic about the Napoleonic wars in Spain, which he intended directing himself, with Cary Grant, Marlon Brando, and Ava Gardner in the leading roles. But when Brando rejected the final script, Kramer chose Frank Sinatra, which meant replacing Ava Gardner, Sinatra's very estranged wife. Kramer wanted to hire Gina Lollobrigida, but discovered she was already signed to co-star with Burt Lancaster and Tony Curtis in UA's *Trapeze*.

Carlo Ponti heard about Kramer's problem and phoned him to nominate Sophia for the role. Kramer knew her only from *Life* and other magazines, but he was interested and agreed to fly to Rome from his production headquarters in Madrid to view some of Sophia's work.

After Ponti screened *Woman of the River* and *The Miller's Beautiful Wife* for him, Kramer made a take-it-or-leave-it offer of $200,000 for Sophia's services. Ponti, who'd been prepared to accept anything just to get Sophia established in Hollywood movies, couldn't believe his luck, but he kept his cool and said, "I'll have to ask her."

When Kramer actually met Sophia and heard her faulty English, he became nervous. He phoned Ponti afterward and told him there'd be trouble if she didn't improve by the start of filming. Fortunately, there was time for that. The contract still had to be drawn up, signed, and then ratified by UA headquarters in New York.

The deal also hinged on Cary Grant, whose contract gave him the right to approve his costars. When Stanley Kramer told him about Sophia, Grant exploded. "My God! You want me to play with this Sophie somebody, a cheesecake thing? Well, I can't and I won't."

Grant then telephoned Arthur Krim, the president of United Artists, and told him he was quitting the project if "Sophie whatever her name is" stayed in. Krim succeeded in pacifying him, at least for the time being. "You haven't even met her," Krim said. "She has what it takes to be a big star. Go to Spain, start the picture. If you don't like her, we'll pay her off and hire someone else."

In Rome, Sophia enrolled for English lessons with an Irish woman named Sarah Spain, a former schoolteacher who also worked at the local studios as an interpreter for American and British actors. Sophia had a good musical ear and a flair for mimicry, which made learning languages fairly easy. Sarah Spain taught her grammar and pronunciation and put her through hours of reading aloud from Shakespeare, Dickens, Shaw, and T. S. Eliot. "Sarah was not a tutor, she was a persecutor," Sophia recalled. "She bullied me until I was dizzy."

When the script for *The Pride and the Passion* finally arrived, it became plain that Sophia's dialogue would not strain her ability to speak English. The role of the peasant girl Juana was more visual than verbal; most of her lines amounted to a few words or a sentence or two at most. Still, Sophia needed to be intelligible. The movie was being shot in the traditional Hollywood way, with the dialogue recorded live, rather than dubbed later, as in Italy.

The Pride and the Passion had started out as *The Gun,* a novella by C. S.

Forester, author of *The African Queen* and the Horatio Hornblower books. The new title shifted attention away from the original's main and nonhuman character, a gigantic cannon with a forty-foot barrel that guerrillas are dragging clear across Spain to destroy a French fortress at Avila and drive the invaders from the country. Sophia would portray the mistress of Frank Sinatra, the guerrilla leader, who has coerced Cary Grant, a British officer sent there to make sure that the cannon isn't captured by the French, into overseeing the military operation.

Stanley Kramer had been preparing the project for eighteen months. It was a classic example of the "runaway" production that nearly shut down the Hollywood studios in the 1950s. If made in the United States, the epic would have cost $10 million, but in the depressed economy of Spain, then still a dictatorship under Francisco Franco, United Artists could get away with spending only $4 million. Kramer needed ten thousand extras for some of the battle scenes. Back home, unionized extras got $60 per day, plus meals. In Spain, he could hire extras from the ranks of farm laborers, who normally earned 50 cents a day, for $2 per day, and they would be happy to bring their own food.

By the time filming began, in April 1956, Carlo Ponti had landed Sophia two more starring roles in European-based productions. She would join Robert Mitchum and Clifton Webb in 20th Century–Fox's *Boy on a Dolphin,* to be filmed in Greece as soon as she finished *The Pride and the Passion.* After that, United Artists wanted Sophia again for the John Wayne adventure *Legend of the Lost,* to be shot at Cinecittà and on location in North Africa. Big-time stuff, but when you start out costarring with names as big as Cary Grant and Frank Sinatra in your first major Hollywood movie, there's going to be a demand for your services even before the film has been released.

Sophia had been tipped off about Cary Grant's objections to her casting, so she was extremely apprehensive when she arrived in Madrid and learned that she would be meeting him for the first time at a cocktail party for the press. She changed outfits six times to relieve her anxiety, then arrived at the reception to find that Grant would be an hour late. When he finally strolled in and Stanley Kramer introduced them, he called her "Miss Lorbrigida . . . or is it Miss Brigloren? . . . I can't remember Italian names."

Sophia giggled, but before she could chat with Grant, Frank Sinatra arrived and photographers wanted the three stars to pose together. Wedged between two men who were among the idols of her adolescence, she had an eerie feeling that she was only dreaming and that it couldn't possibly be happening.

Sophia and Grant never did get a chance to talk that evening, but before he left, he was overheard telling Kramer, "My God, Stanley, you were right about her. I can't understand my prejudices. That girl is magnificent. What's the matter with me?"

Because of the size and complexity of the production, Sophia would spend four months in "Windmillville," Sinatra's name for the flat plains region around Avila where most of the filming took place. In her first lengthy trip away from home, Sophia was accompanied by her Ponti-appointed chaperon, Basilio Franchina, who served as her interpreter and dramatic coach on the set and provided companionship between Ponti's weekend flying visits from Rome.

Cary Grant and his actress-wife, Betsy Drake, traveled to Spain via Monaco, where they attended the wedding of close friend Grace Kelly to Prince Rainier. Frank Sinatra, who'd once had a joyless affair with Kelly and had not been invited to the royal nuptials, brought to Spain an entourage of Hollywood cronies that included his current flame, the young jazz singer Peggy Connelly.

The international press corps based in Madrid was taking bets that a romance would ignite between the Italo-American Sinatra and *paisana* Loren, but if Sinatra had any plans in that direction he got off to a bad start. As soon as he discovered Sophia's faulty English, he tried to play the wise guy and taught her expressions like "It was a fucking gas" and "How's your cock?" which caused her extreme embarrassment when she innocently used them in conversations with strangers. When Sophia realized that Sinatra had taken advantage of her naïveté, she confronted him on the set in front of the entire company and called him "a mean little guinea son of a bitch."

From then on, Sinatra kept needling Sophia with one of his pet expressions, "Okay, baby, you'll get yours." Sophia couldn't understand what Sinatra meant. Was it a sexual promise or a threat of bodily harm? She kept her distance and never did find out.

To everybody's surprise, Cary Grant turned out to be the costar who really seemed to fancy Sophia. He wasted no time in letting her know by sending big bouquets of roses every day. Since Grant was a notorious skinflint and also reputed to be gay or bisexual, his behavior seemed a bit bizarre for a man who also never had a reputation for getting romantically involved with his leading ladies.

Grant had been married three times, for nine months to film actress Virginia Cherrill in the early 1930s, for three of the World War II years to the super-rich Woolworth heiress Barbara Hutton, and since 1949 to Betsy Drake. After divorcing his first wife, Grant shared a home for six years with the rugged action star

Randolph Scott, which started rumors and speculation about the nature of their relationship. Grant always claimed he did it to save on the rent, and left it at that. The current Mrs. Grant had been a struggling stage actress when he "discovered" her and made her his costar in the 1948 film *Every Girl Should Be Married*. Nineteen years younger than Grant, Betsy Drake was a short-haired "Peter Pan" type, causing much speculation about the intimate side of the marriage.

Grant started taking Sophia out to dinner after work, discreetly at first, with Mrs. Grant joining them. But it soon escalated to midnight suppers for two at romantic hilltop restaurants. The wife stayed behind at the hotel and seemed to be remarkably understanding.

Tall, dimpled, and always impeccably dressed, the fifty-two-year-old Cary Grant was regarded as one of the world's handsomest and most debonair men in any field of endeavor. Nearly thirty years older than Sophia, he was also six years older than Carlo Ponti. But with his full head of hair, streamlined build, and perpetual suntan, Grant looked considerably younger and more virile than her short, potbellied, and balding lover.

A romance developed, but how far it went beyond courtship is known only to Sophia and Grant. Since he knew just a few words of Italian, he did most of the talking and Sophia mainly listened and tried her best to understand. He told her about his real self, Archibald "Archie" Leach, a poor British boy from a broken home who'd joined a troupe of acrobats and traveled the world before settling in America to become an actor. By the year of Sophia's birth, he'd changed his name to Cary Grant, had made about fifteen movies, and been married and divorced.

As she grew to know him, Sophia sensed that Grant had truly fallen in love with her and wanted to marry her. She would later claim that he actually proposed, which made her wonder if he might be a bit crazy, given their radically different backgrounds and ties. But she didn't want to hurt him, either, so she told him that she'd need time to think it over when the film finished and they were no longer seeing each other every day.

Sophia also undoubtedly realized that Grant could make a wonderful pawn in her relationship with Carlo Ponti. If she could convince Ponti that she really intended becoming Mrs. Cary Grant, Ponti might finally do something about getting a divorce and marrying her. It smacked of a real-life soap opera, with too many characters and too many plot complications to be resolved easily or quickly.

Meanwhile, Sophia and Grant continued with the on-screen romance of

Juana and Captain Trumbull, which ends tragically when she's killed in the cross fire of the massive guerrilla invasion of French-controlled Avila. Before that, Grant spends half the movie avoiding Sophia and sticking to duty, but he finally loosens up when she taunts him with "Captain, I have an idea you'd like to act more like a man than a cold piece of English mutton."

A few scenes later, Grant happens to run into Sophia just after she's taken a nude swim in a pond. She's standing with just a horse blanket wrapped around her when he's irresistibly drawn to her and they start making love. The camera view discreetly pans toward the sky, and the scene fades without showing any graphic details.

In 1956, a time before movies were given audience ratings for their United States release, Hollywood's self-imposed censorship code prohibited full or partial nudity. Sophia splashed around in a flesh-colored net swim suit in the few moments before Grant entered the scene. Her wardrobe for the rest of the movie didn't amount to much more, a series of low-cut peasant blouses and tight skirts designed to emphasize her best points.

The filming gave Sophia her first lesson in working with colossal Hollywood egos. Though Cary Grant may have been in love with her, both he and Frank Sinatra seemed to love their profiles more and were always vying to get the best angles from cinematographer Franz Planer. As a result, Sophia's nose became as prominent as some of her other features; in certain shots that caught her in full profile it looked like a ski jump. But experience is the best teacher, and she learned what to avoid in the future.

Cary Grant did help Sophia in other ways, realizing how important her English-speaking debut would be to her career, and to her acceptance by the average American moviegoer. "He didn't want Sophia to have the image of an Italian sex symbol. He didn't want her to fall into that pit. He thought she was beyond that," Stanley Kramer recalled.

"When they were in a scene together, Cary was very thoughtful and very helpful to her. He never hesitated to say, 'Why don't we do another take? I don't think her line was clear there,' or 'I think she can do a little bit better, don't you think so, Sophia?' He encouraged and bolstered her."

When United Artists flew over some artwork being considered for the advertising campaign, Grant demanded revisions when he saw the giant cannon depicted rather phallically and aimed in the direction of Sophia's crotch area. He also objected to the photograph of her and requested that the cleavage be airbrushed to more modest dimensions.

Producer-director Kramer was aware of the romance between Sophia and Grant, but tried not to care: "It was just an added complication for me. It was the toughest movie I ever made, with ten thousand extras, over a thousand horses and animals, and a squadron of helicopters filming aerial views of the chases and battle scenes."

In July, midway through production, Sophia and Grant may have gotten too cozy for Betsy Drake to tolerate any longer. Mrs. Grant suddenly decided to go home to Beverly Hills, packed her things, and drove to Gibraltar to board the next ship bound for the United States. Unluckily, it turned out to be the Italian liner SS *Andrea Doria,* which five days later collided with the Swedish SS *Stockholm* in heavy fog about sixty miles from Nantucket Island, Massachusetts. Fifty-two people died when the *Andrea Doria* sank to the bottom of the ocean, but Betsy Drake was one of several hundred passengers rescued by another passing ship, the SS *Île de France.*

Had his wife been killed or injured, Grant no doubt would have taken temporary leave of *The Pride and the Passion,* but he stayed put and didn't seem bothered by the fact that she might need him after such a traumatic experience. When contacted by the Associated Press for a statement about his wife's rescue, Grant said, "I love her so much that, for once in my life, words fail me." What he really felt can only be guessed at, but later on, after he'd returned home, servants heard him arguing with Drake and shouting, "I wish you'd gone down with the ship. It might have saved us both a lot of problems."

Mrs. Grant's decampment gave him more freedom to court Sophia, but that would have to end, at least temporarily, when production did. That happened sooner than expected due to Frank Sinatra's homesickness and his rage over the primitive telephone service in Spain, which made it very hard for him to keep in touch with his cronies back in Hollywood and Las Vegas. He was also brooding over Ava Gardner, who was as near as Madrid, but having an affair with a bullfighter and driving Sinatra crazy with jealousy.

With seven weeks of filming still remaining, Sinatra finally decided to bolt. "Hot or cold, on Thursday I'm leaving the picture. So get a lawyer and sue me," he told Stanley Kramer. And off Sinatra went, forcing Kramer to improvise while he waited for the UA legal department to perform a miracle.

Kramer tried to work around Sinatra by using a double in the action scenes and finishing the dramatic scenes in which only Sophia and/or Grant appeared. Meanwhile, Sinatra caved in to the threat of a $15 million breach-of-contract suit and agreed to do his remaining dramatic scenes, provided that Kramer filmed them in Hollywood. That forced a further delay since, among other things, both Sophia and Grant were due to start new projects and wouldn't be able to re-group with Sinatra until February or March of the coming year. In the meantime, Kramer would make the necessary studio arrangements and proceed with the editing and musical scoring of the completed portion so that the movie's release wouldn't be overly delayed.

Despite Sinatra's vanishing act, Stanley Kramer held the traditional "wrap" party for cast and crew to celebrate the end of the filming in Spain. Neither Sophia nor Cary Grant attended. They'd said their good-byes privately and taken off in opposite directions to start their next movies. Ironically, his was en-titled *An Affair to Remember*.

HOLLYWOOD STAR

SOPHIA briefly returned to Rome to see her family and to try to clarify her relationship with Carlo Ponti. In Spain, Cary Grant had cautioned her that should she decide to remain with Ponti, she must marry him if she intended to have a career in Hollywood movies. Grant knew from his own experience that puritanical gossip columnists like Louella Parsons and Hedda Hopper, and pressure groups such as the Catholic Legion of Decency would try to crucify her if they discovered her liaison with a man who had a wife and two children.

Sophia wanted to get married to Ponti as soon as possible. Ponti's response discouraged her. As a lawyer himself, he knew that his present marriage could only be dissolved through an annulment from the Roman Catholic Church. There was also the possibility of obtaining a divorce in some other country with liberal rules, such as Mexico or Switzerland, but such a decree wouldn't be recognized by the Italian authorities. Ponti was exploring an annulment on the grounds that he was a lapsed Catholic at the time he wed, but his advisers doubted that the Vatican would accept it.

Cary Grant, as well as Romilda, had also raised doubts in Sophia's mind about Ponti's sincerity. Perhaps Ponti didn't really want to marry her. Perhaps his legal problems were just a convenient excuse. Sophia didn't want to believe it to be true, but she'd seen how her father had avoided marrying her mother, so she couldn't rule it out either.

Ponti had fabulous news for Sophia on another front. Cary Grant had no sooner returned to California than he requested Sophia for his costar in *Houseboat,* a future project that was part of a three-picture deal he had with

Paramount Pictures. As a consequence, Paramount had contacted Ponti about a multipicture contract with Sophia. If he got everything he wanted in the deal, Ponti would be the producer of some of the films, which would give them more reason to be together, married or not.

By this time, Ponti had ended his partnership with Dino De Laurentiis. Conflicts arising from their loyalties to their lovely ladies were secondary to a personality clash; both were Little Caesars who wanted to rule their own empires. Appropriately enough, their last coproduction was *War and Peace*. De Laurentiis took over some of their Italian commitments, starting with Fellini's *Nights of Cabiria*. Ponti formed a company called Champion Film, which commenced with Pietro Germi's *The Railroad Man* and Alberto Lattuada's *Guendalina*.

In September, Sophia left Rome for Athens, again accompanied by Basilio Franchina and also by Ines Bruscia, a former "script girl" whom Ponti had hired as Sophia's full-time secretary-helper. The CinemaScope adventure *Boy on a Dolphin* was a pet project of Spyros Skouras, the Greek-born president of 20th Century–Fox, who had hoped it would do as much for tourism in his native land as Fox's recent smash hit, *Three Coins in the Fountain,* had done for Italy. The new film used the same director, Jean Negulesco, and cinematographer, Milton Krasner, as well as one of the principal stars, debonair Clifton Webb.

When Sophia signed for the movie, Robert Mitchum was supposed to be the leading man, but he got caught up in production delays on John Huston's *Heaven Knows, Mr. Allison,* which sent producer Samuel Engel scurrying for a replacement. Alan Ladd replaced Mitchum, which delighted Sophia because she'd adored him in the American films she'd seen right after the war. Ladd's patrician blondness was a rarity among Italian men. She considered him *"un uomo molto seducente."*

Like Sophia's previous film, *Boy on a Dolphin* had an inanimate object as the motivating character. This time, it was a gold and bronze statue of a young boy riding on the back of one of the deep seas' friendliest creatures. Portraying a peasant who supports herself by diving for sponges, Sophia finds the statue at the bottom of the Aegean chained to the remains of a ship that sank 2,000 years ago. Needless to say, the statue is worth millions of dollars, but the field of buyers is quickly narrowed down to Alan Ladd, an archaeologist who works for governments trying to retrieve lost treasures, and the sinister, super-rich Clifton Webb, who covets it for his private collection.

Spyros Skouras had done so much charitable work for Greece over the years that he was able to command special armed protection for the production unit.

As luck would have it, the filming coincided not only with a political crisis in Greece, but also with Egypt's seizure of the Suez Canal, which promised to plunge the Middle East into war. The U.S. State Department had already started evacuating American personnel from the area.

Several scenes were filmed around Athens and the Acropolis, but most of the outdoor and underwater work took place in the vicinity of Hydra, a rocky island in the Aegean with boat connections to Athens. The production rented luxury yachts and cabin cruisers to serve as floating residences for some of the stars and VIPs. Clifton Webb, who never traveled anywhere without his elderly mother, Maybelle, was one of Fox's most prized contract stars, thanks to the success of his *Mr. Belvedere* films, so he got the largest and best furnished. Alan Ladd's wasn't far behind, with a deck long enough for him and wife Sue to practice their golf shots.

Sophia opted to stay on land. There were only two rental houses on all of Hydra, so she took one to be with her little entourage, while director Jean Negulesco and his wife, Dusty, agreed to share the second with scriptwriter Ivan Moffat.

After being enchanted by Cary Grant, Sophia expected to be at least charmed by Alan Ladd, but their first meeting disquieted them both. In the time since Sophia had last seen him in *The Great Gatsby,* the forty-three-year-old actor had lost his chiseled handsomeness from too much boozing. His bloated features and stocky physique startled Sophia, but she was even more surprised by his stature. Thanks to camera magic and his own charisma, Alan Ladd suggested a big man on screen, but he was only 5'6".

Sophia quickly discovered that Ladd had a complex about his size. In the presence of taller people, he kept his distance or tried to get them to sit while he stood to minimize the discrepancy. When he met Sophia, he must have been as shocked as she was but for the opposite reason. Her Amazon size and youthful voluptuousness were more than he could compete with. She would very likely wipe him off the screen.

Throughout the filming, Ladd was icy toward Sophia and rebuffed her efforts to establish a friendly working environment. "We spent hours together every day for two months," she recalled. "The political climate at the time was very dangerous. All this should have made us close, but no. He was always polite but never seemed to want to have any social contact. I liked Alan, but he didn't seem to like me. I couldn't understand it."

In all of his Hollywood movies, Ladd either had similarly petite leading ladies such as Veronica Lake, or worked eye-to-eye with taller ones by standing on a box that was out of the camera's view. Ladd found that too demeaning now, so Jean Negulesco had to devise ways of reducing Sophia's height. "Holes were dug in the ground for her to stand in," the director said later. "For a scene of Sophia and Alan strolling side-by-side, we had to build a very long trench for her to walk along."

Due to Ladd's puffy and haggard looks, Negulesco tended to favor Sophia in the camera shots. Ladd would later claim that the director "fell in love" with Sophia and gave her all the good closeups. "All you ever saw of me in most scenes was the back of my neck," he said. "I very quickly got fed up with it."

Once again, Sophia's costumes were those of a peasant, but Jean Negulesco created something extraordinary in her pearl-diving outfit. It was basically a faded old yellow dress with a cord tied around the waist, but the back of the skirt was brought forward through her legs and tucked into the belt so that her long legs were fully exposed.

Negulesco copied the costume from a photograph he'd seen of a Japanese pearl diver. To test it, he took it to Sophia's house and asked her to put it on and then go soak in the bathtub. "After the first dunking, an explosive vision appeared, with every detail of Sophia's perfect body outlined dangerously. Perhaps too dangerously for the film censors, so I took the dress back and had it double-lined. The second dunking gave us a sensual suggestion, but without the obvious lusty truth. Exactly what I wanted," he recalled.

On the day of shooting, Sophia hitched up her skirt and dived into the sea. But when she surfaced and emerged from the water, Negulesco's eyes boggled: "I had not anticipated the ice-cold temperature of the water and its effect on Sophia's lovelies, which were pointing at us with daring accuracy. The still photographer dropped his camera. The soundman raised his boom. The Greek laborers were thunderstruck. It was simply too good to film only once. I did take after take, to my enjoyment and the crew's appreciation. 'The dripping yellow dress,' as it came to be called, made Sophia a poster girl all over the world when the film opened."

While working with Sophia, Negulesco developed a theory that she was at her best as an actress when portraying barefoot peasant types. In the one scene where she had to dress fancy for her first meeting with millionaire Clifton Webb, her high-heeled shoes distracted her concentration.

"The shoes were uncomfortable; they were her enemy," Negulesco remembered. "At the first shot where her feet were out of view, she took them off. She suddenly became free, secure with the dignity of a peasant. She looked radiant and noble. I thought to myself, if she could always remember to take off her shoes, to be the free Sophia, with no rules, with no makeup, no acting tricks, she could become a legend."

The film was finished on schedule, which freed Sophia to spend Christmas in Rome before starting her next film. Returning to Italy promised to be an ordeal. During one of Ponti's flying visits to the Greek locations, Sophia had gone to the Athens airport to meet him. Although they always tried to be discreet when they were out in public together, Sophia's emotions seemed to overtake her. When Ponti stepped off the plane, she ran to him, kissed him passionately, and continued to nuzzle at his neck as he proceeded through customs and immigration. Some of the paparazzi who were always stationed at the airport to ambush arriving celebrities snapped away, which may have been Sophia's intention. Perhaps she thought that exposing the affair would force Ponti into moving faster on his promises to marry her.

Years later, she practically admitted that. "I adored Carlo," she said. "He was my man, my only man. I wanted him desperately as a husband and as the father of my children. Finally it had to come to the point when I knew he was not going to make the decision unless I put him on the spot. After all, it's universal, not just Italian, for a husband to try and get the best of both worlds—a nice situation with his family, and just as nice a situation going for him with his mistress. This was not what I had in mind for Carlo and me."

Unfortunately, publication of the airport photographs in the Italian press started an avalanche of trouble not only for Sophia and Ponti, but also for Ponti's wife and two children, who became prey for the paparazzi as well. Sophia's international filming commitments proved something of a blessing, removing her from the direct line of fire for months at a time.

In Rome on Christmas Day, Sophia and Ponti attended a party in John Wayne's hotel suite to meet him and the other principals involved with *Legend of the Lost,* which was due to begin production on the second day of 1957. Wayne had decorated his Christmas tree with little flags of all the nationalities involved. Because of the crisis in the Middle East, the main location had been shifted from Egypt to the seemingly safer northwestern portion of Libya, which borders on Algeria and Tunisia.

In a sense, Sophia would be working for John Wayne. His independent Batjac Productions (named after a fictitious shipping firm mentioned in his 1942 *Reap the Wild Wind*) had made a deal with United Artists for three pictures, starting with this one. UA then contracted with Robert Haggiag of Italy's Dear Film to put up some of the financing, which explains how Sophia and compatriot Rossano Brazzi were signed as Wayne's costars.

Legend of the Lost was the brainchild of its director, Henry Hathaway. He was a crusty veteran of westerns and action films who'd been carrying the idea around for years before finally hiring the prolific Ben Hecht to develop the plot and Robert Presnell Jr. to write the screenplay. Wayne wanted to stick close to home and film it in California's Mojave Desert, but Hathaway argued that audiences would be able to detect that the dunes were built by bulldozers and that the sandstorms were created by wind machines.

Critics often complained that John Wayne always portrayed John Wayne, but this time around he was Joe January, a hard-boozing desert guide who's stranded in Timbuktu, which is depicted as somewhere in the middle of the Sahara. The script put Sophia back in rags as Dita, described as a "slave girl" to accommodate the Hollywood censorship code but apparently one of the town whores from the way she struts around. Rossano Brazzi is the catalyst when he arrives to form an expedition to find out what happened to his long-missing father, an archaeologist who'd been searching for an ancient treasure believed buried beneath the desert.

In the first meeting of the three characters, Sophia tells Brazzi, "I hate men. If I could only start over." Brazzi assures her that "sin is a wound that can be healed," but Wayne sneers, "If you want to scrub her soul, it may take a little time." Off they go into the Sahara, where Wayne and Brazzi spend less time digging for treasure than drooling over Sophia.

It took John Wayne's company four months to prepare for production; all the technical equipment and most of the supplies and food had to be shipped to Libya from California or Italy. Batjac chartered a DC-3 to use as an air ferry between Rome and the locations once filming started.

Sophia took along her usual entourage, this time to reside in the oasis settlement of Ghadames, where the only hotel, a dilapidated twelve-room remnant of the Italian colonial period, would be home to the entire cast and crew. Everybody had to share the one bathroom. Outdoor temperatures fell so low at night that the walls of the guest rooms were lined with blankets made by the local Berber population.

After Alan Ladd, John Wayne was a leading man Sophia could truly look up to, measuring well over six feet and taller than Cary Grant. But Wayne lacked Grant's charm and seemed interested in Sophia only as someone who might boost his producer's share of the box-office takings. When they acted their first passionate love scene, Sophia gave it all she had, knowing full well what being seen in the arms of America's number-one action star could do for her career.

Wayne hadn't been kissed with such intensity since Maureen O'Hara tangled with him in *The Quiet Man.* He was doubly pleased because no costly retakes were necessary. To show his appreciation, he slapped Sophia on the behind and grinned, "Oh, you gorgeous investment, you!"

The chances of an actual Loren-Wayne romance seemed slight owing to the presence of his fiery, and considerably younger, third wife, Peruvian-born Pilar Pellicer. Because of the health risks in North Africa, their baby daughter, Aissa, remained in California with relatives, which enabled Mrs. Wayne to be with her husband full-time. No doubt some of the gossip about Sophia and Cary Grant had put her on guard.

Pilar Wayne first caught sight of Sophia at one of the early-morning buffet breakfasts in the hotel's restaurant. "I couldn't believe this was the gorgeous Loren everybody was raving about," she remembered. "Her eyes were unexceptional, her mouth too wide, her figure hidden by loose clothes. But when I saw her again a few hours later, fully made up and dressed for her role, she looked like a different person, absolutely breathtaking. Sophia could assume beauty the same way she assumed a role, an ability she shared with many of Hollywood's most compelling female stars."

John Wayne rapidly became disenchanted with Sophia when he discovered the details of her private life. According to Pilar Wayne, "The Duke" disapproved of Carlo Ponti's flying visits and Sophia's apparent fondness for Rossano Brazzi when Ponti wasn't around.

"It soon became obvious that Sophia and Rossano were close friends. They spent all their off-camera time together," Pilar Wayne recalled. "Duke didn't approve of any of it. He'd grown up in an era where boys could be boys, but girls were supposed to be ladies. Duke could excuse the behavior of Ponti and Brazzi, even though they were both married men, but he couldn't excuse Sophia's. But she had my unspoken sympathy."

The Waynes may have misinterpreted Sophia's relationship with Brazzi, whose wife, Lidia, managed his career and traveled everywhere with him. The Brazzis were longtime friends of Ponti and often socialized with him and Sophia in Rome. If Sophia and Brazzi were romantically involved, there was no real evidence beyond their obvious mutual affection.

But it's easy to understand why there might have been more to it. For

Sophia, the forty-year-old Brazzi, incredibly handsome and romantic, may have been the ideal Italian lover in ways that Carlo Ponti could never be. Long a major star in Italy, he'd recently achieved international success in *Three Coins in the Fountain* and had just signed for the movie version of *South Pacific*. For Brazzi, Sophia may have been just another diversion from his marriage of convenience. Mrs. Brazzi, who'd grown quite stout since they wed in 1940, reportedly tolerated her husband's philandering so long as it didn't threaten her control of his career or the lavish lifestyle that it purchased for them.

Late one night during the filming, Sophia had a near-death experience resulting from a faulty gas heater in her hotel room. Carbon monoxide fumes woke her up, but she'd already inhaled too many and didn't have the strength to put up much of a fight. Finally, she dragged herself to the edge of the mattress and rolled over onto the floor. The shock revitalized her slightly, and she was able to crawl to the door, unlock it, and get into the hallway before she lost consciousness.

Rossano Brazzi found her and called for help. Why he didn't attempt to revive Sophia himself isn't clear, but the company doctor quickly arrived and took over. When the commotion subsided and Sophia seemed out of danger, people began to wonder about Brazzi's role in the drama.

Crew members were also speculating about the closeness between Sophia and the forty-two-year-old British cinematographer Jack Cardiff, whom she'd first met in Rome while he was working for Ponti and De Laurentiis on *War and Peace*. An Oscar winner and renowned for his mastery of color in classics like *The Red Shoes* and *The African Queen,* Cardiff was the sort of friend Sophia needed to look her best on screen, so she may have just been playing up to him for the usual professional reasons.

But Phil Stern, the American photographer hired by United Artists to snap the publicity and advertising stills, later said that Jack Cardiff became so obsessed with Sophia that UA had to fly in a second cinematographer from Rome to concentrate on Wayne and Brazzi, who were complaining that Cardiff wasn't shooting their closeups with the same loving care.

On Sundays, the company's only rest day, Sophia and Cardiff usually went off by themselves for a picnic in the desert, but no one else, including Mrs. Cardiff, ever went along.

"At the daily communal meals, Jack always sat opposite Sophia and ate little while drooling over her. It was like an Italian *opera buffa,*" Phil Stern recalled.

After six weeks in Libya, production shifted to Rome's Cinecittà for the interior scenes of the lost city supposedly buried under the Sahara. The Waynes felt it was now safe for baby Aissa to join them at their rented villa outside Rome, so they flew her over from Los Angeles in the care of a registered nurse.

One evening they invited Sophia and Ponti to dinner to meet Aissa. "We couldn't get Sophia out of the nursery," Pilar Wayne remembered. "I never saw anyone behave with a baby the way Sophia did. She wanted a child of her own so badly."

That seemed unlikely to happen until Sophia found herself a husband. She wanted to avoid the shame and humiliation that her mother had suffered. Also, from the standpoint of Sophia's booming career, it just wouldn't be practical. She'd made three major movies in less than a year. At the rate that offers were coming in, she seemed likely to be booked solid for several years to come.

By the time Sophia finished *Legend of the Lost,* Ponti had completed his negotiations for a five-picture deal with Paramount Pictures. The Paramount contract was nonexclusive, which gave Sophia the right to work elsewhere, provided there was no conflict in production schedules. When the distinguished British director Carol Reed cabled that he wanted to team Sophia with William Holden in his next production for Columbia Pictures, she accepted instantly without even asking for a script, and left it to Ponti to work out the details.

By 1957, all the big Hollywood studios had phased out the longtime system of star rosters, so Sophia's Paramount deal was something of a tribute to Carlo Ponti's bargaining prowess. For the previous four years, the Oscar for Best Actress had been won by the star of a Paramount film—Shirley Booth for *Come Back, Little Sheba,* Audrey Hepburn for *Roman Holiday,* Grace Kelly for *The Country Girl,* and Anna Magnani for *The Rose Tattoo.* Ponti convinced Paramount that Sophia not only had the same kind of talent, but also had a long future because of her youth. Since winning their Oscars, Kelly had retired to become a princess while the middle-aged Booth and Magnani had proved box-office duds in their subsequent Paramount films.

Ponti had the support of Paramount's global sales chief, George Weltner, who thought that Sophia would be a major asset in the foreign market. Since the end of World War II, and especially since TV decimated theater attendance in the United States, the Hollywood studios had become increasingly dependent on foreign revenues, which sometimes accounted for 50 percent or more of a film's total gross. Hollywood had a long history of foreign-born stars whose films did well in America and even better abroad, starting with Pola Negri and Vilma Banky in the silent era, Greta Garbo and Marlene Dietrich in the 1930s, and most recently with Audrey Hepburn. There was something about their foreign heritages that made it easier for non-American moviegoers to identify with them.

Sophia's potential as a younger and more beautiful version of Anna Magnani was put to the test in her first Paramount project. Staff producer Don Hartman got the assignment and chose Eugene O'Neill's *Desire Under the Elms* as the vehicle.

There was a certain logic to it. Swedish-born Greta Garbo had made her "talkie" debut in O'Neill's *Anna Christie*. Also, O'Neill was the most revered American playwright, a winner of the Nobel Prize and four Pulitzers. Though he died in 1953, the posthumously produced *Long Day's Journey into Night,* along with hit revivals of several of his classics, had made O'Neill a Broadway phenomenon in recent years. Novelist Irwin Shaw, a longtime friend and disciple of O'Neill, was selected to adapt *Desire Under the Elms* to Sophia's needs.

Simultaneously, Paramount was preparing to reteam Sophia with Cary Grant in *Houseboat,* which would be filmed right after *Desire Under the Elms.* The romantic comedy had been turned over to the team of writer-director Melville Shavelson and writer-producer Jack Rose, who'd worked very successfully with Grant and his wife Betsy Drake on *Room for One More.* Drake, who'd contributed the basic story idea for *Houseboat,* was again supposed to star opposite her husband, but his sudden infatuation with Sophia changed that. Still in psychological turmoil from her ordeal on the *Andrea Doria,* Drake didn't seem to care. More interested in getting better, she'd enrolled in an experimental therapy program that used the drug lysergic acid diethylamide, or LSD.

Prior to starting *Desire Under the Elms,* Sophia had to be in Los Angeles to finish the remaining scenes of *The Pride and the Passion* with Cary Grant and Frank Sinatra, so she expected to be in the United States for a minimum of six months. She tried to persuade her mother to come with her, but Romilda feared flying and refused. Sophia's sister, Maria, who had dreams of becoming a pop singer like the Italian-American Connie Francis, was all too happy to go in her place.

Needless to say, Carlo Ponti would also accompany Sophia, but would travel separately with her aides Basilio Franchina and Ines Bruscia for the sake of appearances. As Sophia's impresario, Ponti had an excuse for being with her, but he thought it best to stay discreetly in the background for as long as their unmarried relationship continued. Ponti knew that America was awash with scandal magazines such as *Confidential, Top Secret,* and *Whisper* that could ruin

Sophia's Hollywood career before it even got started. One called *Suppressed* had already run a cover story hinting that Sophia had a sordid past as a prostitute.

Although it might have seemed like Ponti was neglecting his own career to be with Sophia, he had several Italian productions in work in Rome that were being supervised by his associate, Marcello Girosi. While in Hollywood, Ponti would have an office on the Paramount lot, making arrangements for the films that he would personally produce under the terms of Sophia's contract.

Ponti had arranged to rent a house belonging to director Charles Vidor, who would soon be leaving for a film in Europe. In the meantime, a suite and several rooms at the Bel-Air Hotel, in a secluded area to the west of Beverly Hills, would be home for them and their entourage.

Sophia had a tearful parting with her mother in Rome. It was Sophia, rather than the Greta Garbo lookalike, who would finally be getting that long-dreamed-of trip to Hollywood.

Sophia and Ponti had hoped to be in Los Angeles in time for the annual Academy Awards ceremony, but last-minute complications prevented them. It turned out to be a night of glory for Ponti and ex-partner De Laurentiis when their production of Fellini's *La Strada* won the Oscar for Best Foreign-Language Film. The award had historic significance because this was the first competitive vote for the category. In prior years, Best Foreign-Language Film had been an honorary selection of the Academy's board of directors.

To reach Los Angeles ahead of Ponti and the others, Sophia and sister Maria took the polar air route from Rome and arrived on April 8, 1957. Thanks to the combined efforts of the publicity departments of Paramount, 20th Century–Fox, and United Artists, all of which had stakes in Sophia's future, the press turnout at the airport was a mob scene. When Sophia stepped off the plane wearing the latest in low-cut Italian couture, photographers climbed up poles or stood on each other's shoulders trying to snap the best views of her cleavage.

The next day, 20th Century–Fox threw a lavish party at Romanoff's, then the chicest restaurant in town, to welcome Sophia to the Hollywood community. Because of the production delay in *The Pride and the Passion,* Fox would get to theaters first by releasing *Boy on a Dolphin* for the Easter holiday season. UA now hoped to have Sophia's freshman effort finished in time for summer release, with *Legend of the Lost* scheduled for Christmas.

To make it a bit easier on Sophia's nerves, Clifton Webb, who became her friend while they were working together in Greece, volunteered to play host at Romanoff's. To nobody's surprise, Alan Ladd failed to show, but Gary Cooper,

Barbara Stanwyck, George Raft, Gene Kelly, Joan Crawford, Danny Kaye, James Stewart, Merle Oberon, Errol Flynn, and Rock Hudson were among the many stars who attended.

Sophia also scored a coup by attracting both Louella Parsons *and* Hedda Hopper, rival gossip hens who rarely attended the same party. Hedda and Louella even agreed to pose for pictures more-or-less together, with Sophia in the middle, a historic "first," according to photographers in the room.

Making a very conspicuous late arrival was Jayne Mansfield, who'd become the top blonde at 20th Century–Fox since its contract problems with Marilyn Monroe. Wearing an even tighter and lower-cut dress than Sophia, she sashayed over to the guest of honor's table to say hello. As she leaned over, Mansfield's right breast popped out of its minimal safety net and almost into Sophia's mouth. Clifton Webb, seated next to Sophia and in direct danger from Mansfield's left breast, raised a hand to shield his face and hissed, "Puhleeze, Miss Mansfield, we're all wine drinkers at this table."

Sophia, who'd never been quite that bold in her own publicity-seeking days, had to admire Mansfield's *impudenza*. When she'd regained her composure, Sophia agreed to pose with her as photographers begged for more. After Sophia went back to her table, Mansfield told a reporter, "She said that she'd never wear a dress like mine. I'm not sure just how I should take that remark."

Cary Grant had had scenes to shoot that day and was unable to attend the party. But as soon as Sophia had arrived in town, he had resumed sending a bouquet of red roses every morning. Grant phoned her several times daily and didn't seem perturbed if Carlo Ponti happened to pick up first. Filming the remaining scenes for *The Pride and the Passion,* which usually took place in the evening after Grant finished work in *Kiss Them for Me* (which also featured Jayne Mansfield), gave them a reason to be together.

Ray Walston, another featured actor in the film, recalled: "We used to break at about 6:30 every night. All of a sudden Sophia Loren started showing up. You could tell that she and Cary were very fond of one another."

Frank Sinatra caused no production problems this time and *The Pride and the Passion* was finally finished. Stanley Kramer threw a second "wrap" party and Sophia took along her sister, Maria, to meet everybody. In the midst of the celebrating, Sinatra got up to sing. Maria Scicolone, meanwhile, had been getting tipsy on champagne. When Sinatra started "Three Coins in the Fountain," she couldn't resist joining in. Sinatra was amused, liked what he heard, and sang two more duets with her.

The next day, Sinatra phoned Sophia and told her that she ought to encourage Maria to pursue a professional career. He recommended a vocal coach and promised to help Maria get a record contract and night club bookings when the time came. Sophia wondered if her sister had the necessary ambition to succeed, but she was all too happy to pay for lessons, if only to keep Maria occupied every day while she worked at the studio.

Desire Under the Elms was now ready to start and promised to be a radical departure from Sophia's previous Hollywood-financed films. After Cary Grant, Frank Sinatra, Alan Ladd, and John Wayne, starring opposite 300-pound Burl Ives and spindly newcomer Anthony Perkins came as a shock, though producer Don Hartman assured Sophia that both were magnificent actors. Director Delbert Mann was a recruit from television, but had won an Oscar for his work on his first movie, *Marty,* which also received Oscars for Best Picture of 1955 and for Ernest Borgnine's performance in the title role. (Mann had also directed Paddy Chayefsky's original teleplay in 1953.)

Though the story took place in rural New England during the 1850s, Paramount opted to film almost all the scenes on the sound stages of its Marathon Street studios in central Hollywood. There would be only one day of exterior work, in the rugged mountain countryside near Santa Monica. Photography would be in black-and-white, which in the Hollywood of 1957 was standard for movies of stark dramatic content.

First performed on the stage in New York in 1924 with Walter Huston, Mary Morris, and Charles Ellis in the leads, *Desire Under the Elms* had created a censorship furor because of the play's references to incest and infanticide. When the play opened in Los Angeles in 1926, the whole cast was actually arrested and charged with obscenity. By 1957, liberalization of Hollywood's Production Code finally made it possible to film the play without any major changes.

In writing the screenplay, Irwin Shaw was the first of many Hollywood writers who had to contend with Sophia's foreign accent. She could never sound like a native-born American, so some explanation would have to be provided for the character's origins. Ironically, during the Depression, O'Neill had been so hard up for cash that he had written a screen treatment that specified that the leading female character could be changed to a European immigrant to enable a major star like Garbo or Dietrich to play the role. The proposal had landed in the O'Neill archives.

As the young Italian immigrant Anna Cabot, Sophia portrayed the newly-married third wife of seventy-year-old farmer Ephraim Cabot, a slave-driving tyrant who literally worked his previous wives to death after they bore him three sons. As much a monster as her elderly husband, Anna has married him only for his wealth. She schemes to get it by seducing his eldest son, Eben, who stands to inherit everything, having already purchased his step-brothers' interests when they moved away. When Eben realizes what Anna is really after, he rejects her, but not before she's become pregnant. Anna then convinces her husband that he's the father and that the child should be his sole heir. After the baby is born, Anna's conscience, plus a sudden realization that she truly loves Eben, unleashes a tragic chain of events.

In O'Neill's original play, the new wife was middle-aged, which made her old enough to be her stepson's mother and underscored the incestuous relationship to the slow-witted in the audience. There was no attempt to age Sophia beyond her twenty-three years, so the element of Greek tragedy was softened in her pairing with twenty-five-year-old Anthony Perkins. Since the part also required an experienced dramatic actress, Paramount might have been better off casting Anna Magnani, who also had a contract with the studio at the time.

"The role was the most challenging that Sophia had tackled up to that time," director Delbert Mann recalled. "She had to play a deeply emotional part with many long and involved speeches in a language that was still largely foreign to her. I was worried about her accent, about the degree of understanding she would have, and frankly, about my problems in communicating with her in an actor-director relationship. I need not have been, for Sophia is a remarkable woman. She had little or no formal training in acting, but her instinct was faultless, and she was wonderful to work with because her response was so pure and so true."

In Burl Ives and Anthony Perkins, Sophia found herself teamed with two Method actors who were protégés of director Elia Kazan. Ives had been known primarily as a folksinger when Kazan turned him into a dramatic actor in the movie *East of Eden* and then on the Broadway stage as Big Daddy in *Cat on a Hot Tin Roof*. Kazan had also given Perkins his first break on Broadway, replacing lead actor John Kerr in the long-running *Tea and Sympathy*.

Burl Ives was easier for Sophia to get along with. He was a kindly man, with a lilting voice that set her at ease when he told her stories about his early days bumming around America as a banjo-picking troubador. Now forty-seven, Ives had to be aged considerably with a white wig and false beard to portray Sophia's septuagenarian husband. With his round face and portly physique, he gave her a preview of what Carlo Ponti might look like at seventy, though Ives was much taller at 6'1".

Sophia was surprised to discover that Burl Ives wasn't the only singer in the cast. Anthony Perkins had a second career with RCA Victor, recording teen-oriented soft rock songs like "First Romance" and "The Prettiest Girl in School." Fan magazines had him pegged as one of the top heartthrobs of the day, but he was more interested in becoming a serious actor. He said at the time that his portrayal of Eben Cabot was patterned on Laurence Olivier's Heathcliff in *Wuthering Heights,* but with "an added nasty streak."

Amusingly, Perkins swore by the teachings of the Actors Studio but had never even auditioned there for fear of being rejected. But he'd learned all about the Method from observing other actors and taking copious notes as they worked with their directors on the motivations for their characters. It must have helped, since he won an Oscar nomination for his first major screen role in William Wyler's *Friendly Persuasion* and was scheduled to star on Broadway in *Look Homeward, Angel* after finishing *Desire Under the Elms.*

As a romantic partner to Sophia Loren, Perkins was too boyish and sensitive to be believable. Perhaps his homosexuality held him back. Years later, he would claim that he never had sex with a woman until he was forty, a break-through made possible only through extended psychotherapy.

Sophia found Perkins a trial to work with because he was always stopping to ask Delbert Mann for guidance into the mind of his character. Perkins was equally unstrung by Sophia's tendency to hog the camera. "Somebody must have taught her very early on to get her face in every scene," he said later. "All you could see of me, even in *my* scenes with her, would be the back of my head and my ears."

Perkins detected a fatal flaw in the film while it was being made. "It was nothing but talk, talk, talk, talk, talk, talk. When you make a moving picture, it's supposed to move."

Hollywood's most recent attempt at filming O'Neill, the 1947 *Mourning Becomes Electra,* had been no more than a photographed stage play and flopped miserably at the box office. Instead of learning from that mistake, Paramount repeated it by shooting 99.9 percent of *Desire Under the Elms* in the studio. Even the scenes taking place outdoors were photographed under artificial daylight and on sets that had the temporary, just-built look of a stage or television production. All the drama unfolded in static confrontations between the principal characters.

Although Edith Head was Paramount's head costume designer at the time, she hired historical expert Dorothy Jeakins to garb Sophia and the rest of the cast as 1850s New England farm folk. The legendary Wally Westmore did Sophia's makeup, and Nellie Manley, the favorite hair stylist of Marlene Dietrich and Carole Lombard in an earlier era, fixed her hair. The result was a breath-takingly beautiful Sophia who looked more like a gypsy fortune teller than a farmer's wife. Several film critics would later wonder how she managed to keep her eyes open under such generous applications of mascara.

8

MISTRESS

I N May 1957, Sophia Loren earned her second *Life* magazine cover, this time shown flaring the pleated skirt of her dress while perched on stepping-stones in the lily pond of her rented Bel-Air home. *Life* called her "The Movies' $3 Million Italian Doll," which supposedly would be her total earnings from various Hollywood projects, some yet to be produced. No mention was made of the fact that the first released, *Boy on a Dolphin,* had turned out a box-office disappointment.

The distributor, 20th Century–Fox, had certainly tried hard to make *Dolphin* a hit, but the massive advertising campaign focusing on Sophia in her skintight pearl-diving outfit had at least turned her into the sex symbol of the moment. In reviewing the film, William Zinsser of the *New York Herald Tribune* said that Sophia "fulfills the basic clause in her contract. She blazes her eyes, she holds her mouth ajar in hommage to the Marilyn Monroe doctrine, she waggles her hips, she exposes her legs. Can she act? That's a matter of definition."

To capitalize on all the commotion, independent distributors snapped up two of Sophia's Italian movies, both produced in 1955, that had never been released in the United States. As luck would have it, the films had their American premieres a day apart in New York City, *The Miller's Beautiful Wife,* shown in Italian with English subtitles at a small East Side art cinema, and *Scandal in Sorrento,* dubbed into English for a mainstream 1,500-seat theater on Broadway. With help from a condemned rating from the Catholic Legion of Decency, *Miller's Wife* packed them in and became an art circuit success nationally.

Sorrento, however, proved an instant flop when critics objected to the dubbed American voices emanating from Sophia's and De Sica's throats.

By the time Sophia completed *Desire Under the Elms, The Pride and the Passion* was finally ready for release. Thanks to saturation advertising, the starry cast, and Stanley Kramer's reputation for quality entertainment, the movie shattered box-office records in its opening days, but attendance soon plummeted in the wake of adverse reviews and negative word-of-mouth. The film failed to recoup its $5 million negative cost in the U.S., but eventually broke even with the international release.

Stanley Kramer blamed himself for the failure, recalling later that "Cary Grant had never done well in costume drama. He was really a drawing-room character. But with one of my more blatant bursts of creative misjudgment, I cast him in a role that was not for him. You know, in the tight military pants, the frilled shirt of the British officer."

Kramer believed that he compounded his mistake by putting Frank Sinatra into a wig with bangs and casting him as a leader of Spanish rebels. "Frank looked like he was going to burst into 'Besame Mucho' at any moment," Kramer said. "The movie was a complete bust, but I don't mean that as a dig at Sophia Loren. She was the only one to escape without any embarrassment. It served the purpose of launching her on an international career."

Everybody, especially Paramount Pictures, hoped that Sophia's next teaming with Cary Grant would be a major improvement. Happily, *An Affair to Remember,* the movie that he made with Deborah Kerr directly after *The Pride and the Passion,* was proving a box-office gold mine, so the public obviously still wanted to see him in the glossy romantic comedies that were his trademark.

Before Sophia began working with Grant again, her personal relationships with him and with Carlo Ponti needed to be resolved. The recent *Life* cover story had discreetly mentioned her liaison with Ponti, but now that it was out in the open, the Hollywood press corps had started getting nosy and asking questions that she had no answers for. Dorothy Manners, who did most of the investigative reporting that turned up under Louella Parsons' byline, kept phoning every few days. She wanted to know when Sophia intended marrying Ponti, insinuating that just continuing as his mistress would not be tolerated in Hollywood and could ruin her career.

Whatever was going on between Sophia and Cary Grant seemed a secret shared only by them. Their names were never linked romantically in the news nor in the gossip columns. Many years later, Sophia would claim that she saw Grant frequently and that he was always begging her to marry him. She said that Grant often phoned her at times when he knew that Ponti would be within hearing range of the conversation. What Grant expected to accomplish by that is unknown, but perhaps he was trying to discourage Ponti, figuring what woman in her right mind would marry unattractive Carlo Ponti when she could have Cary Grant?

Close friends of Grant's like Rosalind Russell and her producer-husband Frederick Brisson were mystified by his feelings for Sophia. "It wasn't like Cary to chase after women," Brisson recalled. "We thought it might be the seven-year itch or the male menopause. His marriage to Betsy was going through a bad patch, so he was very vulnerable when he met Sophia. I suspect that Sophia realized that, and frankly, I believe that her only interest in Cary was to make Carlo Ponti jealous. She may have gone too far in Cary's case. She drove him gaga. He wasn't thinking rationally, and she probably wasn't either. Suppose Ponti had given up. Cary and Sophia came from completely different worlds. Marriage would have been an instant disaster."

Whether he'd been pressured into it or not, Carlo Ponti finally promised to marry Sophia as soon as possible. Ponti may have seen public reaction as more of a threat than Cary Grant. The news media back in Italy and now in the United States were becoming relentless persecutors.

In July 1957, while waiting for Paramount to announce a starting date for *Houseboat,* Sophia and Ponti flew to Switzerland for a vacation at the Burgenstock, a superluxurious resort complex high up in the Alps overlooking Lake Lucerne. Audrey Hepburn and actor-husband Mel Ferrer resided there between filmmaking assignments. Sophia and Ponti thought it might suit them as well, but the real reason for the visit was to consult with his Swiss lawyers. Ponti already had them working on a Mexican divorce that would end his present marriage, but there were many details that needed to be taken care of before he could marry again. He was considering the possibility of becoming a Swiss citizen, which would mean paying much lower income taxes than in Italy. Ponti already did most of his banking in Switzerland, where laws were more liberal than in any other country in the world at that time.

Ten days later, the couple was back in Los Angeles and Sophia had begun preparations for *Houseboat.* At Cary Grant's request, the character that was originally to be enacted by his wife, Betsy Drake, had been transformed into glamorous Cinzia Zaccardi, daughter of a famous Italian orchestra conductor who's

making a concert tour of the United States. While traveling with her domineering father, Cinzia rebels and runs away, straight into a chance meeting with Tom
Winston, a widowed Washington diplomat with three young children. He
doesn't know anything about Cinzia, but he likes the way the kids respond to
her and he offers her a job as housekeeper-governess. Cinzia needs to hide
from her father, so she accepts, not expecting that home will turn out to be a
decrepit old houseboat that Tom rents to escape crowded city living.

Producer Jack Rose neglected to inform designer Edith Head of the script
changes, so she had assumed that Sophia would be playing an average working girl when she selected her costumes for the movie. But when Head delivered the sketches, Sophia rejected most of them. "I had envisioned someone in
blue jeans, shorts, sweatshirts, the very casual sort of things you would wear if
you were living on a houseboat and taking care of kids," Head said later.
"Sophia couldn't have been more charming—or more horrified—as she told me
in her lilting version of English, 'I do not wear jeans.' "

Edith Head had only to glance at Sophia's big posterior to understand why.
"I asked her what she did like to wear and she invited me to her house to see.
I took a good look through her wardrobe. It was very high fashion, very elegant: dresses, shoes, jewelry by top Italian designers. Sophia turned out to be
the exact antithesis of the earthy, highly emotional Italian actress I'd expected.
She was the most poised person with whom I'd ever worked, thoroughly organized, dignified and slightly formal. She wasn't about to call me 'Edith,' at least
during our first meeting. And I liked that."

Sophia told Head that she preferred soft colors—beiges, pale mauve, soft
olive-green. "Those are colors that complement her eyes, which are soft green,
like a tiger's," Head said. "Sophia also disliked frills, the plainer the better. She
was quite right. The closer she resembles a statue, the better she looks and the
better proportioned her clothes appear."

After four straight films as a peasant character, *Houseboat* gave Sophia her
first shot at the full Hollywood glamour treatment. Head designed some beautiful outfits that delighted her, but Sophia was startled to find that Cary Grant
demanded to see them first. "In his contemporary films, Cary always provided
his own wardrobes," Head recalled. "Since he was *the* most beautifully dressed
man in the world, I had complete trust in his choices. But before he made them
he needed to know what Sophia was wearing in each scene so that the clothes
he selected complemented hers. He worked out a color scheme for his things
throughout the picture. He had a discerning eye, a meticulous sense of detail."

Grant fretted over one of Sophia's dresses, the fabric of which was flaked with 14-karat gold. Grant insisted on coming to Sophia's fitting and rehearsing the party dance scene in which she would wear it. As soon as they embraced, Grant's fears were confirmed as the gold started rubbing off on his suit.

"Sophia couldn't stop laughing that deep, infectious laugh of hers," Head recalled. "I sent at once to the studio paint shop for some lacquer and a spray gun. It was such an instant drying lacquer that Sophia didn't have to disrobe. I sprayed it on and the gold stayed put. Sophia quipped, 'I feel like the Oscar, sprayed on.' "

Before *Houseboat* started production at Paramount's studio in Hollywood, Sophia and Grant headed a group of actors and production crew that was flown to Washington, D.C., to shoot some of the exterior scenes, including an evening concert with fireworks at Watergate Stadium. Unaccompanied by their mates, Sophia and Grant both stayed at the Hotel Statler, but whether they spent any of their nonworking hours together is a matter for conjecture.

During Sophia's visit to the capital, the Italian Embassy threw a cocktail reception in her honor. Among scores of government dignitaries attending was a certain married senator from Massachusetts. Nearly four decades later, a dual biography entitled *Jack & Jackie* would claim that "Jack," whose wife was away on a trip to New York at the time, fell hard for Sophia and invited her back to his house on N Street for a champagne supper.

The story goes that Sophia declined, but that "Jack" kept bombarding her with phone calls and that she finally agreed to a rendezvous. George Smathers, a friend of the future president, recalled, "I never saw Jack strike out with anybody if he really wanted to get together with them. He just would not take no for an answer, and he just kept at it until he wore them down. Miss Loren was no exception. She went with Jack all right, and I understand they had a wonderful time." No public comment was made by Sophia following the publication of the claim in 1996, but friends say she was furious and denied it.

By the time that *Houseboat* started full production in Hollywood in August, Sophia's personal relationship with Cary Grant seemed to have cooled. Actress Martha Hyer, who played Sophia's romantic rival in the film, recalled that "Cary was completely smitten with Sophia and driving her crazy. One day I picked up the phone in my dressing room and got a line crossed with theirs. He was pleading with her to marry him, promising her a trip around the world on a tramp steamer, the children she'd always wanted, anything, everything. I wanted to interrupt and shout, 'If she won't, I will.' Sophia listened to him very quietly, saying little."

According to his friend Frederick Brisson, Grant soured on Sophia when she went off to Switzerland with Carlo Ponti, but fell back in love with her when they started playing their romantic scenes in the film. "Cary thought he'd lost her. He believed it would be too painful working with her again, so he tried to get her removed from *Houseboat,* but it was too late. There was a moment in the film where they had to make love in a rowboat. Sophia responded to him so passionately that Cary thought she couldn't be acting and that he still had a chance with her."

Grant's mood seemed to depend on what gossip column he'd read that morning. Any linking of Sophia's name with Carlo Ponti's would send him into a rage, usually aimed at the director, Melville Shavelson. "Cary had to take it out on somebody and I was the most convenient, although after the picture was over he apologized for giving me such a hard time," Shavelson recalled. "He objected to the photography, he objected to portions of the script, he objected to things which in normal situations he would not have minded at all. His problem was with Sophia. And that made it hard going for everybody."

Shavelson felt sorry for Sophia and tried to console her. "She often came to me crying over Cary's behavior towards her. She made it clear so many times to him that Carlo Ponti was her man, but apparently Cary just couldn't understand that. He couldn't comprehend this father fixation that many Italian women have, this need for the care, the comfort, and the guidance which Sophia certainly got from Carlo Ponti."

Sophia recalled later that "Cary thought psychoanalysis might help me. But I felt that I knew as much about myself as any psychiatrist could possibly discover. Anyway, my complexes have been good to me. They help to make people what they are. When you lose them, you might also lose yourself."

Some of Grant's moods rubbed off on Sophia, and one day she laced into child actor Paul Petersen, who was portraying the eldest of Grant's three kids. Petersen was supposed to start crying in the scene, but after twenty takes he couldn't manage the tears and Sophia finally lost patience and slapped him across the face. "You do not take money for nothing," she said. "You are being paid to cry. So cry!" She slapped him again, and the tears flowed. Afterwards, overcome by remorse, she picked him up in her arms, smothered him with kisses, and apologized.

On the morning of September 18, 1957, syndicated columnist Louella Parsons announced to the world that Sophia Loren and Carlo Ponti had been married by proxy in Mexico. The news surprised even the bride and groom, whose attorneys had taken their time informing them and hadn't counted on Louella Parsons having spies everywhere.

In a matter of weeks, a Mexican court had voided Ponti's eleven-year marriage to Giuliana Fiastri and freed him to wed Sofia Scicolone, which was still Sophia's legal name. Amusingly, two male attorneys substituted for Sophia and Ponti at the proxy wedding ceremony. Sophia's stand-in had a mustache and beard.

The new Mrs. Ponti found out about it during breakfast when she opened the *Herald-Express*. "Since we were deeply involved with each other long before the proxy wedding, seeing it in Louella Parsons' column was almost like reading about two other people," Sophia said later. "We were already man and wife in our eyes. Passionately joined to each other. A paragraph in a gossip column hardly did it justice."

That night, the Pontis dined alone by candlelight to celebrate. In lieu of a wedding present, Carlo promised Sophia that he would build "the most beautiful house in the world" for them to live in.

Needless to say, Cary Grant was furious about the marriage, but he tried to conceal his feelings. He, too, first learned about it from Louella Parsons' column. When Sophia came to work that day, he merely said, "I hope you'll be very happy," and gave her a cool kiss on the cheek.

Ironically, the script for *Houseboat* had a similar scene, but with more pungent dialogue that seemed to echo their personal relationship. When the lovers are about to split after a major disagreement, Sophia tells Grant, "It was a lovely interlude. I enjoyed every minute of it—until we both had too much champagne and spoiled it all."

"It was just an interlude, was it?" Grant asks. "Yes, an interlude," she answers. He turns on her and says, "For a girl who's had so much experience lying, you're not doing very well at this moment."

The finale of *Houseboat* had yet to be filmed. It became a classic case of fantasy mixing with reality as Sophia and Grant get married in a sumptuous religious ceremony set to Felix Mendelssohn's music. While Sophia's real-life proxy marriage robbed her of the opportunity, she could still be a bride in the magnificent long white gown of antique lace that Edith Head designed for her.

For the bastard Sofia Scicolone, who used to clip pictures of brides and movie stars from magazines to paste in a scrapbook, it was a dream coming true, but also an ordeal. "I cared very much for Cary and I was aware of how painful it was for him to play the scene with me, to have the minister prothe same age bracket as male leads William Holden and Trevor Howard, so it really didn't matter that much which actress played the part.

The Key gave the newlywed Pontis a convenient excuse for not returning to Italy, where the news of their Mexican legal maneuvers had struck the Vatican like a thunderbolt. In the official Vatican newspaper *L'Osservatore della Domenica,* a legal adviser to the Vatican on marital matters wrote that

> Civil divorce and a successive civil marriage are gravely illicit acts and have no judicial effect whatever before God and the Church. Those responsible are public sinners and may no longer receive the sacraments.

> The code of Canon Law regards as bigamists those who contract a new marriage—even if only a civil one—although they are bound by a valid marriage. It punishes both parties with the penalty of infamy [loss of rights]. If they set up life in common, this is termed concubinage and may be punished even with interdict [denial of certain sacraments] and excommunication.

Though the article failed to mention the Pontis by name, a reference to "the recent proxy wedding in Mexico of a beautiful Italian film star" made it plain who the sinners were. Other Catholic publications also condemned the marriage; a weekly Catholic film magazine said that back in the Middle Ages, the Pontis would have been burned alive or stoned to death in a public square for all to see.

Relatives and friends sent the Pontis copies of the latest indictments. Sophia said later that she read them all "with a terrible feeling of dread and indignation. I was being threatened with excommunication, with the everlasting fire, and for what reason? I had fallen in love with a man whose own marriage had ended long before. I wanted to be his wife and have his children. We had done the best the law would allow to make it official, but they were calling us public sinners. We should have been taking a honeymoon, but all I remember is weeping for hours."

Ponti promised to fight. "We're married and we're going to stay married," he told Sophia. "If this Mexican marriage is not recognized, we'll find some other way. This is all just a dust storm that will blow over. We are the victims of ignorance. It is the ones who are denouncing us who lack morals. We are the moral ones. Whatever has to be done, we will do. You are my wife and nobody will ever change that, and that's all there is to it."

nounce us man and wife, and to take me in his arms and kiss me," Sophia recalled. "It was painful for me, too, his make-believe bride. I could not help
thinking of all those lovely times we spent in Spain, of all the souvenirs I had in
my memory. I'm very romantic and vulnerable, and I would cherish forever
what Cary brought into my life."

Grant, who'd never won an Oscar and had been nominated only once in his
lengthy career, perhaps should have gotten some sort of prize for playing the
scene with such a happy look on his face. One can only guess how he really
felt as he swapped the sacred vows with Sophia and came as near to being her
husband as he ever would. Immediately after finishing *Houseboat*, he left for
England to work opposite Ingrid Bergman in *Indiscreet*, which conveniently
spared Sophia from further tribulations.

The Pontis remained in Los Angeles to sort out their next commitments.
Paramount had agreed to Ponti producing Sophia's next film for the studio, but
a property had yet to be selected. Ponti proposed teaming Sophia with Ingrid
Bergman and Audrey Hepburn in Chekhov's *Three Sisters*, but Paramount
wanted to wait until the results were in on *Desire Under the Elms* before com-
mitting to more theatrical classics.

Paramount wanted something more contemporary, but rejected Ponti's suggestion of *Journey with Anita*, which director Federico Fellini and his scriptwriting partner Tullio Pinelli planned to make in Italy. Fellini hoped to team Sophia
with Gregory Peck in the story about a famous writer who falls seriously in love
with an occasional girlfriend while they're taking a long trip to the country to
visit his sickly father. The script was more erotic than any of Fellini's previous
films, including a scene that would have required Sophia to strip naked and roll
in the dew-soaked grass. Paramount decided it could not get Production Code
approval and passed. Fellini never did make the movie, but many years later he
sold the idea to Universal, which turned it into *Lovers and Liars* for Goldie
Hawn and Giancarlo Giannini.

While Paramount's story department tried to find other projects, Sophia had
to fulfill her commitment to Columbia Pictures for director Carol Reed's next,
which by now had been titled *The Key*. Filming would take place in England at
the MGM-owned Boreham Wood Studios near London. In the hope of jacking
up Sophia's salary, Ponti had dawdled about actually signing the contract, but
he quickly settled for the offered $225,000 when Columbia started negotiations
for Ingrid Bergman to take over Sophia's role. Although Sophia and the considerably older Bergman might not have seemed interchangeable, the latter was in

When the couple left Los Angeles for England, they flew indirectly via Paris so that Ponti could catch a connecting flight to Rome to spend a few days secretly consulting lawyers. Sophia traveled on alone to London's Heathrow, where she found a flock of reporters and photographers waiting for her in the VIP lounge. Asked to comment on the Vatican's condemnation, she replied, "Do I look like a sinner? Come on, tell me. And is my husband a criminal? Have we done something terrible by getting married? There are many other Italians who have gone through what we did in Mexico and are now living in Italy without being molested by the Church. But because Carlo and I are celebrities, they have decided to use us as scapegoats."

While in Rome, Ponti instructed his lawyers to try again for a Vatican annulment, this time by going straight to the Sacred Rota, the court of final appeal. When he rejoined Sophia in London, Ponti visited the Italian Embassy and pleaded with the ambassador, Count Vittorio Zoppi, for governmental support. Ponti said the adverse publicity was making Italy the laughingstock of the world for its antiquated divorce laws.

The Pontis' latest temporary home was a suite at the Edgwarebury Country Club in Hertfordshire, not far from the studio where *The Key* was being filmed. By the time of Sophia's arrival, director Carol Reed had already completed most of the scenes in which she didn't appear, including all the World War II naval action that took up about half the movie.

Sophia was literally the key to *The Key,* which was based on Dutch writer Jan de Hartog's novelette *Stella,* her character's name in the film. Yet another shady lady, the Swiss refugee lives in the port city of Plymouth and shares the key to her apartment (and her body) with a succession of tugboat captains involved in dangerous rescue operations in the English Channel. The first skipper, who was also Stella's fiancé, was killed on the eve of their wedding. Ever since, she's been trying to forget him with others, only to find that they, too, are likely to become casualties of the war.

The Key marked the official career rebirth of the blacklisted American screenwriter Carl Foreman, who was able to make a three-picture production deal with Columbia Pictures after he agreed in 1956 to testify before the House Un-American Activities Committee and received a clean bill of health as a "disillusioned Communist." But from 1951, when Foreman took the Fifth Amendment, he could only get writing work using aliases or without any screen credit at all, as in the case of *The Bridge on the River Kwai,* which had just entered release when *The Key* started production.

While working on *Kwai*, Foreman had become friendly with William Holden and talked him into signing on for the first effort of his independent company, Open Road Productions. Besides scripting *The Key,* Foreman was serving as producer. He wanted David Lean to direct, but the latter had already committed to a project about Lawrence of Arabia, so Foreman decided to take a chance on Carol Reed. By the end of the 1940s, three successive Reed films, *Odd Man Out, The Fallen Idol,* and *The Third Man,* had been such triumphs that he was considered Britain's greatest film director after Alfred Hitchcock. In 1952, he was granted a knighthood as Sir Carol Reed, but his movies after *The Third Man* were critical and commercial disappointments until the most recent, *Trapeze,* with Burt Lancaster, Tony Curtis, and Gina Lollobrigida. Reed had managed to get a good performance out of La Lollo, which augured well for his being able to handle her Italian rival in a more complex dramatic role.

Sophia had never met Sir Carol or William Holden, so Carl Foreman arranged a small dinner party at Reed's house in London to introduce them. According to Foreman, Sophia made such an impact on both Reed and Holden that they unwittingly began to compete with each other for her affections. "Both Bill and Carol were married at the time, so I can't say whether their interest in Sophia went beyond the platonic. But they seemed to be vying for the possession of her psyche, if not her body," Foreman recalled.

William Holden later remembered his first glimpse of Sophia: "She didn't walk into the room, she swept in. I never saw so much woman coming at me in my entire life. Beautiful women have always thrown me. I really don't know how to handle them, especially when they're actresses that I work with. You have to work with them terribly intimately, particularly in the love scenes, and unless you play it neutral you may well have a situation on your hands. I'd had that difficulty previously with Jennifer Jones, Grace Kelly, Audrey Hepburn, and Kim Novak."

Holden was then thirty-nine and Reed nearly fifty-two, while Sophia was twenty-three. When filming started, she acquired a third admirer in forty-one-year-old Trevor Howard, a star of many Carol Reed films, who portrayed another of Stella's seafaring lovers. Sophia quickly became aware of how all three felt about her and used it to her advantage, but apparently stopped short of becoming personally involved with any of them.

Holden and Howard found it hard to adjust to Sophia's method of acting. During the rehearsal of a scene, she always did a superficial reading, saving her full performance for the actual take. Reed indulged her, but Holden and Howard rarely knew what would come out of Sophia until the cameras started rolling.

"I had little professional training and an inferiority complex when it came to rehearsing with experienced actors," she said years later. "I didn't want to be embarrassed by my inability to turn it on and off as true professionals do. My technique consists simply of following my basic instincts. The actress in me is only released at the moment the camera demands it. The word 'Action!' frees me. I kick away my self-consciousness and I feel liberated, uninhibited, even reckless. The transformation is something that I cannot explain. It is fragile and mysterious, and too much analysis might destroy it."

Carol Reed declared at the time that Sophia was easy to direct. "She trusts you right from the start," he said. "She gives herself to you as an artist. During shooting, she'd ask me, 'What did I do wrong? What can I do to make it better?' I've never known her to pull an act—the headache, the temperament. Usually with such a beauty, there is worry about the looks. Sophia doesn't bother about looks. She's interested in acting."

During the filming, Sophia received her second chance to meet Queen Elizabeth II. Like all the top celebrities in London at the time, she was invited to the annual Royal Film Performance, which this year featured *The Bridge on the River Kwai*. Carlo Ponti stayed at home so that William Holden, one of the stars of the film, could be Sophia's escort for the evening. In her gorgeous white evening gown, and with Holden in white tie and tails, the couple dazzled everybody and were first on the Queen's receiving line.

This time, Sophia remembered to not wear a tiara in her hair, but some of the next day's newspapers criticized her anyway, claiming that Sophia's marital situation made her unfit to be received by the Queen of England. The *Daily Mirror* couldn't resist reporting that on the very day of the Royal Performance, a woman back in Italy had registered a formal complaint against the Pontis that charged them with bigamy and concubinage and could lead to their arrest and possible imprisonment.

The complainant, a Milanese named Luisa Brambilla, had written to the public prosecutor, who, by Italian law, was obligated to investigate any criminal charges that a citizen makes against another citizen. In her letter, Brambilla identified herself as a wife and mother who wanted to "save the institution of matrimony in Italy."

Brambilla was believed connected with Catholic Action, which had a network of local pressure groups throughout Italy. Her letter started a flood of similar complaints from all over the country, including Sophia's home town of Pozzuoli, where thirty-seven housewives signed a petition demanding action against "the bigamists." Actually, only Ponti qualified for that epithet, since Sophia had no other known husband.

At the preliminary hearing scheduled by the public prosecutor, neither Brambilla nor any of the other complainants actually turned up. But the sacks of letters were enough to convince a magistrate to sign arrest warrants charging Ponti as a bigamist and Sophia as his concubine, both criminal offenses in Italy at that time.

The warrants had no legal authority outside Italy, so to avoid arrest, the Pontis would have to exile themselves until a solution could be found. Fortunately, their movie commitments required them to be away from Italy much of the time anyway, but they would still miss the permanence of a home and being with their relatives and friends.

Incredibly, while the Pontis were being pilloried in Italy, Sophia's parents had reconciled and were living together in Rome. In the most bizarre twist yet in the tempestuous Scicolone-Villani affair that had started in 1933, Riccardo had left his wife and two teenage sons to move in with Romilda and Maria in the posh apartment that Sophia provided for them.

Passion and money seemed the motivating factors. Now in her middle forties, Romilda was still a beautiful and voluptuous woman. She apparently rekindled a spark in Riccardo and derived great satisfaction from luring him away from his wife Nella, whom she despised for causing her so much grief over the years.

Now that his eldest daughter was a world-famous movie star, Scicolone thought that he had the right to share in the glory and some of her wealth. He proposed taking over the management of her finances, but Sophia didn't trust him and said that Ponti would continue in that job. Sophia was extremely suspicious of her father, but he seemed to be making Romilda happy and Maria also enjoyed having a *papa* on the scene, so she decided to tolerate the arrangement.

When Sophia finished *The Key* in December 1957, the Pontis returned to the Burgenstock resort in Switzerland, which they decided would be their European residence for the duration of their Italian difficulties. With its proximity to Italy, their relatives and friends there could visit easily by plane or, in the case of the flying-phobic Romilda, by express train to Lucerne.

Although the Burgenstock had three superluxury hotels in its five hundred acres of gardens and parkland, the Pontis selected one of its individual chalets, which had a quaint Swiss exterior but a completely modern interior with enormous picture windows that looked out on the Alps. The two-bedroom duplex had every living convenience, including maids, butlers, and the option of ordering from one of the hotel kitchens if the Pontis didn't feel like cooking.

The Burgenstock also had all the business facilities that Carlo Ponti needed to keep in touch with Hollywood and the production centers of Europe. Due to his legal problems in Italy, Ponti would have to forgo producing more films there, but during the past eighteen months he'd made six. The majority received scant distribution outside Italy, but two, the Pietro Germi–directed *The Railroad Man* and Alberto Lattuada's *Guendalina,* became moderate successes on the international "art" circuit.

While the Pontis were spending Christmas in Switzerland, United Artists opened *The Legend of the Lost* in major cities across America, but the results were just as disappointing as those of Sophia's two previous Hollywood-financed films. Critics called it insipid hokum and downright boring, which was not what the public wanted in a John Wayne film. Sophia received the usual compliments for her "full-blown charms," but they were not enough to save *Legend of the Lost* from becoming her third box-office flop in a row.

Ponti promised to do better for Sophia in the coming year. By the end of 1957, he'd worked out a nonstop schedule of films for her at Paramount that he would personally produce, starting with *The Black Orchid,* a melodrama about an Italian immigrant widow that seemed tailor-made for Sophia, even though the studio had originally intended it for Anna Magnani. After that, Sophia would make the romantic *That Kind of Woman* and an as-yet-untitled comedy based on Ferenc Molnár's play *Olympia,* the exact order to be decided as soon as the scripts were finished and ready to be filmed.

Meanwhile, Sophia's first two Paramount films had yet to be released. Nervous about the commercial chances of *Desire Under the Elms,* the studio hoped to build it into a prestige item and had entered it in the Cannes Film Festival in May. And due to Warner Brothers' decision to rush out *Indiscreet,* the release of *Houseboat* had been postponed until summer to avoid having two Cary Grant pictures on the market simultaneously.

In mid-January 1958, the Pontis flew to Los Angeles for what promised to be an extended stay. They rented a house in the Bel Air hills for themselves and their usual entourage of helpmates. Prior to their arrival, Ponti's coproducer,

Marcello Girosi, had moved his office from Rome to Paramount's Hollywood studio so that he could handle all of the detail work on the several films under development.

Ponti, however, made most of the creative decisions. Before selecting a director for *The Black Orchid,* he screened the work of several that Paramount recommended and chose Martin Ritt. Ritt's recent first movie, *Edge of the City,* an exposé of labor union corruption with Sidney Poitier and John Cassavetes, reminded him of Italian neorealism and had been shot very economically and swiftly in twenty-eight days. Like Carl Foreman, Ritt was a resurrected ex-Communist who'd suffered through five years of blacklisting as an actor and director in television, but the critical acclaim for *Edge of the City* started a new career in movies. He had since done impressive work with Joanne Woodward in *No Down Payment* and had gone on to direct her again with even better results opposite Paul Newman in *The Long Hot Summer.*

Ritt had started out as an actor with New York's prestigious Group Theater and taught classes at the Actors Studio during his blacklisted years, so Ponti saw him as a director who might be able to guide Sophia to an Oscar-winning performance. Ponti had originally intended to hire Vittorio De Sica, but Paramount vetoed the idea because he had no experience working in Hollywood studios. Ponti *was* able to persuade Paramount to hire Alessandro Cicognini, composer of the background music for *The Bicycle Thief* and other De Sica classics, to do the score.

The Black Orchid had a curious history. Joseph Stefano, a young entertainer and composer from South Philadelphia, wrote the script just to prove that he could do better than most of the junk he saw on television. He submitted it to various TV producers, but had no luck until it landed at Paramount's New York story department, which noticed similarities to *Marty,* an Oscar-winning film that had originated as a teleplay. Paramount wanted to turn *The Black Orchid* directly into a movie with Anna Magnani, but she had other commitments and it got passed on to Ponti for consideration.

The black orchid turned out to be a white rose in the person of Manhattan tenement dweller Rose Bianco, the recent widow of a murdered gangster and the mother of an incarcerated juvenile delinquent. When her twelve-year-old son is permitted to come home for the funeral, she promises him a better life in the future, though that hardly seems likely with her paltry earnings from making artificial flowers, the trade she learned back in her native Italy. But when matchmaking neighbors introduce Rose to Frank Valente, a widowed businessman who has problems of his own with an overly possessive grown-up daughter, the stage is set for some heavy-breathing drama before the inevitable happy ending.

Due to a multiple-picture deal that Paramount had with Anthony Quinn, Ponti was forced to accept him as Sophia's costar, even though they did not work well together in *Attila the Hun*. In the intervening four years, Quinn had won his second best supporting Oscar (for portraying Paul Gauguin in *Lust for Life*) and had starred opposite Oscar-winning actresses Anna Magnani (*Wild Is the Wind*) and Shirley Booth (*Hot Spell*), so Ponti had no basis to complain about Quinn's ability to play the role. He could only hope that the chemistry with Sophia would be better this time.

The Black Orchid was filmed largely within the confines of Paramount Studios, utilizing standing sets that had been doubling for the streets of New York and other cities since the 1920s. To "open up" the action, scenes of Sophia's visits to her son were shot at an actual correctional institution near Los Angeles. To gain a further sense of reality, Martin Ritt insisted on taking over St. Paul's Roman Catholic Church for two major scenes, the funeral of Rose's husband and her subsequent marriage to Frank. To save time, both scenes, though separated by the entire movie, were shot on the same day, with Sophia playing a widow in the morning and a bride in the afternoon.

The two stars were on early call that day and shared a limousine to the location. "Sophia hadn't had time for breakfast," Anthony Quinn recalled, "so she asked the driver to stop to get her a pizza. She sat in the car and ate the whole thing. It almost started my ulcer acting up again."

Portraying the traditional Italian widow in permanent mourning, Sophia wore somber black outfits except for the wedding scene, but all were custom designed for her by Edith Head. Wally Westmore concocted some new makeup for Sophia that made her look old enough to be the mother of a young delinquent but without diminishing her beauty.

Due to his training in television, Martin Ritt was accustomed to working fast and without too much rehearsing, which suited Sophia's style of acting. "At first I thought she might be too young for the role," the director recalled. "Here was this all-powerful female playing a woman who was left with a child, supposedly mature, experienced, and a widow, yet Sophia was clearly in the full bloom of her mid-twenties! But she overcame it because she is resolute, but mostly because she has this perfect concentration. She gave herself to me, and to the film, and was rewarded for it. She proved that she was a fine actress and not just a sex symbol."

Since Sophia and Anthony Quinn both had very potent personalities and tended to emote at full throttle, Ritt fought to keep them under control to save their scenes together from deteriorating into unintentional comedy. In their only moment of passionate lovemaking, Ritt demanded seven takes before he was satisfied, reducing the sizzle a few degrees each time.

"Finally, we were playing the scene so small it didn't seem to us to be like acting anymore," Quinn remembered. "But when we saw it in the rushes, it was as powerful as hell. Because the thing Sophia does, and obviously I do, is to overcharge instead of pulling back."

While filming *The Black Orchid,* Sophia received her first invitation to participate in the annual Academy Awards ceremonies, that year being held at the Pantages Theatre in Hollywood. Believe it or not, there would be no advertising breaks during the telecast; the industry itself was sponsoring the event after receiving too many complaints about the numerous commercials in previous years.

To make up for the drab clothes she made for Sophia in *Black Orchid,* Edith Head designed a gorgeous sheath dress for her to wear, made of glimmering pearl silk shot through with gold. Sophia would need all the help she could get to stand out in a crowd that was to include Lana Turner, Elizabeth Taylor, Mae West, Kim Novak, Natalie Wood, Joan Collins, Anita Ekberg, Zsa Zsa Gabor, and other bodies beautiful.

On that night of March 26, 1958, Sophia strolled on stage to present the Best Director award and momentarily looked like she was going to pull a Jayne Mansfield as one of the shoulder straps of her gown came loose. While she adjusted it, she thanked the Academy members for "the recognition you've given Italian artists." Only minutes before, Italy and Federico Fellini had won their second consecutive Oscar for Best Foreign Film, this time for *Nights of Cabiria,* produced by Carlo Ponti's ex-partner, Dino De Laurentiis.

Sophia was supposed to share a joke with emcee Bob Hope, but when she flubbed the setup to his punch line and got a laugh, he wisecracked, "You catch on fast, honey." Sophia rattled off the names of the five nominees, asked for the winner's envelope, and then laughed at herself when she realized she was already holding it. The winner was David Lean for *The Bridge on the River Kwai.* Sophia gave him a big hug when he walked on stage to the music of the "Colonel Bogey March."

When Sophia retreated to the wings, she ran smack into Cary Grant, who was waiting to go on to present the Best Actor award. They embraced, but had no time to chat. As luck would have it, Sophia's current costar, Anthony Quinn, was one of the nominated actors (for *Wild Is the Wind*), but he lost to Alec Guinness of *The Bridge on the River Kwai,* which later in the evening was also named Best Picture.

Anna Magnani, Quinn's costar in *Wild Is the Wind,* was also an Oscar nominee that night. While she lost the Best Actress award to Joanne Woodward of *The Three Faces of Eve,* Magnani had already signed with Paramount producer Hal Wallis for another film with the same director, George Cukor. Due to her age and homeliness, Magnani wasn't the easiest star to cast, but Wallis' scouts had found an ideal property in Alberto Moravia's 1957 novel, *La Ciociara* (literally, "the woman from Ciociara," a region in southern Italy), about a peasant mother and daughter trapped between the German occupiers and the Allied invaders in the final year of World War II. The book had just been published in English under the title of *Two Women,* which would also be used for the film version.

While nosing around the Paramount lot, Carlo Ponti became familiar with the project and suggested to Hal Wallis that Sophia would be a good choice for the role of Magnani's daughter. At fifty-three, Magnani *was* old enough to be Sophia's mother, but she didn't see it that way. When Ponti phoned her in Rome to discuss it, she told him, "Don't make me vomit. I know you're in love with Sophia, but don't try to suggest that she could play my virgin daughter. If anything, that cow should play the mother, not the daughter, she's old enough."

The volcanic Magnani got so upset that she cabled Hal Wallis her regrets and advised him to find some other property for her to do instead. Ponti, meanwhile, purchased *Two Women* from Wallis, with the intention of producing it himself after his other Paramount projects were finished. When the legal situation cleared in Italy, Ponti hoped to film it on the actual locations in Ciociara, with either Roberto Rossellini or Vittorio De Sica directing. Needless to say, Magnani had planted an idea in his head to cast Sophia in the mother's role, which could easily be accomplished by making the daughter younger than in Moravia's novel.

By taking over *Two Women,* Ponti had inadvertently bumped the intended director, George Cukor, who was one of Hollywood's most revered, and not to be treated shabbily. To compensate, Ponti hired Cukor for another of Sophia's upcoming Paramount films. Bizarrely, it was a western, a genre in which the director had never worked before, but since Cukor had a special flair for handling actresses, Ponti hoped he would be able to guide Sophia to a triumph.

Meanwhile, Paramount was getting nervous about *Desire Under the Elms,* which though scheduled to be shown at the Cannes Film Festival in May, had been sitting on the shelf for nearly a year and causing theater exhibitors to suspect it was a bomb. To allay fears, Paramount booked a series of test engagements in several major cities, starting with New York and Los Angeles. In each, *Desire Under the Elms* opened simultaneously in a theater in the art category, where the advertising stressed the Eugene O'Neill connection, and also in a mainstream theater that put the emphasis on sex and depravity. The results were about the same in each; few people attended after the first few days due to unfavorable reviews and word of mouth.

Bosley Crowther of *The New York Times* panned the movie and especially Burl Ives, who reminded him too much of a "Foxy Grandpa." But Crowther wrote that Sophia

> gives a strong performance in the role of the crafty and passion-charged woman who makes for trouble down on the farm. Even though she is shown as Italian and not the New Englander of the play, she is plausibly in the spirit of the tempestuous drama that unfolds. She is initially the spitfire who can tempt the wild young man with cogent wiles. Then she dissolves into a woman who is raptly and recklessly in love.

Other influential critics differed. *The New Yorker* praised Sophia's "breath-stopping beauty," but noted that she "conducts herself as if her only problem is to keep her eyes open under a most generous application of mascara. . . . The three stars' acting styles are so diverse that they seem like independent turns in some sort of vaudeville."

After a few more desultory openings, Paramount chalked *Desire Under the Elms* off as a loss and hoped that the Cannes Festival showing would improve the movie's chances in the European market.

Ironically, the only film of Sophia's enjoying box-office success in the United States was the four-year-old *Attila,* which Joseph E. Levine had acquired for $75,000 and was distributing himself through a company called Attila Associates. Levine, who made a fortune in 1956 with the Japanese-made *Godzilla,* had staked $500,000 of it on launching *Attila the Hun* with the largest saturation advertising campaign on radio and television in the film industry's history. As a result, the movie had grossed a huge $2 million in its first ten days of release (the average price of a movie ticket in 1958 was 51 cents!).

"You can fool all the people all of the time if the advertising is right and the budget is big enough," Levine was fond of saying.

Sophia was horrified by what Levine had done to the film, cutting twenty minutes of expository scenes to speed up the action and dubbing all the voices, including her own, in England with actors who spoke in aristocratic tones. The ads boasted of "raging ravishers roaring out of their Asian wastelands to lay waste a pleasure-gorged empire. . . . See Anthony Quinn as the scourge of God, and Sophia Loren as the scourge of *men!*"

By the time Sophia finished *The Black Orchid,* Columbia was preparing to release *The Key,* which would break industry tradition by opening in England and Europe simultaneously with the United States. Unfortunately, when Columbia's Hollywood executives screened the final cut, they decided that the unhappy ending to the love story between Sophia and William Holden would mean death at the box office unless it was changed. Director Carol Reed and writer-producer Carl Foreman disagreed, but were willing to compromise by shooting a more upbeat conclusion for the American release only.

Accompanied by Ponti, Sophia flew to London to rejoin Holden for the one brief scene. *The Key* was so near to having its London premiere that the Pontis stayed on to attend and, prior to that, to visit the Cannes Film Festival for the showing of *Desire Under the Elms.* In Cannes, where the couple were out in public for the first time since the start of their legal troubles in Italy, the paparazzi swarmed after them wherever they went. Paramount set up a press conference so that Sophia could answer questions in return for their leaving her alone for the balance of her visit.

Asked what attracted her to Ponti, Sophia said, "I needed a father, a lover, a husband, a guide. Carlo is all four. He teaches without I know it. Natural, like a child being born."

Plainly, Sophia's everyday English still needed work. When a reporter called her a sexpot, she replied "I am a sexy pot, yes, but I act roles which have a common feeling with people, and they like me because they know I come from them."

Desire Under the Elms won no prizes at Cannes. Instead, it went on to flop in Europe.

Back in London again for the premiere of *The Key,* Sophia participated in another Royal Film Performance, this one a shade less regal, with Princess Margaret rather than her elder sister as the guest of honor. But it provided another chance for Sofia Scicolone to outdazzle the royals, courtesy of producer

Carl Foreman, who bought her the Yves St. Laurent gown, and Carlo Ponti, who reportedly paid $125,000 for her double-strand diamond and ruby necklace.

Due to the last-minute decision to change the ending for the American release, *The Key* opened in England and Europe a month in advance of the United States. The reviews were generally excellent, and many critics thought Sophia gave her best English-speaking performance so far. Leonard Mosley of London's *Daily Express* called her work

> touching and tender. She has never looked lovelier, which is no mean achievement when you remember that she is hardly ever seen in anything except her night clothes. In the hands of a less talented actress, this could have been just another story of a kind-hearted woman in a back bedroom. Miss Loren gives the role an extra dimension and lifts it above tawdry origins. She helps make *The Key* a strange, sombre, compelling film.

The movie also won acclaim at a special showing in conjunction with the opening of the Brussels World's Fair and went on to become a hit throughout Europe, where its World War II content seemed to strike a responsive chord. In the United States, however, *The Key* fared less well. Even with an upbeat ending, it was probably too serious a drama to appeal to summertime vacationers. In the final tally, it grossed about $7 million abroad, but only slightly over $2 million in the United States.

9

BLONDE IN PINK TIGHTS

⟋⟍

As soon as *The Key* was launched in Europe, the Pontis hurried back to Los Angeles to complete preparations for Sophia's next movie, *That Kind of Woman,* another drama with a World War II background, but this time about the battle between the sexes on the American homefront. Ponti had selected Sidney Lumet, who'd made his movie debut the previous year with the highly praised *Twelve Angry Men,* to direct.

That Kind of Woman grew out of Robert Lowry's 1945 short story, "Layover in El Paso," which Paramount acquired for filming after it won critical acclaim in a 1957 anthology of the best American short fiction written during the World War II years. Lumet recommended his friend, the blacklisted Walter Bernstein, to write the screenplay, but both Lumet and Bernstein warned Ponti that there might be problems with the House Un-American Activities Committee.

"Ponti rattled off a stream of Italian," Bernstein recalled, "and then his partner, Girosi, who spoke much better English, turned to us and said, 'Mr. Ponti would like to know who has to be fixed and how much it will cost.'" When Lumet explained that all that was required was a show of courage, Ponti not only hired Bernstein but also promised to use him on one of Sophia's next films if the script turned out well.

Robert Lowry's original story told of two high-priced hookers and two naive soldiers on furlough, who meet on a train bound from Los Angeles to New York; due to the overcrowded wartime conditions, they get bumped in El Paso and have to stay overnight. Bernstein had to turn that slender premise into a vehicle for Sophia Loren and also accommodate Sidney Lumet's insistence on filming it in New York. Lumet was a product of the Broadway theater and New York–based television. He loathed the artificiality of movies shot on Hollywood sound stages and refused to work there.

With his experience with the Italian neorealist directors, Ponti could be accepting and also encouraging, since he wasn't happy with the look and texture of the three Hollywood-based movies that Sophia had made so far. When Lumet proposed authentic locations and the hiring of Boris Kaufman, the Oscar-winning cinematographer of *On the Waterfront,* Ponti instantly approved.

By the time Lumet and Bernstein delivered a camera-ready script, *That Kind of Woman,* whether intentionally or not, had traces of Sophia's own life woven into it. The title character, Kay, is the mistress of a New York munitions tycoon who also uses her to lure admirals and generals into recommending his company for government contracts. Slight mention is made of Kay's origins, but she's an Italian immigrant who worked in a factory before discovering an easier way to provide for herself. While Kay and her friend Jane, who also works for the millionaire, are returning from a Florida assignment in the company of a male bodyguard, they become pals with two GIs on the train. By the time they arrive in New York, romances have bloomed, but the women are whisked away in their employer's limousine and the soldiers will spend their seven-day leave trying to find them.

Kay's friend Jane was such an important character that Paramount wanted to team Sophia with another of its contract stars, Shirley MacLaine, but Carlo Ponti feared she might end up stealing his wife's thunder and nixed the idea. Ponti wouldn't stand for *any* actress getting costar billing with Sophia, so at Sidney Lumet's recommendation Barbara Nichols got the part. The one-time beauty-contest winner from Queens, New York, was coming up fast in the Monroe-Mansfield league and had recently given memorable performances in *Sweet Smell of Success* and *The Naked and the Dead.*

After rejecting Shirley MacLaine, Ponti was forced to accept Paramount's choice of Tab Hunter for the costarring role of Sophia's GI lover. Physically at least, the twenty-seven-year-old hazel-eyed blond could easily pass for a yokel soldier boy, but he wasn't much of an actor. Hunter was, however, the current teen dreamboat, with a string of hit records as a pop singer. Paramount hoped that Hunter would pull in the younger moviegoers who'd stayed away from Sophia's previous films.

The role of Sophia's millionaire protector, known only as "The Man" in the film, went to fifty-two-year-old George Sanders, which may have been wish fulfillment in the case of his real-life counterpart. Unlike Carlo Ponti, Sanders was tall, suave, and handsome, and would never need an English interpreter to be understood.

Paramount set a starting date of September 15 for *That Kind of Woman*. While Marcello Girosi went to New York to work with Sidney Lumet on selecting the locations and studio facilities, the Pontis remained in Los Angeles for conferences on their other Paramount projects.

The western to be directed by George Cukor now carried the working title of *Heller With a Gun,* after the Louis L'Amour novel on which it was based. Paramount had originally purchased the book as a vehicle for Alan Ladd when he was under contract to the studio, so Cukor had his hands full tailoring a script to suit Sophia Loren. Dudley Nichols of *Stagecoach* fame had already written a script during the Ladd era, but he was now terminally ill with cancer and unable to help Cukor with revisions. Ponti was delighted with Walter Bernstein's work on *That Kind of Woman* and assigned him to the task.

Ponti also decided that he wanted Bernstein to fashion the script for *A Breath of Scandal,* which would be based on the Ferenc Molnár play *Olympia* and a 1932 movie version written by Sidney Howard. Ponti, who seemed to fluctuate between hiring newcomers and old masters to direct Sophia, thought that one of the latter would suit the film's turn-of-the-century Viennese schmaltz. Paramount recommended the Hungarian-born Michael Curtiz, who'd directed films in Austria before moving on to Hollywood and every sort of classic from *The Adventures of Robin Hood* and *Yankee Doodle Dandy* to *Casablanca* and *Mildred Pierce.* Ponti hoped they would be able to start production in the spring of 1959.

Sophia still owed Paramount a film on her own, without Carlo Ponti as producer. The studio head, Jack Karp, asked her if she'd be interested in teaming with no less than "The King" himself, Clark Gable. The actor was winding up a three-picture deal with Paramount after starring with Doris Day in *Teacher's Pet* and Carroll Baker in *But Not for Me.*

Sophia needed no coaxing. Paramount assigned the packaging to Melville Shavelson and Jack Rose as a reward for their work on *Houseboat,* which had not yet been released but was testing well in a series of sneak previews around the country.

While *Houseboat* promised to be a hit, Paramount was worried about *The Black Orchid.* Ponti, who wasn't the most impartial judge, believed Sophia's performance worthy of an Oscar. To prove it, he persuaded the studio to enter the movie in the Venice Film Festival in August. In the back of his mind, he also hoped that if Sophia and the Ponti-produced movie did win some prizes, the Italian government would express some pride in their achievement and maybe drop the criminal charges against them.

The annual Venice Film Festival was older than the one in Cannes and, in Italy at least, carried more prestige. Benito Mussolini, who appreciated the influential power of film, founded the international competition in 1932 and it resumed after the war, minus, of course, the dictator and the trophies named in his honor. The screenings and award ceremonies were held at the Palace of Film on the Lido, the swank beach resort just across the bay from Venice.

That summer, while waiting for *That Kind of Woman* to begin, the Pontis rented a house on the French Riviera near the Italian border. As the time of the Venice festival approached, rumors flew that they would be arrested as soon as they set foot on Italian territory. While it wasn't essential for them to attend, they certainly wanted to be there if there were any major prizes to be accepted.

"Should we go or shouldn't we? In the end, we decided it would be too much like slapping our country in the face if we were to turn up there together," Sophia recalled. "Though I dreaded leaving Carlo, I decided to face it out alone. I thought that as a woman I was less likely to be treated badly."

Ponti's associate, Marcello Girosi, and Pilade Levi, Paramount's top executive in Italy, pleaded with the festival officials to intercede with the government so that Sophia wouldn't be hassled. The festival was one of Italy's most important cultural events, received publicity all over the world, and packed Venice's hotels and restaurants. Nasty happenings were likely to smear its image and decrease attendance in the future.

No doubt Paramount also spread some money around to ensure Sophia's safe conduct. To avoid tougher airport security, she took the train from Nice across northern Italy, well out of reach of the Pontis' tormentors in Rome and Vatican City. When she arrived in Venice just hours before the closing night ceremonies, Paramount had arranged a royal reception. Paid demonstrators pelted her with flowers or waved signs that said SOPHIA, WE LOVE YOU and WELCOME HOME TO ITALY!

A floral-decorated fleet of gondolas awaited Sophia in the Grand Canal, where she boarded a speedboat that whisked her to the gala on the Lido. During the three-week festival, the judges had screened nearly a hundred movies entered by thirty-six countries, including Italy. Who the finalists were for the Best Actress prize was known only to the judges, but Sophia won for *The Black Orchid*. Best

Actor was Alec Guinness for England's *The Horse's Mouth*, while Japan's *The Rickshaw Man* received the Gold Lion of St. Mark as Best Picture.

Clutching her prize, a gold cup named in honor of Count Volpi de Misurata, Sophia expressed her thanks to the audience and left as fast as she could. Paramount had chartered a private plane to fly her back to Nice, where Ponti would be waiting for her at the airport. "Receiving the award meant nothing to me until I could share it with Carlo. He was the one who had created me," she said later.

Sophia's victory in Venice proved of no help to the Pontis' legal problems in Italy. The International Catholic Film Office criticized the award as "immoral" and urged moviegoers to boycott *The Black Orchid*.

In light of the Venice prize, Ponti wanted Paramount to release *The Black Orchid* in the United States as soon as possible so that Sophia's performance could qualify for the 1958 Oscar race. Paramount, however, had already promised producer Don Hartman that it would push *Desire Under the Elms* and also knew that Columbia had similar designs on getting Sophia nominated for *The Key*. Paramount also had *Houseboat* booked solidly through the Thanksgiving and Christmas holidays and didn't want to compete against itself with a second Loren film. Paramount persuaded Ponti to wait until next year, which wasn't that far away and would give Sophia a shot at the 1959 Oscars.

Meanwhile, the Pontis had plenty to occupy them in *That Kind of Woman*. Sophia flew to Los Angeles for costume fittings with Edith Head while Ponti arranged their temporary living quarters in New York. He subleased an apartment on Park Avenue for the duration of the two-month production schedule, which promised to wear Sophia to a frazzle, since she appeared in nearly every scene.

Budgeted at $2.5 million, the black-and-white *That Kind of Woman* was reportedly the most expensive film made entirely in New York up to that time. Locations included Grand Central and Pennsylvania Stations, the Staten Island ferry, Central Park, a restaurant in Little Italy, the Brooklyn Bridge, Fifth Avenue, Sutton Place, an Irish bar on Third Avenue, and the 125th Street railroad stop in Harlem. To save a trip to Florida for the opening scene, the Long Beach terminal of the Long Island Rail Road "doubled" for the Miami station.

All of the interiors, including those taking place on the train to New York, were shot at Gold Medal Studios in the Bronx or at Fox-Movietone in Manhattan. Daily rehearsals were held near Times Square in the lower lounge of the Paramount Hotel, the former site of Billy Rose's legendary nightclub, the

Diamond Horseshoe. Sophia remembered seeing it depicted in an old Betty Grable musical that she saw at least ten times back in Pozzuoli.

Sophia had problems from the start with Sidney Lumet, whose style of directing entailed lots of rehearsing and helping the actors to psychoanalyze the characters they were portraying. He also wanted to stress the darker side of the kept woman Kay's relationship with her sinister and older protector, which may have been cutting too close to reality for both Sophia and Ponti. They wanted a lighter and more romantic "woman's picture" that would appeal to the masses. Will Kay remain a rich man's concubine or marry the penniless young paratrooper who dreams of becoming a farmer if he survives the war?

Love, of course, will be the deciding factor, but with Tab Hunter as her costar, Sophia had to struggle to make it seem believable that she could ever seriously fall for him, let alone desire him for a husband. The tall and naturally blond Hunter had sensational looks, but slight acting ability. His name, changed from Arthur Gelian, had become generic for talentless pretty-boy stars manufactured by the Hollywood studios. His voice was once described as a "baby baritone," and his clean-cut masculine image had recently been smeared by *Confidential* magazine, which claimed he'd been arrested in 1950 for participating in an all-male "pajama party."

Tab Hunter's homosexuality was no shock to Sophia, but it was apparently one reason why their love scenes lacked fire. "Sophia is a very tactile actress," Sidney Lumet recalled. "Nothing less than total contact with the men in her movies is tolerable. If she doesn't have that, she can't function at all. If you put her in the arms of someone who's not responsive to women, or even worse, someone who can barely pretend that he is, then there's going to be problems."

Lumet later claimed that he fell in love with Sophia himself: "Most everybody who works with her does. She literally takes your breath away when she walks into a room. She's got wit, she can sing bloody well, and linguistically she's extraordinary. What she doesn't understand in words, she understands in your eyes. She was totally cooperative from the word go. She always knew what to do and was a total joy from beginning to end."

Sophia felt at ease residing in New York, which reminded her somewhat of Rome and was so different from the more isolated lifestyle in Beverly Hills or Bel Air. She had moments of misery, however, whenever she received bad news from Italy or read something nasty about her marital situation in the newspapers and magazines. Sidney Lumet admired the way Sophia coped, refusing to let it affect her job or the production schedule.

"Out on the locations, there were times of distress when she'd climb into the back of the studio limousine and cry for twenty minutes. Then, when we needed her, the assistant director would knock on the window, and wham, out she'd come, a bit red-eyed but ready and smiling for work," Lumet recalled.

Sophia had a new problem to contend with, her sister Maria's romance with jazz pianist Romano Mussolini, the youngest son of Il Duce. The lovers had been trying to keep it secret due to Maria's fear that her family wouldn't approve, but they were eventually ambushed by paparazzi while sneaking out the back door of a Rome nightclub.

Sophia was furious when she found out about the affair. First and foremost she felt betrayed, since she and her sister had always been completely open and honest with each other. Second, she loathed anything to do with Benito Mussolini, who ranked in infamy just behind Hitler and Stalin. Last but not least, she knew that the thirty-one-year-old Romano had a long history of romancing women and then dumping them. Maria had just turned twenty and was too innocent to be involved with such a cad.

The press in Italy went wild with stories and headlines like SOPHIA'S SISTER LOVES A MUSSOLINI and SOPHIA AND MUSSOLINI: WILL THEIR KIN MARRY?, which only added to the scandal that was already raging over the disputed Ponti marriage. The two cases seemed to be competing for front-page coverage, but whichever grabbed the most space, Sophia Loren always got dragged into it in a negative way. The chances of the Pontis receiving clemency from the government seemed more remote than ever.

In her exile from Italy, Sophia could do little more than telephone Maria in Rome and try to talk her out of the Mussolini affair. But Sophia's opposition only made her sister more determined to get her man. Maria not only loved Romano but had also found a mentor. A brilliant musician, he was helping her to realize her dreams for a career as a jazz singer.

When *That Kind of Woman* wrapped, the Pontis moved to Los Angeles for the editing of the movie and to get ready for the filming of *Heller with a Gun*. Meanwhile, *Houseboat* had entered release, and for a change Sophia found herself in a box-office hit. Paramount had wisely slanted the frolic toward the family audience, but some of the advertising copy had naughty undertones: "Blundering, wondering Cary Grant playing mama and papa to three kids, aided by Sophia Loren, who knows the best way to play house."

Cary Grant's popularity in romantic comedies was considered the main reason for the success of *Houseboat* (it eventually earned rentals of $8 million worldwide). But Paramount was delighted finally to have Sophia associated with a hit, which would make it easier to get better deals with exhibitors on her future releases.

Through a distribution deal with RCA Victor Records, Paramount also released a 45-rpm single of Sophia's two songs from the movie, "Almost in Your Arms" and "Bing, Bang, Bong." Neither of the tunes by Jay Livingston and Ray Evans landed Sophia on the best-seller charts, but "Almost in Your Arms" went on to an Oscar nomination for the Best Song of 1958.

By January 1959, director George Cukor and writer Walter Bernstein still hadn't hammered out a complete script for *Heller with a Gun,* but they gave Carlo Ponti enough to start casting the major roles. As a vehicle for Sophia Loren, the title was misleading, since it referred to the gunslinging cowboy hero of Louis L'Amour's novel. Bernstein suggested changing it to *Heller in Pink Tights,* and Ponti agreed. They might also have found a better word than the archaic "heller," which stumped many people when the movie came out. "Hellion" or "hell-raiser" could have done the trick.

Sophia's role as Angela Rossini, the star of a traveling theatrical troupe, was straight from Louis L'Amour's book except for the inevitable Italian name change, but George Cukor greatly expanded the story so it became more of a tale of showbiz on the American frontier. Cukor, who came from a theatrical background himself and was an expert on stage Americana, looked to the career of pioneer actor-manager Joseph Jefferson for inspiration.

Cukor and scripter Bernstein retained Louis L'Amour's hero, King Mabry, the role that Paramount had originally intended for Alan Ladd, but built up the character of actor-manager Tom Healy, owner of The Great Healy Dramatic & Concert Company. Angela Rossini and Healy are affectionately if not passionately involved until she falls for Mabry when he rescues the troupe from marauding Indians.

In twisting the plot around, Healy became the more important of the two male leads. Cukor recommended Kirk Douglas or Gregory Peck, but Paramount considered them too expensive and insisted on Anthony Quinn. It may have seemed like lunacy to team him again with Sophia, but Quinn had one picture remaining on his Paramount contract.

Sophia and Ponti were furious, but since Paramount was bankrolling the $4 million production, they had to accept Quinn. They were not made any happier by Paramount's choice of Steve Forrest for the role of King Mabry. The younger brother of the more famous Dana Andrews, Forrest had recently ended an inauspicious five years at MGM, but Paramount seemed to think he could be their next Alan Ladd.

The old-time theatrical background enabled Cukor to incorporate characters that were composites of oddball types he'd actually known as a young assistant stage manager. He hired the former child star Margaret O'Brien, now pushing twenty-one, to play the troupe's reluctant ingenue, and future Oscar-winner Eileen Heckart to portray her domineering actress-mother. He also found supporting roles for two old friends who'd once been major Hollywood stars, Ramon Novarro and Edmund Lowe.

Cukor had never been happy with the "look" of Technicolored westerns, so he hired George Hoyningen-Huene, who'd previously worked with him on the Judy Garland version of *A Star Is Born,* to be visual and color consultant. The Russian-born Hoyningen-Huene had been a famous fashion photographer and illustrator since the 1920s and was an expert on art and design. Cukor left it to him and the director's assistant, Gene Allen, to do the historical research and to choose sets, costumes, and lighting effects appropriate to the 1880s. Cukor told them that he wanted a movie that looked like a cross between Frederic Remington's paintings of the Old West and Toulouse-Lautrec's renderings of music hall performers.

To suit his color schemes, Hoyningen-Huene recommended that Sophia be a blonde. She loved the idea, provided that she didn't have to dye her hair, so a dozen wigs in various styles were ordered for her. One was of short, bright red hair for a scene in which she had to do a male impersonation in a play being put on by the Healy troupe.

Hoyningen-Huene's presence caused friction with Edith Head, who had to report to him and ended up copying costumes that he sketched for her or found in old books and magazines. Though Head received screen credit as the film's designer, her main contribution was as Sophia's wardrobe mistress.

By delegating the technical details to others, George Cukor could concentrate on preparing his cast of actors, especially Sophia, whom he adored. He thought she had the most potential of anyone he'd worked with since Judy Holliday, who had given an Oscar-winning performance in the film that he made of her Broadway hit *Born Yesterday.* Cukor's mental image of Sophia in *Heller in Pink Tights* was a blend of Lillie Langtry, the English society beauty turned actress who made many triumphant tours of the United States, and Adah Isaacs Menken, an American superstar of the 1850s famed for pulse-pounding melodramas like *Mazeppa.*

As actress Angela Rossini, Sophia would play a scene from *Mazeppa,* where the captive heroine is stripped naked and sent to her death strapped to the back of a wild stallion, as well as moments from other works in the touring troupe's repertory. To give her some insight into what those thespians were really like, Cukor took her to meet his Austrian friend Fritzi Massary, the legendary operetta diva and stage actress, now seventy-seven years old, who'd been living in Beverly Hills since fleeing Europe in the 1930s to escape Nazi persecution.

One of Massary's greatest triumphs, way back in 1911, had been in Offenbach's *La Belle Hélène,* a snippet of which Sophia had to perform in the movie. She sat spellbound as Massary reminisced in a voice that had aged into a hoarse, double-bass croak. Massary demonstrated the bravura acting techniques used on the stage and recalled some of the legends she'd known, including those ferocious rivals Sarah Bernhardt and Eleanora Duse. Sophia came away inspired and charmed.

Just before production began, the Motion Picture Academy announced the nominations for the 1958 Oscars. Paramount had been pushing for *Desire Under the Elms* with a big campaign in the trade press, and Columbia had done the same for *The Key,* so the Pontis were hoping that at least one of them would pay off in a nomination for Sophia as Best Actress, but it was not to be.

Sophia received some consolation from her second consecutive invitation to be one of the Oscar presenters, this year in the category of Best Song, a nominee for which was, of course, "Almost in Your Arms" from *Houseboat.* *Houseboat* was also nominated for Best Original Screenplay, which in a way honored Sophia as well. Much of the script had been rewritten to her specifications when she took over the role originally intended for Cary Grant's actress-wife, Betsy Drake.

Edith Head whipped up another spectacular gown for Sophia to wear to the televised ceremonies. The producers thought it would be fun to team Sophia with another *paisano,* Dean Martin. When they strolled onto the stage of the Pantages Theatre to introduce the movie and recording stars who would perform in a medley of the five nominated songs, Martin peered down Sophia's cleavage and jokingly clutched the podium to save himself from collapsing.

After the medley, which included Eddie Fisher crooning "To Love and Be Loved" to wife Elizabeth Taylor in her front row seat, Sophia and Martin returned to announce the winning song. Passing the sealed envelope to Sophia, he cracked, "You open it, honey. I don't do sight bits." She responded with a baffled "What?" and proceeded to reveal Alan Jay Lerner and Frederick Loewe as the winners for the title song from *Gigi*.

By the time that the last and most important Oscar for 1958's Best Picture had been handed out (also to *Gigi*), the show was running twenty minutes *ahead* of schedule, which caught NBC unprepared to fill the balance of the allotted time slot. Mitzi Gaynor had already started belting "There's No Business Like Show Business" as the finale, so all the winners and presenters were sent back on stage and told to sing three hundred encores if necessary.

Jerry Lewis, the last of the evening's six cohosts, borrowed a baton from the orchestra leader and began conducting the star-studded chorus. Sophia, who didn't know the lyrics to the Irving Berlin song, stood there looking bewildered until Dean Martin swept her into his arms and started dancing with her. Soon the whole stage was filled with whirling couples, including Cary Grant and Ingrid Bergman, Natalie Wood and Robert Wagner, Maurice Chevalier and Rosalind Russell, and Bob Hope and Zsa Zsa Gabor.

Dean Martin guided Sophia toward the podium and grabbed one of the display Oscars. Jerry Lewis cracked, "And they said that Dean and I would never be on the same stage again." Martin replied, "He needs me." Sophia seemed lost, as did many of the others. After five minutes she couldn't take any more and asked Martin to take her backstage for some alcoholic refreshment at the bar.

To capitalize on the Oscar season, Paramount decided to get a headstart on the next year's by releasing *The Black Orchid* with advertising and publicity pitching Sophia Loren's performance as the one to beat in 1959. The plan was to open the movie slowly and only in prestigious, small-seat "art" theaters, where the studio hoped it would run for months and then cross over into commercial success.

Unfortunately, the reviews weren't the raves that Paramount and the Pontis craved. Bosley Crowther, whose opinions in *The New York Times* usually determined the success or failure of movies in the art category, compared it unfavorably to the similar *Marty* and expressed disappointment in Sophia's performance. Crowther called her acting "too cool and crisp. The role needs the input of a highly emotional type like Anna Magnani." One can only guess how the Pontis reacted to that comparison, but some of the Paramount brass must have kicked themselves because the movie had originally been intended for Magnani.

Without any major critical acclaim, *The Black Orchid* quickly wilted as an art release and was shifted into mass release on double bills with another

Paramount disappointment, *The Trap*. By the time of the 1959 Oscar nominations, *The Black Orchid* had been forgotten.

Sophia finally started work on *Heller in Pink Tights* without a finished script. It was the only way that Ponti could avoid delaying their next project, *A Breath of Scandal,* which would be shot on location in Vienna and needed to be finished before the summer tourist invasion.

George Cukor and Walter Bernstein had blocked out the western scene by scene, but big chunks of dialogue needed to be filled in and were often written a mere day in advance or even on the spot. With Sophia as both star and wife of the film's producer, Cukor lavished most of his attention on her role, and the other main actors had to fend for themselves.

That was especially hard on Anthony Quinn, who had seemed miscast as the dashing company manager. "Tony didn't have the pages," Walter Bernstein said later. "I was literally writing and rewriting as we went along. He couldn't go home and read the script and work on his character. Nobody knew what they were getting the next day. That was very tough on everybody."

The action in *Heller in Pink Tights* starts in Cheyenne, Wyoming, and moves south by southwest to a mythical boomtown called Bonanza, where Sophia and Quinn decide to stop touring and build a permanent theater. All of the interior scenes and some of the exteriors were shot at Paramount's Hollywood studio, with its famous outdoor Western Street doubling for Cheyenne. On Paramount's huge Stage 16, art directors Hal Pereira and Gene Allen built three adjacent sets of the interiors of a frontier theater, saloon, and gambling casino. The theater had three hundred working gaslights, a full-sized stage equipped with a treadmill, tiers of box seats, and a horseshoe-shaped balcony.

Exteriors were also filmed in Arizona, on several immense ranches between Tucson and the Mexican border, to capture the various types of western terrain. By that time, Carlo Ponti had left for Austria for conferences on *A Breath of Scandal,* so Sophia had only her secretary, Ines, for companionship. They stayed with the rest of the company in a motel outside of Tucson and cooked pasta on a hot plate in their suite whenever they tired of the local Mexican-American fare.

Sophia found George Cukor difficult to work with. Like De Sica, he acted everything out for her first and made her copy him, but he was less flexible than De Sica and demanded an exact imitation of *his* performance, permitting Sophia to add nothing of herself. His technique threw her at first, but she decided to go along with it since Cukor had directed Greta Garbo in *Camille,* Ingrid Bergman in *Gaslight,* and practically all of Katharine Hepburn's best performances.

"I didn't speak English very well then and Cukor, naturally, corrected me," Sophia recalled. "But he insisted that I repeat phrases exactly the way he said them. The least 'oh' or 'ah' that sounded wrong, Cukor made me repeat it. I felt myself a complete prisoner of Cukor's sounds. And I found that unfair. It was always a case of 'You can do it, you *will* do it.' He put me through so much that I lost nine kilos. In the first scenes of the film, I'm plump. By the end I'm transparent."

In *Heller in Pink Tights,* Cukor gave the blond Sophia a grand entrance worthy of a screen goddess. She's seen briefly in the opening scene, peering out a coach window while the troupe is being chased by a sheriff's posse for not paying its bills, but she doesn't get the full treatment until the caravan arrives safely in the next town. To persuade people to buy tickets for that evening's performance, Anthony Quinn introduces the actors to a crowd gathered in the street. As the star attraction, Sophia is saved for last. The camera starts on her shoes and travels up her elegantly gowned body until reaching her face. She teases the crowd with magic, playing peek-a-boo behind a silk scarf that changes a different vivid color every time she threads it through her hands.

Throughout the film, Cukor's visual consultant, Hoyningen-Huene, used color to dramatize Sophia's splendor. In a scene in a seedy hotel room, her blue and white costume creates a glow reminiscent of Manet's "Nana." To justify the movie's title, she wore shocking pink tights, instead of the traditional white, for her nude scene as Mazeppa. That moment was re-created exactly as it was in the 1880s, with Sophia strapped to a real horse that was docked on a moving treadmill to create the illusion of galloping.

While working on the movie at Paramount in Hollywood, Sophia had an unsettling encounter with Marlon Brando, who was getting ready to make *One-Eyed Jacks* and had an office on the lot. She'd never met Brando before, but one day while she was relaxing in her dressing suite with the front door open, he just walked in and started nosing around.

"On the walls, I had hung some paintings that I loved and that always traveled with me wherever I went," Sophia recalled. "Marlon stood studying them and, after a long silence, shook his head and said, 'You're sick. Emotionally disturbed. You should see a psychiatrist.' I asked him why, and he told me, 'Pictures always reveal the state of mind of their owners. You're suffering. Deep down you have a secret emotional wound.'

"I didn't yell at him. I only said, 'Never mind, at least I keep it secret. Too bad you don't do the same.' "

Brando may have hit on something, but Sophia was aware of his reputation as a weirdo and didn't take him seriously. She knew, however, that her nerves were being stretched to the breaking point by the controversy over the legality of her marriage. Nearly two years had passed since the Mexican proxy wedding, but the opposition in Italy still stood its ground.

GOODNESS GRACIOUS ME

℘

THE Pontis' legal advisers were now recommending a new strategy, in effect, nullifying the Mexican proxy marriage and starting over. Sophia would become a single woman again, and Ponti could no longer be charged as a bigamist. They could probably return to living in Italy if they maintained separate residences and carried on discreetly until a better solution could be worked out.

Sophia and Ponti decided to risk it. There was an urgent business reason to do so. Sophia's upcoming movie with Clark Gable required location work in Italy. Paramount had received assurances from the government that she wouldn't be prosecuted if she did the job in the required amount of time and left, but she preferred to be legally clear for peace of mind.

Meanwhile, Ponti returned from Europe for the final weeks of *Heller in Pink Tights*. With *A Breath of Scandal* due to roll in Vienna, Ponti had all but fulfilled his four-picture contract with Paramount. While only *The Black Orchid* had so far been released, its dismal grosses made Paramount reluctant to sign any new deals with Ponti until the other films had been put to the box-office test. Consequently, after Sophia's non-Ponti teaming with Clark Gable, neither Sophia nor Ponti would have any Hollywood commitments. It was all very worrying, and more reason for them to try to end their problems at home so they could resume working there.

A Breath of Scandal was a step in that direction. Ponti sold a share in the production to Titanus Film, which took over some of the financial burden from Paramount and provided him with an Italian partner for future deals. The project was also an attempt to boost Sophia's popularity in the European market.

Ponti believed that her previous Paramount films had been geared too much to the American taste and lacked appeal to audiences elsewhere.

Ponti persuaded Paramount to buy the property, based on Ferenc Molnár's *Olympia,* when he discovered its similarities to the same author's *The Swan,* which had been the basis for Grace Kelly's next-to-last movie before she retired to become Princess of Monaco. *The Swan* was a box-office hit, mainly because its release coincided with the worldwide news coverage of Kelly's royal wedding. But it also provided an exquisite showcase for her beauty and talent. It was the sort of sumptuously romantic vehicle that Sophia needed if she was ever to rank among the Hollywood goddesses.

With Ferenc Molnár's signature attached to it, *A Breath of Scandal* promised to be Sophia's most sophisticated film yet. His blithe stage comedies like *The Guardsman, The Play's the Thing,* and *The Glass Slipper* were acclaimed for their ingenuity and irony. His dramatic masterpiece *Liliom* was the nucleus of Rodgers and Hammerstein's *Carousel.*

Molnár's *Olympia,* first performed in his native Hungary in 1927, had been previously filmed in 1929 by MGM under the title of *His Glorious Night,* with the celebrated stage beauty Catherine Dale Owen as the princess. It marked the "talkie" debut of the great silent star John Gilbert, but his high-pitched voice didn't match his dashing image and the movie was quickly withdrawn from release after adverse audience reactions. Although Gilbert learned how to modulate his voice for subsequent movies, he never regained popularity, and he died a disillusioned alcoholic in 1936.

Needless to say, Paramount had no intention of reminding the public of the inglorious Hollywood ancestry of *Olympia*. Along with the new title *A Breath of Scandal,* the story of Princess Olympia got a major character makeover. Her hussar-lover was transformed into an American tourist from Pittsburgh, Pennsylvania.

Molnár might have turned over in his grave, but the American playwright Sidney Howard had already done extensive revisions on *Olympia* when it was first produced on Broadway in 1928 (with Fay Compton and Ian Hunter in the leads). Walter Bernstein's latest changes were intended to accommodate the casting of the main roles.

The story takes place in turn-of-the century Vienna. Princess Olympia, whose romantic escapades are always scandalizing the emperor's court, has been temporarily banished to the country, where she has a chance meeting with the American and spends a romantic but chaste night alone with him in a hunting lodge. The next day, she quickly forgets him when she's summoned back to Vienna and told that she is to marry Prince Rupert of Prussia. The American, meanwhile, has fallen in love with Olympia. Forgetting that he's not back home in the land of free choice, he tries to persuade her father, Prince Philip, to let her marry him. Permission is denied, but when the American refuses to give up, matters get very complicated. He finally promises to desist if Olympia will spend one more night with him. The princess, of course, winds up falling madly in love with the commoner, and in the end they elope to Pittsburgh.

To play opposite Sophia Paramount tried "borrowing" Rock Hudson from Universal, but had to settle for that studio's John Gavin, a newcomer who'd recently made an impact romancing Lana Turner in *Imitation of Life*. Since neither Sophia nor Gavin were experienced in the frothy, droll style required of Molnár, director Michael Curtiz insisted on surrounding them with a cast of skilled actors who would make them look better just by the association and might even be able to teach them something. Maurice Chevalier, whose long career had recently been revived by his endearing performances as Audrey Hepburn's father in *Love in the Afternoon* and as the elderly libertine in *Gigi*, got the role of Sophia's father, Prince Philip. Her Italian accent and his French might make it hard to believe that they were related, but in the movie they were Austro-Prussian, so what did it matter?

For box-office insurance, Paramount wanted one more established Hollywood "name" in the cast and hired Angela Lansbury, a fine character actress who hadn't yet broken into the star ranks, to portray a nasty, gossipmongering countess. Britisher Isabel Jeans, who'd acted with Chevalier in *Gigi* and was a peerless player of sophisticated comedy, landed in the role of Sophia's mother, Princess Eugenie.

Sophia and Ponti were so delighted with art director Gene Allen's contributions to *Heller in Pink Tights* that they selected him as visual consultant. This time, the enduring regal splendors of Vienna made Allen's job easier. Some of the most incredibly beautiful palaces, buildings, and parkland in the world were just waiting to be photographed. Also at his disposal was the costume factory and warehouse of the Vienna State Opera. Edith Head, who was preoccupied with other projects, approved the choice of Ella Bei, of the Knize fashion house, to design Sophia's princess wardrobe. Some of the plunging necklines and bare-shouldered evening gowns may not have been historically accurate, but when they revealed so much natural beauty, who cared?

The Pontis took over the largest suite at the Imperial Hotel for the duration of the filming. Almost immediately, problems developed with seventy-year-old Michael Curtiz, who as the Hungarian-born Mihály Kertész possessed an affinity for the material but hadn't worked outside the walls of Hollywood studios since 1926. He went a bit gaga from culture shock and fell more in love with Vienna than he did with the script. He seemed to be turning the film into a travelogue, making the city, rather than Sophia Loren, the real star.

Worse even, Sophia found Curtiz impossible to work with. His thick Hungarian accent and tendency to bark commands in garbled English like "Please stand a little closer apart," threw her completely. "Sophia didn't understand a word Curtiz said, and yet I found him a very good director," Angela Lansbury recalled.

Curtiz also wasn't one of those "acting" directors who performed a scene first and gave Sophia a path to follow. She needed all the help she could get because Molnár's style of comedy was much subtler than the broad humor of some of her previous films.

Since it was too late to change directors, Ponti let Curtiz continue with the movie but, without telling him, also arranged for Vittorio De Sica to fly in from Rome to work with Sophia. Ponti's offer of $2,500 a day in cash was an irresistible lure to De Sica, a besotted gambler who went out every night to hit the roulette tables of Vienna's casinos.

Curtiz never found out about it, but after he left the set for the day, De Sica was often called in to reshoot scenes that Sophia and/or Ponti felt that she could have done better. De Sica may have improved Sophia's performance, but when critics later reviewed the film, many thought she still had a lot to learn about comedy technique.

And whether directed by Curtiz or De Sica, Sophia's romantic moments with John Gavin fell flat. If possible, he was an even more wooden actor than Tab Hunter.

Due to their commitments in Vienna, the Pontis missed attending the world premiere of *That Kind of Woman,* which Paramount had optimistically booked into the 5,868-seat Roxy Theatre in New York City. The film's locations were expected to be an added crowd-puller. "New York has her picture taken with more power and poetry than ever before," the ads proclaimed.

The critical reviews were mixed, with some raves for Sophia's performance and snide remarks about her teaming with Tab Hunter. Bosley Crowther, who thought that Hunter looked young enough to be her son, said that the only valid explanation for Sophia's attraction to him was that "deep down, she must have a yen to keep this big, tousle-haired inarticulate kid from going off to that terrible war and getting killed."

John McCarten of *The New Yorker* called Sophia "an anatomical marvel" but poked fun at the movie's melodramatic plot:

> George Sanders is so rich that he can hire a spy, Keenan Wynn, to follow Sophia while he's busy counting his money, which seems a full-time job. The burning question is, will Sophia give up her sugar daddy for a paratrooper who in civilian life is a sap-tapper in Vermont?

Supported at the Roxy by a stage revue with the singing duo of Cindy & Lindy as headliners, *That Kind of Woman* ran only three weeks, the final two to virtually empty houses. Small wonder that after a series of similar disasters, the beloved "Cathedral of Motion Pictures" was demolished in 1961 to make way for an office building.

Paramount might have been better off releasing *That Kind of Woman* on the "art" circuit, but the flop at the Roxy soured the specialized exhibitors on giving it a second chance to prove itself. Paramount grabbed whatever commercial bookings it could get, and the film landed in the same scrap heap as *Desire Under the Elms* and *The Black Orchid*.

In Hollywood, Sophia Loren's latest box-office failure, her second within the year, had studio executives worrying. One told *Daily Variety:* "Sophia's been badly mishandled. She's been overexposed, which is Ponti's fault. He has the Italian weakness for the fast buck, and he's throwing Sophia away. He'll accept any cockeyed offer if they come up with the money. He says, 'What exposure? She's only making four pictures a year.' He's crazy. One or two a year is enough. Sophia's still young enough to become a great star, but I'm afraid that she'll burn out before she can get there."

Over at Paramount, panic buttons were being pushed. George Cukor had delivered a first cut of *Heller in Pink Tights* that set some of the executives at the initial screening to snoring and the others to wondering what it was all about. The domestic and foreign sales heads considered it unreleasable unless it was drastically cut and changed into a conventional western. Since Cukor had gone off to Europe to finish Columbia's *Song Without End* (director Charles Vidor had died in the midst of it), *Heller* was shelved pending his return.

Paramount wasn't too happy, either, with reports of the problems in

Vienna with *A Breath of Scandal,* so a call went out to make sure that
Sophia's next project, which now had the title *Bay of Naples,* didn't become
another troublemaker. With Clark Gable involved, there could be no delays.
His contract specified nine-to-five hours, and he wouldn't tolerate even a
minute of overtime.

Everybody pitched in to get a good script. Ponti recommended bringing
Vittorio De Sica into the project to work with Sophia and to add an authentic
Italian flavor to the screenplay that Melville Shavelson and Jack Rose had al-
ready written. De Sica picked Suso Cecchi D'Amico, who'd collaborated with
him on *The Bicycle Thief* and was one of Italy's best screenwriters, to flesh out
Sophia's role and to add minor characters and situations that were typically
Neapolitan. Inevitably, bits and pieces of the real Sophia were woven into the
final result.

She portrayed Lucia Curcio, who dreams of becoming a movie star but is currently performing in a honky-tonk nightclub on Capri to support herself and an
orphaned nephew. Fernando, or Nando as everybody calls him, is the illegitimate child of Lucia's sister and an American playboy, both killed in an accident.
His existence is a shock to his uncle, Philadelphia attorney Michael Hamilton,
who learns the secret only when he arrives in Naples to settle his brother's estate. Aunt Lucia and Uncle Mike immediately clash over the custody of Nando,
who at age eight has become a cigarette-smoking, wine-guzzling pickpocket
and con artist.

When Clark Gable first read the script, he suggested the title *Americano, Go
Home,* but Paramount vetoed it as too politically controversial for a romantic
romp. Gable did, however, portray a mild version of the typical "ugly American,"
growling and criticizing everything Italian until Sophia managed to melt his
heart.

Carlo Angeletti, a nine-year-old Italian who used the singular professional
name of Marietto and was well known in Europe, got the role of Nando.
Though he barely spoke English, Marietto had a gift for mimicry similar to
Sophia's and could recite long, difficult speeches in any language after the dialogue coach acted them out for him.

Sophia herself would be getting on-the-set advice from Vittorio De Sica, who
ended up with a costarring role in the movie as compensation. He portrayed a
Neapolitan lawyer whom Gable hires to gain custody of Nando. The casting
aroused great interest in Italy, where De Sica held a regal position comparable
to Gable's in Hollywood.

While the Pontis were winding up *A Breath of Scandal* in Vienna, their lawyers paved the way for the couple to return to Italy to make *Bay of Naples*. The Mexican proxy marriage was discovered to be invalid because the lawyers handling it had neglected to provide the two witnesses required by law. Carlo Ponti could no longer be charged with bigamy in Italy, but the public prosecutor first had to see the Mexican certificate to make sure. Meanwhile, the prosecutor's office was about to recess for the summer, so it seemed that the case had landed in a neutral zone for the time being. It was highly unlikely that the government would attempt anything while Sophia was working in a production that pumped $4 million into the economy and also promised to be a boon to Italian tourism.

But Sophia and Ponti still had to be on their guard and try to avoid compromising situations while they were back in Italy. Accompanied by her usual entourage, Sophia took the train from Vienna to Rome to begin rehearsals. Ponti would join her later during the locations in Naples, where law enforcement tended to be more relaxed than in the capital.

Expecting to be attacked by paparazzi at the Rome terminal, Sophia detrained a stop earlier, where Ponti had arranged for a limousine to drive her to her mother's apartment. The press mob waiting for her in Rome met only her entourage and thirty-five pieces of luggage. Within the hour, reporters were camped outside Sophia's front door and refused to leave until she made a statement.

"I hope to settle this situation of my marriage. Then, if God grants it, I hope to have the greatest joy of my life—a baby," she said.

Most of the interior scenes for *Bay of Naples* would be shot at Cinecittà in Rome, but they were outnumbered by exteriors scheduled for Naples and Capri. Robert Surtees, who'd recently finished filming *Ben-Hur* in Rome and had two Oscars to his credit, for *King Solomon's Mines* and *The Bad and the Beautiful,* was hired as cinematographer. That seemed to guarantee that both Italy and Sophia Loren would never look more beautiful. Ironically, Sophia had passed through Surtees's lenses once before, as a dress extra in *Quo Vadis*.

Clark Gable was fifty-eight at the time of *Bay of Naples*, which made him the oldest of the Hollywood "legends" that Sophia had been teamed with so far. Gable was only three years the senior of Cary Grant, but had aged more severely and had lost much of his rugged handsomeness from neglect, chain-smoking, and heavy drinking. In his two most recent films, one with Doris Day and the other with the even younger Carroll Baker, he'd switched from playing the swaggering lady killer to a reluctant love object, sort of poking fun at his macho image.

Gable traveled to Italy with his fifth wife, former movie starlet Kay Williams, and her two youngsters, Bunker and Joan, the products of her previous marriage to multimillionaire Adolph Spreckels II. Paramount housed them in a rented villa near Rome for the duration of the filming. Gable had become a devoted family man since marrying Kay, a vivacious blonde fifteen years his junior. She seemed to fill the void left by his beloved Carole Lombard, who had died in a plane crash in 1942. The Gables intended having children of their own, but their first attempt had ended in a miscarriage. They hoped the trip to romantic Italy, which coincided with their fourth wedding anniversary, would change their luck.

Because of Gable's family commitments, Sophia barely got to know him. During the lunch breaks, she cooked spaghetti for him several times and hooked him on pasta. By the time production ended, Gable's weight had soared to a lifetime high of 230 pounds. Because his scenes weren't always shot in consecutive order, his jowls and heft ping-ponged noticeably throughout the film.

After Gable met Sophia for the first time, he said to one of the crew, "Jesus, is that all mine for the duration? That girl makes you think—all the wrong thoughts!"

After working several days with Gable, Sophia grew upset over his tendency to grab the best camera angles. "I know he's considered 'the King' and a very great star, but I don't think he's being fair with me," she complained to director Mel Shavelson. "Somehow he manages to position himself so that my worst side is always turned toward the camera. He doesn't have to worry about his career anymore, but I have to worry about mine."

Shavelson promised to speak to Gable, who responded with a growl and a few curses. "What the hell's she talking about? She's lucky. *Both* sides of my face are lousy, and my backside isn't that good-looking either. You just tell me what side she wants to show and I'll get out of her way!"

Sophia's friend Marcello Mastroianni idolized Gable and kept pestering her to arrange an introduction. Unlike Sophia, Mastroianni had been resisting all offers to work in Hollywood, so it seemed like this might be his only chance to meet "the King."

"Sophia finally fixed it, but it was only for a few minutes," Mastroianni recalled. "In cases like that, you have too much to say, so you end up saying practically nothing. I found Gable to be the only exception, at least in my mind, to the actor as an amorphous entity waiting to be shaped by a director. He had so much personality that he had no need to do characters in the way that we normally say an actor does a character."

Sophia's role gave her two more opportunities to sing and dance, this time with support from guitarist Paolo Bacilieri. She performed one of her songs, the satirical *"Tuo Vuo' Fa' l'Americano?"* ("You Want to Be an American?") in the Neapolitan dialect and in English, and the mambo, *"Carina,"* in Italian and English.

For the musical numbers, the Italian designer Orietta Nasalli-Roca whipped up a couple of revealing costumes, both worn with tights and high heels to emphasize as much of Sophia's long and shapely legs as possible. The first consisted of just a straw hat and a mannish blouse that stopped just below her crotch. The second was a slinky sleeveless dress with a multislit skirt.

Bay of Naples was the occasion for Sophia's first visit to Naples since becoming a Hollywood star as well as a central figure in a bigamy case. In the same streets where she nearly starved during the war, people hung out of windows and shouted at her with love or damnation.

Sofia Scicolone had never been able to afford the ferry fare to Capri, so she ended up making her first visit in the company of Clark Gable. Needless to say, there was a romantic interlude in a rowboat in the legendary Blue Grotto, where the light reflecting off the water creates effects of breathtaking beauty. The lovers strip naked and take a swim, but the camera work was carefully arranged to show them in silhouette so that body doubles who were a bit svelter than Sophia and Gable could be used.

Carlo Ponti sneaked into Capri to help Sophia celebrate her twenty-fifth birthday on September 20, 1959. He brought her a magnificent diamond and ruby necklace and the latest news from their lawyers. Leaks from within suggested that the public prosecutor's office was divided on the bigamy issue and would delay going to court until it had overwhelming evidence to support its case. Normally, a complaint from the wronged spouse would be enough to convince any judge, but Giuliana Ponti had not taken any legal action or made any public statements that indicated that she considered her husband a philanderer.

As soon as *Bay of Naples* wrapped, the Clark Gables returned to California so the kids could go back to school and he could mull over an offer from United Artists to costar with Marilyn Monroe in *The Misfits,* a contemporary western written by her husband, Arthur Miller.

But with the last of her Paramount commitments behind her, Sophia found herself at liberty. The Pontis' experience in Hollywood had not fulfilled its promise. Sophia may have become a world star, but Ponti had failed her as a producer. Their Paramount collaborations suggested that, in Ponti's case especially, he should stick to productions that relied more on his European expertise and connections.

Ponti also had an ego of his own, and longed to resume making movies beyond just those that were vehicles for Sophia. His legal problems in Italy stood in the way of going full blast, but in the meantime he was dickering with several French companies on coproduction deals that did not involve Sophia's participation.

Very quietly, Ponti had also optioned the movie rights to Nobel Prize winner Boris Pasternak's *Doctor Zhivago,* thanks to help from his friend Giangiacomo Feltrinelli, who had been the first to publish the novel after it was smuggled out of the USSR. Ponti, of course, intended it as a showcase for Sophia as Zhivago's great love, Lara, but the project was an immense undertaking and he put it on a back burner until he could find the creative talent and financing that he needed.

In the more immediate future, Ponti planned to star Sophia in *La Ciociara,* the property he'd acquired from Hal Wallis and Paramount after Anna Magnani refused to portray Sophia's mother. Ponti assigned Vittorio De Sica and his long-time partner, Cesare Zavattini, to write the script. Ponti hoped that by the time he was ready to start *La Ciociara* his legal problems would have cleared and he could film it on the actual locations in Italy. If not, he knew he could find similar terrain in Spain or Yugoslavia.

Meantime, Sophia and Ponti were living like fugitives in Rome. "We were constantly under surveillance, so our life became an exercise in studied confusion," Sophia recalled. "Some nights we stayed in my mother's apartment, or with friends. We regularly changed the apartments we rented, often taking them under assumed names. When we were invited to dinner, we always arrived and left separately, or with a group of guests. Of course, we never appeared together in public. It was a silly and strenuous way of life, but I must confess that the cops-and-robbers aspect of it made it rather exciting. We were like two lovers trying to avoid a murderously jealous husband."

One day, Ponti decided it was time to get started on that "most beautiful house in the world" that he'd promised Sophia on their wedding day two years ago. He drove her to the sleepy village of Marino, about twenty miles southeast of Rome at the foot of the Alban Hills, to show her the place he had in mind. It was a dilapidated estate called Villa Sara, which he'd bought very cheaply as an investment right after the war but had never bothered with since. German officers residing there during the war had stolen or ruined most of its furnishings and fittings, but there were still traces of its centuries-old magnificence.

"When I first saw it all, I was very discouraged," Sophia remembered. "I told Carlo, 'The place must have been beautiful once, but how can we put it all back together?' And he said what he always says to me, 'Wait five minutes, and everything is going to be all right.' I am an impatient Neapolitan, and he is a patient Milanese."

Actually, it would take more like five years than five minutes. But Ponti immediately put the job in the hands of Imerio Maffeis, an architect and landscape gardener, and interior decorator Ezio Altieri.

Meanwhile, after several months of living in the shadows, Sophia begged Ponti to make a deal somewhere that would take them away from Italy again. Unfortunately, Ponti's bargaining power in Hollywood had just decreased again due to the box-office failure of *Heller in Pink Tights,* so none of the studio chiefs were responsive to his phone calls and cablegrams.

Surprisingly, *Heller* received some excellent reviews. Bosley Crowther, who said it reminded him a bit of *La Strada* in its depiction of entertainers living in a perilous world, called it "colorful, humorous, sentimental, and even exciting." He found Sophia "remarkably appealing, as warm and natural as she has been in anything since that little pizza item in *The Gold of Naples.*"

But the public wasn't buying it, which may have been Paramount's fault in the marketing. Pitching *Heller in Pink Tights* to the western action fans instead of sophisticates was a mistake, as was the confusing title, which caused some people to wonder if it was about a transvestite gunfighter. The movie later turned a profit in the European release, thanks to director George Cukor's cult following and the novelty of Sophia Loren in a western, but that was still in the future and of no help to the Pontis in their present bargaining predicament.

Ponti finally struck lucky with British producer Dimitri de Grunwald, who wanted to team Sophia with Peter Sellers in a romantic comedy based on George Bernard Shaw's *The Millionairess.* Ponti at first disapproved, claiming that Sophia was too big a star to be matched with Sellers, who was then known only as a comic character actor with some successes on the art circuits in England and America. "It is not right for Sophia to play with this comedian after working with Clark Gable, Cary Grant, Frank Sinatra, John Wayne, and so on," he told the producer.

But de Grunwald persisted, and the salary of $200,000, plus the opportunity to leave Italy for twelve weeks with all expenses paid, caused Ponti to accept on Sophia's behalf. The studio financing the movie, 20th Century–Fox, questioned Sophia's box-office draw and proposed replacing her with Ava Gardner. But de Grunwald held out for Sophia because he needed her more youthful sensuality to create sparks between the two main characters.

After her experience in the worlds of Eugene O'Neill and Ferenc Molnár, Sophia wondered how she would cope with George Bernard Shaw, arguably the greatest playwright in English after William Shakespeare. She relaxed a bit when she learned that her director would be Anthony Asquith, who was not only a master at translating Shaw to the screen (starting with *Pygmalion* in 1938), but also a "directing" director who really cared about his actors.

But Ponti had doubts as well, and again insisted on bringing Vittorio De Sica along to help Sophia bridge the gap between her Italian sensibility and the peculiarities of Shavian wit. Since De Sica was a star in his own right, he couldn't be expected to take the job for a consultant's fee. He demanded, and got, a role in the movie for his customary salary of $5,000 per week.

Peter Sellers' close friend Wolf Mankowitz, a novelist and playwright whose works included *Expresso Bongo* and *A Kid for Two Farthings,* wrote the script for *The Millionairess.* Since Shaw's death in 1950, the executors of his estate had become more tolerant of tampering with his genius (*Pygmalion,* for example, had been transformed into the Broadway musical *My Fair Lady*). Mankowitz updated the setting from Edwardian London to the present, deleted some of the plot complications, and altered the leading characters to better fit the talents of the star actors.

Sophia, of course, had the title role, Epifania Ognisanti di Parerga by name, whom Shaw modeled after Nancy Astor and other rich and powerful women he'd known personally. The character was the quintessential Shavian superwoman and required a dynamic actress. Edith Evans was Shaw's choice for the first London production in 1940 (canceled due to the Blitz) and Katharine Hepburn had a triumphant success with it in New York and London in 1951. Hepburn reportedly threw a fit when she learned that Sophia had been signed for the movie, which she coveted for herself. But at fifty-three, Hepburn could no longer pass for a young woman under the magnification of the movie screen, though she might have still been able to create the illusion in a stage production.

Epifania inherited her wealth from her father, a self-made industrial tycoon. Before his death, to make sure that she married someone like himself, he makes her promise that whenever a man proposed, she will give him £150 and tell him that if he can run it up to £50,000 within six months, she is his. But her father had forgotten that many men are scoundrels, and Epifania quickly lands in a bad marriage with an adventurer who wins the bet through criminal means. Seemingly too late, Epifania meets a struggling immigrant doctor who might have made a worthier husband.

For the movie version, Wolf Mankowitz zipped through Epifania's marriage and established her as recently divorced and still looking for a husband who can pass her father's test. The film now focused mainly on her romance with the doctor, who runs a clinic in the impoverished East End of London. Shaw might have been horrified, but the doctor's nationality was changed from Egyptian to Indian so that Peter Sellers could do another of the uncanny ethnic impersonations that helped to make him famous on the BBC Radio series *The Goon Show*.

In the movie, Epifania and Dr. Kabir play tit-for-tat with each other. He counters her financial test with one of his own. If she can prove that she's capable of earning her own living within three months, starting with only a small sum and the clothes on her back, they will marry. Provided, of course, that he also succeeds in multiplying the money that she hands him.

Mankowitz squeezed Vittorio De Sica into the film by making him the owner of a sweatshop bakery where Epifania gets a job and promptly uses her inherited business acumen to turn it into an ultramodern, moneymaking operation. To give the film an authentic Shavian touch, the role of Epifania's eccentric lawyer-adviser was expanded for one of England's greatest stage and film actors, Alastair Sim.

Sophia was guaranteed the full glamour treatment with the hiring of Oscar winners Jack Hildyard as cinematographer and Paul Sheriff as production designer. To make sure that she was truly dressed like a millionairess, de Grunwald and his coproducer Pierre Rouve selected Pierre Balmain, then the chicest and priciest of all the French couturiers, to design her wardrobe. Publicity claimed it cost $75,000, which made a nice bonus for Sophia because the producers promised her that she could keep it at the end of filming.

En route to London, Sophia stopped over in Paris so that Balmain could personally supervise the final fittings. In addition to the expected low-cut gowns, Balmain came up with some trendy suits and flamboyant hats. But his most awe-inspiring contribution was a black satin merry widow corset, which Sophia would wear with long stockings for a strip scene in Dr. Kabir's examining room.

To publicize the start of *The Millionairess,* the producers arranged for Sophia to take the boat train from Paris to London for a press reception at Victoria Station. Peter Sellers would be there to greet her with roses and champagne. The two stars had never met before, which promised some lively photo opportunities if nothing else. Carlo Ponti had remained in Paris for business meetings and planned to join Sophia at a later date, so there would be no dubious husband around to give nosy reporters a chance to turn the party into a tribunal.

Peter Sellers was then thirty-four years old, had spent his entire career acting nonromantic character roles, and had never even been near a sex symbol like Sophia Loren. At first meeting, he found her the most tantalizing and beautiful woman he'd ever met. But when he got home that night, he tried to hide his infatuation by telling his wife, Anne, that Sophia was "ugly, with spots."

For Sophia, it apparently wasn't love at first sight, but Sellers charmed and amused her in the few minutes they had together before she was taken to her latest home-away-from-home. The producers had rented a house for her and the customary entourage in Hertfordshire, several miles from the studio. Vittorio De Sica opted for a flat in London's Mayfair so he could be near all the gambling clubs.

Rehearsals started the next day with director Anthony Asquith, who immediately told everyone to call him "Puffin," a nickname given him in childhood because of the resemblance of his nose to the beak of that species of seabird. Now verging on sixty, Asquith came from wealth and power (his father had been a prime minister of England, his mother a queen of high society), but he was unpretentious, always wore faded old coveralls on the set, and everybody loved him.

"Puffin never ordered actors about. He guided them—gently and intelligently, but above all unselfishly," Sophia recalled. Critics often described Asquith's directorial style as "unobtrusive." Actors were hardly aware of his participation in the collaboration.

From day one, it became evident to those working on *The Millionairess* that the make-believe romance between the two stars could develop into a real one. "I am quite certain that Peter was deeply smitten with Sophia. To him, she was heaven brought down to earth," Dimitri de Grunwald said later. "But there is nothing that will convince me that Sophia returned his passion with anything more than the mutually narcissistic feelings such stars go in for when the limelight is on them, and the romantic content of the film may have helped. Peter would come and hold Sophia's hand like a boy finding his way into his first affair. The nice way of describing her attitude is to say she was kind to him. The other way is to say that her attitude gave him greater hope than was warranted."

De Grunwald added that "I believe that no man could ever cause Sophia to leave Ponti. She once told me, 'Without Carlo, I am nothing,' perhaps doing herself less than justice. 'If Carlo were not here,' she said, 'what would I do? I couldn't earn a crust of bread. No one would want me, not even for a *Vogue* cover!' "

Another production executive had his own theory: "I've always felt that Sophia is one of those actresses who need to feel that their leading men love them before they can give a good performance. Peter had no experience playing romantic roles. He misread the signals and developed a delusion that Sophia had fallen in love with him."

Sophia discovered Sellers to be completely different from the man she first met, who was quite ordinary looking and peered at the world through black-framed glasses. He was one of those actors who are possessed by their roles and become that person twenty-four hours a day for the duration of the job. As Sellers once described himself, "I have no personality of my own. I have nothing to project. I don't know what to do with myself until I get something to hide behind. Then I'm off. I don't have any problems once I get a character to explore."

In the guise of Dr. Kabir, Sellers gained a handsomeness and self-assurance that may have caused him to believe that he could win Sophia Loren in real life. Like his character in the film, he was hooked from the moment he met her. In that scene, Kabir checks Epifania's heart with a stethoscope and exclaims, "Goodness gracious me, I have never heard such a pulse. It is like a slow sledge hammer. It is a pulse in a hundred thousand. I love it. I cannot give it up."

The scene also required Dr. Kabir to massage Epifania's naked back. Before Sellers walked on the set, Sophia removed her bra and lay face down on the examining table. When Sellers arrived, the sight of her body exposed for his touch perturbed him. "When we do the take, do I really have to massage you?" he asked.

She laughed. "Of course, darling."

"It's all right, then, is it?," he asked urgently.

"Yes, of course, it's all right," Sophia said mockingly. "You're supposed to be a doctor, aren't you?"

Sellers finally did the scene, gently massaging Sophia's back from the nape of her neck down to her waistline. Years later, he would be unable to remember how many retakes were required, if any. "I always thought they faked that kind of stuff," he recalled. "But there she was with her bra down. There was this magnificent, fantastic woman, a really very, very beautiful woman. All I can say is that I don't think I have ever been in love with anyone the way I was with Sophia."

As the filming progressed, the stars grew cozier. Sellers took Sophia for meals at his favorite Chinese restaurants and she cooked pasta for him at her rented house in the country. He taught her to speak in Cockney slang, which she did, hilariously, but with a thick Italian accent.

But Sophia proved hopeless at mimicking the singsong Indian accent that Sellers used as Dr. Kabir, which he had first learned while performing in camp shows in India and Ceylon during his RAF service in World War II. Amusingly, switching Kabir to Indian from the Egyptian in Shaw's original play caused *The Millionairess* to be banned in Egypt, where the censors took it as an insult to their national pride.

Sellers lived with wife Anne and their two young children, Michael and Sarah Jane, on a magnificent seven-acre estate, including a twenty-room manor house, swimming pool, and tennis court, at Chipperfield, about twenty miles from London. One evening he threw a supper party in Sophia's honor and hired a band for dancing. While his wife played hostess to the hundred guests, Sellers spent most of his time dancing with Sophia or showing her off to his friends.

Actor-comedian Graham Stark recalled being grabbed by Sellers and told, "Here, Gra, come over and meet this angelic vision." Stark found himself mesmerized by Sophia's "great slash of a mouth. Only the sheerest of scarves covered her bare shoulders and plunging neckline on that untypically hot English summer night. She gave every appearance of being entranced by Peter's wit and flattery."

Several days later, while driving to the studio with scriptwriter Wolf Mankowitz, Sellers confessed that he was in love with Sophia and that he'd decided to tell his wife. Mankowitz laughed, "I'm in love with Sophia, too. Aren't we all?"

Sellers shook his head. "No, I'm serious. She finds me very funny. I make her laugh a lot."

Mankowitz advised Sellers that it wasn't a good idea for a man to tell his wife about such matters, but if he was determined to do so, to make sure he knew the difference between fantasy and reality. "Are you having an actual physical affair with Sophia?" he asked.

"No," Sellers said, "but I'm going to tell Anne that I'm in love with her."

Sellers did, but as Mankowitz predicted, Anne promptly departed with the two kids and moved in with friends. A reconciliation later took place, but the episode contributed to a divorce not long after that.

Several decades later, the ex–Mrs. Sellers said in an interview: "Peter was cast opposite this stunningly beautiful woman, which Sophia was and still is. He just got totally carried away with it, and he became besotted by her. I'm not sure if the feeling was returned, but he felt it was, and it was very genuine to him."

It also started to look genuine to Sophia's Sicilian friend and chaperon, Basilio Franchina. According to Sellers, Franchina took him aside one day and told him that when Ponti found out about Sellers' feelings, "there will be trouble!" Sellers replied, "Well if he has to find out about it, it's just too bad."

Carlo Ponti's arrival in London did bring trouble, but for a different reason. During Sophia's trip to Heathrow Airport to meet him, someone broke into her bedroom and stole a fortune in jewelry that she'd locked away in a bureau drawer. When summoned to the scene, police theorized that the thief had squeezed through a small window on the ground floor and crept upstairs while the servants were watching television in the lounge. It hinted suspiciously of an inside job. But thirty-four years later, an elderly professional burglar named Ray "The Cat" Jones took credit in his published memoirs. Jones claimed that he and a cohort rented a Rolls-Royce and, disguised as a chauffeur and passenger, had been parked in Sophia's posh neighborhood for several days studying her comings and goings. Jones never explained how he knew where she hid the jewels, but he said that he sold everything to a fence for £44,000 (about $106,000 at the time).

Sophia broke down and sobbed. "It is so unjust," she said to the police inspector. "The value of the jewelry is secondary. I can earn money to buy some more. It is what it symbolizes in my life. I pulled myself up out of the slums of Naples, where we were always so terribly poor. The jewelry was the proof that I would never be poor again."

When she calmed down, Sophia dictated a list of the missing items: a ruby necklace; a sapphire and diamond necklace and matching sapphire ring; an antique diamond necklace and matching diamond earrings and ring; an antique emerald necklace and matching emerald earrings; a pearl necklace with one white and one black string; a three-string white pearl necklace; two diamond brooches; an antique Russian brooch in three pieces; a gold evening bag; a two-

and-a-half-yard gold chain; an antique gold brooch of a snake, with rubies and emeralds for eyes; a heavy gold bracelet that snapped open to reveal a watch.

Carlo Ponti said that the stolen jewels were worth about £200,000 (then $480,000). " . . . And they weren't insured. They weren't insured!" he kept moaning for the next several days to anyone who'd listen.

Producer Pierre Rouve later recalled the period following the robbery: "It took place on a Saturday. I knew that Sophia didn't get any sleep that night or the next day either because the police were swarming all over the place. I thought we'd have to cancel her scenes on Monday, but at seven in the morning her Rolls-Royce drove through the front gate. She went straight to her dressing room and carried on as if nothing had happened, though we all knew how shattered she was. Later that morning, somebody else's nerves cracked—those of Peter Sellers. He fainted and had to be taken to hospital. We needed, of course, to go on working, so we spent the rest of the day shooting closeups of the tired, greatly upset Sophia—and they turned out to be absolutely gorgeous!"

When Sellers recovered (apparently from frayed heart strings), he went shopping at Asprey's, the royal jeweler, and bought her a bracelet for £750 to start a new collection. Ponti, however, seemed more concerned about Sophia's safety and hired twenty-four-hour guards with German shepherd dogs to patrol the house and grounds.

Vittorio De Sica raised Sophia's spirits by telling her, "Listen, my love, we are both from Naples. The good Lord has given us other things. It is only jewelry. What is two hundred thousand pounds? You are a woman with beautiful gifts from nature. Look at them!"

"You look at them," Sophia laughed, with understanding written all over her face.

Some good news from America also brightened her mood. Her film with Clark Gable, which Paramount had retitled the more provocative *It Started in Naples,* had opened to excellent business and favorable reviews, making it Sophia's first unqualified hit since *Houseboat.* Bosley Crowther of *The New York Times* again gave evidence of being a devoted fan, writing that "the major thing to look at is Miss Loren, and all else is background for her, strong light to put her femininity into profile."

Sophia was also delighted to hear that Clark Gable and his wife, Kay, were expecting a baby. She hoped that the nights that the couple spent together on romantic Capri were what finally changed their luck.

Sophia's own chances of motherhood seemed remote. While she longed for children, she didn't want to suffer what her mother did with her illegitimate brood. A family would have to wait until she and Ponti were legally married, which still seemed a long way off.

For the time being, however, Sophia was legally a single woman and free to marry anyone she wanted, which is perhaps why she never really discouraged Peter Sellers's attentions. Perhaps she enjoyed flirting with him, and as in the case of Cary Grant, she may have seen Sellers as a means of making Ponti jealous enough to find a speedier solution to their legal predicament.

As *The Millionairess* continued, Sellers became bolder. "I adored Sophia and I had the feeling all the time that it was mutual," he recalled. "She loved my jokes and we got on famously. One day I told her that I was in love with her. A day or two later she came on the set in a beautiful white dress by Balmain. She was in a wistful mood. I said to her, 'Anything wrong? Has anything upset you?' 'No, no,' she said, 'I'm fine.' And then she said, 'I love you, that's all.' "

Sophia once gave her own version of the relationship: "Peter's marriage was falling apart and he was in need of love. I was there and he fell in love with me. I didn't encourage him, nor did I discourage him. When Peter looked at me with those soulful eyes, I just smiled back and he was pleased. He knew I wouldn't take off with him. It was all a very sensitive wounded man's game.

"I knew he'd get over it and that his love for me would help him through a crisis in his life—and it did."

But Sellers showed no signs of giving up when the filming ended. Wacky though it might seem, he came up with the idea of recording a long-playing album with Sophia. Sellers had a contract with EMI for a series of comedy albums and wanted to make the next one a tie-in with *The Millionairess*. A novelty song entitled "Goodness Gracious Me," inspired by the examination room scene between Epifania and Dr. Kabir, would be the only real link to the movie. The rest of the material would be a mixed bag of sketches and musical numbers, some just solos by Sellers that enabled him to do impersonations of everybody from Alec Guinness to Ukulele Ike.

Sophia readily agreed. The $25,000 advance against royalties would go nicely toward buying some new jewelry, and Sellers promised her two solo tracks where she could prove that she was Italy's answer to Ella Fitzgerald and Peggy Lee. The project was turned over to producer George Martin (later the magician behind the Beatles) and took several months to prepare. Sophia, in the meantime, returned to Italy with Ponti, but flew back to London for a week when

Sellers and Martin had everything ready. The album was titled *Peter Sellers &*
Sophia Loren: England's Gooniest Meets Italy's Loveliest.

"Goodness Gracious Me," set to a pulsating heart rhythm, had Sophia complaining of love pains and the Indian-accented Sellers exclaiming, "My stethoscope is bobbing to the throbbing of your heart." The recording was such a
gem that EMI rushed it out as a single in England, where it hit the top of the
charts and sold 200,000 copies.

Two of the other duet numbers seemed wish fulfillment on the part of
Sellers. In "I Fell in Love with an Englishman," written and composed by his
friend Leslie Bricusse, Sophia attends a party and is irresistibly drawn to a sim-
pering English twit who spills tea down his trousers. In "Bangers and Mash,"
she portrays a war bride from Naples who will cook only Italian and denies her
Cockney husband all his favorite dishes.

In her solo turns, Sophia sang Rodgers and Hart's droll "To Keep My Love
Alive," about a much-married lady who kills her husbands as soon as the romance starts to cool, and the tongue-twisting novelty "Zoo Be Zoo Be Zoo."
The latter title rhymes conveniently with "means I love you," which is the point
of the song.

The album concluded with the duet "Fare Thee Well," with Sellers alternat-
ing between the singing voices of Bing Crosby and Noel Coward. "Let's forget
the past and make this last," he croons to Sophia as the song winds down to a
joke finish.

"Aren't you going to show me Rome?" he asks.

"Yes," she replies, "but first I want to show you the Fontana di Trevi."

"Ahh, 'Three Coins in the Fountain,' so romantic. Are you going to throw a
coin in the fountain, Sophia?"

"No, darling. I'm going to throw you in it!" They both collapse into laughter,
followed by sound effects of their getting into a car and driving off together.

O S C A R   N I G H T

ℒ⅁

PETER Sellers's romantic obsession with Sophia continued long after they finished *The Millionairess*. Sophia was always coy about her own feelings, but she once said, "I love Peter very much, in my own way. It is not the way I love Carlo. That is the kind of love which leaves a scar on you. But with Peter it is different. He is really a great, great friend. I consider him a member of my family. I think it is rare for a man and a woman to have that kind of relationship when she is passionately in love with someone else."

By the completion of *The Millionairess*, Carlo Ponti had assembled all the pieces of *La Ciociara*. With the approval of author Alberto Moravia, Vittorio De Sica and Cesare Zavattini wrote a script that retained the tragic flavor of the original novel but heightened the drama and dropped the technique of narration by the title character. The story drew heavily on Moravia's own experiences in Ciociara during World War II, when he and his writer-wife, Elsa Morante, went into hiding there to avoid imprisonment for their antifascist views. As luck would have it, De Sica himself was a native son of Ciociara, born in the small town of Sora.

The rural province situated between Rome and Naples owes its name to the word *cioce,* a type of shoe worn by peasants. The recently widowed Cesira hails from Ciociara, but is running a grocery store in Rome when the Germans invade the capital in 1943. After several bombing raids, Cesira panics and, with her thirteen-year-old daughter Rosetta in tow, flees for safety to the little village where she grew up. By train, mule, and on foot, dodging machine-gun fire from snipers and low-flying planes, they finally reach Sant' Eufemia and move into one of the few undamaged houses with other refugees and local peasants. Among them is Michele, a bookish and idealistic farmer's son known as "the professor." Young Rosetta develops a crush on Michele and flirts with him, but he's more attracted to her mother. Both women become dependent on him for protection.

As the war rages on, the village is suddenly endangered by Allied troops moving up from the south toward Rome. A group of escaping German soldiers abducts Michele and forces him to guide them across the mountains to safety in Austria. Without Michele, Cesira decides that she and Rosetta must move to a safer place. While bedding down for the night in a bombed-out church, they're attacked by some Allied Moroccan soldiers and brutally raped. They barely survive, and the trauma turns Rosetta into a compulsive wanton. Her mother is about to give her up as a lost soul when the sudden news of Michele's death causes Rosetta to break down and admit that she needs help.

In Moravia's novel Cesira was fiftyish, which would have been stretching it a bit for the twenty-six-year-old Sophia Loren, so the script made her thirty-five. The daughter Rosetta, meant to be Sophia's role in the aborted teaming with Anna Magnani, now reverted to a budding adolescent of thirteen, which slanted the dramatic fireworks in the mother's favor. It would no longer be the acting duel that the Magnani-Loren combination had promised.

Since De Sica was a master at finding and directing young actors, Ponti left it up to him to select Rosetta. After auditioning over a hundred girls, De Sica chose Eleanora Brown, who had a luminous sweetness and dignity. She looked enough like Sophia to be her daughter, though with a less prominent nose. The casting was contrary to Moravia's novel, where the mother and daughter looked completely different and would never be taken for kin.

To raise the 530 million lire (about $850,000) needed to make the movie, Carlo Ponti arranged a coproduction deal with a French company, Les Films Marceau-Cocinor. In order to collect a government subsidy, at least one of the stars had to be of French nationality. The role of Michele went to Jean-Paul Belmondo, whose ugly-handsome charisma had just won him overnight fame in Jean-Luc Godard's À bout de souffle (Breathless). Since Belmondo could speak only French, other actors would dub his voice for all but the postsynchronized version released in France.

Vittorio De Sica hadn't made a film in the neorealistic style since The Roof in 1956, so La Ciociara was a chance to redeem himself after wasting most of the interim years taking high-salaried acting jobs in order to support his two families and pay his gambling debts. He told Sophia that if she worked really hard with him, they would both have something to be proud of.

"It won't be easy," he warned her. "You will have to be convincing as a woman ten years older than you really are. We will shoot this with no makeup, and we will dress you as a peasant woman really dresses. You have actually lived this story yourself, Sophia. You survived the war, you know all there is to know about it. If you can become this woman, without any thought as to how you look, without trying to restrain your emotions, letting everything flow into this character, I guarantee that you will give a wonderful interpretation of it."

In preparing for the part, Sophia remembered her mother's "fears, connivances and sacrifices, and especially the way she fiercely protected us against the scourges of war," she said later. "With my own memories to draw upon, you would think I would have had an easy time of it. But it was very hard for me to relive my girlhood terror and at the same time to transform the reality of my feelings into the role I was acting. In memory, I still looked at my experiences with the eyes and emotions of a girl, but the role demanded that I see them with the eyes of a tortured woman."

Sophia credited De Sica for rescuing her. "He stands behind the camera as you work and he is acting with you," she said. "His face lights, his eyes dance, his mouth, his shoulders, his arms, his whole body acts with you—almost as if he carries you along with him! And it becomes contagious—like he spills his emotion into you and through you into the camera. Then—most wondeful of all—when you see the picture on the screen, it flows over into the audience. It's like a miracle!

"De Sica gave me the confidence to go far beyond where I had ever gone before, into an area where I would not have dreamed to venture. Thanks to his support, I even dared to play certain key moments out of control, as a skier will throw all restraint to the winds in order to achieve a new mark."

During the climactic scene where Sophia breaks down crying after telling her daughter that Michele is dead, she saw De Sica standing by the camera, weeping too. "It's so wonderful to have a director who is a perfect mirror," she recalled. "Each time I played the scene, I would see him crying, and each time he was crying in a different way."

Alberto Moravia helped De Sica to select the location sites in Ciociara. In the fifteen years since the war, the countryside had been restored to its natural beauty, but with the help of gritty black-and-white photography instead of color, the change would not be noticeable. When filming started, De Sica encouraged Sophia to spend time circulating among the peasant women to study them and to try to learn their gestures and mannerisms.

"The people of Ciociara at first seemed harsh and uncommunicative," she recalled. "They are of fiery character, but they are very frank, sincere, and reliable when you get close to them."

The decision to shoot *La Ciociara* in Italy may have caught the public prosecutor's office by surprise, but midway through production Sophia and Ponti received a summons to Rome to testify before the magistrate who was investigating the bigamy charges that had been filed against them. The couple's lawyers coached them carefully beforehand. Sophia was cautioned to remain calm and not to let the fiery actress in her take over.

Judge Giulio Franco called Sophia first and dispatched Ponti to the waiting room. Before the judge could get started, Sophia asked him if she could meet Luisa Brambilla, the Milanese housewife who filed the first complaint denouncing the Pontis as bigamists. When the judge refused her request, Sophia said that she wanted Brambilla to know that Ponti's marriage, in the connubial sense, had long been over by the time she started living with him.

"Are you married?" Judge Franco asked Sophia.

"No," she answered, and "No" again to his next question, "Are you married to Carlo Ponti?" She waved her handbag and said, "My passport is here. It says I am Sofia Scicolone, spinster."

The judge dismissed her and called in Carlo Ponti. The question "Are you married to Sofia Scicolone, also known as Sophia Loren?" was answered by an immediate "No."

Frustrated, Judge Franco said he could not make a decision solely on the basis of the defendants' testimony. The bigamy charges would have to stand until their lawyers could prove that the couple's Mexican marriage was invalid.

Meantime, the evidence against Sophia and Ponti was too flimsy to risk arresting either or both of them. The matter would continue to hover over them like a storm cloud, capable of raining trouble at any time.

As the filming of *La Ciociara* progressed, news arrived from Los Angeles that Clark Gable had died suddenly of a heart attack at age fifty-nine. Vittorio De Sica, who'd worked with Gable and Sophia in *It Started in Naples,* shut down production for the day. Sophia was inconsolable and cabled flowers to the pregnant widow, who four months later gave birth to John Clark Gable.

Before *La Ciociara* was finished, Joseph E. Levine arrived in Italy on one of his frequent shopping trips for product for his distribution company, Embassy

Pictures. Since releasing *Attila* in 1958, Levine had fallen out with Ponti over business dealings. "When Carlo invited me to see rushes of Sophia's latest movie, I didn't want to go," Levine said later. "But in this industry you can't afford to hate anybody for long. After seeing a three-minute scene from *La Cockarocha* or whatever they called it in Italian, I bought the American rights."

Levine returned to New York with an 8 × 10 black-and-white scene still that showed Sophia, with her dress torn to shreds after the rape, kneeling in the dirt and weeping with rage. He immediately turned it into a full-page trade press advertisement announcing the acquisition. The photo also become the official logo for the film, which from that time on took on the title of *Two Women* in the English-speaking world.

Meanwhile, moviegoers were getting their first glimpse at some of Sophia's prior work. After holding *A Breath of Scandal* on the shelf for more than a year, Paramount, in November 1960, was finally encouraged to test the waters, when *Life* magazine featured the "Tiger-Eyed Temptress" on its cover for the third time. A short article inside contained several shots of the star in her gorgeous costumes and said that while the movie was all "waltz and schmaltz," it was worth seeing if only to "look at Sophia looking lovely."

A Breath of Scandal opened at a single art theater on New York's Upper East Side, drew a hundred customers on the first day, and quickly folded after bad reviews. Bosley Crowther called it "absolute twaddle" and said that the most scandalous thing about *A Breath of Scandal* was "the fortune squandered upon a slip of an idea." Paramount grabbed whatever bookings it could by making it the bottom of a double bill with *It Started in Naples,* which was rushed back into release to capitalize on Clark Gable's death.

Due to Peter Sellers's fanatic following in England, *The Millionairess* was released there first at Christmas, ahead of the United States and the rest of the world. Though critics moaned over the maltreatment of George Bernard Shaw, the movie was a box-office hit, helped somewhat by the continuing popularity of Sellers and Sophia's single record, "Goodness Gracious Me," and the release of the album containing it.

Unfortunately, the success of *The Millionairess* was not duplicated in the United States, where Sellers was known mainly to art theater patrons who usually relied on critics to choose their movies for them. *The Millionairess* was solidly panned, and Sophia in particular received some of her worst reviews yet.

Bosley Crowther, her often ardent fan at *The New York Times,* wrote:

With the casual air of a showgirl who has no idea what the show is all about—knows only that she's supposed to model those costumes and generate a miasma of sex-appeal—Miss Loren postures and swivels through virtually every scene she plays as a fabulously wealthy Italian heiress who tries to buy herself a Hindu husband and finds she can't.

From the way she performs this lady, it appears her only idea of how to snag the fellow is to run the range of the wiles of a vamp. She lies seductively on sofas, takes advantage of the possibilities of low-cut gowns, occasionally slips out of her dresses and when she isn't rolling her hips, she rolls her eyes. The performance is so calculated and so discordant with the drone of Shavian quips—such as "Is there nothing you can get with money but more money?"—that it's as if Miss Loren is doing an act all by herself. It is not a very good act and it becomes monotonous.

A triumph with *Two Women* seemed essential if Sophia's career was to survive her latest series of flops. By the time the movie wrapped, everybody thought that it stood a good chance with the critics but would be a hard sell because of its downbeat subject matter and the public's apparent apathy toward Sophia Loren. Joe Levine told Ponti to push Sophia for an Academy Award nomination. If she won the Oscar for Best Actress, it would be the first time in history for a performance in a language other than English. Ponti thought it an impossible scheme, which only made Levine more determined to carry it out. To get the ball rolling, he persuaded Ponti to enter *Two Women* in the following spring's Cannes Film Festival, where the first major awards of 1961 would be handed out. A win at Cannes usually marked an actor or actress as a contender for all the film prizes handed out later in the year.

The completion of *Two Women* put a temporary halt to Sophia and Ponti's working relationship. He was involved with two French-Italian co-productions—Jean-Luc Godard's *Une femme est une femme* (*A Woman Is a Woman*) and newcomer Jacques Demy's *Lola*—and traveling frequently to Paris to attend to business. He was also preparing a film for Sophia based on the famous French play *Madame Sans-Gêne*, but the financing and packaging were still under negotiation.

Although Sophia's experience with Hollywood superproductions had been all but humiliating, she decided to fill the gap in her schedule by accepting a $500,000 offer from producer Samuel Bronston to costar with Charlton Heston in *El Cid*. Heston's last two spectacles, *The Ten Commandments* and *Ben-Hur,*

A family snapshot of Romilda Villani and her daughters, Sofia (left) and Maria, taken just before the start of World War II in 1939.

Sofia Scicolone made her first communion at age seven.

By her late teens, she still bore slight resemblance to the future Sophia Loren.

Gina Lollobrigida, the first of Italy's film deities to win international stardom in the 1950s, was eventually eclipsed by the younger Sophia.

Sofia Lazzaro stripped to the waist for her role as a harem slave in *It's Him . . . Yes! Yes!*

With singing voice dubbed by Renata Tebaldi, Sophia wore dark makeup and wigs as Verdi's Aida, her first starring role.

Lecherous aristocrat Vittorio De Sica tried to bed Sophia in *The Miller's Beautiful Wife*, one of the most successful of their acting collaborations.

Charles Boyer was the first of Hollywood's great romantic idols to court Sophia, in the 1955 Italian-made *Lucky to Be a Woman*.

Sophia and Cary Grant practice a Spanish dance for *The Pride and the Passion*. By the time the movie was completed, they had fallen in love.

The world first learned of Sophia's liaison with Carlo Ponti when news photographers caught them together at Athens airport during the filming of *Boy on a Dolphin* in 1956.

Sophia's sponge-diving costume made an even more indelible impression when soaking wet and revealing her natural wonders.

Sophia and John Wayne arrive in Libya for filming of *Legend of the Lost*.

Jayne Mansfield could barely contain herself while welcoming Sophia to Hollywood. Gossip queen Louella Parsons, right, had a ringside seat at the "battle of the bosoms."

Houseboat was the biggest hit among Sophia's Hollywood-made films, but the wedding scene was the nearest that she ever got to becoming Mrs. Cary Grant.

"The King" himself, Clark Gable, romanced Sophia in *It Started in Naples*. The location filming took them back to the region where she grew up in poverty.

Prior to starting *The Millionairess,* Peter Sellers gave Sophia a good luck peck, but a month later her diamond necklace and matching earrings were part of the loot in a $480,000 jewel robbery.

Sophia stripped down to her corset for "Doctor" Sellers and set his heart on fire, both in the movie and in real life.

El Cid was the highest-grossing movie of Sophia's entire career, but costar Charlton Heston received most of the credit for its success.

The marriage of Benito Mussolini's youngest son to Sophia Loren's only sibling in March 1962 made world headlines. In the right background of this wedding photo, Sophia beams approval, but Mama Romilda looks less than happy.

Sophia and a dazed Eleanora Brown in the post-rape scene from *Two Women*. In a proposed earlier version that was never made, Sophia would have played the daughter and Anna Magnani the mother.

Producer Joseph E. Levine, who masterminded the promotional campaign that helped Sophia to win an Oscar for *Two Women*, flew to Rome to present her with the gold-plated statuette. Stage fright kept her from attending the Hollywood ceremonies.

At a film gala in New York in 1962, Sophia finally got a chance to meet her girlhood idol, Rita Hayworth, then forty-seven.

Sophia could joke about the padding that she wore for the role of the perpetually pregnant Adelina in *Yesterday, Today and Tomorrow,* but she cried many tears over her own inability to become a mother.

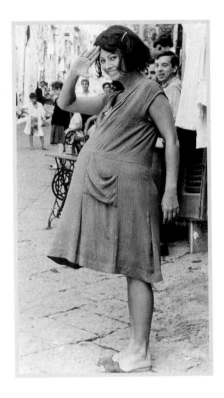

Sophia's see-through outfit as a bordello prostitute in *Marriage, Italian Style* worried movie censors but helped to make her one of the sexual icons of the 1960s.

Vittorio De Sica prepares Sophia for an emotional scene with Marcello Mastroianni in the conclusion to *Marriage, Italian Style.* She received another Oscar nomination for her performance, but lost to the Mary Poppins of Julie Andrews.

Will Sophia Loren look like this at eighty? Makeup artists spent hours transforming her into the elderly character in *Lady L.*

Doctor Zhivago, with Omar Sharif and Julie Christie, was Carlo Ponti's most successful production. Ponti intended casting Sophia as Lara but was talked out of it by director David Lean.

At his seventy-seventh birthday party on the set of
A Countess from Hong Kong, Charlie Chaplin pretended to slash his throat, much to the merriment of Sophia and Tippi Hedren. In the center is Hedren's eight-year-old daughter, future film star Melanie Griffith.

They look like sisters,
but actually it's Sophia and her fifty-eight-year-old mother, Romilda Villani,
snapped off guard during a glitzy movie premiere in Italy in 1967.

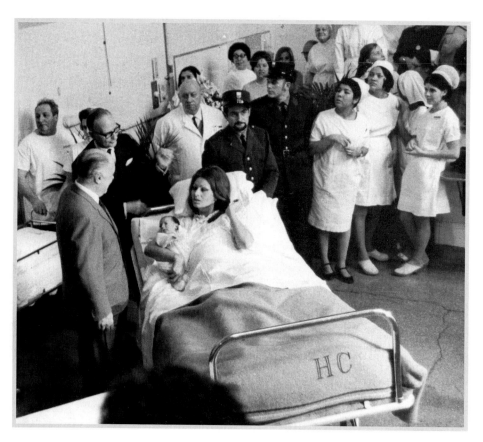

The principals get ready for the mass press conference that introduced day-old Carlo Ponti Jr. to the world. Standing to the proud father's left is Dr. Hubert de Watteville, who helped Sophia to conquer years of childbearing problems.

A rare photo of Sophia and Carlo with Guendolina and Alex Ponti, children of Ponti's first marriage, at a charity ball in Monte Carlo in 1969.

Sophia surveys
the view from the
terrace of the Pontis'
triplex apartment
near the Champs
Elysées in Paris.

Sophia and Marcello
Mastroianni made
an unlikely couple in
The Priest's Wife (1970),
the eighth of the twelve
films in which they
acted together.

What was Richard Burton whispering to Sophia as they took a break from filming a scene for the television remake of *Brief Encounter* in 1974?

In March 1977, Sophia and her considerably older husband were both looking haggard and troubled when he met her at the airport in Paris after she was detained in Rome and grilled by government inspectors about currency smuggling and tax evasion.

During the 1977 Cannes Film Festival, paparazzi wouldn't give up until Sophia agreed to pose with her longtime friend Princess Grace of Monaco.

By 1980 the forty-six-year-old Sophia was a walking advertisement for her self-designed line of eyeglass frames. Here she's shepherding sons Carlo Jr., age eleven, and Edoardo, seven, through arrivals at London's Heathrow to begin a sightseeing holiday.

At age fifty-five, Sophia wore minimal make-up for her role as family matriarch in the Italian TV movie *Saturday, Sunday and Monday,* but her beauty was as luminous as ever. *(From author's collection)*

Sophia turned Walter Matthau and Jack Lemmon into even grumpier old men when she dumped a huge pot of tomato sauce on them in the 1995 comedy hit. It was her first American-made theatrical film in seventeen years.

At a Golden Globes gala in Hollywood, Sophia shared the spotlight with her two grown-up sons and their ladies, Carlo's fiancée, Odile Rodriguez de la Fuentes (left), and Edoardo's inamorata, Elizabeth Guber.

were among the biggest box-office hits ever, and Bronston was being hailed as
the new Cecil B. DeMille. Perhaps Sophia had chosen the right company this
time.

El Cid would run over three hours on screen and take six months to film at
Bronston's studio in Spain, but Carlo Ponti negotiated a contract for Sophia that
spared her from spending half a year away from home. All of the scenes in
which she appeared, regardless of where they turned up in the script, would be
shot first, in a maximum of twelve weeks. While Bronston might have seemed
nuts to accept such a condition, he was getting some of his financial backing
from Italy's Dear Film and needed an Italian leading lady to qualify for government subsidies. Failing Sophia, Bronston would have had to settle for Gina
Lollobrigida, whose international career had been even more disappointing
than Sophia's.

In scriptwriter Philip Yordan's version of the medieval Spanish epic, Sophia
would portray Chimene, wife of the heroic knight Rodrigo Díaz de Bivar, who
is known to his followers as El Cid (The Lord) for rescuing the Christian country from conquest by the Moors. Over nine centuries, the story of El Cid had
been retold so many times that the movie was more fiction than fact. For dramatic purposes, Chimene is portrayed as El Cid's one great love and inspiration.
When he's fatally wounded during a new invasion by the Moors, she helps him
to gain a sort of immortality. His corpse is mounted on his horse and leads the
attack the next day. Believing that El Cid has miraculously returned to life, the
Moors flee in panic and their leader is killed in the stampede. Spain has won,
and El Cid and Chimene pass into romantic myth.

Charlton Heston had already approved Bronston's choice of Anthony Mann
as director, so Sophia went along with it. Ironically, Mann had been a second
unit director on Sophia's first movie, *Quo Vadis,* responsible for the scenes depicting the burning of Rome. He'd since become highly regarded for his thrillers
and large-scale westerns, five of the latter with James Stewart as star. Mann was
everything but the kind of "actor's director" that Sophia favored, but he had a
brilliant camera sense that promised to make *El Cid* a visual masterpiece. He
hired Robert Krasker, cinematographer of such classics as *Henry V* and *The
Third Man,* to make sure.

Sophia brought her usual entourage to Spain, including Basilio Franchina to
serve as "script consultant." Sophia wasn't happy with some of the pseudopoetic
dialogue written by Philip Yordan, so she asked Franchina to translate it into
Italian and then back into a simpler English that she felt more comfortable with.

From the time of her arrival in Madrid, Sophia became the center of attention and was treated like royalty to make sure that everybody, including the stills photographer and unit publicist, got whatever they needed from her during her alloted twelve weeks. Charlton Heston felt neglected, and as a consequence an unspoken chill developed between the two stars. Heston had brought his wife, Lydia, and their young son, Fraser, along on his six-month assignment, so he felt no need to socialize with Sophia and her gang.

In the second half of *El Cid,* the story jumps ahead a full decade, but Sophia refused to change her makeup to balance that of Heston's, which had been aged with worry lines, a dueling scar on the nose, and a gray-flecked beard. "Perhaps Sophia was right," Heston recalled. "In every scene she was in, her glowing image was an enormous asset to the film. Still, she could've made something of Chimene's suffering, too. A director with more guts to stand up to her would have made sure that we saw not only the beautiful Chimene, but Job's wife later on."

Toward the end of her twelve-week contract, Sophia caught the flu and had to spend several days in bed, which left less time later on for the last scene on Sophia's schedule, a lengthy one that depicted El Cid's death and required many complicated camera setups. "By the end of the first day," Heston recalled, "we just got to my entrance, where I'm carried in unconscious, with an arrow in my chest. We shot for two days more; John Fraser was excellent as King Alfonso, Sophia was deeply moving . . . but at the end of her last day of work, we still had not gotten to my closeup."

Among film actors, it's expected that you go on playing the scene when the camera shifts away from you to them. "Don't worry, Chuck," Sophia said. "I'll come back in the morning, before I leave for the airport, and do the off-camera with you."

Heston knew he could do it without her, but he was touched by her offer. Unluckily, several hours after Sophia left the studio, she tripped on the stairs in her duplex hotel suite and fractured her shoulder. Needless to say, Heston acted his last closeup without Sophia. When he went to visit her before she left for Rome, she asked, "What would we have done if I'd fallen last month?"

Fortunately, it was a minor fracture and Sophia could cope while she waited for it to heal. Meantime, she had something more upsetting to deal with in the ongoing romance between her sister, Maria, and Romano Mussolini. The two-year affair had reached a point where Romano, in the expected Italian tradition, went to visit Mamma to get her consent to marry. The seventy-five-year-old

widow of Il Duce didn't exactly say "No!" but she begged her son to find someone more respectable than the sister of a movie star, both of whom happened
to be *bastardi* as well. The press got wind of the meeting and had a field day
dragging the names of Mussolini, Scicolone, Loren, and Ponti through the mud.

Sophia found herself caught in the middle. She'd never approved of
Romano, but Maria was madly in love with him and threatening suicide if she
couldn't have him for a husband. Deciding that Maria's happiness came first,
Sophia got travel directions from Romano and arranged for Ponti's chauffeur to
drive her to Rachele Mussolini's home for a surprise confrontation.

Signora Mussolini resided well north of Rome near Bologna, in the village of
Forli, where her husband is buried in the local cemetery. When Sophia pulled
up in front of the house in Ponti's Rolls-Royce, the old lady, who lived alone,
sized her up as royalty and invited her in for a glass of wine. Before she knew
it, Sophia was being taken on a tour of Villa Carpena. In a room that had been
converted into a chapel, Donna Rachele showed her several relics of Benito
Mussolini, including an eye and a portion of brain that had been removed for
scientific research while the corpse was in the custody of the Allied victors of
World War II.

"It was very macabre, but when she talked about it, she didn't cry," Sophia
recalled. "She was an old woman, but still beautiful. She was very small, and so
thin, with piercing blue eyes, and absolutely white hair. When she spoke about
Mussolini, she still called him Il Duce. Sometimes she was bitter. She said he
was surrounded by bad people. But she never tried to defend him. She loved
him very much and was still in love with him in spite of his mistresses and the
way he treated her. For her, at any rate, it was a love story, and she didn't care
what the world thought."

Donna Rachele decided that movie stars weren't as bad as she had imagined.
Inviting Sophia to stay for lunch, she took her into the kitchen to help her prepare a meal of veal and pasta. "My admiration for her became boundless,"
Sophia said. "Despite her age, she was full of life and energy, very intelligent
and intuitive, interested in what she could do for other people, willing to fight
for what she believed in. I found her not at all fascist, in fact still a socialist,
which she was when she first met Mussolini."

When Sophia left, Donna Rachele made her promise to send Maria for a visit.
That encounter was equally successful. "When I met Romano's mother, I wanted
to marry him even more," Maria remembered. "From the first day I walked into
her little farmhouse, which smelled of freshly baked cake, with strands of fettuc-

cine hanging to dry in front of the fire, we hit it off famously. I love babies and old people, and Rachele Mussolini was the most fascinating elderly woman I had ever met. She was wise and compassionate and considerate."

No marriage date was set. Maria wanted a big wedding with all the trimmings, Romano did not. It would be months before one of them finally conceded.

Meantime, Sophia and Ponti were still in a muddle over matrimonial matters, but about to start a new professional alliance with Joe Levine's Embassy Pictures. Ponti had worked out a deal for six movies, some starring Sophia and others not, that would avoid some of the pitfalls of their Paramount contract. All the films would be produced in Italy or France, with Europe as the primary market. Depending on their success there, they would go the subtitled art route in the United States and the U.K. or be dubbed into English for commercial release.

The arrangement put Levine at minimal risk because he was investing only a portion of the financing for each film, the amounts depending on how many other partners Ponti had in the European markets. Ponti stood to profit the most because he wasn't spending any of his own capital and could also get government subsidies in countries that gave them to encourage local production.

While Sophia's fractured shoulder was healing, Ponti whipped together the first project in the deal. *Madame Sans-Gêne*, a title that referred to the lady's carefree spirit and would be shortened to just *Madame* for the American release, was based on a comic play written in 1893 by the French master Victorien Sardou. It was famous for two legendary performances, the first by Gabrielle Réjane, a rival of Sarah Bernhardt, who introduced it on the stage and in 1912 starred in a three-reel film version of it. In 1925 *Madame Sans-Gêne* helped to make Gloria Swanson the undisputed queen of the silent movie world. While she was filming on location in France, Swanson's real-life romance and marriage to a nobleman received unprecedented news coverage and turned *Madame Sans-Gêne* into an international box-office smash.

Sophia's version would be tarted-up Sardou, injecting more sex and deeper plunging necklines than were permissible in the eras of Gabrielle Réjane and Gloria Swanson. Like *El Cid,* the story, set in Napoleonic times, blended fact with fiction. The title character, Catherine Huebscher, is a laundress who used to do Napoleon Bonaparte's washing when he was just a nobody. Their paths keep crossing through the years, but never romantically. She's in love with a sergeant in the emperor's army. When they marry, she becomes a camp follower and they get involved in a series of heroic deeds that Napoleon rewards with rapid advancements in his court. Before long they're the Duke and Duchess of Danzig, and on their way to becoming King and Queen of Westphalia.

Madame Sans-Gêne required spectacular battle scenes and hundreds of extras, not to mention period sets and costumes and one of the most sumptuous wardrobes ever designed for Sophia (by Marcel Escoffier and Itala Scandariato). Ponti raised the $6 million budget not only from Joe Levine's Embassy but also from three other companies, in Italy, France, and Spain. Because of the setting and some of the principal participants, it was decided to shoot in the French language, which caused no problems for Sophia. She'd become fluent in French while dubbing many of her films for that market and spoke it, in the opinion of some critics, with better results than she did English.

Robert Hossein, a darkly handsome tough-guy star who was France's equivalent of Burt Lancaster, took the role of Sophia's lover-husband. When Peter Sellers learned of the project, he nominated himself for Napoleon Bonaparte, but he also wanted $750,000 in salary, so the part went instead to the distinguished French actor Julien Bertheau, for the equivalent of $25,000.

Ponti selected a director adept at showcases built around voluptuous female stars. Christian-Jaque (real name Christian Maudet) had created and also been married to one of them—Martine Carol, France's number-one sex symbol prior to Brigitte Bardot—and had also done notable work with Bardot and Sophia's rival, Gina Lollobrigida. La Lollo's performance in his 1951 *Fanfan la tulipe* had made her an international sensation. Of course, that was a decade ago, but Christian-Jaque had directed over fifty films by the time of *Madame Sans-Gêne* and was considered one of the best in Europe for lighthearted romantic pulp.

In May 1961, Sophia took time off from the filming to attend the screening of *Two Women* at the fourteenth annual Cannes International Film Festival. Though the movie was officially entered under Italian nationality as *La Ciociara,* Joe Levine took over the promotional campaign at Cannes and spent so much money that it sometimes seemed like no other movies were competing.

Sophia stole the show at the festival. Her appearance at the screening of *Two Women* made a startling contrast to the dirty, ragged Sophia that the audience saw in the film. "I was knocked out by her terrific performance, and then the lights went on and she stood up to take a bow," critic Vincent Canby remembered. "She was dressed to the nines and looked like eighty billion dollars. It was just dazzling to see this extraordinary-looking woman after she'd just given a performance that was sensational. It brought the house down. It was fabulous."

To no one's surprise, Sophia won the award for Best Actress. Since the judges kept their voting secret, only they knew who'd been her closest competition, but gossip claimed Ingrid Bergman for *Goodbye Again,* Claudia McNeil for *A Raisin in the Sun,* and Silvia Pinal for *Viridiana. La Ciociara* also shared an award with three other Italian films for Best National Selection shown during the festival. Whether it had been considered for Best Picture is anybody's guess, but the voting ended in a split decision between Spain's *Viridiana* and France's *Une aussi longue absence.*

In expectation of a triumph at Cannes, Carlo Ponti and Joe Levine had arranged an overlapping theatrical release for the movie that varied from country to country. In Italy and the rest of Europe, *La Ciociara* received conventional, mass-appeal distribution and played the biggest theaters and circuits. In the United States and Great Britain, *Two Women* opened only in a subtitled version in a limited number of art theaters for extended engagements. The American premiere at the Sutton Theatre on New York's East Side was geared to run at least until the year-end film awards were made.

Sophia hoped that her Cannes prize, which came in the form of a Lalique crystal water pitcher, would lead to an Oscar by next April. Omens were good in the New York reviews, which included a not-unexpected rave from Bosley Crowther:

> The beauty of Miss Loren's performance is in her illumination of a passionate mother role. She is happy, expansive, lusty in the early phases of the film, in tune with the gusto of the peasants, gentle with her child. But when the disaster strikes, she is grave and profound. When she weeps for the innocence of her daughter, one quietly weeps with her.

Many critics compared Sophia's performance favorably to the best of Anna Magnani, who was originally supposed to play the role, but the lady herself disagreed. After she saw the movie, Magnani made news in Italy by accusing Sophia of copying her gestures and her earthy technique. "Anna believed her characterization had been appropriated," her director-friend Franco Zeffirelli recalled. "I think that in my whole career I have seldom seen anything as tragic as the way she reacted to that experience. She said, 'There is no longer any place for me in the cinema.' She withdrew from public view, which was senseless because she was a great original actress and had nothing to fear from Loren or anyone else."

When Sophia finished *Madame Sans-Gêne,* she flew to New York to do the English dubbing of *Two Women.* An English version would be needed eventually since about 85 percent of the theaters in America and Britain refused to show subtitled films, which were difficult to follow for moviegoers who were poor readers or got stuck in a seat with an obstructed view. Many of the foreign films that Joe Levine imported, such as *Attila* and the *Hercules* series, were released only in dubbed versions, which also made them easier to sell later to television, where subtitles were even more of a reading problem because of their diminished size.

Sophia spent three weeks dubbing *Two Women* at Titra Sound Studios, working with a dialogue director and actors who were selected to be the voices of Jean-Paul Belmondo, Eleanora Brown, and the others in the cast. They listened to the original soundtrack through earphones and watched the movie projected on a screen in front of them as they went through it scene by scene.

Italian is spoken more rapidly than English, which gave Sophia problems. Much of her original dialogue had to be rewritten in English, using fewer words so she didn't sound like a chipmunk. The director also demanded an authentic Italian accent to her voice, rather than the posh Angloese that she favored in her Hollywood and British movies. Her pronunciations of words like "daughter" (daw-tah) and "water" (waw-tah) would never do for an Italian peasant mother.

In an interview at the time, Sophia said, "I get ill whenever I see the early movies where someone dubbed my voice. The voice is a very important thing in a character. It comes with the body. If you have another voice on the body, you have an entirely different person."

Upon completion, the English-dubbed version of *Two Women* went into a vault until needed for the movie's commercial release. In the meantime, critics and opinion-makers were to be shown only the subtitled Italian prints, so that they could be exposed to the full power of Sophia's original performance. Joe Levine started running a series of bimonthly ads in the two daily Hollywood trade papers, quoting the latest raves to remind the industry that the film should be remembered when Oscar season rolled around.

The critical and box-office success of *Two Women* restored some of Sophia's luster at the major Hollywood studios and brought a flurry of new offers. Although she was part of Ponti's European coproduction deal with Joe Levine, she also had the freedom to go on working independently as before in English-speaking, Hollywood-financed movies. Two that caught Sophia's fancy in outline form were *Seven Pieces of Maria,* a musical comedy that would team her with Danny Kaye, and *The Third Dimension,* a suspense shocker in the mold of *Psycho.* She promised United Artists, which was producing both movies, that she would do them if she liked the scripts.

Meantime, the response to *Two Women* seemed to demand an immediate re-match of Sophia with Vittorio De Sica. Ponti had several projects in mind, one of which he sold to 20th Century–Fox when Joe Levine deemed it too expensive for his small independent company to take on. *The Condemned of Altona* would be based on the great French stage play by Jean-Paul Sartre and filmed in English with an all-star cast, including Spencer Tracy if he was willing. Cesare Zavattini and Abby Mann, author of *Judgment at Nuremberg,* were collaborating on the script.

Zavattini and Mann were also drafting a screenplay for *Children of Sanchez,* based on Oscar Lewis's bestseller about the wretched life of a poor Mexican family. A deal with Levine hinged on Ponti and De Sica getting approval from the Mexican government to film there, which seemed problematical due to the disturbing content of the story.

In the interim, Sophia and De Sica became two of the main ingredients in the next Ponti-Levine collaboration, *Boccaccio '70,* which marked a return to the anthology format that had always been so popular in Italy. Producer Antonio Cervi gave Ponti the idea for a film by four directors who were modern-day equivalents of Boccaccio and had suffered similar problems with the censors of artistic expression.

De Sica would direct Sophia in an episode entitled "The Lottery," scripted by Zavattini. Federico Fellini and Anita Ekberg, one of the stars of his recent *La Dolce Vita,* would be reunited for "The Temptation of Dr. Antonio." Luchino Visconti's episode, "The Job," would feature his protégée, the ex–juvenile star Romy Schneider. Mario Monicelli, the least known internationally of the four directors, would direct "Renzo and Luciana," with newcomers Germano Gilioli and Marisa Solinas.

One of the advantages of anthologies like *Boccaccio '70* was that the episodes could be filmed separately and simply spliced together when all were completed. Since Sophia and De Sica knew each other so well by this time, their forty-five-minute segment took only a month to film, permitting them to go on to other things while Ponti still had three other directors and casts to deal with. Fellini, using color photography for the first time, got carried away with his episode and spent six months, longer than it had taken him to make *La Dolce Vita.*

Inspired by a true story, "The Lottery" was reminiscent of Sophia's *pizzaiola*

episode in De Sica's *The Gold of Naples,* with the locale shifted farther north in
Italy to the Po River valley. The lusty Zoe works in a traveling carnival, where
she runs a shooting gallery owned by her brother-in-law. Every Saturday night,
to boost business, they sell tickets to a lottery, with a rendezvous with Zoe as
the prize. When Zoe acquires a steady boyfriend, she vows to be faithful and
tries to get out of her obligation to the latest lottery winner, a meek church sex-
ton who's never slept with a woman before and won't give up the chance.

With two nonfamous actors in support, Sophia was the whole show in "The
Lottery," which made better use of her physical attributes than her acting talent.
Through much of the episode she wore a low-cut red dress that looked several
sizes too small. In one scene, she strips off a red blouse to wave at a marauding bull and he charges away, seemingly terrified by the sight of her tightly-
packed brassiere.

Later, when all the episodes of *Boccaccio '70* were put together, Sophia
would no longer be able to hog the spotlight. She would be competing for attention with Anita Ekberg's massive bust and Romy Schneider's total nudity.
Fortunately, her "husband" happened to be the producer, so "The Lottery" was
positioned as the final episode in the movie, which would send audiences
home with Sophia Loren still lingering in their thoughts.

While Ponti was overseeing *Boccaccio '70* in Rome, Sophia decided to accept the $300,000 offer from United Artists for *The Third Dimension* and left for
Paris to prepare for the production. First stop was the salon of Guy Laroche,
who would design her wardrobe, hers to keep when the filming finished.

The Third Dimension was another of those English-language movies of
mixed nationality, cofinanced by UA, France's Filmsonor, and Italy's Dear Film.
Paris-based newspaper columnist Art Buchwald called them "movies without a
country" and quipped that they were becoming as much a part of the international scene as the Duke and Duchess of Windsor.

Crazy though it might seem, *The Third Dimension* reteamed Sophia with
Anthony Perkins. But in the four years since they made *Desire Under the Elms*
together, Perkins' huge success as the psychopathic motel-keeper in Hitchcock's
Psycho had made him Hollywood's top choice for roles on the neurotic-lunatic
fringe. Ironically, while Sophia won her Cannes prize for *Two Women,* Perkins
had received the Best Actor award for *Goodbye Again,* in which he romanced
the considerably older Ingrid Bergman.

Anatole Litvak, who directed *Goodbye Again,* was also directing *The Third
Dimension* and was the main reason why Sophia signed on. The Russian-born

director was revered for his wizardry with actresses, including Olivia de Havilland in *The Snake Pit,* Barbara Stanwyck in *Sorry, Wrong Number,* Bette Davis in *All This and Heaven Too,* and Vivien Leigh in *The Deep Blue Sea.* More recently, he had guided Ingrid Bergman to an Oscar with her performance in *Anastasia.*

Scripted by Peter Viertel and Hugh Wheeler, *The Third Dimension* gave Sophia the chance to run the emotional gamut in the role of Lisa Macklin, un-happily married to a jealous and paranoid American executive who's suddenly killed in a plane crash. While she's arranging the funeral, hubby Robert returns from the dead, but only she knows. He miraculously survived the crash and wants Lisa to help him collect on a $120,000 insurance policy, after which he promises to vanish and let her get on with her life. She agrees to hide him in their apartment, but the next few months become a nightmare during the in-surance company's investigation. When Lisa finally receives the big check and drives Robert to his escape point, he announces that he never intended leaving her behind. If she doesn't accompany him, he swears to turn them both over to the police and implicate her in the fraud. Lisa goes berserk, runs him over with the car, and dumps his body in the river. Later, while telling her tale to a new admirer, she seems to be rapidly and permanently losing her mind.

The teaming of Sophia and Tony Perkins made big news in France, where the Cannes Festival awards are taken very seriously. They were the current royal couple of the film world. Director Litvak explained to the press why he chose them: "I was interested in the contrasting personalities of the two. Sophia is outgoing, serene, and cheerful. She has to play the role of a girl from a hum-ble home in Naples who is making good in the sophisticated world of the Paris fashion houses. Well, Sophia knew poverty as a child in Naples and she is cer-tainly a success in the sophisticated world of international picture making. Tony has a gentle boyish quality, which also contains the seeds of violence. I am try-ing to blend the gentle young man I directed in *Goodbye Again* with the dan-gerous quality he revealed in *Psycho.*"

Litvak failed to take into consideration the physical incongruity between the two stars. In a joint interview with Perkins during the filming, Sophia told a re-porter, "When I play opposite Tony, he makes me look like his mother, even though I'm younger than he is."

Perkins laughed and added, "I've got to do something drastic about my in-ability to age. Sophia just seems more grown up, more adult. I'm still asked for an ID card when I go to a bar. I don't think they'd ask for hers."

Sophia seldom saw Perkins away from the studio, but she became very chummy with the debonair American actor Gig Young, who portrayed her suitor and confidant in the movie. Then forty-eight years old, Young had recently separated from his actress-wife, Elizabeth Montgomery, which may have made him more susceptible to Sophia's charms.

"Gig was immediately smitten with Sophia, who seemed to return the feelings," Young's biographer, George Eells, recalled. "They made the rounds of Paris together and had a bittersweet parting when the filming ended. Later, when Gig was back in California, he tried phoning Sophia in Rome through an intermediary in case Carlo Ponti answered the phone, but she kept hanging up. He finally got the message and that was the end of it. He never saw or spoke to her again."

The Third Dimension went through an amusing series of title changes before it was completed. Concerned that it might be mistaken for a 3-D movie, United Artists cranked it up a notch to *The Fourth Dimension,* then tried *All the Gold in the World* and *Deadlock* before finally settling for *Five Miles to Midnight.*

While Sophia was working in Paris, the campaign to get her nominated for an Oscar for *Two Women* went into high gear. By this time, she had repeated her Cannes victory at the Cork Film Festival in Ireland and had also won prizes handed out by groups of film critics in Italy, Germany, Belgium, and Japan. In December 1961, voting took place for the awards that were always a major influence on Oscar voters, those given by the New York Film Critics, a circle that in those days represented the opinions of eight daily newspapers, including the upper-crust *Times* and *Herald Tribune* and the blue-collar *Daily News* and *Mirror.*

By the end of 1961, Sophia's main competition for any Best Actress awards that were being presented for that year seemed to narrow down to Geraldine Page for *Summer and Smoke;* Piper Laurie, *The Hustler;* Audrey Hepburn, *Breakfast at Tiffany's;* Natalie Wood, *Splendor in the Grass;* Deborah Kerr, *The Innocents;* Monica Vitti, *L'avventura;* Marilyn Monroe, *The Misfits;* Claudia McNeil, *Raisin in the Sun;* Vivien Leigh, *The Roman Spring of Mrs. Stone;* and Anouk Aimée, *La Dolce Vita.* Along with Sophia's work in *Two Women,* those were the most praised performances by the lead actresses of the movies released in the United States that year.

During the voting of the New York Film Critics for Best Actress, Sophia ended up in a tie with Geraldine Page on the first ballot with four votes each, followed by Piper Laurie with three and eight others with single votes (most newspapers had more than one critic voting). Sophia finally won with eleven votes to Page's seven and Laurie's one. Her victory marked the first time in the New York Film Critics' twenty-seven-year history that a woman or man had won the acting prize for a performance in a foreign language.

Foreign-language movies were ineligible for the New York Film Critics' Best Picture award, which went to *West Side Story*. *Two Women* was, of course, in the running for Best Foreign Film, but *La Dolce Vita* won.

As one of the winners of the most prestigious film critics' awards in America, Sophia seemed guaranteed an Oscar nomination. Joe Levine immediately stepped up the trade paper ads and ordered his publicity staff to make sure that every eligible Oscar voter had seen *Two Women* by nomination time. Private screenings, preceded by cocktails and a buffet supper, were set up in Los Angeles, New York, Chicago, London, Paris, Rome, Tokyo, and virtually every spot in the world where the Motion Picture Academy had members.

While Sophia was making news with *Two Women*, *El Cid* had its world premiere in New York at the Warner Theatre. Allied Artists, which controlled the American distribution, opted for a two-shows-per-day, reserved-seat policy at $3.50 per ticket, which quickly proved a mistake. Switched over to continuous runs at the current standard price of $2.00, *El Cid* took off and became a smash hit, not only in the United States but everywhere. It eventually turned out to be the biggest grosser of Sophia's entire career, earning worldwide rentals of $25 million in its first year of release.

Amusingly, soon after *El Cid* opened in New York, Carlo Ponti saw some photographs in the trade papers of the huge electric billboard on the northwest corner of Broadway and 47th Street and threw a fit. Though Sophia's contract specified equal billing with Charlton Heston above the title, the Warner Theatre's sign placed only Heston's name above *El Cid* and had Sophia's below it. Ponti immediately ordered his attorney in New York to file a damage suit in Sophia's behalf.

The case was eventually laughed out of court by Justice Samuel Hofstadter, who commented that "the egocentricity that appears to be indigenous to show business is here manifested by the passionate insistence of a well-known motion picture actress to have her name emblazoned on Broadway not only in the same size of type as her coactor but also on the same line. There is a genuine question whether Miss Loren is really in danger of suffering the loss of prestige and other damage."

Allied Artists had been intending to push Sophia for an Oscar for *El Cid*, but her reviews were nothing special—Bosley Crowther called her "lovely, agile and a latent force, but little more"—and the plans were dropped. Joe Levine gave a sigh of relief because the two efforts would probably have canceled each other out.

As 1962 began, Sophia had no urgent need to go back to work. With two hit movies in current release and *Madame Sans-Gêne, Boccaccio '70,* and *Five Miles to Midnight* lined up behind them, there was a limit to what the market would bear. Also, Ponti didn't want to make any new deals involving Sophia until Oscar time. If she did win, her current asking price, which was in the middle six figures for mainstream English-language productions, could be jacked up to $1 million or more.

In the meantime, the National Broadcasting Company in the United States was getting Sophia for free for a television special, though she would receive priceless publicity benefits when the program aired. "The World of Sophia Loren" was the latest in a series of one-hour *The World of . . .* documentaries that NBC ran periodically, most recently featuring comedian Bob Hope, evangelist Billy Graham, and Air Force general James Doolittle. Producer Donald Hyatt chose to focus on Sophia because she seemed to symbolize the new international aristocracy of the movie industry.

Not surprisingly, Joe Levine's publicity machine got into the act and persuaded NBC to schedule the telecast for the day that the Academy Award nominees were announced. If Sophia happened to be one of them, the TV exposure should have a positive impact on the Oscar voters who might be watching.

NBC started filming "The World of Sophia Loren" while she was winding up *Five Miles to Midnight* in Paris, which enabled them to follow her around the city and also do interviews with Tony Perkins, Anatole Litvak, and columnist Art Buchwald. Back in Rome, Sophia and Ponti agreed to an interview in their apartment, provided there was no discussion of the bigamy scandal. Vittorio De Sica dropped by to sing Sophia's praises. The whole thing turned out to be more of a valentine than a documentary. Alexander Scourby did the majestic narration, and Robert Emmett Dolan composed a song, "Sophia," for the soundtrack.

Just hours before the telecast on March 6, 1962, Sophia got the Oscar nomination that she had been hoping for. The other Best Actress nominees were Geraldine Page for *Summer and Smoke;* Audrey Hepburn, *Breakfast at Tiffany's;* Piper Laurie, *The Hustler;* and Natalie Wood, *Splendor in the Grass.*

The joyous news couldn't have come at a better time for Sophia, who was still in shock from a tragic accident only three days before. What should have been a happy occasion—the wedding of her sister, Maria, to Romano Mussolini—turned into a nightmare during its last, postceremony hours.

The longtime lovers had finally decided to make it legal by getting married at the Church of St. Anthony in Predappio, the town where Il Duce was born and later entombed. It promised to be a wedding worthy of the Circus Maximus, but Sophia went along with it to please Maria. Her only demand was that their father should stay away. There was enough for the paparazzi to feast on without dragging the Scicolone sisters' illegitimacy into it.

Carlo Ponti was delegated to give the bride away, but the Catholic Church authorities said no because of his dubious marital situation. Arturo Michelini, a close friend of the Mussolini family and the leader of a local neofascist group, replaced him. Ponti wisely decided to remain in Rome and sent Sophia and her mother on their own in his chauffeur-driven Rolls-Royce.

Thousands of curiosity-seekers and the expected wolf pack of reporters and photographers jammed St. Anthony's and the town square during the wedding service, which ended with the overwrought Maria fainting and Romano carrying her out of the church in his arms. After fighting through the mob scene in the town square, the groom also collapsed and had to be revived with an injection of vitamin B_{12}.

Prior to the wedding banquet, Rachele Mussolini insisted on taking everybody to the cemetery to put flowers on her husband's grave. As soon as the newlyweds left for their honeymoon, Sophia and Romilda returned to Rome. Just as their Rolls-Royce was driving through the outskirts of Predappio, it collided with a man on a Vespa motor scooter. The rider, who turned out to be a twenty-five-year-old schoolteacher named Antonio Angelini, was killed instantly.

Sitting in the Rolls, Sophia and Romilda broke down in tears when they discovered what had happened. As soon as the police arrived, they walked the two women and the chauffeur to a store across the road and questioned them for two hours while paparazzi swarmed outside. The three were finally released and no charges were made, pending further investigation.

The tragedy deeply depressed Sophia, who was also reacting to her sister's wedding. "When Maria married," she recalled, "I suffered terribly. I thought it unfair that she should want to leave me for a husband, that she should prefer another person to me. On her wedding day, I was more jealous than a father. This feeling lasted only a few days, but it still frightens me when I think of it."

Jealousy turned into a mild case of envy when Maria soon tested pregnant.

On December 30, just a shade over nine months after the wedding, she gave birth to a daughter, making the new Zia Sophia very happy indeed. The parents considered calling the baby Benita, after her famous grandfather, but the name Benita Mussolini seemed one handicap too many to start life with. Instead, she was dubbed Alessandra, in honor of Il Duce's father, Alessandro, but within the family she would always be known as Sandra.

Unintentionally, Alessandra's parents quickly caused Sophia grief and more moral censure when they picked her to be the godmother at the christening. The bishop reviewing the application decreed that "the public sinner" should not be permitted to participate in a sacred ceremony. Sophia decided to brazen it out. When she turned up at the church, trailed by the usual pack of paparazzi, the officiating priest took pity and went on with the service to avoid the ugly spectacle of turning her away. But the next day Sophia was pilloried by the Catholic press and also denounced on the radio by the Vicarate of Rome for violating canon law.

Meanwhile, the campaign to win Sophia an Oscar for *Two Women* intensified. The week before balloting closed, *Time* magazine featured Sophia on the front cover and ran a gushing article that started out with a backhanded compliment:

> Her feet are too big. Her nose is too long. Her teeth are uneven. She has the neck, as one of her rivals has put it, of a "Neapolitan giraffe." Her waist seems to begin in the middle of her thighs, and she has big, half-bushel hips. She runs like a fullback. Her hands are huge. Her forehead is low. Her mouth is too large. And *mamma mia,* she is absolutely gorgeous.

Noting how far she'd come since her starlet days, *Time* said that "a short time ago, all the serious attention being paid Sophia Loren would have seemed as preposterous as the suggestion that Jimmy Hoffa might someday win a Nobel Prize."

By this time, Joe Levine's Embassy Pictures had reportedly spent over $150,000 in trade paper advertising, in addition to another $100,000 on buffet suppers and screenings for Oscar voters in every city where the Academy had members. "I nursed that picture like a baby," Levine said later. He seemed to have several factors in his favor: the novelty of Sophia's foreign-language performance, a probable split in the Paramount bloc of votes between Audrey Hepburn and Geraldine Page, Fox's minimal support of Piper Laurie, and

Hollywood's disapproval of Natalie Wood's current and very flagrant live-in relationship with Warren Beatty.

As the big night of April 9 drew nearer, Sophia couldn't make up her mind
whether to attend the ceremonies or not. Ponti, who was miffed that *La Dolce
Vita* rather than *Two Women* was nominated for the Best Foreign Film, thought
they should decline Joe Levine's offer of a chartered jet to fly them to Los
Angeles. He believed that Hollywood had it in for them because of their string of
flops at Paramount and other studios, but he left the final choice up to Sophia.

"I decided that I could not bear the ordeal of sitting in plain view of millions
of television viewers while my fate was being judged," she later remembered.
"If I lost, I might faint from disappointment; if I won, I would also very likely
faint with joy. Instead of spreading my fainting all over the world, I decided it
was better that I faint at home."

In 1962, years before satellite TV made it possible for the Oscar ceremonies
to be beamed "live" worldwide, Sophia could only sit and wait for the results to
be phoned in or broadcast on the next day's news. Due to the nine-hour time
difference between Italy and California, it was already 4:30 A.M. in Rome when
the show began. Sophia and Ponti stayed up all night, and upon advice from
Joe Levine invited photographer Pier Luigi to join them just in case there was
cause for celebration.

By 6:00 A.M., Sophia couldn't stand it anymore. "Someone else got it and no
one has the courage to call me," she told Ponti. He advised her to forget it and
go to bed. She changed into green pajamas, but couldn't fall asleep. Small wonder, since she smoked five packs of cigarettes and drank at least two pots of
coffee before turning in, according to the calculations of Pier Luigi.

Sixty-five hundred air miles away in the Santa Monica Civic Auditorium, the
presentation of the Oscar for the Best Actress of 1961 fell to Burt Lancaster, who
goofed as he read the list of nominees and forgot to mention Sophia Loren. As
people in the audience called it to his attention, he apologized and then had to
repeat himself as he tore open the envelope and proclaimed Sophia the winner.

Red-headed Greer Garson, who gave the longest acceptance speech in the
history of the Oscars when she won for her 1942 performance in *Mrs. Miniver*,
substituted for Sophia and was mercifully brief this time.

"I am delighted to accept for this wildly beautiful and talented girl," said
Garson, who was twenty-five years Sophia's senior. "We do wish her good
health and happiness along with the award, which is the first ever given for a
performance in a foreign language. History has been made tonight!"

A CLASSIC TEAM

WHEN the phone rang at 6:45 A.M. Rome time, the caller was Cary Grant, who'd stayed home in Beverly Hills that night to watch the Oscars on the portable TV in his bedroom.

"Darling, do you know?" he asked.

"Know what?" Sophia screamed.

"Oh, darling, I'm so glad I'm the first to tell you. You won!"

Sophia, in her dressing gown, began jumping up and down with joy, urged on by Pier Luigi, who was clicking away with his Rolliflex. Ponti, who'd been handed the telephone receiver, asked Grant, "Sophia win? Sophia win? True? True?"

As soon as Grant hung up, calls came from Joe Levine, William Holden, Frank Sinatra, Peter Sellers, Tony Perkins, John Wayne, Clifton Webb, and many others. Though Sophia's Oscar reflected glory on her native land, no congratulations were received from the President of Italy, hardly surprising in view of her dubious marital status.

Magnums of champagne were popped open to celebrate as Vittorio De Sica and Sophia's relatives arrived to kiss and hug the new Queen of the Cinema (or at least until next year's Oscars). Sophia's mother said later that "it was like an unforgettable fairy tale, a compensation for all the sacrifices I'd made in my life."

Like many "stage mothers," Romilda Villani had turned into the star she helped to create, at least in her own mind. "When the Oscar was given for *Two Women,* it was given to me. I am Sophia. The applause was mine. I was fulfilled. . . . Everything that I wanted for myself happened to Sophia. I live in her reflection, and it makes me happy," she once said.

For Sophia, the morning passed in an ecstatic blur: "I vaguely remember tele-graph boys delivering bundles of messages from every corner of the world, re-porters and cameramen overrunning the apartment. At the end, exhausted, I lay on my bed between Mammina and Maria. We had no need of words. We knew we were all thinking of our first home in Pozzuoli and the distance we had trav-eled."

That afternoon, Sophia decided that she must do something to thank the world, and donated a pint of blood to the Red Cross. "Good Neapolitan blood," she told the nurse who drained it. "Concubine's blood," sneered a news report in one of the Roman Catholic newspapers.

Sophia's Oscar triggered the broadest possible distribution for *Two Women*, which in the United States and Britain meant finally releasing the English-dubbed version to get bookings on major theater circuits like RKO and Odeon. Embassy Pictures temporarily withdrew the subtitled prints, which caused moviegoers to miss some of the performance that had just won Sophia an Oscar, though few complained. The dubbed *Two Women* earned over $6 mil-lion in rentals in the U.S., as against $2.5 million from the subtitled art release.

Bosley Crowther of *The New York Times* found the English version of *Two Women* to be "a remarkably effective job" and recommended that all quality foreign films be dubbed so that they could reach a larger American audience. He argued rather convincingly that most foreign soundtracks were "faked" any-way, with the voices usually postsynchronized and often by ghosts. In the "orig-inal" version of *Two Women* that won Sophia her Oscar, for example, Jean-Paul Belmondo's voice came from an Italian actor. Crowther also felt that foreign movies usually had so many subtitles that he devoted most of his attention to reading them. He said he never got the full impact of *Two Women* and *La Dolce Vita* until he saw the dubbed versions.

Most of Crowther's peers disagreed with him, and the dubbing versus subti-tled controversy has raged on until the present day, with no resolution on the horizon.

Sophia's Oscar brought scores of offers for new movies, but none for the mil-lion-dollar fee that Carlo Ponti now believed she was worth. Meanwhile, Sophia was part of his package deal with 20th Century–Fox for *The Condemned of Altona,* so there was no need to commit to anything beyond that just yet. Ponti also had his hands full with several of his Levine coproductions that didn't in-volve Sophia, including Jean-Luc Godard's *Le mépris* with Brigitte Bardot, and was traveling frequently to Paris and New York on business.

Ponti and Joe Levine had by now completed *Boccaccio '70* and planned to follow the same prestige formula that they had with *Two Women,* starting with the 1962 Cannes International Film Festival in May. A huge gala for the press and industry VIPs was scheduled in Sophia's honor to make up for the snub she received from the Italian government when she won the Oscar.

Unfortunately, the Cannes screening of *Boccaccio '70* was greeted with boos and an angry demonstration outside the theater, though it had nothing to do with Sophia Loren. Cineastes were outraged by what Ponti and Levine had done to the movie in the editing room. The episode directed by Mario Monicelli was removed entirely, and Federico Fellini's drastically shortened from ninety to fifty-four minutes. The producers claimed that the cuts were necessary to get a movie of comfortable endurance length that would not require an intermission, but the Monicelli and Fellini fanatics were not convinced. Before *Boccaccio '70* was even released, it became permanently tainted in the realm of film criticism.

Even in its compacted three-episode version, the movie ran close to three hours, which required some ingenious marketing. In June, Joe Levine arranged the American premiere to open New York's brand-new Cinema I and Cinema II, which were separate theaters built on top of each other and forerunners of the multiplex concept that took hold in the movie industry in the 1980s. The subtitled *Boccaccio '70* ran in both theaters on a staggered schedule so that there was a performance starting every ninety minutes.

The combination of the generously exposed anatomies of Sophia Loren, Anita Ekberg, and Romy Schneider incited the Catholic National Legion of Decency to award *Boccaccio '70* a Condemned rating, which, together with the sexy ad campaign, was probably why the movie did blockbuster business. The reviews, which are usually the deciding factor for an art house release, were not good, especially for Sophia.

Bosley Crowther savaged both the star and director of the concluding episode:

De Sica is obvious and unbecomingly gross . . . the display of Miss Loren's charms in "The Lottery" is excessive to the point of tedium, and the portrayals of her various grunting suitors are more callow than comical.

How Carlo Ponti, her husband and the producer of this film, could have allowed her and Signor De Sica to revert to such an artless crudity after their powerful creation of *Two Women* is an incidental mystery.

Boccaccio '70 crossed over into mainstream success with an English-dubbed version. It also made history by being the first movie with a Condemned rating to ever play the Loew's circuit, which proved either how much the moral climate had changed or how desperate exhibitors had become for commercial successes.

Counting the hefty grosses, Carlo Ponti went a bit giddy and announced plans for *Boccaccio '71,* this time with Sophia as the star of every episode but with a different director, scriptwriter, and cast for each. To make it a multinational production, he envisioned De Sica, Jacques Tati, and Billy Wilder as directors, but the project was soon forgotten as those already on Ponti's slate took precedence.

By September, he was ready to start Sophia's fourth collaboration with De Sica as director, which would also be their first to be shot in the English language. The studio, 20th Century–Fox, had insisted on it, even though De Sica's only previous movie in English, *Terminal Station,* had been a critical and box-office disaster, though possibly through no fault of his own. David O. Selznick, who produced it with his wife Jennifer Jones and Montgomery Clift as stars, took over the final cut and the ineffable *Indiscretion of an American Wife* was the result.

Ponti was talked into producing *The Condemned of Altona* by De Sica, who'd attended the premiere of Sartre's drama in Paris in 1956 and had been trying to film it ever since.

"A critic once described me as 'the poet of suffering,' " De Sica said in 1962. "Certainly the horror, the pain, and the suffering of the war years brought profound changes into my approach to life, and I suppose, therefore, it was natural that when I saw Sartre's play I was immediately filled with a burning desire to translate this indictment of oppression into cinematic terms. Set in postwar Germany as a study of fanatical Nazism, it remains an accusation against all dictatorships."

Ponti considered it too ponderous to work, but he owed De Sica more than he could ever repay for his contributions to Sophia's success. The recent smash hit of the all-star *Judgment at Nuremberg,* a similarly heavy dose of *angst* over Nazi war crimes, further encouraged Ponti and 20th Century–Fox to proceed. Ponti also raised cofunding from Italian and French companies, so it became yet another pot of Euro-American goulash in order to qualify for government subsidies.

Ponti might have started out by changing the title, which confused everybody, including Fox board chairman Spyros Skouras, who announced it as *The Condemnation of Altoona* during a speech at the annual stockholders' meeting.

The film is set not in that Pennsylvania city, but rather in a palatial estate called Altona near Hamburg, Germany, that belongs to the Gerlach family. Papa Gerlach, whom Sartre patterned after Gustav Krupp, controls a titanic industrial empire that served the Nazis during World War II but has survived and become even richer than before.

Sophia was cast as Johanna Gerlach, a stage actress married to Gerlach's youngest son, Werner, who is scheduled to run the family business when his father retires but wants out because of its shameful past. Werner's older brother, Franz, was really supposed to take over, but he had been killed after being found guilty of war crimes during the Nuremberg trials. In a not too surprising plot twist reminiscent of the one in *Five Miles to Midnight,* Franz is not only still alive, but being hidden, in a rather deranged condition, in Altona's attic by his sister, Leni. When Johanna discovers the secret, she sets off a bizarre chain reaction by being romantically attracted to Franz, who isn't as nutty as he seems and convinces her that he's innocent of the Nuremberg charges that he caused the deaths of hundreds of Russian peasants.

Abby Mann, who'd scripted *Judgment at Nuremberg* and collaborated with Cesare Zavattini on *The Condemned of Altona,* tried to persuade Spencer Tracy, one of the stars of the former, to take the role of Papa Gerlach. But Tracy passed, claiming that he would be uncomfortable playing a non-American character. His close friend Fredric March, who'd costarred with Tracy in *Inherit the Wind,* took over, but March wasn't a box-office favorite and the film's commercial chances may have suffered as a result.

Ponti signed Austrian-born Maximilian Schell to portray Franz Gerlach. On the same night that Sophia won her Oscar, Schell received one for Best Actor for his performance as the German defense lawyer in *Judgment at Nuremberg,* so the teaming seemed dictated by the Academy Awards, even though the deal had been made previously. Schell was a chum of Abby Mann, who'd given him his first big break in the original TV production of *Judgment at Nuremberg.*

At the insistence of 20th Century–Fox, contract star Robert Wagner got the role of Sophia's husband, Werner Gerlach. If a girl from Pozzuoli could portray a famous German stage actress, then a boy from Detroit, Michigan, would presumably be accepted as a German aristocrat. The mixture of so many different accents coming from German characters in the movie would eventually drive critics and moviegoers wild.

To satisfy some of the cofinancing arrangements, the role of Franz and Werner's sister, Leni, had to go to a French national. When Fox suggested

Jeanne Moreau, Ponti thought she might be too much competition for Sophia and refused to consider her. They finally settled for Françoise Prevost, an accomplished actress whose credentials as a star were debatable.

To make things easier for De Sica, most of *The Condemned of Altona* was shot at Cinecittà in Rome so that he could use his usual Italian crew. Most of the action took place indoors anyway, with an abundance of scenes that amounted to long monologues—a favorite device of Sartre—by one or another of the main characters.

The only location work for the black-and-white CinemaScope movie took place in Hamburg and Berlin. Although American film companies had never been permitted to work in East Berlin, Ponti got clearance to shoot two scenes there, at the Bertolt Brecht Theatre. To establish Sophia's character as a stage actress, the moments showed her working with members of the esteemed Berliner Ensemble in Brecht's *The Rise and Fall of Arturo Ui*. Sophia had never acted on a theater stage before, but Helene Weigel, Brecht's widow and director of the Berliner Ensemble, coached her and she got through without De Sica demanding too many retakes.

Throughout the filming of *The Condemned of Altona,* Sophia had to contend with gossip that she had become personally involved with Maximilian Schell. It would be easy to understand why. With his dark hair streaked with blond for the movie, Schell was a handsome man who adored women and was said to have a batting average that surpassed Warren Beatty's.

One person who did believe the gossip about Sophia and Schell was Peter Sellers, who was still gaga about her and kept track of her movements through mutual friends. Sellers' heartbreak and jealousy turned into hatred for Schell. When he was offered a costarring role with Schell in *Topkapi,* he rejected it. Sellers's lovesick rage may have cost him the Oscar that his replacement, Peter Ustinov, received.

Known to his friends as R.J., Robert John Wagner added some complications to whatever was going on between Sophia and Schell. "The night before a crucial scene," Wagner recalled, "Schell gives me this big talk about our playing brothers and getting into the *essence* of the relationship—you know, that actors' bullshit talk. So the next day I start my scene, and Schell takes a script and goes over behind the camera and shakes his head the whole time I'm working. Can you imagine? In all my years, I've never seen *anybody* do something like that. What was really pissing him off was that I was having this thing with Sophia. She liked me, and that drove Max *wild*."

Wagner's "thing with Sophia" apparently never went beyond friendship, though he'd recently been divorced from Natalie Wood (they remarried in 1972) and was open to a new relationship. "They were very obviously attracted to each other," scriptwriter Abby Mann said later, "but Sophia's husband just happened to be the producer and was always coming around. I think R.J. was afraid to make a move because Ponti was such a power in the European film industry at the time. R.J.'s contract with Fox was about over and he wanted to make a fresh start in Europe. Ponti could really make it tough for him if he was caught fooling around with Sophia."

During the filming, the Pontis celebrated the fifth anniversary of their Mexican proxy wedding. Though its legality was still under challenge in Italy, they had become the oddest and most speculated-about married couple in the movie world. Anyone who saw the towering Aphrodite standing alongside the short and pudgy older man couldn't help wondering what—besides his wealth and power—she found so attractive.

Sophia's stock answer to those who asked her was always, "All I can tell you is that when I am without him, it is as though I were without oxygen." She also never failed to mention that Ponti was a father figure, a replacement for the one she never had.

"From the first moment I met Carlo, I felt that I had known him all my life, ever since I was born," she claimed. "I see men every day who are more handsome, but they are like cardboard compared to my Carlo."

Skeptics in the European scandal press kept insinuating that the marriage was a sham, that Ponti was a skirt chaser and that Sophia stayed with him and played the adoring wife only bcause he had total control over her wealth. The gossip columns often linked Ponti with other actresses he'd "discovered," most notably Sylva Koscina, an exotic import from Yugoslavia, and Virna Lisi, the latest in a line of blue-eyed blondes that had started even before May Britt.

Incredible though it might seem, *The Condemned of Altona* turned out to be Sophia's fiftieth movie since starting out as an extra in *Quo Vadis* in 1950. Of course, the first dozen or so movies in that twelve-year period were only bit parts, but at age twenty-eight she had already chalked up more credits than most movie stars do in a lifetime career. Now also an Oscar winner, Sophia seemed to have earned the right to demand a million-dollar fee, which Ponti finally negotiated for her on her next movie, *The Fall of the Roman Empire*.

It was partly a matter of luck. The global success of *El Cid* caused producer Samuel Bronston to rush into preparing another historical epic for the same stars and director. Even before the script was submitted to Sophia and Charlton Heston, Bronston started a huge and authentic reconstruction of ancient Roman temples and buildings on the acreage of his studio near Madrid.

Unfortunately for Bronston, Heston hated Philip Yordan's screenplay and backed out by promising to sign for one of the producer's other upcoming films. Sophia wasn't happy with the script either, but with Heston eliminated, Ponti had a bargaining advantage. If Sophia dropped out as well, Bronston would really be stuck because Sophia Loren and the Roman Empire went together as naturally as spaghetti and meatballs. Bronston had originally planned to pay Sophia and Heston $750,000 each, but he agreed to hike Sophia to $1 million, which still left him with $500,000 to offer the male lead.

In the end, Bronston gained financially. To replace Heston, he hired the Irish-born Stephen Boyd, Heston's costar from *Ben-Hur,* who was an equally stunning piece of beefcake but worked cheaper, at $300,000 per picture. The remaining $200,000 went to Alec Guinness, which might seem stingy compensation for one of the world's greatest actors, but it was for an overblown cameo role that would take only two weeks to film.

To protect Sophia's interests, Ponti insisted that Basilio Franchina, their longtime associate and an ex-history professor, should be hired to do some rewriting of the script and to serve as technical adviser. Franchina wound up with co-screenplay credit with Philip Yordan and Ben Barzman. British historian Edward Gibbon's six-volume *The Decline and Fall of the Roman Empire* was cited as their source material, no doubt because it was a work in the public domain.

Sophia's was the only female role of any importance, though by no means the cause of the fall of the Roman Empire. She portrayed Lucilla, daughter of the Stoic philosopher-emperor Marcus Aurelius, who has chosen his adopted son, Livius, to succeed him. The emperor's own son and heir, Commodus, is too demented to trust, but a supporter who wants him on the throne murders Marcus Aurelius before the transition can take place. Lucilla, who's been in love with Livius since childhood, tries to persuade him to take over as her father wished, but he would rather remain a commander in the armed forces. Commodus thus proclaims himself emperor and turns into the licentious monster that Marcus Aurelius feared. To stop Lucilla from interfering, he marries her off to the barbaric Sohamous of Armenia. In the complicated story that takes up more than three hours of screen time, Lucilla is eventually widowed and brought back to Rome to be burned at the stake. Commodus has discovered that he's not really

Marcus Aurelius's son, which means that Lucilla is the only true heir to the Roman empire. Just in the nick of time, Livius arrives to rescue Lucilla and kill Commodus, but the reunited lovers realize that Rome is beyond redemption, and they leave to find happiness elsewhere.

Ironically, Sophia was the only true Roman in the cast. In addition to Stephen Boyd and Alec Guinness, who was supposed to be Sophia's father but hardly sounded like it with his impeccable stage actor's diction, her costars included Christopher Plummer as Commodus, James Mason, Anthony Quayle, and Mel Ferrer. Omar Sharif, an Egyptian star who would soon become famous internationally through a supporting part in *Lawrence of Arabia,* played Sophia's Armenian husband, though most of his scenes ended up being cut to shorten the movie's running time.

Budgeted at $20 million, *The Fall of the Roman Empire* was reportedly the most expensive film produced up to that time (*Cleopatra* cost more, but only because of a false start and a year's delay while Elizabeth Taylor recuperated from a near fatal illness). Samuel Bronston obtained some of his financing from a longtime partner, the American tycoon Pierre S. Du Pont, but the bulk of it came from selling off the distribution rights in advance of production. Paramount Pictures and the Rank Organization were the largest of eight companies involved; after the movie recouped its negative cost, they would share fifty-fifty with Bronston in the profits.

Though Sophia was being paid twice as much as for Bronston's *El Cid,* Carlo Ponti negotiated the same limited contract, meaning that all her work had to be completed within twelve weeks. Since she figured in only about 25 percent of the scenes, director Anthony Mann could easily accommodate her as before.

When Sophia learned that she would be working with Alec Guinness, she grew a bit terrified. "After all, he was a brilliant actor, and one of the few with 'Sir' before his name," she recalled. "I thought that he would be rather pompous. I expected him to be just like 'Sir Eric Goodness,' the impersonation that Peter Sellers did on our record album, but he wasn't. He was marvelous; we loved each other. At a party, we danced the Twist together. He did it very well."

Sophia and Guinness discovered that they might have met before. In 1943, while serving as a lieutenant on a British supply ship, he spent some time in Pozzuoli and frequented a refreshment stand on the quayside that sold coffee and imitation brandy to the soldiers and sailors. The local ragamuffins swarmed around begging for chocolate and chewing gum. Two decades later, after

Guinness told the story to Sophia, she knew all about it as one of the kids who congregated there.

One night during the filming, Guinness invited Sophia to dinner at one of Madrid's top restaurants. A windy rainstorm was raging as he arrived at her apartment building in a hired limousine to pick her up. Sophia came down to the lobby in a shimmering long white dress. "New," she announced proudly. "First time I wear. For you!"

Guinness opened an umbrella to escort her across the wide sidewalk to the car. Halfway there, Sophia slipped and fell full length into a large puddle, ruining her dress, bruising both hands, and grazing her face. Guinness helped her to get up. For a moment, she seemed in shock, but then said, "I'll put on another dress."

When Guinness took Sophia back to her apartment, he tried to dissuade her from going out at all in such terrible weather, but she wouldn't hear of it. "No, no," she said, "I want to come. Give me five minutes please."

"And within ten minutes," Guinness remembered, "she reappeared in another dazzling outfit, hair rearranged, washed, scented, and with a small Band-Aid on her chin. 'You like this dress, too?' she asked. When I said that indeed I did, she shrugged happily, saying 'I think it is more prettier than the other. But I have lots of dresses, all pretty.' "

They went out and had a wonderful meal together, but Guinness insisted on taking Sophia back to her apartment early. He thought that the combination of the accident and his company might have been too much for her.

Critics would later complain about the paucity of scenes between Sophia and Guinness, whose Marcus Aurelius dies early on and is never seen again in the movie. Some wished that could have happened instead to the Livius of Stephen Boyd, who turned out to be another of those vapid leading men who got wiped off the screen by Sophia's overwhelming presence.

While she was winding up her scenes in *The Fall of the Roman Empire,* Sophia's backlog of movies was starting to catch up with her. *Madame Sans-Gêne* and *Five Miles to Midnight* received their first distribution in Europe and were box-office hits, especially in France, where the historical background of the first film and the pseudo-Hitchcock style of the second seemed the reasons for success. In a poll of French exhibitors, Sophia replaced Brigitte Bardot as the country's most popular female star (the second place Bardot was followed by Jeanne Moreau and Michele Morgan).

Unfortunately, neither movie clicked in the English-speaking world. Critics, who can make or break a suspense chiller, roasted *Five Miles to Midnight,* calling the script moronic and the reteaming of Sophia with Tony Perkins another disaster. One reviewer noted that they seemed to be acting in separate movies and that Perkins "twitched his way through like a person undergoing electric shock treatments." Even Bosley Crowther had to admit that "Sophia Loren is given very little opportunity to display her acknowledged talent for acting."

With its title misleadingly shortened and eroticized to *Madame,* the Napoleonic epic suffered a cruel fate for a $6 million production. Considered too commercial for art theaters and too tedious for mainstream audiences, it was released in the United States only in an English-dubbed version. In New York, the traditional launching pad for foreign films, Joe Levine couldn't get a Broadway or East Side booking, so it wound up having its American premiere as part of a double bill on the Loew's neighborhood circuit. New York was then in the grip of a lengthy newspaper strike, but reviews in other media were bad and Levine pulled the plug. Large sections of the United States never saw *Madame.*

Sophia finished *The Fall of the Roman Empire* just in time to fly to Los Angeles for the Academy Awards show on April 8, 1963. As winner of the 1961 Oscar for Best Actress, she was expected to hand out the 1962 Best Actor award, a reversal-of-the-sexes tradition that started at the second annual ceremony in 1930. Though it wasn't mandatory, Sophia wanted to be there to make up for having been absent on her night of triumph. Ponti accompanied her. None of his films were in the running this year, but he wanted to oblige Joe Levine, who'd worked another miracle for the Italian film industry by shepherding several nominations for producer Franco Cristaldi's *Divorce, Italian Style.*

The Pontis' friend Marcello Mastroianni was, in fact, one of those nominees, but he opted to stay home because he didn't think he had a chance of winning. He commissioned Sophia, who would be opening that particular envelope, to accept for him just in case.

Frank Sinatra emceed the ABC telecast that night. When Sophia walked on in the final minutes, Sinatra introduced her as "the greatest pizza maker in the world." Laughing, she promised to send Sinatra her favorite recipe, and then proceeded to thank the Academy members "for the award you made to me and my country last year." She then read the list of nominees for Best Actor, which besides Mastroianni included Burt Lancaster for *Birdman of Alcatraz;* Jack Lemmon for *Days of Wine and Roses;* Peter O'Toole for *Lawrence of Arabia;* and Gregory Peck for *To Kill a Mockingbird.*

Peck was out of his seat before Sophia finished announcing him as the winner. She bussed him on the cheek as he accepted the Oscar and then read from a speech that he pulled from his pocket. When they finally walked off stage, Sophia asked, "Now when are we going to do a movie together?" If Peck could have foretold the future, he would have answered, "Two years from now."

Sophia lingered backstage to learn who would succeed her in the category of Best Actress. Ironically, the presentation had fallen to last year's Best Actor, Maximilian Schell, which may have given Sophia another reason for hanging around. Anne Bancroft turned out the winner for *The Miracle Worker,* edging out Bette Davis (*Whatever Happened to Baby Jane?*); Katharine Hepburn (*Long Day's Journey into Night*); Geraldine Page (*Sweet Bird of Youth*); and Lee Remick (*Days of Wine and Roses*).

Sophia witnessed a classic case of one-upmanship as Joan Crawford paraded on stage to accept the Oscar for the absent Anne Bancroft. Crawford had been consumed by jealousy ever since Bette Davis, her costar in *Baby Jane,* got nominated and she didn't. Now Crawford was taking her revenge by waving the Oscar in the air as though it belonged to her instead of to Anne Bancroft.

Later, at the gala ball sponsored by the Motion Picture Academy's board of governors, Carlo Ponti transacted a little business. Impressed by the total of seven Oscars that went to Best Picture *Lawrence of Arabia,* he strolled over to congratulate director David Lean and casually asked him if he would be interested in taking on *Doctor Zhivago.* Lean said yes, very much so. They made a date to discuss a deal.

Ponti hurried back to Sophia with the good news. Lean's 1957 *The Bridge on the River Kwai* had also won seven Oscars, including Best Picture. Perhaps in a couple of years, they'd all be back in Hollywood to collect some for *Doctor Zhivago.*

Meanwhile, Ponti was having problems with 20th Century–Fox over *The Condemned of Altona,* which had turned out such a depressing talkathon that the studio was trying to get out of its contract to release it. Whatever happened, Ponti realized that, in the case of future teamings of Sophia and Vittorio De Sica, the movie was a blunder. They should stick to homegrown projects like *La Ciociara,* though not necessarily in that tragic vein.

After *Divorce, Italian Style* was such a hit in America and Marcello Mastroianni came close to equaling Sophia's feat of winning an Oscar for a foreign-language performance, Joe Levine urged Ponti to add Mastroianni to the Loren–De Sica equation and come up with something wonderful. Ponti and De Sica put their heads together and arrived at *Ieri, oggi e domani*

(*Yesterday, Today and Tomorrow*), a multi-episode comedy in the mold of *Boccaccio '70* but with a difference. Instead of separate casts and directors for each of the three stories, Sophia and Mastroianni would play the leading roles in all, under De Sica's command.

With her husband as the producer, *Yesterday, Today and Tomorrow* wound up being slanted in Sophia's favor. Each episode was titled after the character she portrayed. "Adelina," written by the great actor-playwright Eduardo De Filippo and Isabelle Quanantotti, told of a Neapolitan slum-dweller who sells bootleg cigarettes and evades arrest by having babies nonstop until her husband's potency is exhausted and she can no longer take advantage of a law that prohibits the imprisonment of pregnant females. "Anna," Cesare Zavattini's adaptation of a story by Alberto Moravia, concerned the unfaithful wife of a Milanese tycoon and her lover, a struggling writer whom she drops as soon as she realizes that he can never provide her with Rolls-Royce convertibles and all the other luxuries that she's become accustomed to. "Mara," also scripted by Zavattini, revolved around a Rome call girl and one of her steady clients, an oversexed playboy who resents the time she spends with a young neighbor studying for the priesthood.

Since last working with Sophia in *Lucky to Be a Woman* in 1955, Marcello Mastroianni had won international fame comparable to hers, but at a less elevated level due to his reluctance to work outside Europe. He had yet to make any English-language movies or to sign a Hollywood contract. In the United States especially, he was known mainly to moviegoers who patronized art cinemas or might have seen the dubbed versions of *La Dolce Vita* and *Divorce, Italian Style,* which were the first of his films to get wide American distribution.

Carlo Ponti was convinced that Sophia and Mastroianni could become Italy's equivalent of Katharine Hepburn and Spencer Tracy in a series of ribald comedies. He had already assigned De Sica and Eduardo De Filippo to developing a script for the next one, which would be based on De Filippo's phenomenally successful stage play *Filumena Marturano.*

Yesterday, Today and Tomorrow began filming in the summer of 1963, with each episode to be shot on location in the city where it took place. De Sica decided to start with the Rome-based "Mara" to end Sophia's anxiety over the final scene, in which she had to perform a torrid striptease in front of Mastroianni. She'd never even seen a real stripper in action, yet the script required her to be so sexy and provocative that her aroused one-man audience howls like a coyote.

De Sica arranged for Jacques Ruet, the choreographer for the fabled Crazy

Horse Saloon in Paris, to fly to Rome to teach Sophia a few tricks. "I had three
or four sessions with him to learn the basic moves, struts, and teases," she recalled. "But then, using those routines, I had to mold them, with De Sica's help,
into my own personal interpretation."

Sophia also received great help from designer Piero Tosi, who provided two
layers of black lingerie, starting with a camisole with garters for her long stockings, and a scanty bra and panties underneath. On the day of the take, she insisted that the set be cleared except for De Sica, Mastroianni, and the required
camera and sound crew.

"The scene had a fully clothed Mastroianni stretched out on the bed, with
music flooding the room from a record player," Sophia remembered. "I smiled
at Mastroianni. He smiled at me. And then I let him have it. Slowly, sensuously,
tantalizingly, I removed my clothes, letting each article dangle provocatively in
front of his eyes while my body undulated to the throbbing music. . . . De Sica
caught it all—the interplay, the timing, the sexiness, the carnal thunder my tease
set off in Marcello. No scene ever gave me more pleasure."

As remarkable as Sophia's striptease was Mastroianni's reaction when she
abruptly stops and tells him that she can't go any further because she's
promised the student priest that she will remain chaste for one week if he
doesn't quit the seminary. Mastroianni's look of incredulity and one-word utter-
ance of "*Cosa?*" ("What?") helped to make the scene one of the most memorable in the history of the Italian cinema.

Amusingly, just as everybody was getting ready to start the Neapolitan
episode of *Yesterday, Today and Tomorrow,* the real-life counterpart of
"Adelina"—Concetta Musscardo—threatened to shut down production unless
she received compensation. Musscardo, known locally as "Black Market
Connie," was so much a part of Neapolitan folklore that she seemed fair game
for fictional treatment of her tendency to get pregnant whenever she was due
for a jail sentence. But since Musscardo was rumored to have friends in the
Camorra, the Neapolitan Mafia, Ponti agreed to shell out 2 million lire (about
$3,200) to pacify her and to avoid possible strong-arm tactics.

Sophia would spend most of "Adelina" wearing padding under her costumes to simulate pregnancy. As soon as the filming started, she began to feel
like she really was pregnant, but blamed it on too much empathy with the
character she was playing. Still, it wasn't like her to be sick *every* morning, so
she phoned her doctor in Rome and arranged for him to come to Naples to
examine her.

She turned out to be pregnant. "It was a moment of great joy for me," she recalled. When she told Ponti that night, he was thrilled, but also began to worry
about the child's future. In the eyes of Italian law and of the Catholic Church,
the parents were unmarried (or at least to each other). Their progeny would be
stigmatized for life.

Sophia later revealed that the couple had not been practicing birth control
for a long time. She attributed not getting pregnant to her strenuous work
schedule, which had been averaging three or four pictures a year. Why it should
happen now was anybody's guess.

Her gynecologist saw no reason why Sophia couldn't finish *Yesterday, Today
and Tomorrow,* which had another month of filming in Milan after Naples. She
and Ponti decided to keep their news secret for the time being to prevent the
paparazzi from pouncing. UN BASTARDO PER SOPHIA? wasn't a headline that they
were looking forward to.

Two days prior to leaving Naples for Milan, Sophia felt more than the usual
morning sickness and arranged to be driven to her doctor in Rome. He found
nothing seriously wrong, but thought she might have been working too hard.
He advised her to rest in bed for several days and to be more careful when she
resumed filming.

Sophia followed instructions, but within hours of arriving in Milan, she
started to feel real pain. She later recalled the experience: "When I first discovered I was pregnant, I felt the complete woman. Here was the first child of my
life, the complete expression of my love with Carlo. I cried with happiness. I
thought that everything else I had was nothing compared to this gift that God
had given to me. I prayed for that baby. I promised that after motherhood I
wouldn't ask anything more of life. Then suddenly I felt this stabbing pain, as
though hands were reaching out to take the baby from me."

Carlo Ponti got on the phone, and within minutes a local doctor arrived. He
gave Sophia an injection and recommended a few days of bed rest. He arranged
for a nurse to stay overnight just in case.

"That evening, the stabbing pain started again," Sophia recalled. "I told the
nurse that I thought I should go to a hospital immediately. I became very
scared. I found myself crying, 'Oh God, don't let me lose my baby.' "

Sophia didn't want to call for an ambulance because she knew it would also
bring the paparazzi racing. While Ponti arranged for a car to pick them up, the
nurse helped Sophia to get into a robe and they took the hotel service elevator
down to the street. Sophia was in agony and almost passed out, but she man-

aged to get into the car and was rushed to the hospital's emergency room. Sadly, it was too late.

"I felt terribly crushed," Sophia said. "I had been pregnant, and suddenly the life had gone. My world was suddenly not so beautiful. It didn't look as if I could make babies."

Sophia liked to describe herself as a frustrated Mother Earth, a woman who would never feel complete until she had produced at least one child. But her heartbreak over the miscarriage may also have been due to a fear that if she continued childless, she would not receive a fair share of Ponti's wealth when he died. Ponti's will reportedly made Sophia an equal beneficiary with the two children by his first marriage.

Some of the couple's friends claim that from the beginning of the relationship, all of Sophia's earnings were paid directly to Ponti-owned companies and she had no money of her own. Everything, including bank accounts, investments, homes, art collection, and so forth, was in Ponti's name only. Because of her husband's secretive ways, Sophia never knew what percentage of the Ponti fortune came from her own labors, but the prospect of inheriting only one third apparently wasn't making her very happy.

Within hours of the miscarriage, Sophia's gynecologist arrived from Rome. After performing a curettage, he couldn't discover any major reason for pessimism. He prescribed bed rest and urged Sophia to get back to work as soon as she felt stronger. Being involved would relieve her depression and start her on the right track toward a successful pregnancy the next time.

When Sophia returned to *Yesterday, Today and Tomorrow,* De Sica welcomed her back with tears in his eyes. Mastroianni, who'd been told that Sophia was sick but nothing more, reacted less emotionally after she told him the whole truth. He looked at Sophia for a moment and then walked away without saying a word. He never spoke to her about it later on, perhaps believing that recalling such a traumatic experience would only upset her more.

None of Sophia's personal sorrow was evident in her performance in "Anna," the remaining episode of the movie. She had at least one good reason to be happy. The exquisite Rolls-Royce "Silver Cloud" convertible used in some of the scenes was hers for the keeping when production ended, another of the advantages to living with a producer who was a master at such deals. The manufacturer was all too happy to get worldwide exposure worth millions in exchange for just one car that retailed then at $28,000.

Amusingly, when Christmastime came around, Sophia decided to give the

Rolls to Joe Levine in appreciation for all that he'd done for the Pontis over the years. The gift, of course, didn't cost Sophia anything, but Levine ended up paying $3,000 to have it shipped to New York and another $15,000 in import tax. Still, that was much less than the same model Rolls sold for in the United States.

Sophia took a much-needed break when *Yesterday, Today and Tomorrow* finished, but with Carlo Ponti as a companion, it could never be a vacation from the movie business. Their joint deals, as well as those that Ponti had on his own, were always hovering in the air and keeping the phones and telex machines busy twenty-four hours a day because of the variances in time between Rome, London, New York, and Los Angeles.

In October 1963, *The Condemned of Altona* opened in the United States to unfavorable reviews and near empty theaters. One critic called it "stupid and inexplicable, with acting and direction as heavy-handed as the script." Many expressed regret that Sophia and De Sica had fallen so far since *Two Women*. Ponti had struck out again in his attempts to produce home runs for the major Hollywood studios.

He was also having problems with some of his coproductions with Joe Levine. Both were appalled by Jean-Luc Godard's *Contempt (Le mépris)* and demanded extensive cuts in the tedious dramatic scenes, plus the addition of more nude footage of star Brigitte Bardot. Godard reacted by going to court in France, which only resulted in the movie finally being released in three different versions, French, Italian, and English, all flops.

Sophia got dragged into Ponti's ordeal with Bette Davis, costarring with Horst Buchholz and Catherine Spaak in his Levine coproduction, *The Empty Canvas,* which was filmed in Rome that autumn. It was Davis's first experience working in a European studio and with a director who spoke minimal English, the Italian Damiano Damiani. Not surprisingly, the temperamental Hollywood legend found fault with everything, starting with her wardrobe, which she rejected. When Ponti couldn't get anywhere with her, he asked Sophia to intercede. Sophia took Davis to the salon of designer-friend Simonetta and helped her to select new dresses and gowns.

Sophia tried to be a friend to Davis throughout production, taking her shopping and sightseeing, and inviting her to dinner parties at home. But the fifty-five-year-old Davis seemed to resent any actress younger and prettier than she was, and they never became close. The coddling didn't seem to help *The Empty Canvas,* which became a low point in Davis's career, memorable only for her bizarre blond wig and for her use of a Texas-Louisiana drawl to portray the rich American mother of her German costar.

In addition to his European coproduction deals with Joe Levine, Ponti was looking for a home for *Doctor Zhivago,* which required the multimillion-dollar financing that only a major Hollywood studio could provide. After David Lean agreed to direct, the rest was easy. Metro-Goldwyn-Mayer, which had been on the rocks in recent years and was trying to make a comeback under its new president, Robert O'Brien, wanted the movie desperately. When Ponti realized that, he carved out a deal with MGM for three more pictures beyond *Zhivago,* with subjects to be decided later.

Ponti made it plain to David Lean that he expected Sophia to be cast as Lara. "Fine, providing you can convince me she can play a seventeen-year-old virgin," Lean said. Flabbergasted, Ponti left it to MGM's president to decide. O'Brien agreed with Lean, which explains why Julie Christie finally got the role after Lean saw rushes of her work in the still-filming *Darling.*

Lean was a crusty Briton who took no orders from producers. As soon as Ponti realized that, he gave Lean a free hand in the decision-making and was seldom heard from during the two years it took to produce and edit the movie. "I didn't see him again until the night of the world premiere," Lean once joked.

With Ponti's new deal at MGM, which was in addition to the one that he had with Joe Levine, life became more complicated than ever, a division of time between the projects that involved Sophia and those that didn't. At present, she was contracted for another De Sica–Mastroianni teaming and would undoubtedly land in some of Ponti's MGM films.

United Artists was also pursuing Sophia for a rematch with Peter Sellers in *A Shot in the Dark,* a mystery comedy that was a hit on the Broadway stage in 1961 with Julie Harris as a French parlor maid suspected of murder and William Shatner as the detective on the case. But Sellers didn't like the play in its present form and wanted to turn it into a vehicle for the "Inspector Clouseau" character that he'd played so successfully in *The Pink Panther.* Sophia balked when she read the revision, which reduced her role to that of Sellers's slapstick stooge, so she passed and Elke Sommer eventually took the part.

Franco Zeffirelli spoke to Sophia about teaming with Mastroianni in Shakespeare's *The Taming of the Shrew,* which the director intended filming on the actual locales in Italy. Sophia was willing, but Mastroianni declined because of his inadequate English. Several years later, Elizabeth Taylor and Richard Burton were looking for a joint project, and Zeffirelli stumbled on his stars.

Six weeks after finishing *Yesterday, Today and Tomorrow,* Ponti was ready to roll with Sophia's next collaboration with Mastroianni and De Sica. Because Mastroianni's *Divorce, Italian Style* had been such a hit in America, Joe Levine insisted that the new movie be titled *Marriage, Italian Style,* which probably made box-office sense. But anyone expecting a sequel, or in this case a pre-quel, would be disappointed because the two films had nothing else in common beyond their ribald humor.

In view of Sophia and Ponti's ongoing marital tribulations, the title of *Marriage, Italian Style* may have been too personal for comfort and certainly seemed capable of provoking their Italian adversaries. Based on a play written in 1947, long before the couple even met, it had nothing to do with their own relationship, though the two main characters were reminiscent of Sophia and Ponti in certain ways.

Marriage, Italian Style had been filmed once before, in 1951, under its original title *Filumena marturano,* with actor-author Eduardo De Filippo and Tamara Lees in the leading roles. De Filippo updated it to current-day Naples, but Filumena remained the driving force of the story. The role was one of the juiciest and most demanding in Italian stage repertory, providing Sophia with a real challenge after the three comparatively simple parts she'd acted in *Yesterday, Today and Tomorrow.*

Filumena ages twenty years in the story, which flashes back and forth in a period between the present and wartorn 1943, when she started working as a prostitute in a Naples brothel. Her very first client is Domenico Soriano, a pros-perous businessman who becomes her ardent swain. Domenico is a confirmed bachelor-playboy and has no intention of marrying Filumena, but he sets her up as his mistress, providing her with an apartment and a job managing a *pastic-ceria* that he owns. As time passes, Filumena never gives up hope that Domenico will marry her, but he keeps finding excuses not to. Filumena walks out several times, but always returns and finally winds up as his live-in house-keeper and companion to his invalid mother.

When Domenico becomes involved with a much younger woman and announces wedding plans, Filumena concocts an elaborate plot to snare him for herself. Pretending to be fatally ill, she persuades Domenico to marry her on her deathbed so that her soul can go to heaven. Once she's Signora Soriano, Filumena springs back to life and demands her wifely rights. Domenico accuses her of fraud and vows to get an annulment. Filumena trumps him by revealing the existence of three sons that she's been secretly supporting for years, one of whom she claims is Domenico's. He refuses to believe her, but as he investigates, he comes to the conclusion that he might have fathered all three boys. As he finally resigns himself to having an instant family, Filumena weeps for joy.

Coming so soon after *Yesterday, Today and Tomorrow, Marriage, Italian Style* proved an ordeal for De Sica, who at sixty-two wasn't as resilient as he used to be. "Vittorio was really a tired man during the shooting," Mastroianni recalled. "But he could still find the time to protect Sophia. She had a difficult role, and he did everything possible to make it easier for her. There was a great sense of mutual trust in the way they got along with one another. They understood each other's sense of humor; they had their deep bond of being Neapolitans."

The movie had nothing to match the eroticism of Sophia's striptease sequence in the two stars' previous collaboration. But the costume that Piero Tosi designed for her in some of the bordello scenes created the sexiest sensation since her water-soaked pearl diver's dress in *Boy on a Dolphin*. The transparent, tight-fitting black negligee had a built-in bra with small embroidered spiders to hide her nipples. Underneath, she wore only black bikini panties, which gave an almost unobstructed view of her voluptuous, bell-shaped figure and long, shapely legs. Photos and pinup posters of Sophia in the outfit have sold in the hundreds of thousands in the decades since.

VILLA PONTI'S
TREASURES

W I T H *Doctor Zhivago* filming at studios in Spain and virtually on automatic pilot as far as Carlo Ponti was concerned, he started negotiating with MGM on his next projects. They settled on two: *Operation Crossbow,* a World War II espionage thriller that Ponti had been developing with two Italian writers, and *Lady L,* which had already cost MGM several million dollars in losses due to an aborted filming in 1961. Ponti made sure that Sophia would be in both. MGM was delighted to get her for *Lady L* after their previous experience with her longtime rival Gina Lollobrigida, whose inadequate performance in the title role caused them to pull the plug after two weeks.

1964 promised to be the Year of Sophia Loren. With two De Sica–Mastroianni movies and *The Fall of the Roman Empire* due for release, she would be on theater screens everywhere, and at the same time be building up a stockpile for the future. While readying the two MGM projects, Ponti made a separate deal for Sophia to play the title role in *Judith,* a cloak-and-dagger epic set in the first year of Israel's statehood. Ponti may have been a silent partner in the movie, which had a mysterious pedigree and credited an inexperienced Israeli named Kurt Unger as the producer. Paramount Pictures had taken on the distribution and also contributed some of the $6 million budget, allegedly at the instigation of studio chief Jacob H. Karp, who was a power in the United Jewish Appeal and who reportedly saw the film as helpful to Israel's image.

As if Sophia didn't have enough to occupy her, she also signed up for her second American television special, this one to be filmed in color for ABC under the title *Sophia Loren in Rome.* It was the latest in a series of travelogues that had previously featured Elizabeth Taylor conducting a tour of her native London, Jacqueline Kennedy showing off the White House, and Princess Grace touting the sights of Monaco.

In addition to her $100,000 fee, Sophia demanded participation in writer-director Sheldon Reynolds's script. Her longtime associate Basilio Franchina contributed most of Sophia's dialogue and helped to select location sites. In her opening spiel, Sophia would say: "You cannot tell Rome's story in an hour, but for an hour you can feel it, and permit it to touch you."

The special ran less than an hour due to the commercial breaks, but Sophia had more costume changes than she did in some of her movies—a suit and three dresses, all designed by Marc Bohan of Christian Dior and hers to keep afterwards.

Sophia Loren in Rome would be telecast in November 1964, but filming took place that spring before she started her next movie. While working with the American production crew, Sophia always carried a deck of cards with her and would call for poker partners during the breaks. She displayed an incredible knack for drawing winning hands. Some might call it cheating, but if you're an adored superstar and the chips are only hundred-lire coins (about 16 cents then), you can usually get away with it.

Sophia's tour itinerary included all the expected fountains and ancient ruins, plus Rome's notorious traffic jams and a staged accident that demonstrated how crowds gathered at the slightest bumper denting. There was also a stop at Marcello Mastroianni's villa on the via Appia. Though Mastroianni tried his best to speak English with Sophia, he was so hard to understand that ABC later printed subtitles on the scene for the broadcast.

By the time of the filming of the TV special, Sophia and Mastroianni were well on their way to becoming the hottest screen couple of recent years. *Yesterday, Today and Tomorrow* had opened to rave reviews and record-breaking business. In the United States, where it was following the route of *Two Women* and being shown only in art theaters with English subtitles, it was shaping up as one of the most successful foreign-made releases of all time.

Ironically, *Yesterday, Today and Tomorrow* was doing much better business than *The Fall of the Roman Empire*, which opened in the U.S. at the same time on a reserved-seat, road show policy. Savaged by the critics as a ponderous bore, it eventually had a moderate success in the international market but never came anywhere near recouping its $25 million investment. Producer Samuel Bronston went bankrupt and never made another film.

As in the case of *Two Women*, Joe Levine started pounding the Oscar drums early for *Yesterday, Today and Tomorrow*. The movie seemed assured of nominations, but there could be a complication. He was committed to releasing *Marriage, Italian* Style in December. The two movies were likely to be competing with each other for awards, but he should be so lucky.

The earnings from the duo would hopefully make up for the losses that Ponti and Levine were suffering on some of their other joint projects. After the flop of Jean-Luc Godard's *Contempt*, Levine backed out of Ponti's next Godard, *A Woman Is a Woman*, with Jean-Paul Belmondo and Anna Karina, which was taken up by other distributors but also bombed. Additional disappointments for Ponti and Levine were Claude Chabrol's *Landru*, or *Bluebeard* as it was titled outside France, and Marco Ferreri's *The Ape Woman*, with Annie Girardot and Ugo Tognazzi. In the United States, the subtitled movies played in art theaters only and quickly disappeared.

With Sophia booked solidly ahead for MGM and Paramount projects, Ponti and Levine had to do some fast thinking about their next coproduction. Marcello Mastroianni seemed their best box-office insurance, so Ponti put some scriptwriters to work and came up with *Casanova '70*, deliberately reminiscent of the hit *Boccaccio '70* and a similar modernization of a ribald classic. Set up as an Italian-French coproduction, the movie would costar Virna Lisi, Michele Mercier, and Marisa Mell, with Mario Monicelli, director of the discarded fourth episode of *Boccaccio '70*, at the helm.

Obviously, with Ponti juggling so many movies at once, Sophia had to contend with frequent separations while he traveled on business. One of their longest started in the summer of 1964, when Sophia left Rome for Israel to begin *Judith*. Ponti, meanwhile, settled in London for the duration of *Operation Crossbow*, which was being filmed at Pinewood Studios.

Although Sophia was the top-billed star of both movies, *Operation Crossbow* was something of a cheat in that respect. She appeared in just a few scenes, amounting to about ten minutes of screen time, and would film them when she finished *Judith*.

Sophia would naturally be the whole show in *Judith*, which was based on an unpublished novella by Lawrence Durrell, the Anglo-Irish writer best known for *The Alexandria Quartet*. Named after the Biblical heroine, Judith is a European Jew who survived the Nazi concentration camps. On the eve of Israeli independence, she arrives in Palestine to hunt for the Nazi husband who betrayed her and abducted their infant son.

Paramount hired JP Miller, author of *Days of Wine and Roses,* to write the script. Since Durrell's original work was hardly more than a sketch, Miller spent six weeks in Israel doing research and living on a kibbutz near Tel Aviv. Though Miller was a self-described Texas goy, he developed great sympathy for the Israeli cause and injected a strong dose of anti-Arab politics into the story.

When Paramount sent the script to Sophia, Carlo Ponti read it first and was horrified. Sophia was a huge box-office attraction in the Arab world. *Judith* could ruin her there and start an Arab boycott of all her films. Miller tried toning down the script, but when Ponti still wasn't satisfied, the writer quit and requested that his name be removed from the credits. Paramount then turned the script over to John Michael Hayes, who'd just adapted Harold Robbins's *The Carpetbaggers* for the studio. Hayes's changes satisfied Ponti, but whether they would the Arabs was too soon to tell.

The final scenario boiled down to Judith working for the Haganah underground, which suspects that her ex-Nazi husband is now collaborating with the Arabs and needs her to identify him. A romance develops between Judith and the Haganah leader, but takes a back seat to the hunt for the fugitive war criminal. When Judith's husband is finally captured, she's overjoyed by the revelation that their son is still alive. But before she can learn the boy's whereabouts, the father is killed by a stray shell during an Arab attack. The film ends inconclusively, with Judith's lover vowing to help her to locate her son.

Peter Finch, who'd been dividing his time between British movies and the London stage after an unsuccessful bid at Hollywood stardom, accepted the role of the Haganah leader. Jack Hawkins would portray a British major, with the German actor Hans Verner as Judith's husband.

Sophia may have been the only star to work with all three of the major Hollywood directors bearing the family name Mann (none of them related). After Delbert Mann and Anthony Mann, she got Daniel Mann for *Judith*. The most lauded of the Manns, Daniel had guided Sophia's compatriot, Anna Magnani, to an Oscar in *The Rose Tattoo,* and did the same for Shirley Booth in *Come Back, Little Sheba* and Elizabeth Taylor in *Butterfield 8.*

Whether Mann could help Sophia to win an Oscar for *Judith* seemed improbable, but not impossible. The script gave her many highly charged emotional scenes, though they were mixed with moments of unintentional hilarity. The opening scene, where Judith is smuggled into Palestine to skirt British immigration restrictions, became one of the most memorable of Sophia's career, but for the wrong reasons. After a huge packing case is unloaded from a cargo ship and broken open, Sophia emerges like a magnificent Venus on the half-shell, all glowing and dewy-eyed despite an arduous sea voyage that obviously proved too much for her dead stowaway companion.

Once Judith moves into a kibbutz, Sophia's wardrobe consists mainly of tight blouses and the briefest of shorts. Moviegoers would later howl and whistle at some of her bouncy gyrations, which outdid those of her old rival, Silvana Mangano, in *Bitter Rice*.

Judith was filmed in the Mediterranean port city of Haifa and in Nahariya, a coastal town near Israel's northern border with Lebanon. At the time, an uneasy truce existed between Israel and the Arab countries, supervised by a United Nations emergency force since the cease-fire following hostilities in 1956. The Israeli Army assigned a squadron of commandos to guard Sophia and the rest of the company, but there were no problems.

Daniel Mann later described the filming as a happy experience because Israel was still a young nation and most of the locals who worked on the movie had actually lived through the events depicted in it. Many of the extras were simply re-creating their arrivals on the beaches from illegal ships. One woman, who came straight to Israel from one of the Nazi concentration camps, once again fell on her knees for the movie cameras and kissed the sand.

Since Sophia's costar, Peter Finch, had a reputation for romancing his leading ladies, the production crew watched eagerly for something to develop. Some members believe it did, but the two stars never confessed to anything more than mutual affection and respect. "Sophia is not a woman you ever make a pass at if you happen to be alone with her," Finch said later. "She is one of those marvelous natural creations you feast your eyes on and leave it at that. Her whole attitude is professional, with no emotional undertow to drag you off course, and what a sense of humor! I once caught her gorging on a mountain of spaghetti and she said, 'I'm making up for two thousand years of Neapolitan poverty.'"

Years later, when news reached her that Finch had died suddenly from a heart attack at age sixty, Sophia told a reporter: "Peter was one of the gentlest, kindest, and most talented partners it has ever been my luck to work with. I know these may be the conventional words you speak in such sad circumstances, but they are true."

Sophia may have forgotten by then, but during the filming of *Judith,* Finch was so addicted to alcohol that she feared he'd kill himself. After work, he usually went out and got absolutely plastered. Finch didn't just stagger on his feet.

He also became violent, one night smashing furniture in the cocktail lounge of his hotel.

After three months in Israel with *Judith,* Sophia took off for England to join Ponti for the completion of *Operation Crossbow.* With the exception of *Doctor Zhivago,* the epic about an Allied attempt to destroy a German base for V-2 rockets was the most expensive undertaking of Ponti's career so far. Most of MGM's $12 million went to the visual effects, which included a spectacular chase through an underground rocket factory and a climactic chain-reaction explosion that was one of the most colossal ever filmed. Ponti assigned the direction to Britisher Michael Anderson, who was best known for the Oscar-winning *Around the World in 80 Days* but had also made *The Dam Busters,* one of the classics in the field of World War II sagas.

Operation Crossbow was Ponti's attempt to copy the 1961 blockbuster hit *The Guns of Navarone,* but with more basis in historical fact. But secret mission "Crossbow" was a fictitious blend of many operations by the Allies intended to destroy German rocket bases.

Although Sophia received top billing in *Operation Crossbow,* the real stars were the up-and-coming George Peppard, Tom Courtenay, and Jeremy Kemp, who portray a trio of Allied scientist-officers parachuted into Nazi-occupied Holland to find the source of the V-2s that are currently terrorizing England. For box-office insurance, Ponti hired a supporting cast of well-known "names," including Trevor Howard, John Mills, Lilli Palmer, Paul Henreid, Anthony Quayle, and Richard Todd.

Sophia makes a short but highly dramatic appearance halfway through the movie as the wife of a Dutch engineer who works in the Nazi rocket factory. Unwittingly, she almost causes George Peppard's arrest when he turns out to be using forged identity papers in her husband's name. Rather than betray Peppard, Sophia vouches for him to the Nazi authorities and ends up being executed when her lie is discovered.

Due to *Operation Crossbow* being filmed randomly in bits and pieces that were later edited together in the correct order, Sophia never got to work with most of the huge cast of actors and extras. Costar Tom Courtenay recalled: "When you see the film, there's a scene where George Peppard says good-bye to me and then turns to greet Sophia, but all three of us were never on set together. In fact, I finished my scenes before Sophia started hers. I never met her at all."

In December 1964, *Marriage, Italian Style* entered release and repeated the success of *Yesterday, Today and Tomorrow*. Bosley Crowther, who seemed to have forgotten that he'd blasted Sophia's collaboration with De Sica in *Boccaccio '70,* wrote that

> Whenever Vittorio De Sica gets together with Sophia Loren to make a motion picture, something wonderful happens . . . a film so frank and free and understanding of a certain kind of woman—and man, too—that it sends you forth from the theater feeling you've known her—and him—all your life. Miss Loren is delightfully eccentric, flashy and formidable, yet stiff in her middle-class rigidity and often poignant in her real anxieties.

Ponti and Joe Levine were deadlocked over which of their two De Sica–Loren–Mastroianni movies should get the major push for 1964 awards. Neither film received any prizes from the New York Film Critics, which suggested that the two canceled each other out in the voting. As Oscar time rolled around, the producers decided to hedge their bets by supporting *Yesterday, Today and Tomorrow* for Best Foreign Film and *Marriage, Italian Style* for the categories that had no language restrictions, such as Best Actor and Best Actress.

Although Sophia's next movie would be MGM's *Lady L,* Ponti had a batch of new deals brewing for her. Crazy though it might seem, Arthur Miller wanted Sophia for the film of his controversial stage play, *After the Fall,* which critics had blasted as shameless exploitation of his now deceased second wife. With the utterly different Sophia Loren playing the self-destructive main character, Miller intended to prove that the play was *not* about Marilyn Monroe. Ponti didn't care whether it was or it wasn't. It seemed a wonderful dramatic role for Sophia, and Miller had already persuaded the revered Fred Zinnemann to direct the film.

Alfred Hitchcock also coveted Sophia—and Mastroianni—for a comical murder mystery based on the director's own idea. The story revolved around an Italian couple that runs a hotel in New York and staffs it with immigrant relatives, one of whom turns out to be an assassin for the Mafia.

A third possibility for Sophia was Ponti's own production of the life story of Mother Cabrini, the Italian-American nun who was the first U.S. citizen to be canonized. But as soon as Ponti announced his plans to the press, the project was immediately denounced by the Mission Sisters of the Sacred Heart of Jesus, the order that Mother Cabrini founded. Its spokesperson, Mother Ursula, president of Cabrini College in Pennsylvania, said that "Miss Loren is the worst possible choice to portray a holy woman. In the first place, there are bigamy charges against her in Italy. Secondly, she doesn't have the physique. Mother Cabrini was a small, slender woman. Miss Loren is bulky."

None of those projects ever got off the ground, but a fourth did. Producer-director Stanley Donen, whose *Charade* with Cary Grant and Audrey Hepburn had recently been a box-office smash, wanted to team Sophia with Gregory Peck in a similar romantic thriller entitled *Arabesque*. Donen intended to start production in England at the end of April, which suited Sophia perfectly because she expected to be finished with *Lady L* by then. Although Donen had no script to show her yet, she agreed to do it because of the opportunity to work with Gregory Peck, which she had asked for two years before at the Oscar ceremonies.

The new year of 1965 promised finally to bring a resolution to matrimonial questions. In January, after two years of legal maneuvering that included buying an apartment in Paris to prove residency, Sophia and Ponti became citizens of France. Premier Georges Pompidou personally signed the papers and was immediately blasted by the leadership of the Left for buckling under to the couple's wealth and fame.

Ponti's French citizenship also passed automatically to his wife, Giuliana. After six months as a citizen, she would be eligible to sue for a divorce under French law. Mrs. Ponti now seemed to control the destiny of her successor, but evidenced no outward signs of hostility. After thirteen years of putting up with Ponti's liaison with Sophia, she was happy to finally be relieved of all the embarrassment and humiliation it had caused her.

Meanwhile, Sophia and Ponti were getting ready to start *Lady L,* their second collaboration for MGM. Set up as a French-Italian coproduction, the movie would use Paris studios for the interior scenes, with location work in Nice, Monte Carlo, and Switzerland, as well as at the awe-inspiring five hundred-room Castle Howard in Yorkshire, England.

Based on the novel by Romain Gary, *Lady L* told the life story of eighty-year-old Lady Louise Lendale, a pillar of the English aristocracy who started out as a laundress in her native Corsica, later worked as a chambermaid in a Paris brothel, and eventually married the impotent heir to a landowning fortune. Along the way, she also kept up a passionate love affair with an outlaw anarchist who is the real father of her three Lendale children and has been working as the family's chauffeur for many years.

Ponti scrapped most of what he inherited from MGM's aborted 1961 *Lady L* (directed by George Cukor, with Gina Lollobrigida, Tony Curtis, and Ralph Richardson in the leads) and started over by signing Peter Ustinov to direct and to write the script. Ironically, Ustinov had portrayed the depraved Nero in Sophia's very first movie, *Quo Vadis,* but in recent years he'd been dividing his time between acting, directing, and writing stage plays and movie scripts. Ustinov's acclaimed 1962 screen version of *Billy Budd,* based on a complex and seemingly unfilmable novel by Herman Melville, encouraged Ponti to select him for *Lady L,* which had similar problems due to a kaleidoscopic plot that covered eight decades spanning two centuries.

MGM, which already intended to release Ponti's *Doctor Zhivago* as a reserved-seat, roadshow attraction, instructed him to deliver the same with *Lady L.* Ustinov happily complied, because a movie running three hours or so would enable him to develop the characters more fully and to retain the heart and soul of Romain Gary's novel.

Ponti struck lucky in the casting. Paul Newman "owed" MGM a movie under a long-term, nonexclusive contract with the studio, so he accepted the role of Armand, Lady L's anarchist lover. Newman had become Hollywood's hottest male star since his riveting Oscar-nominated performances in *The Hustler* and *Hud.* Sophia was thrilled to get him.

Ustinov selected close friend David Niven to portray Sophia's husband, Lord Lendale. Though a veteran of pre–World War II Hollywood, Niven had become more popular than ever since starring in *Around the World in 80 Days,* winning an Oscar for *Separate Tables,* and playing the debonair jewel thief in *The Pink Panther.* At age fifty-five, Niven was old enough to be Sophia's father, but in portraying her husband, he would require less makeup than she did in the scenes of their old age.

Sophia's main worry about *Lady L* was the aging, which required her to grow gradually from a teenage virgin into a wrinkled dowager. Going on thirty-one herself, Sophia was well past innocence but still a long way from maturity. Her oldest screen age so far had been forty-six, in portions of *Marriage, Italian Style.*

Fortunately, the script used a flashback technique, and the elderly Lady L appears only in the opening and closing scenes, while she's reminiscing with her authorized biographer. Ustinov shot those moments first to relieve Sophia of the ordeal of spending four hours in makeup every morning while the ravages of fifty years were applied.

"When Sophia first saw herself made up to be eighty, she burst into tears,"

Ustinov recalled. "We all carry a hidden old man or woman within us. The nose starts slumping or overhanging a bit, the rest of the face shrinks. Sophia suddenly realized that she probably would look like that at eighty, and that's why she cried."

The biggest technical problem, according to Ustinov, was "trying to make Sophia look like a great shelf. You can't have her kind of blooming body for an old woman. We managed to lower the bosom down to her midsection. I could understand why she got so depressed whenever she looked in the mirror."

Paul Newman and David Niven relied mainly on wigs and hair dye as their characters grew older. Newman caused an uproar when he grew a mustache for his role. While doing research, he couldn't find one photograph of an anarchist without a mustache, so he insisted on one. When the MGM brass saw the first rushes, they were horrified and demanded the clean-shaven look that made him a sex symbol. Newman threatened to walk, the mustache stayed, and MGM later regretted not taking a firmer stand.

For all his magnetism, Newman couldn't match Sophia's and the teaming failed to sizzle. Ustinov later blamed it on their different acting styles. "Sophia is almost too good to work with, too obedient," he said. "But at the same time, she is enormously astute. Her feminine instinct has an unerring wisdom to it. She's capable of moving any way a director requires her to, but she'll challenge you if she feels you don't know what you're doing."

Like Anthony Perkins and Anthony Quinn, Newman was another nitpicker from the Actors Studio. "Paul likes discussing everything, sometimes for a couple of hours," Ustinov said. "You had to steel yourself from being worn out by Method conversation about interpretation, which left you groggy at the end. Sophia just waited there as patiently as I did, saying, 'When's he going to stop?' "

Sophia found Ustinov to be less of an instructing director than Vittorio De Sica, but equally effective. "Peter's secret is that he leaves actors free to do what they want in a scene," she said in an interview at the time. "He creates a wonderful atmosphere on the set, one joke after another, and with him it is all spontaneous. He makes me feel like I am relaxing at home with friends rather than working at a studio."

While Sophia and Ustinov were filming in Switzerland, Noel Coward and his longtime companion Cole Lesley invited them to dinner at their mountain chalet in Les Avants. "Two days later," Coward remembered in his diary, "Coley and I stood about for hours in the withering cold watching them shoot some scenes on the lakeside at Montreux. She is a dear, I think, and a hundred per cent professional. Peter seemed to be a bit woolly and indecisive, but he is a brilliant creature and I am very fond of him. I don't think, however, that I would like to be directed by him. He is very slow."

At the end of his visit, Coward told Sophia, "You should have been sculpted in chocolate truffles so the world could devour you."

Midway through the filming of *Lady L*, the announcement of the nominees for the 1964 Oscars caused Carlo Ponti to order champagne and to throw a party on the set. *Yesterday, Today and Tomorrow* had been nominated for Best Foreign-Language Feature, while Sophia was up for Best Actress for *Marriage, Italian Style*. As luck would have it, Peter Ustinov also received a nomination in the category of Best Supporting Actor, for his performance as the grubby police informer in *Topkapi*.

With their commitments to *Lady L*, none of the nominees could attend the Academy Awards ceremony in California in April. Sophia lost out to Julie Andrews for *Mary Poppins*. The other Best Actress nominees were Anne Bancroft (*The Pumpkin Eater*), Debbie Reynolds (*The Unsinkable Molly Brown*), and Kim Stanley (*Seance on a Wet Afternoon*). Julie Andrews reportedly received an overwhelming majority of the vote in sympathy for her losing the movie version of *My Fair Lady* to Audrey Hepburn, whose performance that same year didn't even land her among the Oscar nominees.

Sophia could console herself with the fact that *Yesterday, Today and Tomorrow* won the foreign-language award, nosing out France's *The Umbrellas of Cherbourg*, Japan's *Woman in the Dunes*, Sweden's *Raven's End*, and Israel's *Sallah*. Joe Levine accepted the Oscar in Ponti's behalf. Between them, Sophia and Ponti now had three Oscars to display in their trophy case, including the one he had received for *La Strada*, 1956's Best Foreign Language Film.

The Oscar recognition helped to add several million dollars to the grosses of *Yesterday, Today and Tomorrow* and also bounced off on *Marriage, Italian Style*, which had played only limited engagements at the end of 1964 and now profited from the popularity of the Loren–Mastroianni–De Sica team.

While Sophia was red hot at the boxoffice, MGM decided to launch *Operation Crossbow*, which, of course, was targeted at a different audience from her foreign-language films. It became the first of Sophia's movies (and Ponti's) to premiere at New York's 6,000-seat Radio City Music Hall, where it was the Easter 1965 feature, accompanied by the annual holiday stage show.

Operation Crossbow set new box-office records at the Music Hall, but no one could really tell whether the movie or the Easter pageant was the main draw.

When *Operation Crossbow* entered general release, it did moderate business but never became the box-office blockbuster that MGM hoped for. Sophia's fans may have stayed away when they learned that she appeared in only ten minutes of the two-hour film.

The completion of *Lady L* forced another temporary separation as Sophia left for England to get ready for *Arabesque* and Ponti returned to Italy to attend to some of his own productions. After viewing some of the rushes of *Doctor Zhivago,* Ponti became convinced that its leading actor, Omar Sharif, would emerge a major star. He wanted to be the first to benefit by teaming Sharif in something with Sophia. Meanwhile, Ponti was about to start his latest co-venture with Joe Levine, *The Tenth Victim,* a futuristic thriller with Marcello Mastroianni and Ursula Andress in the leads and Elio Petri directing.

Sophia's rented home for the duration of *Arabesque* was much smaller than Lady L's castle in Yorkshire, but the Georgian country house near Ascot in Berkshire had every modern convenience and plenty of room for her entourage. Prior to settling in, Sophia stopped in Paris for costume fittings with Christian Dior's Marc Bohan, who designed all of her outfits and the twenty-five pairs of footwear that went with them.

Due to the success of *Charade,* wherein Audrey Hepburn made fashion news in her Givenchy creations, producer-director Stanley Donen was able to persuade Universal to spend a bundle on garbing Sophia similarly. Marc Bohan's bill for what he described in fashion gibberish as "a kind of ornamentation consisting of fantastic interlacing patterns" reportedly amounted to $125,000. Whatever the cost, Sophia's closets would bulge some more when she took them home at the end of production.

Cary Grant, who'd been Stanley Donen's financial partner in several of their movies together, was originally supposed to star in *Arabesque.* But after taking flak from the critics for his love scenes with the considerably younger Audrey Hepburn in *Charade,* Grant decided that he'd grown too old to continue playing romantic roles. He recommended that best friend Gregory Peck, his junior by twelve years, replace him in *Arabesque.* No doubt Grant also nominated Sophia for leading lady. He was still very fond of her, often phoning her long-distance just to chat and gossip.

Arabesque repeated a plot device used in *Charade,* where the audience never knew for certain whether Cary Grant was the hero or the murderer until the climax. This time the mystery surrounded Sophia as Yasmin Azir, the mistress of a murderous Arab tycoon who's plotting to take over the world's oil supply. The two need Gregory Peck, an American exchange professor at Oxford University, to help them decipher a secret message written in hiero-glyphics.

Instead of the Paris of *Charade, Arabesque* used London, Oxford, Ascot, and the English countryside for backgrounds. As he did for *Charade,* Henry Mancini composed the title song and musical score. The title *Arabesque* suggested un-dulating suspense but also played on the word "Arab," a major element in the story. Stanley Donen chose it over *Cipher,* the title of the Gordon Cotler novel on which the script was loosely based.

Friends claimed that Gregory Peck had been taking himself too seriously as an actor since winning the Oscar for *To Kill a Mockingbird.* But Sophia found him amiable and easy to work with, though his technique lacked the comedic sparkle of Cary Grant.

One of their first scenes together required the fugitive Peck to run and hide in a shower stall occupied by the nude Sophia. Since they hardly knew each other, he tried to put her at ease. "Don't be embarrassed," he told her. "It's all in the game. Strictly professional."

Sophia looked Peck straight in the eye and giggled. "What makes you think I would be embarrassed?" she asked as she slipped out of her bathrobe and into the shower. "Absolutely nothing at all," Peck replied, as soon as he caught his breath.

Later in the film, Sophia and Peck are being chased through a cornfield by villains driving a deadly threshing machine. Since suffering a broken ankle in a horseriding accident some years before, Peck had had difficulty running, so he couldn't keep up with Sophia, who kept getting well ahead of him. Finally, he pleaded with her, "Sophia, will you please slow down? Remember, I'm sup-posed to be rescuing you."

Sophia just laughed and said, "Oh, you can do better than that. Just try a bit harder." Waving to director Donen, she shouted, "Make him run faster." But Peck was in such pain that Sophia finally had to cooperate or there would have been no scene.

One day while Sophia was relaxing in her dressing room, one of her child-hood idols phoned to praise her work in *Yesterday, Today and Tomorrow* and to request an audience. When Sophia established that it really was Charlie Chaplin on the line, she invited him to tea at her rented house near Ascot.

The chunky little white-haired man of seventy-six who turned up hardly re-minded Sophia of the bowler-hatted elf of *The Gold Rush* and *Modern Times,* but he handed her a bouquet of red roses and shyly explained the reason for his visit. He had just signed a deal with Universal Pictures for his first movie in ten years and wanted Sophia and Marlon Brando to play the starring roles.

Opening a script outline that he brought with him, Chaplin gave a capsule run-through, acting out all the different parts, including a small one intended for himself. Sophia was too entranced by Chaplin's performance to concentrate on the story. When he finished and told her that she wouldn't have to make up her mind until he had a completed screenplay, she replied, "I don't have to read the script. I make the film for you even if you just want me to read the telephone directory."

After Chaplin left, Sophia phoned Carlo Ponti in Rome and told him to go easy in making a deal. She wanted nothing to stand in the way of working with the man she called "the patron saint of laughter."

While Sophia was in England, a court in Rome held another hearing on the Ponti bigamy case. Lawyers for the public prosecutor's office read from the latest pile of angry citizens' letters, including one that demanded extreme punishment "for that slut, Sofia Scicolone of Pozzuoli."

Ponti's lawyers countered with a statement written by the accused: "I married Miss Loren after obtaining a Mexican divorce from my first wife in order to make my relationship with her legal outside Italy, which does not recognize divorce. The legality of the marriage was necessary above all in Hollywood where we had to go regularly for work—and where an irregular union would have been badly received."

The hearing lasted barely half an hour. The judge pounded his gavel and declared the case adjourned for three months.

When Sophia returned to Italy upon finishing *Arabesque,* Ponti whisked her off to the Soviet Union for the Moscow Film Festival, a biannual event that alternated with one in Karlovy Vary, Czechoslovakia, as the Cannes Festival of the Communist world. *Marriage, Italian Style* was in competition and seemed likely to win something, since few movies from outside the Iron Curtain were entered.

From what she'd heard and read about life in Russia, Sophia expected to be an unknown quantity to the general public, but they mobbed the airport for her arrival and camped in groups outside the National Hotel to watch her comings and goings. Women tried to get as close as possible to examine her clothes and makeup. Few people asked for autographs, but many handed her flowers or left them with the guards outside the hotel, where ordinary folk were forbidden to enter.

For the festival screening, *Marriage, Italian Style* was shown in a huge congress hall about the size of Radio City Music Hall, but with none of the latter's Art Deco elegance. Since the movie had not yet been approved for theatrical release in the USSR, there were no Russian subtitles to help the audience. Instead, the volume of the Italian soundtrack was lowered to a bare minimum so that a Russian interpreter, stationed near the screen with a mike in hand, could do an instant translation of the dialogue.

To no one's surprise, the only award won by *Marriage, Italian Style* at the Moscow Film Festival was the one for Best Actress. Sophia got a standing ovation as she collected the trophy from Sergo Zakhariadze, already chosen the festival's Best Actor for the Russian *Father of a Soldier*. Never one to miss an opportunity, Carlo Ponti immediately annnounced plans to team Sophia and Zakhariadze in an Italian-Soviet remake of *Anna Karenina*.

As a souvenir of their Russian trip, the Pontis purchased a dozen white birch trees for shipment to Italy and the gardens of their "dream house," which they finally moved into that summer after five years of renovation and the expenditure of 2.5 billion lire ($4 million). While all the work was going on, a rumor started in the nearby village of Marino that the Pontis were paying for it from the sale of a solid gold Etruscan statue of a horse that was discovered during the excavations.

While the story probably wasn't true, the six-acre site of Villa Ponti had been a place of human habitation for over two thousand years, according to historians. The current fortresslike house with its fifty rooms was built in the sixteenth century, probably by a prince of the Catholic Church as a summer retreat from Rome's oppressive heat and humidity.

In everything from its rococo interiors to its vast and casual gardens—with a manmade pond and mechanical waterfall—the villa suited a pair of international film celebrities with its mix of Italian flamboyance and Hollywood glitz. During the couple's travels of recent years, Ponti had always found time to shop for embellishments. In Spain, while Sophia was making *El Cid*, he bought a thirteenth-century baptismal font and a fourteen-foot marble table top. From Germany, during the filming of *The Condemned of Altona*, he sent back hundreds of azalea plants. A souvenir of *Two Women* was an exquisite sixteenth-century marble fountain that he found in a crumbling villa near Sorrento and had installed in the patio adjoining the newly built swimming pool.

When he added the pool, Ponti decided to erect a guest house to go with it. The four-story building with its turrets and white marble trimmings was ingeniously colored and "aged" to match the main house. Along with the flower gardens and arbors, there were a vineyard and an olive grove. Ponti hoped eventually to provide his own wine and olive oil for the table.

Excavators checking the foundations of the main house found underneath it twisting catacombs and bits of antique Roman mosaic pavements. The interior of the house was restored to what it looked like in the eighteenth century, when the carved and painted wooden ceilings were first installed. Pastel wall frescoes of the same period portrayed country landscapes and hunting and fishing scenes. Because of its age and decoration, the villa was an official Italian National Monument. Ponti needed permission for all the work and also had to promise never to sell the villa without first offering it to the nation.

The main house had several spectacular rooms that the Pontis used mainly for entertaining guests. The frescoed living room had contemporary chairs and sofas offset by antique everything else. A slab of ancient marble found in the catacombs formed the top of a large coffee table, which had a Louis IX gilded, carved wood base.

The dining room was dominated by a huge antique crystal chandelier. The dining table and serving console were made of a rare Egyptian marble, the chairs white and gold Louis XVI.

Sophia, who as a child in Pozzuoli had had to share a bed with three adult relatives, had a bedroom fit for a queen. Frescoes of the four seasons, originally in a room downstairs, were carefully transferred to light canvas and reset on the walls. Her hand-carved four-poster bedstead and matching furniture were Louis XVI, made in Tuscany. Ponti's bedroom was similarly sumptuous.

Sophia's favorite room among the fifty was her study, which looked out on the gardens and swimming pool. The study was originally the choir section of a seventeenth-century church and housed all her favorite things, including books, snapshot albums, and awards such as her 1961 Oscar. There were five other studies or libraries scattered around the villa, some serving as depositories for Carlo Ponti's huge collections of paintings and antiques, which had far outgrown the space of their Rome apartment. The villa became a veritable museum, with works by Picasso, Renoir, Dali, Bacon, Canaletto, Modigliani, Matisse, Magritte, Sutherland, and other masters decorating the walls throughout.

Ponti's art collection was worth millions (dollars, not lire), but probably no one except the man himself knew how much he'd actually paid for it. Though he regularly bought through established dealers and auction houses around the world, he acquired many of his treasures from private collectors or through barter, that is, accepting paintings or other art works in exchange for distribution rights to some of his films. During the trip to the Moscow Film Festival, for example, he reportedly sold the Russian rights to *Marriage, Italian Style* to the government film monopoly for $100,000 worth of medieval icons, another of his great passions.

The couple never got around to choosing a name for their new home, which by default was usually referred to as either Villa Ponti or Villa Marino. When Sophia first moved in, she told a visitor, "It will take me time to get acquainted. A house is like a person. You must be together awhile to be comfortable."

After their return from the Moscow Film Festival, Ponti started negotiating Sophia's contract for the Charlie Chaplin project, which by now had been titled *A Countess from Hong Kong.* In his eagerness to sign Marlon Brando for the male lead, Chaplin had already promised him top billing throughout the world, or at least top billing after the old maestro himself. The above-the-title credits were to read "Charles Chaplin presents Marlon Brando & Sophia Loren in . . ."

When Ponti found out, he phoned Chaplin's executive producer, Jerome Epstein, and complained, "You can't do this to Sophia. She's at home weeping! Marlon nutting in Japan, Sophia beeg! Marlon nutting in Italy, Sophia beeg, beeg star! Marlon finished in America, Sophia tremendous! At least let them split fifty-fifty: in some countries, Sophia come first, in other countries, Marlon!"

After Epstein explained that he'd already promised Brando and couldn't go back on his word, Ponti then called Charlie Chaplin directly and used scare tactics. Ponti warned him of the budgetary problems that Brando would cause: "Contact [director] Lewis Milestone. The trouble Marlon gave him on *Mutiny on the Bounty!* He was always late; he never knew his lines. Sometimes he never even showed up! At least he can give Sophia Italy—her own country!"

Ponti threw Chaplin into a panic, mainly because the latter's financing deal with Universal required him to pay the overage if production costs exceeded the budget. Also, the egomania over billing was something that Chaplin had never had to deal with before. He'd always been the whole show in his previous movies.

In a fury, Chaplin called Jay Kanter, Universal's international production chief, and told him, "For God's sake, if Marlon doesn't give her a few countries, you're not getting this picture." Ponti threw more fuel on the fire by promising Chaplin financing from MGM or Joe Levine if it came to that.

Kanter, who was an old friend of Brando's and had once been his agent, finally persuaded him to give Sophia top billing in two countries—Iceland and

Togoland. Ponti was furious, and Chaplin got fed up. "Who the hell are they, anyway? *I'm* Charlie Chaplin," he told Jerry Epstein. He considered the project in limbo until the billing was resolved.

Ponti flew to London to plead his case with Epstein, bringing with him a mock ad that solved the dilemma, or so he believed. The names of Sophia Loren and Marlon Brando were arranged in a circle and repeated several times so that you couldn't tell which name came first. Epstein not only rejected it as too confusing, but also delivered a message from Chaplin that they were going to sign Elizabeth Taylor if Sophia didn't accept second billing.

"Carlo sat there frozen—dumbstruck," Epstein recalled. "The blood drained from his face. When he came to, there was no more talk about billing."

Ponti would have to be content with the fact that Sophia had the title role and that *A Countess from Hong Kong* sounded more like her movie than it did either Brando's *or* Chaplin's. The character of Natasha Alexandroff, an exiled White Russian countess reduced to working as a hostess in a Hong Kong dance hall, was modeled after May Reeves, born Mizzi Muller, a European adventuress who'd been a flame of Chaplin's in the long-ago past.

Sophia was taking over a role that Chaplin originally created for his third wife, actress Paulette Goddard. The idea for the script came to him while they were on an ocean cruise to the Far East in 1936. During a stopover in Shanghai, they visited a fleshpot called The Venus, where American sailors danced with so-called "taxi girls," some of whom were stranded foreigners trying to raise money to pay for passage home.

Chaplin's mind went to work and came up with a story that he first entitled *Stowaway.* To escape bill collectors, the ex-countess stows away on a luxury liner to the United States, where she becomes involved with an American multi-millionaire whose wife is due to join him when the ship reaches Honolulu. Chaplin intended teaming Paulette Goddard with Gary Cooper in the movie, but the Chaplins' marriage broke up before he could implement the project, and it sat on a shelf for almost thirty years.

In the dusting off, Chaplin switched the story's port of departure to Hong Kong. Shanghai was by this time part of Communist China. Chaplin didn't relish starting another furor over his alleged Communist sympathies. His original concept of the wealthy American was of a man with presidential ambitions, but he changed him into a globe-hopping ambassador to avoid comparisons with John F. Kennedy, whose assassination was still fresh in memory.

When all the contracts were finally signed, Chaplin held a press conference in London on November 4, 1965, to announce his plans. Sophia flew over from Rome to participate, but the reclusive Marlon Brando opted to stay home in Los Angeles.

Sophia and Chaplin were nearly trampled by the herd of reporters and photographers that invaded the River Suite of the Savoy Hotel. Almost a decade had passed since Chaplin had made his last movie, *A King in New York,* but the big story was not so much his professional "comeback" as his return to public favor after the political and moral witchhunts that caused him to leave the United States in 1952 and to settle permanently in Switzerland.

Even in his heyday, Chaplin had never been accessible to the press, so his sudden turnaround at age seventy-six was a historic moment. Sophia, dressed in a new Dior and dripping in emeralds, had to settle for being window dressing at the press conference. After the main presentation, they each held court in adjacent rooms to answer questions. Chaplin's was packed to overflowing. Sophia drew just a handful of visitors. "Now I know what a real star is," she cracked to one of them.

A Countess from Hong Kong consisted mainly of interior scenes that could be filmed in a studio anywhere, but Chaplin and Universal fixed on London because it had become the epicenter of the Swinging Sixties. All the big Hollywood companies had opened production offices there to take advantage of the talent pool and of tax benefits offered by the British government.

Pinewood Studios was so bulging with major productions like *You Only Live Twice* and *Fahrenheit 451* that Chaplin would have to wait until mid-January before he could start filming *A Countess from Hong Kong.* Sophia was delighted. It gave her some time to rest before Carlo Ponti dragged her off to the world premiere of *Doctor Zhivago,* which was being held December 22 at the Capitol Theatre in New York.

Though Ponti had had slight creative input into *Zhivago,* he wanted to be identified with the movie. It promised to be the first box-office blockbuster of his many English-language projects and could work miracles for his reputation as a producer. MGM, which spent $15 million on the filming, was giving it the royal treatment as a three-hour, reserved-seat roadshow attraction.

Needless to say, having Sophia on his arm at the premiere would swell Ponti's chances of getting his picture in the papers. That night it turned out that way, but the next morning's press also carried reviews of *Doctor Zhivago* that were not only bad but in some cases downright insulting to director David Lean and scriptwriter Robert Bolt for reducing Boris Pasternak's masterpiece to soap opera.

Fortunately, time would write a happier ending to *Doctor Zhivago*. But the critical pans and equally disappointing box-office receipts were not the sort of gifts that Ponti and Sophia were hoping for that Christmas season.

But there was also good news from Paris. Just before the French courts closed down for the holidays, Giuliana Ponti was granted a divorce on the grounds of her husband's adultery. After a ninety-day cooling-off period that gave them time to change their minds, both would be free to marry again if they so wished. Sophia started shopping for a wedding dress as soon as she got back to Rome.

MARRIED WITHOUT
CHILDREN

ᘒᘒ

TAKING some of the joy out of Sophia's wedding plans was the man who traditionally gives the bride away. But in this case, Riccardo Scicolone had suddenly decided to sue his daughter for libel over some withering statements she had made about him in an interview published in a German magazine.

By this time, the reconciliation between Scicolone and Romilda Villani had turned out to be a short one. As Sophia had suspected, Scicolone's main reason for getting back together was to weasel his way into managing and sharing in Sophia's wealth. But no one except Carlo Ponti would ever have control over that. As soon as Scicolone realized it, he resumed his old tomcat ways, and when Romilda caught on, she chucked him out for good. Sophia sided with her mother, but younger sister Maria had grown fond of her father, by now a doting grandpa to Alessandra, and continued their close relationship.

Scicolone, who had originally studied to be an architect but never practiced, became a building contractor and prospered, no doubt helped by the fact that he was Sophia Loren's father. But when she came out in print blaming him for most of her early sufferings and misfortunes, he sued. In the preliminary court hearing in Rome, however, the judge decided that Sophia's statements "do not appear to be of a clearly aggressive significance to the reputation of the complainant."

Dropping the lawsuit, Scicolone retaliated by defending himself in an article that he sold to another German magazine. He claimed that he never gave Romilda and the girls financial support because the war years were difficult and he had no money. To repudiate Sophia's story that she and Maria had to walk around Pozzuoli barefooted, he boasted of paying for one pair of shoes per year for each of them.

"Sophia is too attached to her mother and has never forgiven me for having been unwilling to marry Romilda," Scicolone said. "Maria is made of a different cloth, not like Sophia, and I'm happy that's so. She's diplomatic, and a caring daughter."

Sophia was deeply hurt, but refrained from any further public mudslinging. She told a friend, "If my father ever wants to see me again, he'll have to go to a cinema and buy a ticket like everybody else."

Meanwhile Charlie Chaplin had invited Sophia and Marlon Brando to spend a weekend at his estate in Vevey, Switzerland, so that he could present them with the finished script of *A Countess from Hong Kong* and discuss production plans. After dinner on the first night, Chaplin played a recording of some of the music he'd composed for the background score and proceeded to perform all the scenes and characters himself.

"As he acted them out," Sophia recalled, "the years fell from him like a cloth. He still had the litheness, the grace of a dancer. Enthralled, I watched the swift movements of his body, how he used his hands and feet, the vitality and eloquence of his eyes and mouth."

Brando appeared less captivated. He kept dozing off, with his head dropping to his chest. Sophia was furious, but Chaplin seemed unperturbed. He saved his rebuke for later, when he told Brando that he was too fat and should try to lose at least ten pounds by the time of the filming.

With Universal Pictures paying the rent, Sophia took a duplex apartment overlooking London's Grosvenor Square for the three months. This time, Ponti would be joining her. To take advantage of the British production boom, he'd formed a company called Bridges Films ("bridges" translates into *ponti* in Italian) and had sold its first project to MGM.

Though Sophia wouldn't be in the film, she gave Ponti the idea for it after reading a magazine article about Britain's new breed of celebrity—fashion photographers like David Bailey and Terry Donovan—and their swinging lifestyle. She suggested that he make a movie about that world. Ponti had recently turned down a script by Michelangelo Antonioni, so he asked him if he'd be interested in developing the idea. Antonioni, who'd been living in London with longtime passion Monica Vitti while she filmed *Modesty Blaise,* already knew the milieu. He jumped at the chance to write and direct what would be his first English-language effort.

Sophia, meanwhile, had her first tiff with Chaplin, not surprisingly during the wardrobe and makeup tests. The impoverished countess spends much of the movie in silk pajamas or a dressing gown borrowed from her millionaire cabin mate, but Chaplin wanted her one dress to be appropriate to the character. He reminded Sophia of the shabby outfits worn by the heroines of *City Lights* and *Modern Times*. He sent assistants to several budget department stores to make a preliminary selection and finally settled on a dress priced at about $19.

"When Charlie showed it to Sophia, I thought she was going to break out in hives," producer Jerry Epstein recalled. "He explained that her character was supposed to be penniless. But to Sophia, this was going to be a big, expensive, and glamorous movie, and she wasn't having it. The next time we heard from her, she was phoning from Paris to inform us that she was having her dress designed by Christian Dior. And that was that."

Chaplin had never shot a movie in color before, nor had he kept up with developments in panchromatic makeup, so he was horrified when Sophia arrived for camera tests in her customary though hardly ordinary warpaint. "Go wash your face," Chaplin demanded. "I don't like all that goo."

Sophia obliged. But when she returned, she told Chaplin, "I feel so naked." He said it made her look even more beautiful, but he begged her to do something about her hairdo. "It's too perfect, with every strand in place," he said.

Sophia ran her fingers through her hair and asked, "Is this the way you want it?" Chaplin nodded, but the minute he was called away, she rushed back to her dressing room and remade herself the way she preferred. When production started, Sophia played the same game with him, but he quickly gave up as he became involved with more important details.

After Chaplin introduced her to cinematographer Arthur Ibbetson, Sophia gently explained to them both how to keep her happy during the filming. Call her a crazy Neapolitan, but she believed that her left profile was more suited to comedy, and the right side to drama. So with the King of Comedy in the director's chair, she wanted to show only her left profile or a full face slightly turned to favor the left side.

Trouble was already brewing with Marlon Brando, who had rented a furnished maisonette in London's Belgravia and brought along two pals for companionship: Christian Marquand, a French actor rumored to be his lover, and Esther Anderson, a young Jamaican actress who'd studied with his mentor, Stella Adler. Arriving in December to savor all that he'd heard about Swinging London, Brando collapsed from exhaustion by the time *A Countess from Hong*

Kong started production on January 24, 1966. Early that morning, he phoned Jerry Epstein and claimed he was too sick to come to work.

Chaplin, who was just getting over the flu and not too strong himself, took the news calmly and told Epstein, "I'm not God, if he's sick, he's sick." They started without Brando and for three full days shot around him with scenes featuring Sophia and Chaplin's actor-son Sydney, who had the role of Brando's business associate. On the fourth day, they were supposed to move to another sound stage for a ballroom scene that required two hundred extras and had to be shot in two days because the space was booked for another movie. Brando swore that he'd be there.

"At eight-thirty A.M.," Jerry Epstein recalled, "Sophia and Charlie arrived to start rehearsals. Two hours went by and no Marlon. Chaplin was fit to be tied. It's so demoralizing to have two hundred people hanging around drinking tea, eating cheese sandwiches, and playing cards as their makeup disintegrates. Word finally came that Marlon had left the house and was on his way. Charlie paced like a caged animal, nervously tapping his fingers on the table when he sat down with us. Sophia told him, 'When Marlon gets here, you must tell him off. You mustn't let him get away with this behavior.' "

Sensing that Sophia was winding Chaplin up for an explosion, Epstein asked her to stay out of it. He didn't want a fracas on the set in front of all those extras. Suddenly news came that Brando was in his dressing room and getting ready for the scene. "He finally came on the set like an innocent little boy," Epstein recalled. "Charlie stormed at him like a tornado. He grabbed Marlon by the arm and said, 'Listen, you son-of-a-bitch, you're working for Charlie Chaplin now. If you think you're slumming, take the next plane back to Hollywood. We don't need you.' "

Sophia sat watching with a Mona Lisa smile on her face, according to Epstein, who suspected she took it as recompense for losing the billing battle to Brando. "Marlon turned into a little kid confronting Big Daddy, all sweet and aplogetic," Epstein said. "But Charlie cut him short and said, 'Listen, I'm an old man and I manage to be here on time. From now on, you're to be on the set every day, ready to shoot by eight-thirty, just like me.' Marlon nodded, wide-eyed. Thereafter, even if he'd been up until dawn, Marlon would arrive punctually, dressing in his limousine as it sped him from London to Pinewood."

Since Sophia already had a negative impression of Brando from that time in Hollywood when he inspected the paintings in her dressing room and advised her to consult a psychiatrist, there was no love lost between them when they finally started working together. Perhaps if Chaplin hadn't been the third point of the triangle, things might have been different. But Sophia adored Chaplin and Brando despised him, so there was no way that the two stars could be friends.

For Sophia, Chaplin was another "acting" director like De Sica, but more dictatorial. He acted everything out for her in advance, then expected her to mimic him exactly rather than add any touches of her own, as De Sica expected. He left nothing to chance, even instructing Sophia for two hours on how to put on a brassiere inside out for one of many visual gags in the film.

Many people on the set who observed Chaplin directing Sophia and Brando thought he was much better at acting the characters than they were. Chaplin told them where to stand, how many steps to take, and how many beats to count before turning. "This is the easiest picture I've ever made. I don't have to do anything, Charlie's doing it all," Brando said at the time, no doubt sarcastically. Inwardly, he was seething. Chaplin's methods left him no latitude.

Brando later described himself as a mere marionette in the director's hands, calling Chaplin "the most sadistic man I'd ever met. He was an egotistical tyrant and a penny-pincher. He harassed people when they were late, and scolded them unmercifully to work faster."

Perhaps because he resented her kowtowing to Chaplin's every whim, Brando treated Sophia roughly throughout production and often called out "There goes Soviet Loren" when she happened to pass by on the set. He told a friend that Sophia's fondness for Italian cuisine made her breath "worse than a dinosaur's."

Once while they were standing together waiting for a retake Brando playfully pinched Sophia's bottom. She slapped his hand and warned, "Don't ever do that again. I am not the sort of woman who is flattered by it."

When it came to filming their first kiss, all hell broke loose. According to the script, Sophia and Brando start out quarreling and wind up in a passionate clinch. After the first take, Sophia broke away and told everyone within earshot, "Do you know what he just whispered to me? That I've got long hairs growing out of my nose!" Gesticulating like a Neapolitan fishmonger, she asked, "How can you expect me to play love scenes with him?"

After Chaplin calmed her down, Sophia agreed to a retake. This time, Brando treated her more tenderly, but also with less passion than Chaplin wanted. On the third try, Brando was so rough that Sophia again exploded: "He bit my lip. Look, it's bleeding! Doesn't that method actor know how to fake passion?"

Sophia stormed off to her dressing room for first aid. When the bleeding stopped, she forced herself to do a fourth take with Brando. Chaplin shouted "Perfect!" when it was over. But from then on, Chaplin would have problems getting his lovebirds to sing harmoniously.

"I had to keep reminding them it was a love story," Chaplin complained later. "The antipathy between them was evident on the screen when each clasped the other as if embracing a werewolf."

Meanwhile, Sophia received some disturbing but not unexpected news. The Arab League condemned her for *Judith,* which had just opened in the United States, and barred all Sophia Loren movies—past, present, and future—from being shown in Arab countries. Arabs residing elsewhere were also urged to observe the boycott. Sophia's "crime" of participating in pro-Israeli propaganda was declared the worst cinematic insult to the Arab world since Elizabeth Taylor had converted to Judaism in 1959.

Paramount had delayed releasing *Judith* for over a year while it tried to milk every dollar it could out of Sophia's *Fall of the Roman Empire.* Nonetheless, the Bronston epic proved a flop with only $1.7 million in U.S. rentals. Though *Judith* premiered at New York's Radio City Music Hall, it quickly became another disaster. While the Arab League would try to claim credit, it seemed just a case of a bad movie that few wanted to see.

Bosley Crowther perhaps summed it up best in *The New York Times:*

Sophia Loren is lending her name and her presence to a routine cloak-and-dagger fim that, without her, would get no more attention—and would deserve no more—than a quickie on the lower end of a double-bill. Even with her, it comes out a disappointing picture, more lurid and loud than lustrous.

Taking some of the sting out of Sophia's latest flop was the sudden turnaround of Carlo Ponti's *Doctor Zhivago,* which had become number one at the box office and promised to unseat the 1959 remake of *Ben-Hur* as MGM's highest-grossing film since *Gone With the Wind.* The success was attributed to a combination of saturation advertising, ecstatic word of mouth about the stirring love story, and the music of Maurice Jarre's "Lara's Theme," which topped the best-seller charts all over the world.

Early in March, Sophia and Ponti rushed for the champagne when *Doctor Zhivago* was nominated for ten Academy Awards, including those for best picture, direction, and scriptwriting. A notable exception was Julie Christie, who got the role of Lara after David Lean ruled out Sophia. Christie did get nominated for Best Actress, but for her performance in *Darling,* which was released four months prior to *Doctor Zhivago* and turned her into an international star almost overnight.

While filming *A Countess From Hong Kong,* Sophia became very chummy with Chaplin's wife, Oona, the daughter of Eugene O'Neill, author of *Desire Under the Elms.* Her husband's junior by thirty-seven years, Oona Chaplin was on the set every day to make sure that he was relaxed and protected. When he finished a take, Chaplin would always look to her for approval. Sophia was very touched, and no doubt found a bond with Mrs. Chaplin in her own relationship with a considerably older man.

Sophia was also slightly envious of the Chaplins for having produced eight children. The eldest, twenty-two-year-old Geraldine Chaplin, just happened to be a star of *Doctor Zhivago,* but Sophia had never met her until she turned up on the set one day to play a bit part, along with her younger sister Josephine, as a favor to their father. Forty-year-old Sydney Chaplin, who had one of the major supporting roles, was their half-brother via his father's second wife, actress Lita Grey.

Sophia loved to play with Chaplin's youngest child, four-year-old Christopher, whom Oona often brought to the studio. As she got to know Oona better, Sophia began to confide in her. One day, she shyly asked her to talk to Chaplin about giving her a few days off to get married. Mrs. Chaplin was only too happy to. By the next day, Carlo Ponti was en route to Paris to make arrangements for the second weekend of April.

To avoid a news media circus, Ponti tried to keep everything secret. The civil wedding ceremony would take place in Sèvres, a suburb of Paris, where Ponti knew the mayor and could count on his confidentiality. In case of a leak, the newlyweds would spend their necessarily brief honeymoon at the Hotel Lancaster instead of at their apartment on Avenue Georges V, an address known to every newshound in Paris and beyond.

Getting Sophia from London to Paris without arousing suspicion was the trickiest part. Though she managed to slip through Orly Airport without being followed by paparazzi, there were, by the next morning, a few stationed outside the house where she was staying with friends. Sophia managed to get rid of them by dressing her hostess in her clothes and dark glasses. The lookalike left in the chauffeured car intended for Sophia and led the paparazzi on a chase to nowhere. Sophia, meanwhile, exited by a back door and was driven to Sèvres by her friend's husband.

On a previous trip to Paris, Sophia had found her bridal outfit at Christian Dior, a pale yellow dress with a matching overcoat. En route to Sèvres, she stopped at a florist to buy a small bouquet of lilies of the valley as a final touch.

Sophia's sister, Maria, and Basilio Franchina had flown over from Rome to be witnesses at the ceremony. Conducted in French by Mayor Charles Odic, it was over in ten minutes.

"I cried, of course," Sophia remembered, "but Carlo had been part of me for so long, I felt as though I'd been married to him almost from the day I was born. We now had a piece of paper with a rubber stamp on it. Okay, it was official. But it was rather like reading a theater program long after you'd seen the play."

Ponti, who'd given Sophia several wedding rings in the past, this time surprised her with one containing an 84-carat emerald. "Diamonds are very cold. I don't like them very much," she once said.

As soon as the ceremony was over and she'd dried her eyes, Sophia rushed to a phone to call her mother, whose fear of flying had kept her in Rome. "Well, Mammina, you were always pessimistic, but it's happened. I'm finally Mrs. Carlo Ponti."

"Ah, yes," Romilda Villani replied, "but not in white, and not in the church."

The Pontis decided in future to observe two wedding anniversaries each year, September 17 for their Mexican proxy marriage in 1957, and April 9 for the French ceremony. It had taken them almost nine years to make it legal, at least outside Italy. The bigamy case against Ponti was still on the docket there, and further confused by a dispute over his change in nationality, which may have been an additional criminal offense.

The newlyweds took their group to lunch at a posh restaurant outside Paris and succeeded in keeping the marriage a secret until it was finally announced by the mayor of Sèvres a week later. The Paris press corps was so incensed that it later voted Sophia its *Prix Citron* (Sour Lemon Award) as the most uncooperative celebrity of that year.

After staying overnight at the Hotel Lancaster, the Pontis returned to London for what promised to be a big week, including Charlie Chaplin's seventy-seventh birthday party and the presentation of the 1965 Academy Awards. Due to their work schedules, the couple were unable to attend the Oscar ceremonies. Ponti was about to start production of his MGM project with director Michelangelo Antonioni, which by now had been titled *Blow Up* and would feature David Hemmings and Vanessa Redgrave in the leading roles.

During his glory years in Hollywood, Charlie Chaplin had never permitted reporters or photographers to visit the sets of his movies, but to please Universal he relaxed the rule on *A Countess from Hong Kong* so long as they kept out of his way and didn't expect interviews. Since Marlon Brando had an even more hostile attitude toward the press, Sophia, by default, got most of the coverage. After seeing one too many magazine covers of Sophia, Chaplin complained to the publicity department, "For God's sake, she's getting all the attention! Her husband isn't making this movie. I am!"

Even Brando started to get envious. "When I die," he told a friend, "Sophia will probably show up at my funeral and get into all the photographs."

The "surprise" party on Chaplin's seventy-seventh birthday on April 16 was an attempt to pacify him. Even Brando joined the celebration on the set, which attracted scores of press. Universal splurged on a huge white-frosted cake with five tiers and a replica of the Little Tramp at the top. Before carving the first slice, Chaplin clowned and pretended to be slashing his throat with the knife.

Sophia made a new friend at the party, an eight-year-old American named Melanie whose mother, Tippi Hedren, was portraying Brando's wife in the movie. Keeping in touch over the years, Sophia watched her bloom into Melanie Griffith, one of the brightest stars of the 1980s.

Three days after Chaplin's party, Sophia and Ponti held a celebration of their own when *Doctor Zhivago* won five Oscars, though not the most coveted one for 1965's Best Picture, which went to *The Sound of Music* (*Darling, Ship of Fools,* and *A Thousand Clowns* were the other nominees). But Robert Bolt won for his script, and Maurice Jarre for the musical score. The other Oscars were for color photography, art direction, and costume design.

How *Doctor Zhivago* would have turned out if Carlo Ponti had insisted upon Sophia as Lara can only be guessed at, but two of her own movies would soon be competing against it. Without bothering to consult each other first—studios rarely if ever did—Universal and MGM both picked May 1966 as the release date for *Arabesque* and *Lady L,* despite the fact that *Judith* was still in release and doing miserable business.

Like *Judith, Arabesque* had its world premiere at New York's Radio City Music Hall, but only because Stanley Donen's previous *Charade* had broken box-office records there. Unfortunately, the critics found *Arabesque* a pale copy and Music Hall business was only fair, better than *Judith* but not up to the previous year's *Operation Crossbow,* which had had the benefit of an Easter holiday booking. Not surprisingly, *Arabesque* earned Sophia another blast from the Arab League for the movie's depiction of Arabs as terrorists and assassins.

Two weeks later, while *Arabesque* was still running at the Music Hall, MGM opened *Lady L* at Loew's State on Broadway and at the much smaller Beekman on the East Side. Peter Ustinov, per instructions, had made a three-hour movie. After he delivered his final cut, editors at MGM's Hollywood studio tried to remove at least an hour of footage. Ponti was horrified when he saw the first result, which ran 107 minutes and dropped what he considered some of Sophia's best acting moments. To placate him, MGM prepared a second and longer version of 124 minutes and then arranged separate "sneak" previews of each to test audience reactions.

Both versions of *Lady L* received a negative response, though the shorter rated slightly higher, perhaps only because it was seventeen minutes less of an endurance test. The cutting in both versions made the story incoherent at times and destroyed the delicate balance between comedy and drama. MGM decided to use the shorter version in the United States and to indulge Ponti by releasing the 124-minute version in England and Europe, where the Old World atmosphere of *Lady L* was more likely to be appreciated.

MGM tried everything to make *Lady L* a success, including the airbrush removal of Paul Newman's dreaded mustache in the advertising art. But the movie bombed and lost a reported $12 million, including the $2.5 million spent on MGM's aborted first try with Gina Lollobrigida and Tony Curtis.

Luckily for Carlo Ponti, *Doctor Zhivago* was doing such huge business for MGM that it more than made up for the failure of *Lady L* and encouraged the studio to extend their coproduction deal. First up after *Blow Up* would be a teaming of Sophia with Omar Sharif in a romantic fairy tale entitled *Once Upon a Time*. Ponti also agreed to take over two major properties that MGM had owned for years and had similar potential to *Doctor Zhivago*—*The Forty Days of Musa Dagh,* Franz Werfel's novel about the Turkish genocide of the Armenians in 1915, and *Man's Fate,* André Malraux's prize-winning epic about Europeans involved in the ill-fated Chinese Communist attempt to gain control of Shanghai in 1927.

While Ponti was wheeling and dealing, he also sold MGM on adding Sophia to the cast of the studio's $15 million extravaganza, *Say It with Music,* which would weld standards and new songs by Irving Berlin to a script by Arthur Laurents, author of *West Side Story.* Julie Andrews and Ann-Margret had already signed on. MGM was also dickering with Brigitte Bardot to complete an international quartet of stars. While Sophia and BB might have seemed odd choices, they'd both sung on screen before and made recordings, so why not?

Meanwhile, when Sophia finished *A Countess from Hong Kong,* she made good on a promise to Robert Favre Le Bret, head of the Cannes Film Festival, to serve as president of the jury of the nineteenth annual event in May.

Sophia was only the second woman to preside over a Cannes jury, preceded in 1965 by Hollywood legend Olivia de Havilland, who resided in France and had taken over on short notice when the actual choice, novelist André Maurois, became ill. Maurois was back this year, but as one of the jurors, along with Sophia's friend Peter Ustinov. Also on the panel were French writers Marcel Pagnol, Marcel Achard, Maurice Genevoix, Jean Giono, and Armand Salacrou; Tetsuro Furukaki, former Japanese ambassador to France; Maurice Lehmann, head of the Paris Opera; Richard Lester, American director; Denis Marion, French-Belgian film critic; Vinicius Moraes, Brazilian composer; and Yuli Raizman, Russian director. Sophia was the only woman and found herself in pretty heady company for a high school dropout.

Sophia thought that the two-week stint would be a lark, but it proved one of the most grueling experiences of her professional lifetime. She had to sit through screenings of over a hundred movies, as well as attend all the official galas and cocktail parties. One night, England's Princess Margaret tried to upstage her by arriving thirty minutes late and delaying the start of the British entry, *Modesty Blaise.* Sophia could hardly conceal her delight as the princess was greeted with boos and hisses.

Fortunately, with all the glamour outfits she'd saved from her various movies, Sophia could wear a different dress every time. "Mobs would gather outside the Palais, just to watch her go in and out and to see her fabulous clothes," festival executive Christiane Guespin recalled.

In the midst of the festival, Chaplin summoned Sophia back to London for two days of retakes. After returning to Cannes, she had to arrange private screenings of all the movies she'd missed. "You don't notice the time flying," she said at the time. "You're watching, and suddenly it's four in the morning! Some films are better than others, of course, but you see such fabulous things that you don't want to stop."

Early in the morning of the day of final deliberations, Madame President and the other jurors were picked up by limousine and taken to a conference room at the Palais du Festival, where they would remain under guard until that evening's presentation ceremonies. Sophia had to bring along makeup and a gown to change into; to prevent news leaks, jurors were forbidden to return to their hotels until the awards were announced.

As president of the jury, Sophia was required to make a speech before the voting began. Whether she endorsed any of her own favorites is unknown, but the most coveted award—the *Palme d'Or* for Best Picture—ended up in a tie between the Italian director Pietro Germi's *Signore e Signori* and the French Claude Lelouch's *Un Homme et une Femme*. Denmark's Per Oscarsson was voted Best Actor for *Sult,* while Vanessa Redgrave, at that moment working in Ponti's *Blow-Up* in London, received the equivalent award for her performance in *Morgan*.

By midsummer, Ponti was ready to start Sophia's next film, her first to be shot in Italy since *Marriage, Italian Style* two years before. With financing from MGM, the project was set up as an Italian-French coproduction, but the principal language used would be English, to make it easier for Omar Sharif and the ageless Hollywood legend Dolores Del Rio, who would portray his mother.

Due to a protest from Columbia Pictures, which had already produced a Cary Grant movie entitled *Once Upon a Time,* MGM told Ponti to come up with something different, and they finally settled on *Happily Ever After*. Ponti assigned the direction to Francesco Rosi, who in Italy was considered one of the masters but had yet to win the international fame of peers like De Sica, Fellini, and Visconti. Rosi also had a hand in the screenplay, sharing credit with three writers who regularly contributed to Ponti's Italian-based productions.

Rosi also happened to be Neapolitan, making him a natural match to both Sophia and the story, which was set in Renaissance Naples circa 1600. Sophia played a peasant named Isabella who captures the fancy of a Spanish prince on the prowl for a bride. Needless to say, she's too lowborn to qualify, but with help from a flying monk who can perform miracles, all ends exactly as the title suggests.

The romantic fairy tale was Sophia's first movie with supernatural elements. To give it a storybook look, Rosi selected Pasquale De Santis for cinematographer. De Santis's fondness for moody lighting and soft focus suited Sophia to perfection. His exquisite work persuaded director Franco Zeffirelli to hire him next for *Romeo and Juliet*.

The filming of *Happily Ever After* took Sophia almost home again. Since Naples had changed too drastically over three centuries, Francesco Rosi selected location sites further south in Matera, the capital of the Lucanian region, and the little town of Padula. Seemingly untouched by time, the region was rich in cathedrals, castles, and splendid landscapes.

Announcement of Sophia's teaming with Omar Sharif triggered another blast from the Arab League, which condemned the Egyptian-born actor for collaborating with a friend of Israel. Rumors began to fly about a romance between the two stars. Fueling the gossip were Carlo Ponti's frequent absences while he was attending to business in London and Rome, which left Sophia sharing Sharif's company during all those lonely nights in remote Matera.

Actually, Sophia and Sharif had been friends for several years, ever since he played her barbaric and short-lived husband in *The Fall of the Roman Empire.* Sharif was a celebrated Lothario and suddenly one of the world's romantic dreamboats as a result of *Doctor Zhivago.* With eyes perhaps even sexier and more soulful than Sophia's, he may have been too much for her to resist, and who could blame her?

As *Happily Ever After* entered its final weeks of production, Sophia turned out to be pregnant again. Her last pregnancy, which had ended in a miscarriage after three and a half months, was three years ago.

Jubilant when all the tests confirmed it, Sophia consulted a specialist on what she could do to avert another miscarriage. Blaming her previous misfortune on working too hard, the doctor instructed her to go straight home to bed and stay there for the full term. When she protested that she had a movie to finish, the doctor told her that if she wanted the baby, the remaining scenes would have to be skipped.

Fortunately, with her husband as her employer, Sophia didn't have to plead to be excused. Ponti promised to find some way of finishing the movie, possibly by using a double or even waiting nine months if necessary.

Ponti also had to do some fast rethinking of Sophia's work schedule. After she completed *Happily Ever After,* she was supposed to be in his next MGM project, *The Girl and the General,* a World War II drama with Rod Steiger as her costar. Ponti made a deal with Virna Lisi to replace Sophia. Lisi, meanwhile, was working for Ponti in yet another of the MGM movies that had him constantly traveling, this one a war thriller entitled *The Twenty-fifth Hour,* which was being shot in Yugoslavia by French director Henri Verneuil, with Anthony Quinn and Michael Redgrave in the male leads.

Sophia took to her bed at Villa Ponti and stayed there. In her terror of another miscarriage, she was afraid even to sit up. She learned how to eat lying flat on her back. She later confessed that the baby growing within her became an obsession. She didn't want to watch television or listen to the radio. She took to wearing earplugs because it made it easier to concentrate on her internal rhythms. The doctor came regularly to give her hormone injections and to check her condition.

Meanwhile, Ponti was dividing his time between London and New York due to a crisis over *Blow-Up*, which MGM intended to open in December to qualify for the 1966 Oscars. Antonioni's baffling mystery about the decadent London scene contained several scenes of nudity and explicit sex that violated Hollywood's self-imposed moral code and caused the Motion Picture Association of America to withhold its seal of approval. MGM, as an MPAA member, would have to make substantial cuts if it expected to release *Blow-Up* in the United States.

While MGM was willing to comply, Ponti and Antonioni weren't. Aside from their mutual loathing of censorship, they knew that the cuts could turn the potential box-office smash into a flop. When Ponti offered to buy back the movie so he could sell it to one of the independent distributors that weren't ruled by the MPAA code, MGM panicked, and its lawyers quickly found a solution to the problem. MGM formed a separate distribution company called Premier Pictures, and *Blow-Up* would be its first release.

With the MGM logo removed, *Blow-Up* still drew fire from the Catholic National Legion of Decency, which gave it a Condemned rating for going "far beyond the limits of moral acceptability for a public entertainment medium." Combined with rave reviews from most critics, the sex controversy made *Blow-Up* an instant hit in America and soon worldwide. It earned $18 million in rentals in its first year of release and was Carlo Ponti's biggest hit after *Doctor Zhivago*.

Due to her confinement, Sophia had to renege on a promise to Charlie Chaplin to attend the world premiere of *A Countess from Hong Kong*, which was being held in London on January 5, 1967. Marlon Brando, who'd previously said no, was coaxed into subbing for Sophia so Chaplin wouldn't have to field the press entirely on his own.

Thanks indirectly to her husband's *Doctor Zhivago*, Sophia's latest film got off to a bad start. Universal held the critics' screening in the same theater where *Zhivago* was being shown in wide-angle Panavision. The projectionist forgot to change the special lens, and when he finally did, the film kept going in and out of focus. By the night of the premiere, most of the reviews were out and declared Chaplin's eighty-first film a disaster. Words like "tedious," "unfunny" and "old-fashioned" were hurled at him, but the unkindest comment of all was a recommendation that he study recent movies like *Blow-Up* and *Who's Afraid of Virginia Woolf?* before he made any further attempts at a comeback.

But everybody whooped it up at the post-premiere party. Brando got so sloshed that at two in the morning he phoned Sophia in Rome to report on all the fun she'd missed. Brando also couldn't stop himself from mentioning the withering reviews.

Chaplin was devastated by the negative response, blaming it on his political enemies and on trendy critics who only endorsed what was hip or avant-garde. "It's about a multimillionaire who gives up his lovely wife to marry a whore. What's so old-fashioned about that?" he asked.

In response to some of the criticism, Chaplin cut six minutes from the movie for its Paris premiere the following week. In the land where *Charlot* still reigned supreme as king of the cinema, the majority of the reviews were raves, with many critics also attacking their English cousins for being so vicious.

Due to Chaplin's troubled history in the United States, Universal decided to delay the American release until the air cleared. Sophia, meanwhile, had more serious things to worry about. After nearly three months in bed, she started feeling like she had during her first pregnancy, only worse mentally because of her fears.

Early in January, while Ponti was away in London on business, Sophia developed such severe stomach cramps that her friend Basilio Franchina rushed her to the hospital by car. Sophia began hemorrhaging in the emergency room, but when her doctor arrived and examined her, he said it was just a minor complication and nothing to worry about.

Romilda Villani, who'd also been summoned by this time, believed differently and thought her daughter might bleed to death if something wasn't done immediately. She screamed at the doctor and begged him to intervene, but he said that if it *was* a miscarriage, he couldn't do anything. Under Italian law, miscarriages were considered an act of God, and the patient had to suffer the consequences without medical intervention.

Sophia spent an agonizing night, but just before daybreak the pain stopped and she knew immediately that she'd lost the baby. The doctor soon confirmed it. Several hours later, he performed a curettage of the uterus, Sophia's second in three years.

Carlo Ponti had by this time flown back from London. When Sophia first saw him, she tried to be lighthearted, with "Well, now I can finish those remaining scenes for *Happily Ever After*." But they both collapsed in each other's arms and wept.

When Maria Mussolini came to visit, she was horrified to find that her sister's room was in the hospital's maternity wing. "Everyone I saw and every sound I heard in the hallways was gay and happy," she recalled. "The private rooms all had pink or blue decorations on the doors. When I got to one that had nothing on the door, I knew it was Sophia's. She was so distraught that I trembled for her. She would tell me: 'I am an actress. I am famous. I have a beautiful home and a wonderful husband. Why can't I have children?' "

Maria might have done better to stay away, since she was expecting another child herself. Her by then very obvious condition probably caused her older sister to fret even more about her own inadequacies. A month later, Maria gave birth to a second daughter, Elisabetta. Like sister Alessandra, now going on five, she would be a substitute child for Zia Sophia until the real thing came along.

Bad medical advice seemed to be at the root of Sophia's dilemma. "When I had my second miscarriage, I really despaired," she said years later. "I had seen some of the best specialists, but they couldn't explain why I was losing my babies. Somehow I couldn't carry a child in the womb for the full nine months. Of course that is tragic for any woman, but for a Neapolitan woman it is almost a disgrace. I felt abnormal, ashamed."

Sophia always declined to name the doctor who treated her. "I hate that man, I really do," she once said. "The two miscarriages were agony for me, and I need never have suffered them. They also ruined my chances of having a large family. After two miscarriages, doctors are afraid to risk a normal birth. They want to give you a cesarean. After one cesarean, you can maybe have a second or third, but that's the finish. No more babies!"

After her second miscarriage, Sophia plunged into depression, and loved ones feared that she might not snap out of it. She shunned company and frequently broke down in tears. "Sophia became obsessed with those miscarriages," Ines Bruscia recalled. "It was the only time she had failed in life, and she didn't know how to handle failure, certainly not as final and tragic a failure as the loss of those two babies."

To snap his wife back into the real world, Ponti tried to persuade her to accept Universal's invitation to attend the American premiere of *A Countess from Hong Kong* in New York in March, but she refused. It turned out a wise decision, because the movie's reception would have depressed her even more. Ironically, for all the drubbing he took, Chaplin went on to earn a fortune in royalties as composer of the movie's theme, "This Is My Song," which became a pop standard as a result of Petula Clark's worldwide hit record.

The disaster of *A Countess from Hong Kong,* preceded by the disappointments of *Lady L, Arabesque,* and *Judith,* was a serious blow to Sophia's career and soured the big Hollywood studios on hiring her again. If she hadn't been Mrs. Carlo Ponti, there might have been no work to take her mind off miscarried babies. But Ponti got her started with the remaining bits of *Happily Ever After* and then activated one of the projects that had previously been set for her in his deal with MGM.

While another teaming of Sophia with Marcello Mastroianni and Vittorio De Sica might have seemed a perfect solution to several problems, both men were booked solid elsewhere and Ponti had to settle for a close approximation. *Questi fantasmi* was a celebrated stage farce by Eduardo De Filippo, author of *Marriage, Italian Style*. Paired with Sophia was Vittorio Gassman, Italy's most popular actor and the one most often cited by critics as its finest. To direct Ponti chose Renato Castellani, best known internationally for a sumptuous version of *Romeo and Juliet* filmed in Italy in 1954 with a British cast.

MGM picked *Ghosts, Italian Style* as the English title for *Questi fantasmi*, which literally translates into "These Ghosts." Set in present-day Naples, the plot concerned a poor married couple who become the custodians and rent-free tenants of a supposedly haunted *palazzo* owned by a longtime admirer of the wife. Through a series of misunderstandings, Sophia, the wife, disappears and is believed to have been murdered by hubby Gassman, who is tossed into jail. After he's released for insufficient evidence, Sophia suddenly turns up, pretending to be a ghost, and scares the wits out of her wealthy admirer, who caused all the trouble. Still believing she's a ghost, he agrees to donate a fortune to a charity in her memory. Sophia and Gassman make off with the money and start a new life in Scotland as caretakers of a castle that turns out to have a real ghost in residence.

The movie was another of Ponti's deals relying on European cofinancing and government subsidies. Mario Adorf, a German actor very popular in Italy, received costar billing as the villain. Ponti hired American writer Ernest Pintoff for the dialogue used in the English-language version, which would be postsynchronized from the original Italian.

As a favor to Sophia and Ponti, Marcello Mastroianni agreed to make a brief cameo appearance as the ghost in the final scene. They all decided later that if he'd been available at the time, Mastroianni would have been a better choice for the role played by Vittorio Gassman. "As an actor, I'm a bit passive and reactive—unlike Gassman, who's a lot more aggressive. That's why I have such good chemistry working with somebody like Sophia," Mastroianni once said. "We complement each other, like Laurel and Hardy. She acts, while I react. With

Gassman, it's different. They're both actors, not reactors. It was bound to be a disaster."

While filming *Questi fantasmi,* Sophia learned of a Swiss gynecologist and obstetrician, Hubert de Watteville, who might be able to solve her childbearing problems. As soon as she could, she flew to Geneva to meet him and to undergo tests at his clinic.

"He gave me an injection of Pentothal, I fell asleep, and he did a complete internal examination," Sophia recalled. "When I awoke he looked very embarrassed. 'I'm sorry,' he said, 'I don't know why you lose your children. The only explanation that occurs to me is that maybe when you are three months pregnant the uterus doesn't close enough. But that is no problem. We can tie it up. Frankly there's no reason why you shouldn't have a normal pregnancy. You're perfect.'"

Dr. de Watteville advised Sophia to take things easy and *not* to rush into getting pregnant again. To make sure that she didn't, he gave her a four-month supply of birth control pills, which was equivalent to a long rest for her reproductive system. At the end of the prescription, she was to phone the doctor for further instructions the instant she thought she might be expecting.

With two completed MGM films awaiting release, Sophia decided to take a work sabbatical until she had a chance to test de Watteville's recommendations. But first she had a commitment to film an American TV special that had been postponed due to her last miscarriage. Produced by David Wolper, *With Love . . . Sophia* was her most elaborate television effort to date, a musical-comedy tour of Sophia Loren's private world, or at least of what she wanted to reveal of it.

Needless to say, the unglamorous Carlo Ponti was nowhere in view, but Sophia's longtime admirer, Peter Sellers, turned up as one of the guest stars. By this time, Sellers had married Swedish sexpot Britt Ekland and lived mostly on a yacht in the Mediterranean to avoid English tax collectors.

As a favor to Sophia, Sellers agreed to appear in a sketch about the previous occupants of Villa Ponti. He portrayed an asinine German officer from World War II times. The American comedian Jonathan Winters played a sixteenth-century sculptor.

In other sections of the TV special, Sophia reminisced with Marcello Mastroianni about their films together and later joined him for a fiery tango in which he repeated the impersonation of Rudolph Valentino that had earned him acclaim in a Rome stage musical the previous year. Their dance started on the patio of Villa Ponti and ended in the swimming pool, with their hands still clapping above their heads as they sank from sight.

Leslie Bricusse, who'd previously composed some of the numbers for Sophia's record album with Sellers, contributed seven songs. Sophia performed three, and the rest were heard on the soundtrack, sung by her Italian-American fan Tony Bennett. Sponsored by the textiles division of Monsanto, the one-hour color program was a veritable fashion show for the house of Dior, which dressed Sophia throughout.

When ABC-TV set a broadcast date of October 25 for *With Love . . . Sophia,* MGM decided to capitalize on it by releasing *Happily Ever After* the following week. By this time the title had undergone yet another change, to *More Than a Miracle,* and it seemed like MGM would need that for the movie to earn back its $6 million budget. Exhibitors were so leery about the historical fantasy that MGM couldn't get a prime Broadway theater for the American launching and had to settle for the shabby New Amsterdam on 42nd Street.

Vincent Canby, who'd replaced the retired Bosley Crowther as film critic for *The New York Times,* deplored all 110 minutes of *More Than a Miracle,* opining that "it seems that one of Miss Loren's most important functions in her private life is to upgrade those motion pictures produced by her husband, Carlo Ponti, that turn into poverty (if not disaster) areas."

Canby added:

> If anyone could save the film, of course it would be Sophia, but even she fails, though she does spend most of the picture in one of those break-away peasant mini-dresses in which she first burst upon the public consciousness. During one sequence, Sophia is entirely hidden in a barrel, which is just another example of how Mr. Ponti has squandered her natural resources.

In desperation, MGM tried yet another title change to *Cinderella, Italian Style,* with more emphasis in the advertising on Omar Sharif's first romantic role since *Doctor Zhivago.* But the public still didn't respond, and the movie became Sophia's fifth loser in a row.

Not surprisingly, MGM decided to shelve *Ghosts, Italian Style.* But its confidence in Carlo Ponti seemed undiminished, thanks to the continuing strength of *Doctor Zhivago,* which had opened as a roadshow and still had a long life ahead of it, and *Blow-Up,* which had become an art house phenomenon.

Thanks to the latter, Ponti had contracted with MGM for two more Antonioni films, the first to be entitled *Zabriskie Point*. With newcomers Mark Frechette and Daria Halprin in the leads (and future star Harrison Ford in a bit part), the $6 million drama would be shot entirely on locations in the southwestern United States, including the Valley of Fire in Nevada.

MGM also gave the green light to Ponti taking on *Man's Fate,* one of the studio's long-owned properties. Ponti promptly signed Fred Zinnemann, that year's Oscar winner for *A Man for All Seasons,* to direct. Zinnemann figured that he would need at least two years to prepare the immense production, which suited Ponti perfectly, because he wanted Sophia to play one of the leading roles.

Ponti was involved in so many deals at the moment that it seemed Sophia would need to make an appointment if she expected to get pregnant again. Using some of his profits from *Dr. Zhivago,* Ponti invested $80,000 in the next film of fledgling director Milos Forman, who'd just had a big international success with *Loves of a Blonde,* made on a shoestring in his native Czechoslovakia. When Forman delivered *The Firemen's Ball,* Ponti disliked it so intensely that he canceled the deal on a technicality, claiming that the movie's running time was two minutes short of the minimum seventy-five specified in the contract. Ponti then began pressuring the Communist state-owned Czech Film Export for the return of his $80,000, which left Forman in a terrible predicament. (He fled to the United States in 1969 and eventually landed on his feet with the multi-Oscar-winning *One Flew Over the Cuckoo's Nest* in 1975.)

After discovering with *Blow-Up* the financial and tax advantages to filming in England, Ponti opened a London office and obtained several commitments from a production-distribution combine funded by the new theatrical movie division of the American Broadcasting Company and Paramount Pictures.

With the offer of a $200,000 fee, Ponti coaxed Marcello Mastroianni into coming to London to play his first starring role in English in *Diamonds for Breakfast,* a comedy caper that marked the movie debut of stage and TV director Christopher Morahan. Mastroianni later recalled: "I told Ponti that the only three things I knew how to say in English were 'fuck,' which was the first word I learned, 'hello,' and 'good night.' He said, 'Stop worrying. I'm the boss and you'll be okay.' "

When Mastroianni reported for work, Ponti hired an English instructor to be on the set to teach him his lines phonetically, like a parrot. With his Italian accent added on, Mastroianni could barely be understood by his British coactors, who included Rita Tushingham and Warren Mitchell, so there were usually several retakes of scenes before everybody got their cues right.

By the time 1968 rolled around, Sophia was still showing no signs of pregnancy. Another flying visit to Geneva resulted only in a stern lecture from Dr. de Watteville, who told her to stop worrying so much and to just relax and let nature take its course.

When she returned to Rome, Sophia agreed to a suggestion from her sister Maria that they spend a couple of weeks at a health spa in northern Italy that was revered for its hot sulfur springs and mud baths. Since the spa catered to victims of crippling disorders like arthritis and rheumatism, Sophia found the surroundings too depressing and wanted to leave after two days. But Maria made her stick it out and Sophia left feeling completely rejuvenated. A month later, she was pregnant.

CONFINEMENT IN
SWITZERLAND

S OPHIA would never forget March 30, 1968. "Carlo was in London when I found I was pregnant," she recalled. "I telephoned him there, but before I could tell him anything, he said, 'What is it?'

" 'I am waiting a baby,' I told him. He said, 'Oh no! Not again!' He was scared for me, afraid I would have another miscarriage."

Terrified of even leaving the house, let alone traveling by plane to Geneva, Sophia arranged for Dr. de Watteville to fly to Rome to discuss strategy as soon as Ponti returned. She remembered later that de Watteville "told Carlo that from that moment on, I would have to live more like an ordinary woman and less like a movie actress. He told me that I needed to be relaxed and very optimistic—and to stay in bed for the next four or five months. And if anything wrong started to happen, then I'd have to stay in bed for all the rest of the nine months."

By the next morning, the Pontis had decided that Sophia should fly to Geneva immediately with de Watteville and plan on staying there under his personal supervision until the baby was born. Ponti got on the phone and booked a suite for Sophia at the Hotel Intercontinental while she underwent tests at the doctor's clinic.

"They did a twenty-four-hour analysis of my urine, which revealed that my estrogen level was very low," Sophia recalled. "The doctor gave me an injection and I was okay, so he started me on a weekly routine of the estrogen test, followed by an injection." Estrogen is the hormone that nourishes the lining of the uterus during pregnancy. The doctor believed that a deficiency had contributed to Sophia's two miscarriages.

De Watteville also placed Sophia on tranquilizers and sleeping pills, which exhausted her initially because she'd never taken such drugs before and her system wasn't used to them. The doctor said later in a press interview that he often prescribed sedatives "because emotional stress can lead to uterine movement and bring on miscarriage. Where there have been repeated miscarriages, there is always such stress in the form of anxiety. Thus we must give sedatives and confidence to break the vicious circle, assuring women that all will be well and this time they will succeed."

Sophia decided to make the Hotel Intercontinental her home for the duration. It had magnificent views of Lake Geneva and the Alps, but was located in a quiet section of town near the European headquarters of the United Nations. The best double room at the hotel rented for 85 Swiss francs (about $21) per night, but Sophia's deluxe suite on the eighteenth floor cost 4,200 francs by the week (about $1,050), astronomical for 1968, especially if it turned out to be a full nine-month tenancy.

Business permitting, Ponti would visit on weekends, but Sophia's only full-time companion would be her trusted secretary, Ines Bruscia. Sophia insisted that her mother and sister remain in Rome until the end of her term. She feared that having family around would be too stressful and emotionally exhausting for everybody.

Sophia's hideaway consisted of a parlor, two bedrooms with baths, and a small kitchen refitted at her expense with appliances and cookware similar to what she had back home. Although Dr. de Watteville had ordered Sophia to stay in bed, she was permitted, for the first months, to get up for an hour three times a day as long as she didn't exert herself. She supervised while Ines prepared their meals, or they just played cards or watched television.

Sophia was reluctant to order from room service, for fear that the deliverer would turn out to be a nut or—even worse—a reporter or paparazzo. "We did our own cooking," she recalled. "Very plain and low in salt or fat. Pasta every once in a while but not in a rich sauce. Sometimes I had a little craving for ice cream and Ines would get some—but no pickles with it."

Only intimates knew Sophia's whereabouts, but when her mother's cleaning lady overheard a phone conversation and sold what she learned to *La Stampa* for 50,000 lire, the journalistic hordes began storming the Geneva Intercontinental. Fortunately, the hotel's Swiss-efficient security guard never allowed her pursuers past the lobby.

Dr. de Watteville acknowledged that Sophia was his patient, briefly explained her history of miscarriages, and begged everybody to respect her privacy so that she could have a successful pregnancy this time. The resulting press coverage was astonishing, both for its worldwide scope and for some of its inventiveness. A German tabloid reported that Sophia was hiding out with a pregnant Neapolitan teenager, just waiting for the baby to be born so she could buy it from the mother and pass it off as her own.

News of Sophia's childbearing problems seemed to touch the hearts of people everywhere, especially those with similar experiences. Cards, letters, telegrams, and flowers arrived from as far away as Japan and Argentina, followed by parcels of baby clothes and toys, many of them handmade by the senders.

Apparently, many from the Roman Catholic world had also forgiven Sophia. Priests and nuns wrote that they were lighting candles for her. Fans sent crucifixes, medals, and figurines of the Madonna and favorite saints.

"Sometimes I felt I wasn't having the baby for Carlo, I was having it for the whole world," Sophia recalled. "When a soldier fighting in Vietnam writes to say he is praying for me, it's really shattering."

Sophia believed that it all helped. "It was a wonderful realization—that people who didn't know me, except through my films, were treating me like their own sister," she said. "I don't know why, but perhaps because in films I'd been portraying human and natural characters—peasants, mothers—the contradiction that I wasn't able to have children of my own made people very upset. They knew me as something else. More than that, they could read between the lines of the gossip columns and news stories to know that this yearning of mine was sincere. That must be why they followed me all the way through with such affection and love."

Dr. de Watteville or members of his staff came every day to monitor Sophia's condition. When she entered the danger zone of her third month, the time of her two miscarriages, she became very apprehensive that it would happen again. She soon started experiencing the same sort of nausea and lightheadedness, but the doctor gave her a massive injection of estrogen, and by the next day the crisis was over and she felt fine again.

Sophia's nervousness continued, but she finally became calmer when Dr. de Watteville brought a sound-amplifying machine to the hotel so that she could listen to the baby's heartbeat. Her worst fears seemed confirmed as the doctor probed her belly with the sounding cup and she heard nothing. But after twenty minutes, she picked up a steady rhythm and started crying with joy.

"I could have listened to that lovely tattoo for the rest of the day," she recalled, "and I was disappointed when the doctor finally disconnected the machine and carted it away. It had been one of the grandest moments of my life."

After four months confined to a hotel suite, boredom set in and Sophia tried to find something to occupy her. "I had a brilliant idea to start answering my fan mail. But the more I answered, the more mail I got back, so it became too much. Instead, I started puttering around in the kitchen, which wasn't too smart because the doctor told me to stay off my feet."

But it inspired Sophia to start writing a cookbook, or at least the basis for one. In a notebook that she kept beside the bed, she began jotting down all the recipes that she and secretary Ines could remember or get from relatives and friends. Every day, Ines prepared one or two of the recipes for their meals and then they cataloged them in a card file, along with the results of their taste tests.

Carlo Ponti popped in frequently from Rome or London, where Fred Zinnemann was doing the advance work for *Man's Fate*. Ponti had also started production of two more MGM ventures. *The Best Little House in London,* a sex romp being directed by Philip Saville, was a showcase for David Hemmings, star of *Blow-Up,* who this time played dual roles as a wicked womanizer and a male virgin.

In Italy, Ponti had Vittorio De Sica back directing Marcello Mastroianni, but working together for the first time in the English language with a romantic tearjerker, *A Place for Lovers*. Sophia's pregnancy had eliminated her from the project, which was originally entitled *Amanti* and revolved around a heroine suffering from an incurable disease. Ponti was delighted when MGM hired Faye Dunaway, a hot property since being Oscar-nominated for *Bonnie and Clyde,* to replace Sophia. He lived to regret it, however, when Mastroianni and Dunaway really fell in love and nearly destroyed themselves, as well as the movie, in the explosive affair that developed.

Although Ponti didn't want to press the issue with Sophia, he was already preparing for her return to filmmaking, which needed to be top grade if it was to erase memories of her long string of flops. Needless to say, Ponti turned to De Sica and writer Cesare Zavattini for help. He told them to develop something with Sophia and Mastroianni in mind for the leads, perhaps with the epic quality of *Doctor Zhivago* as a switch from their rowdy comedies.

As Sophia remained in seclusion in Geneva, her thirty-fourth birthday ticked by, and before she knew it she was writing Christmas cards and dispatching Ines to do her gift shopping. In her final weeks, she relented and sent for her mother and sister for moral support. Carlo Ponti canceled all his appointments and joined them.

Because of Sophia's previous miscarriages, the doctor had always intended a cesarean delivery, but that became absolutely essential when the baby shifted to a breech position, meaning that it would be born feet first rather than the usual head first. There was potential for strangulation if the baby's head got tangled in the umbilical cord.

Since Sophia could choose the date of birth from several the doctor proposed, she was tempted to pick December 25, a lucky day for miracles like the one she was praying for. But the hospital was going to be on a short-staffed holiday schedule and de Watteville didn't want to take any chances, so he recommended they wait until December 29. Early the previous day, Sophia left her suite at the Intercontinental in a wheelchair and was taken down to the loading entrance of the hotel ballroom, where a car was waiting to drive her to Geneva Cantonal Hospital. At five in the morning, there were no reporters or photographers lurking in ambush.

In her room in the hospital's maternity section, Sophia found a bassinet already standing next to the bed. "When I saw it, I had them take it away," she recalled. "I knew I was having the baby the very next day, but I wasn't taking any chances. When a nurse, seeing how nervous I was, tried to occupy me by asking what names I had in mind for the baby, I told her sharply that I didn't know, even though I knew very well. I wouldn't let myself believe until I actually saw the baby."

Sophia had given little thought to the cesarean operation itself until she was wheeled down to the amphitheater the next morning to be prepared for surgery. Terror seized her as she was hooked to a lifeline, had her stomach taped around the area where the doctor intended to cut, and waited for the anesthetic to be given. She recalled later that as soon as she lost consciousness, "I dreamed that the baby had died. I kept hearing a voice saying 'He's dead, he's dead, your baby is dead.' In my dream, I began screaming, 'Don't let him die. I beg you.' "

Sophia also would complain later of receiving insufficient anesthetic, which started to wear off as she was being stitched up and, as a result, caused her excruciating pain. But it seemed worth it as she opened her eyes and the beaming Dr. de Watteville told her, "You have a fine baby boy." But her son had already been whisked off to an incubator per hospital regulations, and she didn't fully believe it until several hours later, when he was finally placed in her arms.

By that time, Ponti was at her bedside. "At last . . . at last, I am a complete wife to you," she told him. Ponti kept kissing her and whispering sweet nothings in her ear.

The baby weighed in at seven pounds, three ounces, and for the time being had a tiny bandage on one buttock. The doctor's scalpel had nicked it during the operation.

In the Italian tradition for firstborns, he was named after his father, with the middle names of Hubert, in honor of the doctor who delivered him, and Leoni, after his paternal grandfather. But Carlo Ponti Jr. quickly became known in the family as Cipi (pronounced "Cheepee"), as the initials CP sound in Italian.

Meanwhile, the news media were clamoring for details of the blessed event. Sophia and Ponti reluctantly agreed to hold a press conference the following day in the hospital's main amphitheater. With many flying in from Italy and other parts of Europe, more than four hundred reporters and photographers attended, causing one to wisecrack that it was probably a larger turnout than for some of Sophia's recent movies.

Sophia was too weak to stand on her feet, let alone answer questions. But she agreed to be wheeled around the amphitheater in a mobile bed, holding the baby in her arms, so photographers could get their photos and TV newsreel shots. Eight of the hospital nurses helped out. Carlo Ponti did all the talking for his wife, while Dr. de Watteville and his team fielded the medical questions.

Ponti drew chuckles when he proclaimed rather grandly, "This child is a triumph for women all over the world." To show the couple's appreciation, he said, they were donating a million dollars toward a new consultation center that de Watteville was planning. The Pontis' gift would be used to buy a row of old residential buildings in downtown Geneva to house the project.

"The rich will pay to be treated there, the poor will not," Ponti said. "There doesn't exist in the whole world something like this. We need it—especially in Europe."

De Watteville then described it as "primarily for women coming from abroad with special problems—women who don't need or can't afford long hospital stays and might find hotels impractical or prohibitive. But it will also be for men—and treatment of sterility and infertility problems."

When the time came to leave the hospital, in the second week of January 1969, Sophia kept finding excuses not to, starting with a fear of exposing Cipi to a current epidemic of Hong Kong flu. She turned her hospital room into a safe zone by having the windows sealed against germs and ordering visitors to wear sanitary masks. She moved Cipi out of the hospital nursery and took over his total care, including the feeding, bathing, and diapering. Sophia later acknowledged that she was being overprotective and suffering from post-partum craziness.

When Cipi was a month old, Sophia arranged for a Catholic priest to come to the hospital to perform the christening. Ponti flew over from Rome for the ceremony, bringing with him Sophia's sister, Maria, the appointed godmother. Dr. de Watteville accepted the Pontis' request that he be the godfather.

It wasn't until mid-February, fully fifty days after Cipi's birth, that mother and son finally checked out, and that was only because the hospital authorities insisted. Sophia had no alternative but to return to Rome, which would be as much of an adjustment for her as for the baby, since she'd been away from home now for nearly a year.

By this time, Sophia had received a vast assortment of baby gifts from all over the world that she would have to take with her. Two of the most striking were "naive" religious paintings by artist-admirers in Yugoslavia and Romania. By age three, Cipi had grown so fond of the "naifs" that he began demanding more. His parents rapidly covered the nursery walls with them, often having to pay exorbitant prices of $750 or more when dealers found out who they were selling to.

Another prized gift was a framed picture of three-year-old Jason Emanuel Gould, inscribed with a message from his mother, Barbra Streisand, that he shared a December 29 birthday with Cipi, as well as a breech birth by cesarean section. The two stars had been a mutual-admiration society since first bumping noses at a gala in London two years ago. "If only I could sing like you," Sophia gushed, to which Streisand replied, "If I was as beautiful as you, I wouldn't have to open my mouth."

Before flying back to Italy, Sophia hired a young Swiss nanny named Ruth Bapst to accompany them and to join the live-in staff at Villa Ponti. Bapst was multilingual and would eventually be expected to teach Cipi languages.

Back home in Rome, Sophia's obsession with the baby continued. She bought a tape recorder and tried to preserve every sound that Cipi made. Tazio Secchiaroli, a still photographer who always worked on Sophia's Italian movies, came once a week to take "candids" for the family album. She also persuaded Ponti to hire a 16-millimeter movie cameraman to visit once a month to make a film of Cipi's progress.

"Sophia's day revolved around the baby," a friend recalled. "If she wasn't spending time with Cipi, she was always talking about him, how much he ate, how much he grew. She always clutched him with both hands, like she didn't want to let him go. She never allowed anyone to touch him except the nurse— not her secretary, not even the grandmother, seldom even the father!"

Photographer Secchiaroli remembered a time when Sophia became convinced that Cipi was losing his voice: "The baby's crying grew a little faint. Sophia panicked, but the Swiss nurse tried to explain that she'd given him some orange juice and the acidity makes the voice go down. Well, Sophia was still so frantic that I think she was ready to phone Geneva. But I told her that I'd seen it happen myself with my own children, particularly when the juice is cold. Sophia looked at me as if I'd saved her life."

Sophia stopped nursing the baby at three months. "He no longer needed it," she said later. "Even after just a month, a mother has given her child all the antibodies he needs. The food and milk preparations they have nowadays are certainly as good as anything a mother can give a baby." Still, she didn't trust the canned variety. Everything had to be prepared by her kitchen staff from fresh ingredients.

Though Villa Ponti was walled in and well protected, Sophia still had to worry about paparazzi. "Photographers with long lenses hide in the hills and sneak pictures of me wheeling the baby in the garden," she said in one of her rare interviews at the time. "It's ridiculous. When you've taken one such picture, there's no sense doing it again and again. But the funniest thing is the captions that go with them. If I'm in old clothes with my hair not combed, they criticize me. They call me a recluse and say I'm obsessed with the baby. Well, of course I'm mad about my child. What new mother isn't? Who can deny it?"

Sophia had slight reason to stray from Villa Ponti because it was the perfect place to bring up a baby. There was even a miniature zoo waiting for Cipi when he was old enough to appreciate it. Ponti had already stocked it with pheasants, rabbits, and ducks. A pair of fawns and some exotic birds were on order.

In the late spring of 1969, Sophia's long break from filmmaking finally came to an end as Ponti made a deal for her first since *Ghosts, Italian Style* two years ago. Released during Sophia's confinement in Switzerland, that film came and went so fast that few people saw it, but it was her fifth expensive flop in a row and left Ponti pushing the panic buttons. He had two prestigious projects lined up that he hoped would reverse the trend, but Sophia herself wasn't keen on the second and Ponti had to drop her from his plans.

That happened to be one of the leads in *Man's Fate*. Sophia liked the script that had been written by Han Suyin, author of *Love Is a Many Splendored Thing,* but the prospect of spending three months on location in the Far East and another four months shooting interiors at Shepperton Studios in England seemed more than the new mother could cope with. She would need to take Cipi with her or leave him in Rome with his nanny, neither of which seemed advisable for an infant.

But Sophia had slight reason to quarrel with *Sunflower,* the film that De Sica and Cesare Zavattini had developed for her and Marcello Mastroianni. Though there would be four weeks of locations in the Soviet Union, most of the production would be centered at Rome's Cinecittà. If any crisis should develop with the baby while the Pontis were away, they could jet home from Moscow in three hours.

Since MGM had already committed $18 million to *Man's Fate,* it wasn't prepared to spend another $10 million on *Sunflower,* so Ponti landed back with his ex-coproducer, Joseph E. Levine. The two had fallen out over the division of profits from *Yesterday, Today and Tomorrow* and *Marriage, Italian Style,* but both were ready to forgive and forget. Ponti needed financing and Levine needed a big prestige movie to impress Avco Corporation, the new owners of his Embassy Pictures.

Sunflower (titled in the plural as *I girasoli* for the Italian release) told of a newlywed Neapolitan couple separated by the outbreak of World War II. After soldier-husband Antonio is sent to the Russian front, Giovanna never hears from him again and finally assumes that he's been killed. Five years later, at the war's end, she tries to get government confirmation of his death, but when the archives prove nothing either way, she decides to go to Russia to continue her search. Something tells her that Antonio might have ended up in a prison camp. After a fruitless week in Moscow, she heads for the Ukraine, where fields bursting with the first sunflowers of summer give her renewed hope that her husband is still alive.

Needless to say, he is, but suffering from wartime amnesia and married to a peasant who saved his life and has since given him a daughter. Antonio doesn't recognize nor remember Giovanna when they meet. It's all too upsetting for her to handle and she rushes back to Italy to try to forget and to start a new life of her own. After she marries and has a son, some of Antonio's amnesia lifts and he gets permission to visit his homeland. Of course, Giovanna and Antonio fall in love all over again. But after a brief affair, they both realize that they must return to their spouses and children.

The highly romantic and tragic soap opera was a radical departure for De Sica and Zavattini, who were under pressure from Ponti to deliver a tearjerker comparable to *Doctor Zhivago*. Ponti made a deal with Mosfilm, the principal Soviet production company, to provide equipment and facilities for the month of locations. It marked one of the first times that the Soviet government permitted moviemakers from the West to work there. Ponti hoped it would lead to a full-scale coproduction deal with Mosfilm. He had not given up on starring Sophia in a remake of Tolstoy's *Anna Karenina,* perhaps with Luchino Visconti directing.

By the time Ponti was ready to start *Sunflower* in the summer of 1969, his previous production with De Sica, the Mastroianni–Faye Dunaway *A Place for Lovers,* had just entered release via MGM and was becoming the laughingstock of the industry. A revered American critic called it "the most godawful piece of pseudo-romantic slop I've ever seen!" Others described it as the finish of De Sica and Mastroianni, and predicted it would ruin Dunaway's chances of becoming a major star. If *Sunflower* had been another MGM production, the studio probably would have canceled it, but luckily for Ponti it wasn't.

Mastroianni later admitted that he signed for *Sunflower* only because of the chance to visit Russia for the first time. He and Sophia were the only cast members to travel from Italy. All the Russian characters were played by locals, including the major costarring role of Mascia, Antonio's peasant wife. De Sica selected one of the top Soviet stars, Ludmila Savelyeva, best known in the West for her Natasha in Sergei Bondarchuk's Oscar-winning version of *War and Peace.*

Since Sophia's movies rarely had roles that gave another actress an opportunity to shine (*Two Women* was the most recent), she wasn't too happy about the choice of Savelyeva. Although they didn't have many scenes together, she thought that Savelyeva could wind up stealing the movie in her showy moments with Mastroianni. Sophia also became resentful of all the time that De Sica spent coaching the Russian.

Sophia vented her feelings to her little entourage on the set, the members of which were always criticizing Savelyeva's performance to De Sica's assistants. It succeeded only in making De Sica more focused on Savelyeva, but as the producer's wife, Sophia may have taken drastic action later. She reportedly made sure that Savelyeva's scenes were cut to the bone in the final editing of the movie.

Sophia found the Russian public even more welcoming than they were dur-

ing her first visit in 1965 for the Moscow Film Festival. "They ask you for an autograph, and give you fruit, flowers, or something in exchange," she said later.
"In restaurants, they were always sending caviar and vodka to our table. They
feel that if you give them something, they must give something in return. It's a
lovely idea. They reminded me of Neapolitans. There is something very open
about them. They wear their friendliness where you can see it—on their faces."

Back in Rome again for the completion of *Sunflower,* the Pontis couldn't resist De Sica's suggestion of turning Carlo Ponti Jr. into an actor for the brief role
of Sophia's baby son. Now going on eight months, Cipi had black hair, large
eyes, and olive skin like his mother, and a round chubby face like his father's.
His *padre* in the film, portrayed by the darkly handsome Germano Longo, was
supposed to be a Neapolitan factory laborer.

Why not? Sophia for a change told De Sica exactly what to do. She had the
director come to the nursery at Villa Ponti with just a few technicians, hand-held
equipment, and the necessary props. Several closeups and medium shots were
required of Cipi in a wooden crib, sucking happily on a pacifier. De Sica predicted his performance would win him an Oscar for the best gurgling of the
year.

Sophia breathed a sigh of relief when *Sunflower* finally finished and she
could go back to being a full-time mother. Ponti had no definite plans for her
next film, but several possibilities were being considered, including *Anna
Karenina* and a Sergio Leone western in which she would be teamed with
Steve McQueen.

To celebrate the completion of *Sunflower,* Ponti told Sophia that he was going to buy her the biggest diamond in the world, a 69-carat whopper coming up
for auction at Parke Bernet in New York. Since Ponti used an intermediary, he
didn't discover until later that he was bidding against such other big spenders
as Aristotle Onassis, Richard Burton, and the president of Cartier. The gem finally went to Cartier for $1.05 million, but Elizabeth Taylor Burton was so up-
set that her husband promptly bought it for her from Cartier for $1.1 million.

The news coverage that Taylor received as owner of the inch-long, inch-thick
diamond elevated her to Queen of the Beautiful People and that, apparently,
was too much for Sophia to bear. When the acquisition came up during an interview she happened to be doing at the time, she told the reporter, "Carlo
could have bought the stone if he wanted. But he had it appraised before the
auction and decided not to bid more than $700,000, which is a long way from
what the Burtons paid. And I assure you, Carlo knows the value of jewelry."

Meanwhile, Ponti was getting ready to start the $10 million *Man's Fate*, which director Fred Zinnemann had been preparing for nearly three years. Liv Ullmann, who'd become a world star through the Swedish films that she made with her director-lover Ingmar Bergman, was signed to replace Sophia as the female lead. Also heading the cast were Peter Finch, David Niven, Max von Sydow, and Eiji Okada, the Japanese star of *Hiroshima, Mon Amour*. One-third of the movie would be shot in Singapore and Malaysia (doubling for the China of 1927), with the rest based at MGM's Boreham Wood studios near London.

Three days before rehearsals were to begin, Ponti and Zinnemann were summoned to a meeting in London with an executive from the Hollywood headquarters of MGM, which had recently been taken over by tycoon Kirk Kerkorian and was undergoing a drastic shake-up under his new production chief, James Aubrey. Studio accountants had noticed that most of Ponti's previous films for MGM had gone considerably over budget, and with the notable exceptions of *Doctor Zhivago* and *Blow-Up,* had also cost MGM millions in losses.

Though MGM had allotted $10 million to *Man's Fate,* Ponti and Fred Zinnemann had already spent over $4 million on preproduction, including scriptwriting, hiring the cast and technicians, building sets, and so forth. With six months of filming still to come, including the location work in the unpredictable weather of the Far East, MGM was getting jittery that costs might double by the time that the movie finished.

MGM took a tough position with Ponti and asked him to sign a guarantee that he would pay for any overages above $10 million. Ponti thought it over and refused. He never put up any of his own money if he could avoid it. MGM threatened to cancel the movie if he didn't change his mind. Ponti guessed they were bluffing. He couldn't believe a studio would pull that on such a prestigious project as *Man's Fate*, directed by Fred Zinnemann, one of Hollywood's greatest.

But when Ponti continued to resist, MGM stuck to its guns and, on November 18, 1969, officially canceled the production of *Man's Fate*. The announcement sent shock waves through the movie industry and earned MGM condemnation from the Screen Directors Guild and other labor unions. Ponti hoped that the groundswell of sympathy would help him to make a deal for *Man's Fate* with another of the major studios, but that didn't happen. One of the reasons was that Ponti would first have to pay back MGM the more than $4 million spent so far. To make up for it, *Man's Fate* would have to be rebudgeted for at least $15 million, which was far more than anyone wanted to spend in 1969–70.

The cancellation had a devastating effect on the career of Fred Zinnemann, leaving a seven-year gap between his last movie, the 1966 *A Man for All Seasons,* and his next one, the 1973 *The Day of the Jackal.*

Ponti rebounded more quickly, but he would never produce another movie for MGM. That alliance ended disastrously a couple of months later, in January 1970, when MGM finally got around to releasing *Zabriskie Point,* Ponti's second venture with director Michelangelo Antonioni. The blistering attack on materialism and the American lifestyle created the same controversy and censorship problems as *Blow-Up,* but did not repeat the latter's success at the box office, causing MGM to lose all of its $6 million investment.

Ponti needed a smash hit to restore Hollywood's confidence in him as a producer. Hopefully, *Sunflower* would be it. Ponti and Joe Levine decided to release the movie in Europe first, with tremendous hoopla. They spent $250,000 on an international press junket in conjunction with the world premiere. How Ponti managed it is unknown, but the President of Italy, Giuseppe Saragat, agreed to be patron of the gala, which would be held at the Rome Opera House on March 15 and benefit the International Red Cross.

Though Sophia wasn't thrilled by the idea, Ponti persuaded her to host a luncheon at their villa in Marino for all the reporters, editors, and columnists who'd been flown in from around the world. It was the first time that press were permitted on the estate. Photographers were barred except those hired by Ponti and Levine to provide coverage. Fifty armed guards were added to the Pontis' usual security crew.

At the premiere the following night, Sophia arrived wearing a spectacular gold lamé gown, but was angrily booed by a pack of paparazzi who'd tried, unsuccessfully, to crash the luncheon party. Later, during the showing of *Sunflower,* the audience broke into thunderous applause at its first glimpse of bit player Carlo Ponti Jr., no doubt egged on by the proud parents sitting in the opera house's royal box.

Further assisted by a gigantic advertising campaign, *Sunflower* opened to record-breaking business in Italy and the rest of Europe. Reviews were not good, but in Europe critics didn't have much power over box-office attendance, which is another reason why *Sunflower* opened there ahead of the United States.

NIGHTMARE IN NEW YORK

⟨ℐᗡ⟩

THE success of *Sunflower* in Europe during the spring of 1970 enabled Joseph E. Levine to secure a booking at Radio City Music Hall for the American premiere, but not until autumn. Since so much depended on the movie becoming a hit, Sophia promised to come to New York at that time to do publicity interviews and help in the national launching.

Sunflower was doing so well in Italy that the local exhibitors started clamoring for another De Sica–Loren–Mastroianni picture as soon as possible. Unluckily, De Sica, along with scriptwriter Zavattini, had already committed to another producer's *The Garden of the Finzi-Continis,* but Ponti did some fast dealing and purchased a script that had been making the rounds and seemed to suit Sophia and Mastroianni. For director, he hired Dino Risi, a disciple of De Sica's who had directed two of Sophia's first Italian successes (titled, in English, *Sign of Venus* and *Scandal in Sorrento*) and had become much admired for his gentle, humorous style.

Again thanks to the European grosses on *Sunflower,* Ponti obtained partial financing from Warner Brothers in exchange for world distribution rights. Warner really wasn't risking much because the budget was only $2 million and Ponti had made his usual arrangements for government subsidies by setting it up as an Italian-French coproduction.

Entitled *La moglie del prete* (*The Priest's Wife*), the latest effort of Mr. and Mrs. Carlo Ponti created an uproar in Italy as soon as it was announced. Just that year, the Italian parliament had finally voted to legalize divorce, much to the consternation of the Vatican, which deemed it part of a plot by the Left to totally destroy its power. The Pontis were accused of more anti-clerical sabotage, which supposedly was their way of getting back at the devout Catholics who had caused them so much grief over the years.

Ironically, one of the first to take advantage of the new divorce legislation was Sophia's sister, Maria Mussolini, who promptly unloaded her jazz pianist-husband after years of putting up with his philandering for the sake of their two children. Once liberated, Maria, who'd never finished secondary school, returned to earn a diploma, and then opened a public relations office, with guess who as her first client.

Adding fuel to the controversy over *The Priest's Wife* was the casting of Mastroianni as a Roman Catholic priest. Mastroianni had long been in the Vatican's bad books for his flagrantly open marriage, which kept him bouncing back and forth between his wife and daughter and a constantly changing harem of beauties such as Faye Dunaway and Ursula Andress.

Scripted by Ruggero Maccari and Bernardino Zapponi, *The Priest's Wife* turned Sophia into Valeria Billi, a headstrong pop singer who's considering suicide over a broken romance but gets talked out of it by a compassionate voice on a telephone help line. Haunted by the voice, she tracks down its owner, who, of course, turns out to be Don Mario. Despite or due to the fact that he's a Catholic priest, Valeria falls in love and chases him until she finally breaks down some of his iron resistance. Their first kiss gradually leads to a sexual affair. They become headline news when Don Mario writes to the Vatican for a dispensation to marry. While he's waiting for an answer, Valeria becomes a celebrity fronting a rock band under the moniker of The Priest's Wife. It all ends sourly when the Vatican fails to rule on Don Mario's request but offers him a promotion to monsignor, his greatest dream since taking the priestly vows. When he tries to persuade Valeria to live with him clandestinely, she gets disgusted and takes off, neglecting to tell him that she's pregnant.

Church celibacy was then one of the most controversial subjects in Italy. The recent Italian Episcopal Conference termed it the major issue of priesthood. The movie's scriptwriters belonged to a new breed of Italian filmmakers who dared to focus on the problems and evils of national life.

Though the Loren–Mastroianni teamings usually played on their Neapolitan heritages, director Dino Risi chose the city of Padua in northeastern Italy as the setting and production location. "Padua is a fortress of Catholicism, which is why we came here," Risi said in an interview at the time. "When Mastroianni in priest's clothes is seen in public with Sophia in her miniskirts, the atmosphere of a hostile city is vital to the scenes."

Though Cipi was now a rambunctious walker of eighteen months, Sophia decided to leave him in Rome with his nanny to test how he would behave in Mamma's prolonged absence. In case of emergency, she had the number of a helicopter service that could fly her home quickly.

Meanwhile, she kept in touch by phone and spoke to Cipi several times a day. Thanks to help from his Swiss nanny, he was starting to talk in three languages. His favorite word at the moment was "again," which he knew in English, Italian, and German.

The church authorities in Padua were hostile to the movie, condemning it in Sunday sermons and in editorials in the parish newspapers. Hundreds of complaints were received from the public over the extras hired to portray priests and black-robed students at Mastroianni's seminary. During their breaks, the men frequently dropped into bars for a drink or stood around in groups ogling women. Many devout Paduans mistook them for the real thing and were deeply offended.

During an interview with Nino Lo Bello, an Italian journalist, Sophia told him, "We are not making a picture against the Church. We are posing a problem that you know and I know is common these days. We read about it every week. And it's a problem the Church will have to face and solve like all the others; if not in the next ten years, then maybe twenty, maybe fifty.

"Personally, I always like to think of a priest as a human being. And he should experience all the problems every human being does. That's why, for me at least, I think a priest should get married and have a family. Only by being married, having the wife and the children to care for every day, can he begin to understand other people's problems much, much better. He should really suffer as we all do—practically, not theoretically."

Sophia strongly denied reports that her troubles with the Church had turned her into an atheist. "It's true that I no longer practice Catholicism. I don't attend church on Sunday, I don't go to Mass or take communion. But I have great faith in God. I pray always, but I believe in relating directly to God instead of through a priest. I wore out the prayer beads while I was expecting my son."

At the end of the filming, Ponti decided it was time for a family holiday. No less than President Tito of Yugoslavia had invited them to join him at his summer retreat. Ponti was then in the midst of negotiating a coproduction deal with the Yugoslav government. The Pontis were the guests of Tito and his wife Jovanka at the presidential estate on the island of Brioni in the Adriatic Sea.

Bringing along some of their own household help from Marino, they were quartered in a beautiful villa near the summer palace. Since Tito spoke little Italian or English, they communicated mainly in German, with Cipi's nanny pressed into service as interpreter when the going got rough.

A month after returning to Rome, the Pontis packed their suitcases again and flew to New York for the American premiere of *Sunflower*. Their residence this time was the Hampshire House on Central Park South, a onetime luxury hotel that had been converted into a cooperative but still offered full restaurant and housekeeping services to residents. Ponti had purchased an apartment there several years earlier, but loaned it to relatives or close friends most of the time. The cost of maintenance was charged off to his business expenses, so he could afford to be generous.

Joe Levine scored a major coup in persuading Radio City Music Hall to book *Sunflower,* which was the first movie in its thirty-seven-year history to be shown with a dubbed English soundtrack. In the six years since the last De Sica–Loren–Mastroianni films were released in the United States, the so-called art circuit for subtitled foreign movies had virtually dried up, so to protect Avco-Embassy's $10 million investment, Levine had to go straight to a conventional release with a postsynchronized version. Needless to say, that was never mentioned in the marketing of *Sunflower*. Everybody hoped that the fact that Sophia and Mastroianni did their own revoicings would create the impression that the movie really was shot in English. None of the other Italian and Russian actors were famous enough for the average moviegoer to know what they really sounded like.

To make sure that *Sunflower* broke all box-office records at the Music Hall on opening day, Sophia agreed to appear on stage prior to the first screening and answer questions fired at her by a group of friendly journalists assembled by Joe Levine. Since her appearances in front of large audiences were limited to the few she made at Oscar ceremonies and film festivals, she was terrified by the prospect of standing all alone before six thousand people on a stage the width of a city block. But she held the spotlight for thirty minutes, innocuously expressing opinions on love, marriage, babies, food, and fashion. She deflated her public image: "People think I have a hundred percent sex appeal, but it is only imagination. Maybe fifty percent is what I've got. The other fifty percent is their fantasies working on it." When a reporter asked, "Now that you're a mother, would you appear nude in a film?" she replied, "Is that a question to answer before six thousand people?"

The second highlight of Sophia's New York visit was a ninety-minute interview with British television host David Frost for his world-syndicated talk show, which was shown in the United States five nights a week on ABC.

Since the 1960 robbery in England, Sophia rarely traveled with a lot of expensive jewelry, so she arranged to borrow some to wear during the Frost interview. Many top dealers were always happy to oblige legendary ladies to gain their goodwill and to land them as customers. Sophia picked out several pieces from Van Cleef & Arpels, including a large diamond solitaire ring. When David Frost spotted it on her finger, he asked her how it compared in value to the $1.1 million whopper that Richard Burton had given to Elizabeth Taylor. After she stopped laughing, Sophia said it was only a chip by comparison, but guessed it might be worth half a million.

In the midst of Sophia's hectic publicity schedule, Carlo Ponti's father died suddenly in Milan. In the best show-must-go-on tradition, Ponti didn't want Sophia to cancel any of her appointments, so he arranged to fly to Italy alone for the funeral. Sophia accompanied him as far as Kennedy Airport and stayed with him until his flight took off. By the time the limousine returned her to the Hampshire House, she felt so exhausted that after checking up on the sleeping Cipi, she decided to retire instead of watching TV in the den with her secretary and the nanny.

As soon as Sophia entered her bedroom, she thought she saw the moving shadow of a man. She ran back to get Ines and Ruth, but when the trio returned, a search of the bedroom turned up nothing. When Sophia calmed down, she asked Ines to bunk with her for the night just in case. Sealing her ears with anti-noise plugs as was her usual practice, she finally fell asleep.

At seven the next morning, Ines got up to make coffee. When she walked into the kitchen, three strangers were standing there, one of them pointing a gùn at two building employees whom they'd forced into opening a back door for them. Ines started to scream, loud enough that Sophia heard a muffled version through her earplugs.

"I thought I was having a nightmare at first," she recalled. "But when I realized I was awake, the screaming seemed so very distant that I thought it must be coming from outside the apartment. But then a man barged into the room carrying a bunch of keys on a large ring. I was still in a stupor. For a moment I thought he was a doctor carrying a stethoscope. I felt my heart jump and I was sick with fright. The sound of screaming and this stranger, who for a moment I mistook for a doctor, meant only one thing to me. My son. He was ill."

"I screamed, 'It's Cipi, isn't it—what is wrong with my baby?' "

The intruder told her, "Don't panic and everything will be all right." It was only then that Sophia realized it was Ines screaming. One of the gang had hit her with a pistol butt.

"My room was in partial darkness," Sophia said. "The man told me to switch on the light next to the bed. It was then that I saw he was waving a gun and wearing dark glasses. 'This is a holdup,' he said. It was like a second-rate gangster film. He started throwing my jewelry around on the dressing table.

" 'This is junk,' he said. 'I want the real stuff. And if I don't get it . . .' Meanwhile, another man came in with the concierge and the manager, holding a gun to their faces. The manager, poor man, was so weak with shock they let him sit down on a chair. I gave the first man a ruby ring which was on the table. He grabbed it, but wasn't satisfied. I still had some jewels from Van Cleef that I wanted to wear to a big party at Rockefeller Center. The man took those jewels too, but he still wasn't happy and said, 'I want the big ring that I saw you wear on the David Frost show.' "

"What a fool I was to place so much importance on it," Sophia continued. "Here I was being threatened by a gunman, my secretary had been beaten, and God knows what was happening to my baby. I shouted at the man, 'It was not my ring. I borrowed it from Van Cleef and gave it back the same night. I implore you to believe me.' He came toward me. 'Where is that ring?' he said. 'You better get it.' "

Sophia begged him to believe her. "He was a man about my own age, maybe thirty-five or thirty-six," she remembered. "I stared at him closely. I didn't realize it was dangerous to look a thief in the face. They are always scared you might identify them. He became furious. He grabbed me by the hair and pulled my head down until I was lying on the floor. Then he emptied my wallet of a few hundred dollars, took the ruby ring and Van Cleef jewelry. Another man came in and shouted, 'Hurry up, let's go.' But the man who was holding me had a sudden thought. Before he left the room he turned and said, 'Okay, where's your kid? Just tell me where the kid is.' "

"When I heard that and thought they were threatening to kidnap Cipi, I began to shake. It was a mixture of an agony of fear for my son, and fury at myself for having such a stupid fascination for jewelry. I had some more diamonds and things on a table in the corridor. I ran past the gunmen. One of them, thinking that I may be going to call the police, grabbed me. 'Take this,' I said to him, handing him a bag of jewelry. He took it and they ran off. I swear from that moment, when I held Cipi in my arms again and saw that he was safe, I was taught the biggest lesson of my life. I deleted the word 'jewelry' from my vocabulary. To own something which could make other people resort to murder and kidnaping is a threat, not a possession. Perhaps I needed diamonds to prove something to myself. Maybe they were the symbols of success in my career. But it is stupid."

As soon as the thieves departed, leaving their two hostages behind, Sophia phoned the Hampshire House switchboard and received no answer. It turned out that there had been a fourth gang member downstairs who held other employees at gunpoint while the robbery was going on. The whole caper took only fifteen minutes and apparently succeeded because of the early hour (seven on a Sunday morning) and the residential status of the Hampshire House, which didn't have the heavy lobby traffic of a hotel.

About six hours later, across the Hudson River in West New York, New Jersey, some teenagers found a paper bag that had apparently been thrown away by the robbers and contained some of the loot. In addition to a gold-plated bracelet and some keys on a chain, there were Sophia's passport and airplane tickets, plus a check for $14,000 that had been paid to her by Avco-Embassy to cover her out-of-pocket expenses during her New York visit.

Not surprisingly, Sophia stayed in New York no longer than it took to help the police department get started with its investigation. The FBI also got on the case and cabled the dealers in Rome, Paris, and London where the Pontis originally bought the jewelery to get descriptions and evaluations. The stolen items were reported to be worth $700,000, $200,000 of which came from those that Sophia had borrowed from Van Cleef & Arpels and were fully insured. The half million dollars' worth of Sophia's own jewelry was not. Insurance companies had considered her a bad risk since her 1960 robbery in London.

Two days later, a mob of reporters was waiting for Sophia and party when they arrived at Kennedy Airport for the flight back to Rome. "I'm not going to wear jewelry anymore. I'll wear my child's arms around my neck," she said, putting Cipi through an actual demonstration before boarding the plane.

Asked if she might perhaps wear imitation gems instead, she smiled. "It's a good idea. I never thought of it. I never wore anything false in my life."

The robbery had its positive side. Several days of tabloid headlines and radio-TV coverage diverted attention away from the negative reviews for *Sunflower*. After a smash opening week at Radio City Music Hall, the pans and equally bad word of mouth finally caught up with the movie and killed it for the American market.

Critics denounced *Sunflower* as a turgid and old-fashioned soap opera, completely out of synch with the bold new breed of movies like *Midnight Cowboy, Easy Rider, M*A*S*H, Five Easy Pieces,* and *Women in Love.* Stefan Kanfer perhaps summed it up best in his review for *Time* magazine: "Why should so many proved talents squander themselves on *Sunflower?* For *pane?* Certainly—but also to counter the sexual revolution with the kind of romantic movie they don't make anymore. *Che mal fortuna*—the pornography of sex cannot be replaced by the opera of soap."

No doubt the dubbed English soundtrack was another factor in the box-office flop of *Sunflower* in the United States. Those moviegoers who insisted on seeing original-language versions with subtitles were given no choice but to stay away. During the Music Hall run, scores walked out and demanded a refund as soon as they noticed the postsynchronized voices. New York City consumer advocate Bess Myerson received so many complaints that she started campaigning for a city law requiring theaters and film advertising to prominently display whether a foreign-made movie was being shown dubbed or subtitled.

The American floppola of *Sunflower* made it next to impossible for Carlo Ponti to interest any of the major Hollywood studios in signing another deal with him and/or Sophia in the same big-budget, multimillion-dollar category. He decided to concentrate on the smaller European coproductions, which were cheap by Hollywood standards. With luck, they could earn a profit without having to worry about getting distribution in the United States, which would be extra gravy if it happened.

That was Ponti's reasoning behind *The Priest's Wife,* which turned out to be a hit in Italy and the rest of Europe, but later bombed in the States (despite Warner Brothers' efforts to please everybody by releasing both subtitled and dubbed versions). *New York Times* critic Vincent Canby, who'd called *Sunflower* "painful to endure," found *The Priest's Wife* slightly better, but "a decade away from *Yesterday, Today and Tomorrow* and *Marriage, Italian Style,* which seemed to have created a new subcategory of film comedy."

Due to the movie's failure in the United States, Warner opted for a smaller world stake in Ponti's next Italian production, which caused him to make up the difference by selling the American distribution rights to United Artists.

Meanwhile, between the death of Ponti's father and the trauma of Sophia's gunpoint encounter with jewel thieves, the couple were too upset to think about moviemaking for the moment. Not surprisingly, Sophia became intensely concerned about security when she returned from New York. At Villa Ponti, new burglar alarms were installed and iron grilles put on the windows. The guards were given walkie-talkies and German shepherd dogs to assist them in their twenty-four-hour surveillance. Barbed wire was installed on all the walls surrounding the six-acre estate.

Since the location of the villa was well known to the public, Ponti had, for several years, been secretly buying up parcels of land in northern Italy, about twenty miles from his native Milan, to build a family hideaway. By the end of 1970, he had turned them into a ranch of over eight hundred acres. Hidden within woods at the center was the Pontis' residence, a remodeled hunting lodge that still had antlers, stuffed birds, and similar trophies decorating the vestibule.

After the New York misadventure, Sophia began spending more and more time at the ranch with Cipi, but she didn't want to move there permanently because the climate tended to be very damp and misty in the fall and winter. Cipi, however, would have been happy to stay there forever, due to all the animals in residence. His father had started another small zoo, and there was also a large herd of cattle.

During the family's summer vacation in Yugoslavia, Tito had boasted so much about his prize Montenegro bulls that he put an idea into Ponti's head to try mating them with some of Italy's finest cows. Though bulls were not supposed to be exported from Yugoslavia, Tito arranged for the Pontis to receive a shipment direct from his farm outside the aptly named Titograd, the capital of Montenegro province.

While looking for ways to keep occupied until another movie came along, Sophia decided to try writing a cookbook, using some of the recipes that she had collected and experimented with during her lengthy hibernation in Geneva prior to Cipi's birth. Longtime friend Basilio Franchina arranged for food writer Vincenzo Buonassisi to help Sophia with the project, which was eventually published worldwide in 1972 in assorted languages (including Japanese!) by Rizzoli, Doubleday, and others under titles ranging from *In the Kitchen with Love* to *Cooking with Sophia*.

Sophia confessed to a lifelong habit of giving food nicknames to loved ones and friends. Carlo Ponti's was usually *Involtino* (roulade), but when he was especially nice to her, she called him *Polpettone* (meat loaf) or *Suppli* (a croquette composed of rice and mozzarella cheese). What Sophia nicknamed her husband when she was angry at him can only be guessed at.

In the spring of 1971, Sophia started her twenty-first starring vehicle with Ponti as producer, a comedy entitled for the Italian release *Mortadella*, which is the word for a certain type of spicy sausage made from pork and beef. Since the nearest equivalent to *mortadella* in American English is *baloney*, it seemed advisible to pick another title for the U.S. release, which became *Lady Liberty*.

Sophia played a volcanic Neapolitan named Maddalena Clarrapico, who's been working double shifts in a sausage factory to save money to fly to New York to marry her longtime fiancé Michele, the owner of a restaurant in Little Italy. When she's passing through customs at Kennedy Airport, inspectors for the U.S. Food and Drug Administration seize a big silver-wrapped *mortadella* that's intended as Michele's wedding present but violates a federal law banning imported meat products. Maddalena refuses to surrender the sausage and lands in detention, to be sent back to Italy if she persists. A newspaper columnist who witnessed the fracas writes a story about it for the next morning's edition and wins Maddalena support from the Italian-American community. But by that time, she has already managed to get released by eating the entire *mortadella* and destroying the evidence.

But Maddalena's troubles are just beginning. She gets into a fight with her fiancé, splits, and seeks help from her defender, the newspaper columnist. They end up spending the night together, but when he turns out to be married with kids, Maddalena quickly decides to go back to Michele if he'll still have her. Unhappily, Michele is eager to take her back, but only because he believes that Maddalena's sudden celebrity will help his restaurant business. When she catches on, she's off to start some new adventure in the land of the free and the brave.

The director of *Lady Liberty* was Mario Monicelli, who'd worked expertly with Marcello Mastroianni and Vittorio Gassman in the past and was best known outside Italy for the comedy caper *Big Deal on Madonna Street*. In an interview at the time, Sophia explained why Monicelli was chosen. "This is his first film with an American background," she said. "Maybe he can see things an American director cannot see any more because they are too accustomed to their own country. Maybe he can show sides of American life that haven't been shown before: the humor, the loneliness, the confusion and wonder of a foreigner who comes to a new country."

For the first time in over a decade, Sophia would be working without a major male costar. In *Lady Liberty* there was room for two. But for the Italian market Ponti wanted at least one native romantic lead, and he selected Luigi Proietti, a popular movie and TV comedian, to play Maddalena's fiancé.

Ponti allotted ten weeks to the New York production schedule, the longest time that the couple spent there since filming *That Kind of Woman* in 1958. Despite what had happened at the Hampshire House eight months before, they were too accustomed to their apartment to want to stay elsewhere. Ponti hired plainclothes security guards to sit in the lobby and outside their front door to make sure they received no surprise visitors this time.

When the casting of Sophia's American leading man began, Ponti selected William Devane, who'd recently won raves for playing the misfit McMurphy in an off-Broadway revival of *One Flew Over the Cuckoo's Nest.*

Working in *Lady Liberty* turned out to be a discouraging beginning to Devane's movie career. "I knew going in that they would have preferred John Guare for the part," he recalled. "They wanted the newspaper columnist to be a Damon Runyon, Jimmy Breslin type of guy. I think that after I started, they were still considering other actors. It was a real fucking madhouse. Sophia would say things to me like, 'It's really not good for us to be working together because we both have sharp features.' That's why she wanted John Guare, because he has a round face with round eyes, which complemented her. She always treated me like a part of the crew until about three weeks into the movie. She overheard me telling somebody about a play I'd written called *The Christmas Dinner.* She asked me if she could read it, so the next day I brought her a copy. She read the play and her whole attitude changed. After that, at least she looked at me."

As luck would have it, while the Pontis were in New York, police finally nabbed two men who were believed involved in the Hampshire House robbery. After Sophia, her secretary, Ines, and several building employees positively identified them, the suspects were arrested and charged not only with robbery, but also with threatening the life of a child.

Before the Pontis returned to Italy, an offer came through for Sophia that would temporarily relieve her producer-husband from the task of providing her with work. Director Peter Glenville had made a deal with writer-producer Dale Wasserman and United Artists to film *Man of La Mancha* and wanted Sophia for leading lady. Glenville, who'd directed Richard Burton and Peter O'Toole in *Becket* and was a close friend of both actors, promised her that one of them would be taking the title role.

Sophia needed no more persuading. She'd been longing to make a musical for years and had loved *La Mancha* when she saw it during its long and record-breaking New York run. She told Ponti to go easy on the pay demands, but he got her $750,000 anyway.

In the meantime, Ponti had another of his own productions waiting for Sophia when they got home. *White Sister* would be the English title for *Bianco, rosso e . . .* , a romantic melodrama that brought Sophia full circle from the bit part she played years ago in *Anna*. Reunited for the first time since then with master director Alberto Lattuada, she portrayed, like Silvana Mangano in *Anna*, a nursing nun torn between her sacred vows and sexual desire.

Coming so soon after *The Priest's Wife*, *White Sister* may have seemed another attempt by the Pontis to provoke their Vatican adversaries. But nuns suffering psychological torment had long been a favorite theme of Italian cinema and pulp fiction, and *White Sister* was intended to be a commercial success. While Ponti had made his usual foreign release arrangements, this time split between Warner Brothers and Columbia Pictures, he was counting on Italy as the primary market. Sophia's leading man was its current rage, Adriano Celentano, often called the Italian Elvis Presley because he was a recording star, entertainer, and movie actor rolled into one.

The movie's English title was a double play on the character's race and white robes. As the story opens, Sister Germana is a nursing missionary in Libya, Italy's former African colony. Germana was once a prostitute, but took the veil after the death of the only man she ever really loved. When Germana is promoted to Mother Superior at a hospital in a small Communist-run town in northern Italy (hence the title *Bianco, rosso e . . .*), she runs into trouble with a patient who's only a common laborer but behaves like he's the head doctor and pokes his nose into everything. The head-on conflict gradually develops into a few kisses and something resembling love. But while Germana is wrestling with her conscience, God seemingly makes the final decision for her. Almost as soon as he's discharged from the hospital, the man dies in an accident, the same fate as the lover who precipitated Germana's becoming a nun.

Notable movie nuns of the past included Ingrid Bergman, Audrey Hepburn, Deborah Kerr, and Loretta Young. Such roles offered a real acting challenge because the robes hid most of the body, while only a portion of the face, from midforehead down, was visible. In Sophia's case, the white framing added an almost ethereal look to her beauty, though some critics later wondered if a real nun would use the eye shadow and false lashes that she rather obviously did.

Since Sophia was still on the Arab boycott list, Ponti had to settle for filming the Libyan exteriors in southern Spain near Almería, which also enabled him to qualify for a government subsidy. As part of that, he was required to hire a Spanish costar, so the role of the Italian hospital administrator went to Fernando Rey, the bearded actor who was a favorite of director Luis Buñuel but also worked frequently in Italian, French, and American films.

White Sister featured several flashbacks into Sister Germana's life before she became a nun, including one that went so far back into childhood that Sophia obviously couldn't play it herself. To ensure a family resemblance, she asked her eleven-year-old niece, Alessandra Mussolini, to take over. Not surprisingly, Alessandra wanted to be an actress just like her aunt.

While Sophia was filming *White Sister*, preparations for *Man of La Mancha* went awry as director Peter Glenville left the project in a dispute with United Artists. As he did with the original play of *Becket*, Glenville wanted to turn *La Mancha* into a big historical spectacle, one that used more of Cervantes' *Don Quixote* than the stage production. UA threw a fit when they saw the proposed $20 million budget and decided to replace him.

Fortunately, that was after Glenville had signed his friend Peter O'Toole for the title role, but UA had to find a new director to take over and put everything together. They hired Arthur Hiller, whose *Love Story* had been a surprise block-buster hit. Hiller had never made a musical before, but seemed adaptable to any kind of script. Since *Love Story*, he'd had two substantial hits with Neil Simon's *Plaza Suite* and Paddy Chayefsky's *The Hospital*.

Ironically, Sophia would now be working for one of Carlo Ponti's chief rivals, Alberto Grimaldi, who took over as producer of *Man of La Mancha* at UA's request. Grimaldi, who'd been a favorite at UA due to a steady run of hits directed by Sergio Leone, Federico Fellini, and Paolo Pasolini, opted to shoot *La Mancha* in Rome at troubled Dinocittà (nickname for the studio complex built in the early 1960s by Dino De Laurentiis), which needed all the activity it could get to stay open.

The Rome base, which was actually fifteen miles south of the city, suited Sophia perfectly because she could commute from home. Filming the Spanish musical in Italy may have seemed a bit loony, but Sophia's previous epic about the fall of the ancient Roman empire had been made entirely in Spain.

Man of La Mancha started out as Dale Wasserman's *I, Don Quixote*, a ninety-minute TV drama with Lee J. Cobb broadcast in 1959 on *DuPont Show of the Month*. A few years later, Wasserman turned it into a musical, with Mitch Leigh as composer and Joe Darion as lyricist. After a successful tryout at the Goodspeed Opera House in Connecticut, they made a deal with New York's new Repertory Company of Lincoln Center, which did not yet have a home, and opened the musical in a temporary theater on the NYU campus in Greenwich Village. Thanks to generally favorable reviews and even better word of mouth, it became the "hottest" ticket in town and eventually moved to Broadway. By the time it finally closed in New York in 1971, *Man of La Mancha* had run nearly six years and spawned productions in forty-five countries in twenty-two languages.

Man of La Mancha gave Sophia two roles to play—a scruffy serving wench named Aldonza, and the hero's virginal dream girl, Dulcinea. Wasserman used a play-within-a-play device, starting out with the imprisonment of writer Miguel de Cervantes during the Spanish Inquisition. When he begins reading his latest work to some of his cellmates, Cervantes is transformed into his own hero, Don Quixote de la Mancha. The story then drifts back and forth between reality and fantasy, but focuses mainly on Don Quixote's wanderings with his devoted servant, Sancho Panza. Fortune blows them, fittingly enough, to a windmill, which in the Don's crazed mind, is a fearsome ogre. Not until a lord of a castle dubs him a knight will he be able to destroy the enchanter. In his delirium, he mistakes a tawdry roadside inn for a castle and its owner as a lord. Even the bawdy Aldonza is elevated to the chaste Dulcinea, whose "name is like a prayer an angel whispers."

The Don confesses to the baffled wench that his mission in life is "to dream the impossible dream . . . to reach the unreachable star." No sooner has the obliging innkeeper dubbed him Knight of the Woeful Countenance than Quixote's mettle is severely tested. A gang of drunken muleteers abducts Aldonza. For a moment, Cervantes becomes himself again as some of his cellmates are removed to be tortured, but back as the Don he finds the gang-raped Aldonza, who pleads with him to accept her for what she is and not as Dulcinea.

As anticipated by Quixote, the enchanter of the windmill suddenly appears, the fantastically costumed Knight of Mirrors, who turns out to be a doctor hired by the Inquisition to cure Cervantes of his delusions. He succeeds all too well in the fierce combat that leaves Quixote mortally wounded. Even Aldonza, insisting now that she is Dulcinea, can't persuade him to become her chivalrous knight again. When he expires, Aldonza sobs, "A man died, but Don Quixote is not dead."

Despite the medieval setting, the musical score for *Man of La Mancha* was written in the contemporary Broadway style and had one song, "The Impossible Dream" (officially titled in the score as "The Quest"), that became a monster hit and perennial standard throughout the world. In fact, it made such a powerful impression that few remembered any of the other songs, although there were a dozen in all, including "Dulcinea," "Little Bird, Little Bird," "It's All the Same," "I Really Liked Him," and the inevitable title number.

The original New York leads in *Man of La Mancha* were Richard Kiley and Joan Diener, both outstanding singers, and Irving Jacobson, a comic actor from the Yiddish theater. While all won acclaim for their performances, none was famous enough to carry an $11 million movie, but the studio hoped that Peter O'Toole and Sophia Loren would pull in the crowds. Thrown in for good measure as Sancho Panza was the roly-poly American actor James Coco, who'd recently finished a long and triumphant run on Broadway in the title role of Neil Simon's *Last of the Red Hot Lovers* and seemed a sure bet for movie stardom.

None of the three stars was a trained singer, although Sophia had done some pleasant vocalizing in a few of her movies and on records. UA hired Saul Chaplin, one of Hollywood's top musical supervisors, to help them out. Chaplin was the miracle man behind *West Side Story*, which used nonsingers in most of the leading roles and wound up winning ten Oscars, including the one for Best Picture. His not-so-secret formula was a mixture of dubbing and an emphasis on *sprechgesang*, a vocal style midway between speech and singing that Rex Harrison used successfully in *My Fair Lady*.

Man of La Mancha started filming in January 1972. Over the years, Sophia had met Peter O'Toole several times at film festivals, so they weren't total strangers, but he treated her like a long-lost friend and bosom buddy. Having done a bit of homework on her background, he insisted on calling her just "Scilicone," which injected some wry speculation into her real name.

"The first time that I used it on her, she just cracked up and fell around the room laughing," O'Toole recalled. "My original impression of Sophia had been of a well-turned-out, extremely skillful piece of machinery. It was only after we began working together that I could see her for what she was. No crap, no artifice—just an extraordinary, sexually attractive lady."

Since the thirty-nine-year-old O'Toole had a reputation as a womanizer, some of the Italian tabloids forecasted an affair with Sophia, though none materialized.

Sophia did develop a close but platonic friendship with the campy James

Coco, who at the time weighed three hundred pounds and told her that the mere sight of food caused him to gain more. "I guess we took to each other because of my Italian roots," Coco recalled. "I felt I had known her forever. She often invited me to her villa and tried out recipes on me."

One day on the set they started reminiscing about their childhoods. "In all innocence," Coco remembered, "I told Sophia that I came from a very poor family. She looked at me like she wrote the book on poverty and sneered, 'What do you know about being poor?' I said that to keep food on the table, we had to grow vegetables in the backyard. 'You had a backyard?,' she asked, like that disqualified us from collecting welfare. 'We couldn't afford a telephone,' I countered. 'We had to go downstairs to the candy store.' 'You lived over a candy store?' she said.

"I thought I had her when I said my father was a cobbler who never earned more than fifty bucks a week in his life, but after a pause, she devastated me with 'You had a father?' "

Whenever time permitted, Sophia loved to drag Coco and/or O'Toole into card games. "Sometimes she would call Peter and me out to the villa on Sunday, our only day off, to play poker," Coco remembered. "She was a real cardshark, a match for any man, or for any experienced player."

"We were totally different characters when we played poker," O'Toole said later. "Sophia swung from cool reserve to a scratching, gesticulating, cursing Neapolitan. I was a bit of the Irish bully and cheat. We ganged up on Coco by concealing deuces and aces—she in her tits and I in my boots. But I will say this for him, and her, they had genuine mirth, and we were all just playing for the fun we got out of it."

Playing a quick hand of poker with O'Toole on the set one day, Sophia suddenly accused him of cheating. As she rose from her chair in a fury, stuffing her stack of chips into her Gucci handbag, O'Toole grabbed it from her and ripped it apart at the seams with both hands.

Without losing her cool, Sophia sat down again, restarted the game, and announced as the stakes the price of a new handbag. And, of course, she won, but by whatever means can only be guessed at. The awed and repentant O'Toole roared, "I love that cow!" as she strolled away.

Making *Man of La Mancha* was hardly all fun and games for Sophia. Though the double role of Aldonza/Dulcinea suited her dramatic talents, it was her most unglamorous since *Two Women*. She wore the same drab (though low-cut) peasant costume throughout and was supposed to look as unwashed and poxy as any wench would have in medieval times. Not the ideal spot to be in for a sex symbol of thirty-seven who was becoming increasingly sensitive about her looks and wanted to expose as little of the ravages of time as possible.

"Sophia gave our still photographer a rough time," the unit publicist recalled. "She went through the contact sheets of his negatives like a hawk, punching holes through everything she wanted destroyed. She had phobias about her large peasant hands and long neck. Whenever she sensed a camera around, she held her head high to conceal the lines at the base of her neck. Nobody was supposed to photograph her without her permission."

Director Arthur Hiller kept sending Sophia back to her dressing room to tone down her makeup and to shake some of the perm out of her long black wig. Peter O'Toole thought it was all a waste. "There is no way that you can deglamorize Sophia Loren," he said later. "The less glossy she is, the more attractive she becomes, especially in the legs-apart, blouse-ripped, eyes-flashing postures."

O'Toole was amused by Sophia's preference for her left profile in the camera setups. "To make sure of it, her contortions were magnificent," he recalled. "Her lightning leg work, ducking, and weaving would shame Muhammad Ali. She didn't want even the cameraman to see that dreaded right profile. If she walked out of a shot and the director demanded a retake, she would glide backwards to her original position rather than turn around. And she was always absolutely open and unblushing about it! I just trotted along on Don Quixote's high heels, poking my head into the lens and hoping for the best."

Sophia and O'Toole did their own singing during the filming. Whatever voices that finally came out of their mouths in the finished movie would have to match their lip movements. Musical director Saul Chaplin realized almost immediately that O'Toole would need a "ghost" except for a few moments where he could talk the lyrics. That postproduction job went to Simon Gilbert.

But Chaplin liked the warmth of Sophia's voice, as well as her Neapolitan sense of rhythm, and decided she wouldn't need a "ghost" when they got around to rerecording the soundtrack in the presence of a full orchestra. When O'Toole heard Sophia singing for the first time, he told her, "Not bad for a wop!" A few days later, when they were acting out a tender embrace, Sophia "accidentally" kneed him in the crotch.

It seemed a bit of a scam that Don Quixote's big show-stopping number, "The Impossible Dream," should be sung by a "ghost." Sophia got a chance to do her own interpretation of it in the touching finale, as Aldonza bids adieu to the dying knight.

Sophia also did what passed for dancing in the big production number where Aldonza is tossed around, mauled, and eventually raped (off camera) by a crew of brutish muleteers. A Broadway critic had once described it as the show's equivalent of the rumble between the teen gangs in *West Side Story*. Choreographed by Gillian Lynne, the scene called for Sophia to punch and kick all of her ten attackers at least once before they finally grabbed her and pounced en masse. At the end of filming it, she had so many bruises on her body that she needed to cover the exposed portions with makeup until they healed.

All that physical exertion apparently caused no internal damage. Within days of finishing her last scene for *Man of La Mancha*, Sophia turned out to be pregnant. O'Toole, who was still in Rome working on the movie, later claimed that he was the first to find out.

"Sophia phoned me from her villa late at night," he recalled. "I think Carlo Ponti was away and she couldn't contact her mother or her sister. 'I want to talk,' she said. 'What about?' I asked. 'I'm pregnant,' she said. 'I had to tell someone.'"

O'Toole wasn't totally surprised: "In recent weeks, she'd been looking pale, and one time on the set she went positively green."

Before leaving Rome, O'Toole gave Sophia a huge ostrich egg. Since she was going to be spending the next nine months in bed anyway, he told her, she might as well try hatching it.

RICHARD AND ELIZABETH

F R O M the first moment that she knew she was pregnant again, Sophia took every safeguard to avoid another miscarriage. Hubert de Watteville predicted that she'd have an easier time because she'd been through it all before. As luck would have it, exactly four years had passed since Cipi's conception, so it was very possible that his new sibling would share that birthday. Since it would be another cesarean delivery, December 29, 1972, was optimistically set as the arrival date.

There was one major change in strategy. Instead of hibernating in Geneva, Sophia would stay at Villa Ponti until her final months. Dr. de Watteville would fly to Rome every two weeks to check her condition; in the intervals, Sophia would be monitored by a Rome specialist whom he trusted.

This time, with three-year-old Cipi to play with and keep her company, it would be more like kindergarten than solitary confinement. The doctor permitted Sophia to go outdoors several times a day, provided she limited it to strolling in the garden or lounging beside the swimming pool.

Sophia broke the news to Cipi by telling him that the *Befana*, the kind old witch who is an Italian equivalent of Santa Claus, would soon be bringing him a baby brother or sister. "I felt I had to tell him immediately because I would no longer be able to run around with him or play any strenuous games. When he started asking why, I didn't want him to worry that I was ill," she recalled.

Cipi adored airplanes, so to prepare him for the time when they would have to move to Geneva for her final confinement, Sophia promised him his first trip there since he was too young to remember. "He was overjoyed. He started looking forward to it. So did I," she said.

Sophia's unexpected pregnancy caused no major problems on the professional front. She'd made no commitments since *Man of La Mancha*. None of the projects on Ponti's current production slate involved Sophia, although, as usual, several were in development for her.

But unless *Man of La Mancha* proved a smash hit, Ponti would have a tough time raising financing for them. *Lady Liberty* had just bombed on both sides of the Atlantic, Sophia's first flop in Europe since *Questi fantasmi,* but her sixth in a row in the United States. Most of America never got a chance to see *Lady Liberty* after United Artists did a disastrous test-run of it in New York as the lower half of a double feature with another of its films that was too weak to stand on its own, the Charles Bronson–Jack Palance western *Chato's Land*.

New York Times critic Vincent Canby, who'd been following the Pontis' collaborations with increasing dismay over the years, wrote that he was starting to suspect that "Carlo Ponti, her producer and her husband, has invented a new film form, the disposable movie, which serves to get his wife's image into theaters and then can be immediately thrown away, like tissues."

Stanley Kauffmann of the *New Republic* chimed in that it was time for Sophia "to sue her producer-husband for nonsupport."

While Sophia was hibernating, Ponti had her frequent teammate, Marcello Mastroianni, working for him in *Che? (What?)*, with Roman Polanski as director. Though Polanski's last movie, the Hugh Hefner–financed *Macbeth,* had lost millions, the huge success of the director's earlier *Rosemary's Baby* sold Ponti on his idea for an erotic spin on *Alice in Wonderland*. Sydne Rome, an American actress who'd become Europe's latest sex bomb, played a wide-eyed innocent who meets some mighty weird characters while she's wandering through the rooms of a millionaire's villa.

Exteriors for *Che?* were filmed at Ponti's own villa near Amalfi, which was entirely secluded in the cliffs and reached by a cable car shaped like a bird cage. Sophia rarely went there because it dated back to Ponti's first marriage and his ex-wife still shared use of it.

The Italian cinema was going through a cycle of soft-core porno movies and gory thrillers, which explains Ponti's switch to *Che?* and *Torso!,* another film he was making at the same time. Graphically entitled *I corpi presentano tracce di violenza carnale* for Italy, it told of a serial killer who preys on beautiful college girls. Sergio Martino directed, with Britons Suzy Kendall and John Richardson heading a multinational cast that also included Tina Aumont, daughter of Maria Montez and Jean-Pierre Aumont.

Though Ponti could no longer count on financing from the major Hollywood studios, he was getting it from somewhere, but exactly where was an industry mystery. Insiders believed it was a combination of foreign tax-shelter money and "up-front" deals, which meant selling the distribution and TV rights in advance to pay for the production. As in the case of Ponti's former partner Dino De Laurentiis, there were also unsubstantiated rumors of funding from the underworld.

As Sophia's confinement continued, Dr. de Watteville pronounced her "absolutely budding with health and happiness" after one of his biweekly trips from Geneva. While she followed the same routine as last time, Sophia found everything much easier now because of Cipi's constant companionship. Though she had always believed it bad luck to dwell on the future, she started praying for a girl this time. By tradition, that would mean another Sophia in the family (or Sofia if they stuck to the Italian spelling). For a middle name, Ponti recommended Penelope, after the goddess of patience in Greek mythology. The expectant mother had certainly been that during her long history of childbearing problems.

And then, in September 1972, calamity struck. There had been forewarnings of it in the past, but everybody considered Sinibaldo Appolloni a harmless *pazzo*. In 1967, he had arrived at the front gate to Villa Ponti carrying a bouquet of flowers and claiming to be Sophia's long-lost husband. Security guards chased him away, and it was another three years before he turned up again, this time also boasting of being Cipi's real father. When the guards examined his "proof," a low-grade copy of a signed photo of Sophia that he probably bought in a collectors' shop, their roars of laughter were enough to send him running.

For what turned out to be his last visit to Villa Ponti, Appolloni sneaked over a side wall of the estate and ran to the front entrance of the villa, where he started pounding on the door and screaming "Give me my son!" When there was no response, he pulled out a hand ax from his knapsack and took a whack at the door.

Meanwhile, Sophia and Ponti were in the back garden with Cipi and his nanny. As soon as they heard the noise, Sophia got so frightened that she couldn't move from her chair. Ponti and the nurse had to lift her up and half carry her into the house through the back door. Once inside, they all went upstairs and barricaded themselves in the master bedroom. By that time, however, the security guards and their watchdogs had overwhelmed Appolloni and were holding him under restraint until the local police arrived.

Sinibaldo Appolloni turned out to have a record of hospitalization in mental institutions and landed back in one permanently this time. A onetime immigrant worker in West Germany, he deserted a wife and two children when he took off in mad pursuit of his movie idol.

The ordeal caused Sophia so much trauma that she thought she'd have another miscarriage. She didn't, but by the next day she decided she couldn't stay at home any longer. Though she wasn't scheduled to leave for Geneva for another month, she phoned Dr. de Watteville to come and get her immediately. The doctor had already promised to accompany her on the trip. She feared that flying at a high altitude might cause her to go into premature labor.

Except for her husband, whose work kept him in Rome, Sophia took Cipi and her whole entourage along to Geneva. This time there was no need to stay at a hotel. As chief underwriters of de Watteville's proposed fertility clinic, the Pontis had purchased a large suite of offices in his present building at 6 rue de Bonnet and converted it into an apartment *pied à terre* similar to the one they had at the Hampshire House in New York. Geneva was, of course, the banking capital of Europe, so Ponti traveled there frequently on personal and business matters.

Although it was now three years since the Pontis had announced their financial support, de Watteville's project was meeting stiff resistance and eventually had to be abandoned. Municipal authorities were difficult about building permits. Rival doctors protested that it would lose them patients, and they probably were right. The publicity over Sophia's first baby started women traveling from all over the world to consult de Watteville.

By December, Sophia was feeling so much better than she did during her first pregnancy that she told Dr. de Watteville that she'd like to try for a natural birth rather than go through another dreaded cesarean. To indulge her, the doctor said yes, but he warned her that if the baby hadn't arrived by the target date, he would have to operate. December 29, Cipi's fourth birthday, came and went. There would be no double celebration party next year.

By the 30th, Sophia wasn't even showing signs of labor, so de Watteville decided to delay the operation. After another five days, he didn't want to risk waiting any longer. Sophia checked into Geneva Cantonal Hospital on January 5, 1973, and at eight the next morning was rolled into the operating theater. Thirty-five minutes later, she gave birth to a son who weighed in at seven pounds, four ounces.

" 'It's a boy,' I heard a voice say," Sophia recalled. "That moment is something that even though you're mostly asleep, you remember each time. It just stays in your mind. . . . When I finally awoke in the early afternoon, I really wanted to see the baby then and there. It happens to every mother. I wanted to know if he was okay, if he had everything, but they kept telling me that they couldn't bring him until the next visiting time. I became very suspicious and finally started ordering: 'Don't tell me! Show me! Bring me my baby!' Instead, what did they bring me? A Polaroid picture of him taken a half hour after he was born! It was beautiful, but I was mad. 'A mother wants her baby, not a picture of him,' I told them. After two hours, they brought him in—and everything was okay. I held him and I thought: 'This is a really pretty baby.' "

Since the Pontis had been pinning all their hopes on a girl to be called Sophia Penelope, it was several days before they decided on the name of Edoardo Gianmaria Leoni. "Edoardo" was a venerable Neapolitan name and also came near enough to "Eduardo" to be a tribute to the Pontis' great friend De Filippo, author of *Filumena marturano* and other works filmed by the couple. Like older brother Cipi, Edoardo soon acquired a family nickname, Dodo.

The baby's arrival gave Sophia no time to fret over some bad news about her most recent movies. *Man of La Mancha,* which premiered in the United States at Christmas, got blasted by the critics and turned out a global disaster. *White Sister,* released at the same time, did well in Italy thanks to the popularity of Sophia's costar Adriano Celentano, but bombed elsewhere. In England, it never even got released.

Although Sophia had insisted on remaining in the hospital for fifty days after Cipi was born, this time around she stayed only the two weeks that were recommended for cesarean recovery. Of course, she now also had a four-year-old son to consider, plus an apartment to return to that was in the same building as her doctor. She decided to hibernate in Geneva with the kids for the balance of the winter, which also gave her time to get her figure back before she had to face the inescapable paparazzi again.

The anesthetic administered during the operation left Sophia totally incapable of breast-feeding the baby, so she had an easier time caring for him than she did with Cipi. Sophia also had help from nanny Ruth Bapst, who was now doing double duty but not complaining as far as anyone could hear.

Meanwhile, back in Italy, Carlo Ponti had both hands full with his latest production, *Rappresaglia,* which with its English title of *Massacre in Rome* might have sounded like another gory slasher epic but was actually the all-too-true story of a Nazi colonel who was ordered by Hitler in 1944 to execute 320 Roman citizens in retaliation for the killings of 32 German soldiers by partisans. The movie was based on a book by Robert Katz that had already been condemned by the Vatican because of its claims that Pope Pius XII refused to intervene to stop the executions.

As soon as Ponti announced the project, Catholic Action groups started protests and an elderly niece of Pius XII filed for an injunction to stop production. Though she didn't succeed, she later sued Ponti, author Katz, and director George Pan Cosmatos for slandering the Pope's reputation and won the case. The three defendants were each sentenced to up to eighteen months in jail, but the charges were eventually dropped after a lengthy appeal.

Massacre in Rome was one of Ponti's oddest multinational projects, teaming Marcello Mastroianni, in the role of an Italian priest who tried to save the hostages, with Richard Burton as the German commandant Kappler (then still living and serving a life sentence in an Italian prison). Ponti and Burton had a close mutual friend in President Tito, which explains the casting. Burton and Elizabeth Taylor had been frequent visitors to Yugoslavia in recent years and he'd even portrayed Tito in the Yugoslav-produced World War II epic, *The Battle of Sutjeska*.

When Ponti signed Burton for *Massacre in Rome,* he decided to make it a two-picture deal, with a teaming with Sophia to follow when they could all agree on a script. Burton's turbulent marriage to Taylor was currently in an off-mode. She was in Los Angeles consulting lawyers about a divorce, while he was in Rome trying to work but spending too much time drowning his sorrows in booze. Some of Burton's benders lasted for days, causing costly delays in the filming. Many of his scenes required umpteen retakes because he had great difficulty in remembering the lines and controlling his trembling. When Burton finally finished the movie, Ponti regretted that they had a contract for one more, but it was too late to cancel.

Burton had flown off to yet another reconciliation with Taylor by the time that Sophia returned to Rome from Geneva with her expanded brood. After six months away, she was only interested in settling in with the baby and restoring the household to normalcy. Ponti promised to go slow on the teaming with Burton. To make Sophia less anxious about it, he signed Vittorio De Sica to develop the project.

During her absence, Sophia had arranged for some construction work at Villa Ponti. Cipi's room was turned into a nursery for the baby, while Cipi got larger quarters consisting of a bedroom, play area, and library. Sophia also had an architect working on plans for a combination schoolhouse and gymnasium in the backyard. The Appolloni incident had left her cautious about the children's safety. With the recent upsurge of terrorism in Italy, educating the boys at home might be necessary. She had already changed her mind about sending Cipi to a local nursery school. He was heartbroken. She'd been promising it to him since Geneva and had even bought him a briefcase and the school uniform.

Sophia was up at six every morning for the baby's first feeding and spent the whole day with the children. "By early evening, I'm dead," she said in an interview at the time. "I'm in bed at eight. I could go straight to sleep then, but I'm ashamed to. If people call up at eight-thirty and they're told 'Sophia's sleeping,' what will they think? So I answer letters in bed and take calls until nine."

Meanwhile, Ponti and Vittorio De Sica settled on *Il viaggio,* a novella by Italy's Nobel Prize laureate Luigi Pirandello, as the vehicle for Sophia's teaming with Richard Burton. *The Voyage* was an old favorite of De Sica's and he'd been scripting it in his mind for years. Working on a crash schedule with a team of three writers, he hammered out a shooting version in six weeks.

At the same time, Ponti was producing two more thrillers for the exploitation market in Italy and abroad, *The Violent Professionals* and *Run, Joe, Run.* Ponti's attempt to do something more audacious with Roman Polanski's *What?* had turned out a total disaster and convinced him to stick to more commercial projects.

But Ponti decided to take a risk on two of Polanski's friends, underground filmmakers Andy Warhol and Paul Morrissey, who came to Rome that spring trying to find a backer for their first 35mm feature, a campy spoof entitled *Flesh for Frankenstein.* When the duo told him that they needed $400,000, Ponti doubted they could make a movie that cheaply, but he challenged them with a counteroffer of $800,000 for two. If they filmed them back to back, using many of the same sets and costumes, Ponti thought they could do it.

After some more brainstorming and Ponti's insistence that both movies carry the name of the King of Pop Art, *Andy Warhol's Frankenstein* and *Andy Warhol's Dracula* were ready for the sound stages that summer. At Roman Polanski's suggestion, photography would be in a polarized 3-D process called Space Vision, which sent bats, blood, and body parts flying off the screen into the audience in full color.

Warhol cast his favorite leading man, Joe Dallesandro, in both movies, with several of his Factory "superstars" in supporting parts. To facilitate some

German tax-shelter funding, Ponti picked the creepy-looking Udo Kier to play Baron Frankenstein and Count Dracula.

Warhol told Ponti that he'd love to get Sophia for a cameo appearance in one or both of the movies. But after Sophia read the scripts and found nuggets of dialogue like "Otto, to know death you have to fuck life—in the gallbladder!", she found it all too disgusting and started to doubt her husband's sanity as a producer.

De Sica, however, didn't share that view. After Warhol asked him, the one-time Clark Gable of the Italian cinema agreed to play an impoverished nobleman opposite Warhol's pal, Maxime de la Falaise, in the *Dracula* movie. By that time, Warhol had gone over budget with *Frankenstein*, so the follow-up was photographed in standard 35mm instead of 3-D to stay within the $800,000 that Ponti alloted for both films.

While director Paul Morrissey was auditioning actresses for some of the minor roles, Carlo Ponti told him that he'd like to meet any youngsters with "star" potential. The only one that Morrissey deemed worthy was twenty-year-old Dalila Di Lazzaro, a stunning blue-eyed blonde whom he selected to work in the nude as a zombie created by Baron Frankenstein from dead body parts.

When Morrissey introduced her to Ponti, the producer couldn't help noticing, among other things, that her last name was almost identical to the one that Sophia had been using when he first met her. Perhaps taking it as a good luck omen, Ponti soon decided to sign Di Lazzaro to a five-year contract, which gossip said included more than just her services as an actress.

In June, Ponti set a September starting date for *The Voyage*. Richard Burton, who was separated again from Elizabeth Taylor and drinking heavily, decided to go to Rome early to dry out. Since he knew the paparazzi would drive him nuts if he stayed in a hotel, he asked if he could take over the guest house at Villa Ponti. Although Mrs. Burton had ditched him for a Los Angeles used-car salesman, he needed room for an entourage that included his valet, a bodyguard, a male nurse, and a secretary.

After Ponti's last experience with Burton, he was all too happy to help if it would keep the actor sober. For the first two weeks, Burton brought along his personal physician to get him started on a no-booze diet and exercise program. The Pontis rarely saw him except when he was out jogging or swimming in the pool.

As the detoxification treatment took effect and Burton became more sociable, Sophia gave him a standing invitation to lunch with her and the children on the terrace. Although Dodo was yet a babe in arms, Burton took a shine to four-year-old Cipi immediately. When Sophia told her son that Burton was going to be acting with her in her next movie, he asked her, "He's not going to thrash you like Peter O'Toole, is he?" Cipi still hadn't gotten over his mother's rough treatment in *Man of La Mancha*.

When Burton promised to thrash O'Toole the next time they met, Cipi became his friend for life. An additional attraction for Cipi was being able to play with Burton's aged one-eyed Pekingese dog, "E'en So," who traveled everywhere with her master and had sixteen offspring scattered around the world.

As Sophia and Burton got to know each other better, he began telling her about his problems with Elizabeth Taylor and his lifelong bouts with alcoholism. Burton dubbed Sophia his *cwtcher*, which is Welsh for *comforter*. He recalled later that "I was very lucky to have her around. She held my hand, larded my ego. It was no small bounty to have such a fabulous woman looking after me, telling me what to do instead of my telling everybody else what to do."

Nine years older than Sophia, Burton was then at the height of his notoriety as a womanizer. Before he became involved with Elizabeth Taylor, he'd made many a romantic conquest among his leading ladies. For all his handsomeness, he was short, squarely built, and had pockmarked skin. But his electrifying voice and brilliant intellect more than compensated for those defects.

With Richard Burton as her houseguest, Sophia inevitably caused the gossip-mongers to wonder what exactly was going on at Villa Ponti. Papparazzi hiding in the surrounding hills with telescopic lenses on their cameras could snap nothing more revealing than the duo swimming in the pool and sunbathing, Sophia in a bikini and Burton in boxer trunks.

Some interaction may have taken place, but the details are known only to the two people involved. For the magazine *Ladies' Home Journal*, Burton later wrote a telegramese appreciation of Sophia that raised more than a few eyebrows:

Tall and extraordinary. Large bosomed. Tremendously long legs. Go up to her shoulders, practically. Beautiful brown eyes set in a marvelously vulpine, almost satanic face. Slightly receding chin, a fabulous nose and a mouth wide and generous like an invitation to rape. Great mother. *Mama mia*. As beautiful as erotic dreams.

Sophia was always coy on the subject of Burton. "Richard and I were good friends, and we'll always be good friends," she once said. "He is very attractive, very brilliant. When he likes someone, and he knows he can trust that some-one, he can really sparkle. But he must feel relaxed—and that's how Carlo and I made him feel in Marino."

Some bad news turned Burton's visit into a two-month tenure. When Vittorio De Sica took the health exam that was required before *The Voyage* could get production insurance, X rays revealed a tumor in one lung. De Sica was then seventy-two and had been a heavy smoker through most of his life. Doctors were extremely pessimistic.

"This came as a terrible blow because we all loved Vittorio," Sophia said later. "The insurance company told us to find another director, but Carlo was only concerned about De Sica's health because he really adored him. He found a cancer specialist in Geneva and took Vittorio there. After a week of tests, the doctor decided to operate. It lasted about four hours, that's how serious it was. Then we had to wait for the analysis of what they removed. It's very rare that anything which looks so bad on an X ray is *not* malignant, but tests showed it wasn't. Some people found it hard to believe and thought maybe the doctor was fooling De Sica and us. But when the insurance company accepted the doctor's report and gave us the policy, it was a very good feeling."

While De Sica recuperated, Ponti pushed back the starting date of *The Voyage* to mid-October, which seemed to give Sophia and Burton even more time for poker, Scrabble, and whatever other games they were playing. But it didn't work out quite that way due to the arrival in Rome of Elizabeth Taylor, who had a contract with producer Franco Rossellini for a film based on Muriel Spark's novel *The Driver's Seat*. Prior to leaving California, Taylor phoned Burton and begged for a reconciliation. How could he refuse?

Since no hotel in Rome could offer the protection that filmdom's royal cou-ple needed, Burton asked the Pontis if Elizabeth could stay with him in the guest house. He borrowed their Rolls-Royce and chauffeur to meet her at Fiumicino Airport. When Taylor stepped off the plane, she was wearing jeans, T-shirt, assorted gold chains, and her 69-carat Cartier-Burton diamond ring. After some gentle kissing and nuzzling for the paparazzi, the couple hopped into the Rolls and drove to Villa Ponti, where Sophia was waiting to welcome her new guest.

"Madame Ponti was wearing a Dior suit, with a Dior handbag, Dior shoes, and Dior gloves," Taylor later dished to a friend. "Can you imagine? She was standing at the front door of her own house, waiting to greet me, in *gloves!*"

Sophia had a lavish lunch prepared. Afterwards, the Burtons retired to the guest house and remained in seclusion. Three days later, the couple's press agent announced that "they're very happy to be together again." A week later, it was a different story. Taylor packed her bags and moved to a seven-room suite at the Grand Hotel in Rome.

Sophia claimed to know next to nothing about what happened. "I didn't want to interfere while they were our guests, so I dropped in as little as possible," she said later. "After ten days though, Richard told me the marriage was over. I felt very sorry for both of them, but I never asked questions. I'm not that kind of person. I mean, if someone wants to talk, they talk without your asking. Otherwise not. There are times when you want to help people, but you are pretty much unable to because it just doesn't concern you. You have to be very careful about helping sometimes. It isn't help when you can't help."

Some of the couple's friends thought that Taylor walked out because she believed that Burton was having an affair with Sophia. His adoptive mentor and namesake, Philip Burton, later remembered a phone call in which Burton blamed his latest marital dilemma on "an involvement with Sophia Loren." Larry Barcher, a member of Burton's entourage, recalled him moaning, "What to do about these two women. Oh, what to do!" Barcher said that "Richard tried to intimate to all of us that he was having a go with both of them."

An intimate of Elizabeth Taylor believed that Sophia and Burton were having an affair. The friend claimed that Sophia hated Elizabeth Taylor and wanted to make her miserable by stealing Burton from her. Sophia was allegedly extremely jealous of the way the news media always treated Taylor like the queen of the movie world, a position that Sophia coveted for herself. Sophia also had a professional ax to grind. Around the time that the Burton-Taylor affair started, during the making of *Cleopatra,* Sophia had been all but set to costar with Burton in two movies, *The VIPs* and *The Comedians,* but Taylor got the roles for herself by offering to work for half the salary that Ponti had been demanding for Sophia.

Another theory about Sophia and Burton was that she was getting even with Ponti for *his* current affair with Dalila Di Lazzaro, which seemed to be getting very serious indeed. Richard Burton may have just been a case of the right man in the right place at the right time.

While Burton stayed on at Villa Ponti, Taylor was soon reported reunited with Dutch-born used-car salesman Henry Wynberg, who took her to Amsterdam one weekend for a shopping spree through the diamond factories. Because of the postponement of *The Voyage* due to De Sica's operation, Taylor had finished *The Driver's Seat* and returned to California with Wynberg by the time that Sophia and Burton finally got around to actually working together.

Set in 1912 in Pirandello's native Sicily, where widows are forbidden to re-marry, *The Voyage* tells the story of the recently bereaved Adriana Braggi, whose ripening love for her brother-in-law, Cesare, is another Sicilian taboo. When Adriana turns out to have a serious heart condition, Cesare vows to help her to find a cure, and they embark on what turns out to be quite a long voy-age from Palermo to mainland Naples and finally to Venice at the outbreak of World War I. The voyage turns into a love affair early on, after a heart specialist tells Adriana that she has no more than two years to live and urges her to fully enjoy whatever time is left.

"It is not the kind of film they do nowadays," Sophia said in an interview at the time. "It goes really against the pornographic or sex films of today, and I think it is worth the attempt. It is a very romantic story, perfect for De Sica be-cause he feels those kinds of things deeply."

The casting of Richard Burton as a Sicilian may have seemed preposterous, but since the Italian supporting actors would eventually be dubbed for the English-language version of *The Voyage,* he might pass. Even Sophia didn't sound particularly Italian when she spoke English, which was usually in a blend of Oxford and American accents.

Since De Sica was still very frail when filming began, Ponti tried to cover himself by asking Franco Zeffirelli to take over the direction if De Sica proved incapable. Zeffirelli refused to consider it, claiming it was immoral for anyone to step into a project that already had De Sica's hallmark on it. He told Ponti it would be better to scrap the movie entirely.

De Sica somehow managed to get through, including an arduous month of locations on Sicily. By that time, Burton had arranged for the *Kalizma,* his and Taylor's 130-foot-long motor yacht, to sail down from its berth on the French Riviera to serve as his floating hotel. The ship had seven bedrooms, including two with huge double beds, which enabled Burton to reciprocate and have the Pontis as his overnight guests on several occasions.

Sophia may have spent a weekend alone with Burton on the *Kalizma.* Taylor later told that to some of her friends, claiming that she heard it from sev-eral of the permanent crew members.

During the filming in Sicily, Burton suddenly received a phone call from a panicked Elizabeth Taylor, who was in a Los Angeles hospital and fearing the worst after an operation for the removal of a possibly malignant uterine cyst. She begged him to come immediately to comfort her while she waited for the test results.

Burton talked Ponti into giving him a few days off and booked himself on a polar flight from Rome to L.A. that took twelve hours. When he arrived at the hospital, he discovered that Taylor had arranged for Henry Wynberg to stay in the room with her in a separate bed. Burton chucked him out and moved in, remaining until Taylor's cancer test proved negative and he decided to take her back to Italy with him on the next polar flight to recuperate aboard the *Kalizma*.

Not surprisingly, "Madame Ponti" was never seen again on the *Kalizma*. The Burtons kept to themselves for the remainder of the filming. When it shifted from Palermo to Venice, they made the trip on a long weekend cruise through the Strait of Messina into the Ionic Sea and up the Adriatic.

A Welsh coal miner's son, Burton later wrote of his time in Venice: "Have spent all night in bed in Elizabeth for real and all day in bed with Sophia for unreal. Not bad when you've come from the bowels of the earth."

Burton described Sophia the actress as a "Very rare lady. Knows her lines. A bit of a governess. Tends to lecture now and then, to wag the finger. Delightfully. Tells me what to do, little knowing that I've done fifty films and endless plays. I always obey. She's always right."

One of Sophia's quirks surprised Burton: "Will not kiss in front of the camera unless her back turned against it. Remarkable. Cannot understand it. I will kiss anybody, including pariah dogs, and I don't care who is looking."

Sophia had a moment in the movie where she breaks down in tears while telling Burton, "I can't marry you or go away with you." The tears seemed to flow so easily that those coworkers who suspected a personal attachment between Sophia and Burton interpreted them as confirmation.

Just before Christmas, *The Voyage* finally wrapped and the Burtons immediately took off by plane to holiday in Puerto Vallarta, Mexico. Their umpteenth reconciliation was by now being trumpeted as permanent. Asked to comment, Sophia told a reporter: "Richard became like one of the family over the last six months. I loved working with him, and want his marriage to succeed. In fact, I'm praying that it will."

Unfortunately, 1974 started grimly for the Pontis. Vittorio De Sica required more lung surgery and doctors doubted that he would survive the year, though the news was kept from him. Due to his heavy gambling losses over the years, De Sica had no money but wasn't the sort who would ask for or accept charity.

To keep him going, Ponti hired him to develop another film for Sophia, realizing full well that it would probably never be produced. The script was to be based on the director's favorite short story, "The Simple Heart," by Gustave Flaubert. De Sica had long wanted to make it with Sophia playing the housemaid whose dedication to her masters continues even after their deaths.

Meanwhile, Ponti was ready and set to go with Sophia's next movie, *Le Testament,* their first to be made in France since the disastrous *Lady L.* This time the omens were better, with no Hollywood meddling and Sophia teamed with Jean Gabin, arguably the greatest French cinema star ever. Gabin was planning to retire when he turned seventy in May, so unless something suddenly came along in the interim, *Le Testament* would be the ninety-fourth and last movie of his illustrious forty-four-year career.

By comparison to Gabin, Sophia was a newcomer, having worked in only sixty-seven movies over twenty-four years. Although she wasn't getting any younger and would turn forty in September, the thirty-year age difference with Gabin shouldn't matter because—surprise of surprises!—they weren't teamed romantically.

Ponti had selected André Cayatte, a filmmaker renowned for his preoccupation with the moral issues of law, criminality, and capital punishment, to write and direct the dramatic shocker. Cayatte, whose most acclaimed earlier works were *Justice Is Done* and *We Are All Murderers,* based his script on Henri Coupon's novel *The Benefit of the Doubt.*

Le Testament was intended as Sophia's crossover into more serious emotional roles that didn't necessarily include a love interest. Ponti seemed more determined than ever for Sophia to take over the mantle from Anna Magnani as Italy's greatest actress. Magnani had died of cancer at age sixty-five the previous September, while Sophia was getting ready to start *The Voyage* with Richard Burton.

Later to be titled *Verdict* for the dubbed English-language version, *Le testament* takes place in Paris and Lyon, a city in southeastern France that has always had close ties to the Italian underworld. As gangster's widow Teresa Leoni, Sophia goes through mental and physical hell trying to get her teenage son, André, acquitted of a murder charge. Convinced that he'll never get fair treatment because of his father's shady reputation, she devises a cold-blooded

plan to sway the verdict by kidnaping the wife of President Leguen, chief magistrate of the Paris court trying the case. The wife is a diabetic and dies without
her medication, but not before Leguen frees Leoni's son. It soon turns out, however, that André really did commit the murder he was charged with. Leguen has
defied justice and his wife is dead, all for nothing. It's all too much for Teresa,
who commits suicide by crashing her car into a wall.

As President Leguen, the white-haired Jean Gabin had what amounted to a
supporting role, but he received top billing as befitted his eminence in European
cinema. Sophia was unconvinced by his talk of retirement. "Jean has got such
energy that I don't believe it," she said at the time. "He adores being an actor. He
gets very excited and very nervous and everything that you can get when you
adore still your profession. If this was going to be his last film, he would not care.
But he cares! He goes to see rushes. He looks at himself and says 'I look good'
or 'I look bad'—he really cares. This man is a rock. He is a magnificent actor, one
of the most expressive and charismatic in the history of film."

Sophia guessed right. Gabin didn't retire at seventy, but he made only one
more movie, *L'Année Sainte* with Danielle Darrieux and Jean-Claude Brialy, before he died, in November 1976, of a heart attack at seventy-two.

For the three-month filming of *Le Testament,* the Pontis decided to move the
whole family to Paris. Although it would be a bit of a squeeze after Villa Ponti,
their residence on Avenue Georges V, a boulevard that runs from the Champs
Elyssées to the right bank of the Seine, was hardly less luxurious. The Pontis
owned the entire nine-story building, but leased out the first six floors and kept
the top three and penthouse for themselves. The resulting triplex apartment
measured about 240 square yards on each floor.

Carlo Ponti had his business office on the top floor, which also contained
several guest rooms and living quarters for the servants and chauffeur. The floor
below consisted of a huge living room with outdoor terrace, plus a suite of
rooms for the two children, their nanny, and Sophia's secretary. Down one
flight were the kitchen, dining room, and separate but adjoining bedroom suites
for Sophia and Ponti.

While Sophia was working in *Le Testament,* she decided to risk sending five-
year-old Cipi to nursery school for the first time. Paris didn't seem as threatening or dangerous as Rome, where kidnaping and snatching people straight off
the sidewalks had become a fact of life.

Not that the Pontis were taking any unnecessary chances in Paris. A bodyguard took Cipi to and from school every day. Their triplex apartment also had

guards posted throughout, all packing hand guns and with heavier artillery in easy reach if needed.

By the time *Le Testament* finished, Cipi was enjoying school so much that Sophia hated to take him out. Since there was no urgent reason to return to Italy, she talked Ponti into staying in Paris until the school term ended. With offices in both places, he didn't really care where they lived as long as he had access to a desk and telephone.

Ponti had another major film in production that didn't involve Sophia but kept him hopping to location sites in Spain, Algeria, Germany, and England. *The Passenger* (aka *Professione: Reporter*) was the last in his three-picture deal with director Michelangelo Antonioni, which had started spectacularly with *Blow-Up* and then gone into limbo after the failure of *Zabriskie Point* and the termination of Ponti's link with MGM. Ironically, *The Passenger* was partially financed by MGM, which had gone through several management changes since then and now distributed its movies through Ponti's other partner, United Artists.

Ponti scored something of a coup with *The Passenger,* which teamed two of the hottest stars of the moment, Jack Nicholson and Maria Schneider. Ponti signed Schneider straight off her notorious debut opposite Marlon Brando in *Last Tango in Paris* and had her under contract for another film after *The Passenger.*

To keep Ponti happy, Antonioni made *The Passenger* a blend of *Blow-Up* and *Last Tango,* with Jack Nicholson as a disillusioned TV journalist assuming the identity of a deceased look-alike gun-runner and Schneider as another sex-driven hippie. In the end, Nicholson is killed by guerrillas hunting the man he-'s impersonating. The seven-minute assassination scene in Nicholson's hotel room was a visual tour de force, filmed from within and outside the set using a huge crane and a new type of camera controlled by gyroscopes.

Ponti was also trying to resuscitate *Man's Fate,* this time with Sophia back in the package as female lead instead of Liv Ullmann. Director Richard Brooks, who'd once come near to making the property for MGM before Ponti and Fred Zinnemann ever got involved with it, was interested again if Ponti could raise the funding. André Malraux, author of the novel, and Han Suyin, writer of the script, were contacting leaders of the Chinese government to get their support for a coproduction deal.

Ponti was desperate to make another big prestige movie like *Doctor Zhivago* and also had offered to buy the screen rights to Nobel Prize–winner Alexander Solzhenitsyn's *The Gulag Archipelago*. Negotiations heated up when Solzhenitsyn was deported from the USSR and settled temporarily in Switzerland, but no deal was ever made.

In the meanwhile, Ponti had nothing definite lined up for Sophia, but an offer came in that was too good to resist and could start a lucrative second career for her in television. Except for the rare self-promoting TV special like *With Love, Sophia,* Ponti had been rejecting anything in the TV acting realm in the belief that if people could see Sophia for free in their homes, they wouldn't buy tickets to her movies. But it had been years since Sophia had had a box-office hit, so it didn't make sense to hold out any longer. Especially now that she was pushing forty and not in great demand for theatrical movies.

The $200,000 offer was from the producers of one of American television's most prestigious programs, *Hallmark Hall of Fame,* which had been presenting five or six dramatic specials per year on NBC since 1952. Their choice of Sophia Loren for a new adaptation of Noel Coward's *Brief Encounter* may seem a bit bizarre, but Hallmark wanted a big star at the top of the cast to hype the ratings. They'd already signed Robert Shaw for the male lead and Alan Bridges as director. Both Britons had recently won critical acclaim for their work together in *The Hireling,* but had slight name value for American TV viewers.

Carlo Ponti carved himself a piece of the action by demanding a coproducer credit. Hallmark also granted him control of all rights for Italy, where he intended to release *Brief Encounter* as a theatrical feature before selling it to television.

Just two weeks before production began in England, Robert Shaw asked to be released from his contract because his current film, *Jaws,* was running far behind schedule due to technical problems with the special effects. Sophia immediately nominated Richard Burton as Shaw's replacement. Why can only be guessed at, but it might have been just because she considered them a good match.

"On the screen, Richard and I look very well together," she said after their *Voyage* collaboration. "It is very believable that we are in love. I'm very pleased with our teaming because it is always so very difficult to find the right partner for me."

In the intervening seven months, Elizabeth Taylor had divorced Burton and was trying to clean him out financially, so Sophia may have had romantic and charitable motives for recommending him. Burton signed on for $200,000, the same fee that Sophia received but $100,000 more than was intended for Robert Shaw. But the price was worth it to Hallmark because Burton's drawing power was at least equal to Sophia's, if not greater.

Since David Lean's 1945 film of *Brief Encounter,* with Celia Johnson and Trevor Howard in the leads, is an acknowledged masterpiece, *Hallmark Hall of Fame* seemed to be risking the impossible with a remake. But the sponsor was mainly interested in selling greeting cards: There weren't many pretested romantic vehicles around that suited two leads past the full bloom of youth.

Brief Encounter started out as the one-act, forty-five-minute play *Still Life,* which Noël Coward wrote in 1935 for himself and Gertrude Lawrence to perform as part of a larger work entitled *Tonight at 8:30.* Set entirely in a railway station buffet, it was nothing more than a sequence of conversations between two lovers, both married to others. They first meet there accidentally while waiting for trains and later regroup every Thursday for tea before their trysts. At David Lean's suggestion, Coward later expanded it into a feature-length screenplay, which added characters, dramatized incidents that were only talked about in *Still Life,* and changed a vital point. In *Brief Encounter* the romance is never consummated, which makes it more a story of anguished yearnings than of illicit passion.

Since Noël Coward had been dead a year by the time of the Hallmark TV version, one can only guess what he might have thought about the changes made by scriptwriter John Bowen, who was himself a respected playwright. Obviously, the role of the plain British housewife, Laura Jesson, needed some major surgery to suit Sophia Loren. Laura became Anna, an Italian war bride, married for seventeen years and the mother of two bilingual sons.

"Other changes were required to make everything more contemporary," Sophia said in an interview at the time. "The woman, for example, used to come into town once a week to go shopping—now she works as well as being a housewife. But the love story remains what it was, because love never dies and never gets old-fashioned.

"The story is painful. Anna loves her husband dearly. She has her own family, her own nest. And suddenly she meets somebody else who gives her what her husband doesn't. She loves her husband—but she finds something exciting, something worth living for with the other man. This is the conflict."

The role of the gallant doctor, Alec Harvey, whose first encounter with Anna is when he offers to help her remove a cinder from her eye, required slight alteration for Richard Burton. Bowen's biggest contribution was the introduction into the plot of the lovers' spouses, who were played by Jack Hedley and Ann Firbank.

David Lean's black-and-white *Brief Encounter* was shot in Carnforth,

Lancashire, on the edge of the Lake District. Alan Bridges wanted to work nearer to London and chose Winchester, a provincial city famous for its Gothic cathedral and for a castle in which King Arthur's actual round table is still on display.

Sophia decided to leave her family behind in Paris. Due to the faster methods employed in television, the filming would take six weeks instead of the three to four months that she usually spent on theatrical movies. Sophia may have also been hoping for some quality time alone with Richard Burton, but if that was true, she probably was disappointed.

Since their last meeting at the end of 1973, Burton's tribulations with Elizabeth Taylor had nearly killed him. By the time she bailed out via a quickie Swiss divorce, he was drinking three quarts of vodka a day and finally collapsed in a coma. He spent six weeks in the hospital recuperating, and left limping from a flare-up of the acute sciatica that had been plaguing him for years.

When Burton arrived in Winchester to begin *Brief Encounter*, he was not only starting to drink again but was also involved concurrently with two women. Traveling with Burton was Jeanne Bell, a black actress who'd once adorned the centerfold of *Playboy* magazine and had played a bit role in *The Klansman*, a movie he'd made soon after *The Voyage*. And waiting for Burton back in London was his new fiancée, the exiled Princess Elizabeth of Yugoslavia, presently in the process of divorcing her merchant banker husband, Neil Balfour.

For all the craziness of his personal life, Burton always strived to be professional and to do the job he was being paid for. In Winchester, he exercised every day to build himself up and also tried to stay out of the pubs. When coworkers dragged him in, he ordered tonic water or an occasional white wine.

Sophia was shocked when she saw how frail Burton had become since their last meeting. He needed an hour in the makeup chair every morning to cover the ravages. Director Alan Bridges tried to use the lowest light levels possible when shooting his scenes. Sophia couldn't really complain about that, since it also made her own flaws less conspicuous.

Since Burton had taken the job on short notice and was due to start a TV film about Winston Churchill's World War II years right after that, he spent his free time preparing and rarely socialized, not even with Sophia as far as anyone could see. "I don't think they ever managed more than a few hands of poker on the set between takes," his friend Brook Williams recalled.

When Ponti suddenly arrived from Paris bringing the two children and their nanny, Sophia again seemed to be trying to put Richard Burton in the past.

While discussing her role in *Brief Encounter* with a reporter visiting the set, she sounded like she was talking about herself as well: "There's no question that you can love two men in a very different way, that you can be married and fall in love with another man—*if* there's that something *missing* with your own husband. But there must be something missing, otherwise you can't fall in love as Anna does in the film. She finally renounces her love. Her husband is kind to her and very understanding and she gives it up. But the renunciation is painful, very, very painful. Tragic. And yet . . . life goes on."

When it came to filming the emotional scene where she tells Burton that she can't desert her husband and children to run away with him, Sophia seemed not to be acting as her eyes filled with tears. No doubt she shed lots more ten years later, when Burton died from a brain hemorrhage at age fifty-eight.

Although Sophia's last two movies hadn't even been released yet, she didn't have to wait long for reactions to *Brief Encounter,* which Hallmark aired in early November to hype the sale of Christmas cards. Sophia's future in television looked dismal after a withering review from America's most influential TV critic, John J. O'Connor of *The New York Times*.

After a long diatribe about the film's "excruciating dullness" and its failure to capture any of the poignancy of the Coward-Lean original, O'Connor wrote that

> Glamorous superstars are notoriously unreliable in depicting relentlessly plain lives. Mr. Burton, in fashionable high-heeled shoes, typically reduces his role to a sonorous reading of the lines. Miss Loren is considerably more effective, but her stunning beauty becomes a distinct and insuperable handicap in a portrait of an ordinary English housewife. . . . Finally, both performers are defeated by a production that falls into a common trap—in attempting to depict boredom, this *Brief Encounter* simply succeeds in being boring itself.

Programmed opposite the hit series *M*A*S*H, Brief Encounter* earned one of the lowest audience ratings in *Hallmark Hall of Fame* history. Not surprisingly, it took another two years to turn up on television in Noël Coward's native England, where Clive James of *The Observer* seemed to be waiting in ambush for it.

James opened his blast with

> "You know what's happened, don't you?" Richard Burton asked Sophia Loren in the retread of *Brief Encounter,* and for a moment I thought his flies had

come undone, or he had slipped a disc. But he went on to advance the theory that they had fallen in love. Hull-down over the horizon, an orchestra of brass and strings loudly agreed with him. The evidence that so ill-assorted a couple must be in the grip of an insane passion had been mounting for some time. Why else would an Italian beauty queen with a wardrobe of exotic if badly chosen clothes pretend to be the humdrum wife of a British solicitor and make goo-goo eyes at a raddled Welsh thespian trying to pass himself off as a promising physician by dying his hair with black boot-polish? To clinch the matter, they had linked hands and run through a field. You have to be crazy to try a stunt like that in street-shoes.

FRIENDS AND LOVERS

I N September 1974, Sofia Scicolone Ponti, aka Sophia Loren, turned forty years old, which set the news media to wondering how the movie goddess was coping with middle age. Her nearly exact contemporary, the eight-days-younger Brigitte Bardot, had already retired from filmmaking at thirty-nine.

"I'm glad to be forty," Sophia said in one of several interviews that she gave at the time. "I wouldn't be any other age. I have never felt better about myself. I wouldn't be twenty again for anything. At twenty I wanted desperately to have children and couldn't. I didn't know who I was or where I was going. But thirty was the really hard birthday for me. At thirty there are no more advantages to be gained from simply being younger than other people. Thirty forced me to face the fact that I could no longer squander time and emotions and expect the well to be always filled."

Sophia noted that "the whole business of age depressed me for a while. But now I know better. In the last ten years I have learned many things—about my-self, about age, about love. I have no regrets. I've done everything that I wanted to and taken the responsibility for what followed. I would rather do something than spend my time wondering what I have missed. Regret only makes wrinkles."

As she entered her fifth decade of life, "I have finally found myself," Sophia said. "I know who I am and what I need. I have never felt younger because I am finally fulfilled. I have two children, a miracle I prayed for all my life, and I love them with an intensity I never thought possible. Cipi and Edoardo changed my life completely and brought it into balance. I will never be unhappy again nor afraid of growing old, because I will grow up with them."

Because of her history of cesarean operations, Sophia said she would have no more children. "A cesarean is *hell*—it's like having major surgery with your eyes open," she said. "Once, yes. Twice. But a *third* time? Never. I'm too afraid."

Sophia described herself as "a liberated woman—in my own terms—which is to live happily with the man I love. I work. I make money. I could live very nicely without him. But I don't want to. I could leave any time I want without fear of being alone. But I don't want to, ever. The more years go by, the more I love him."

At forty, the superstar had no recent box-office hits to her credit and had also reached that awkward age between romantic leads and character parts. Without her producer-husband, her career seemed in peril, especially in the Hollywood industry, where she'd long been out of favor anyway.

One of Ponti's fortieth birthday gifts to his wife was her first teaming in four years with Marcello Mastroianni, a combination that usually hit the box-office jackpot (their last two, *Sunflower* and *The Priest's Wife* were the exceptions, but only in the United States). Though the team seemed to work best with De Sica as director, he was too ill to participate this time. *The Voyage,* which was being edited by other hands, seemed destined to be his last film.

The Italian pop culture was currently going through a retro-phase where the lurid mobster movies from Hollywood's golden age were a major influence, which was Ponti's reason for selecting *La pupa del gangster* as the vehicle. *Gangster's Moll* was the nearest English translation, but the title in that language would be *Poopsie & Company* (later shortened to just *Poopsie* and still later lengthened to *Oopsie Poopsie*).

Sophia portrayed Poopsie, an ex-hooker turned gangster's mistress who does double service helping the police to catch a murderer. Mastroianni played Charlie the Collar, a hood obsessed by Rita Hayworth. Director Giorgio Capitani and scriptwriter Ernesto Gastaldi modeled the movie on Nicholas Ray's *Party Girl,* a Robert Taylor–Cyd Charisse clinker from 1958 that was adored by European cineastes.

Anyone who ever wondered what Sophia Loren might have looked like if she'd been the opposite sex received a glimpse in a scene where Poopsie dons a male disguise. Sophia dressed in a black pin-striped suit, white shirt and tie, and with some of her hair pulled down from under a Borsalino hat to simulate sideburns.

Sophia found Mastroianni in a happier and more contented mood than when they had last worked together. He had finally ended his agonizing affair with

Faye Dunaway, but was still leading two lives: one in Rome with his Italian wife and their twenty-two-year-old daughter, and the other in Paris with Catherine Deneuve and *their* two-year-old toddler, Chiara.

"I live between two worlds, having the best of both," Mastroianni said in an interview at the time. "The nicest thing is that both women understand. They didn't in the beginning, but they do now—and it's wonderful!"

Faced with a similar dilemma, Sophia was far less understanding. After a year of mentoring Dalila Di Lazzaro, which included sending her to New York to learn English and to take private acting lessons with a teacher from the Stella Adler Studio, Ponti decided she was ready to play a choice supporting role in *Poopsie*. While Sophia might have been tolerant of her husband's philandering, she wasn't going to risk having the movie "stolen" from her by such a gorgeous young thing. Di Lazzaro's part was reduced to a glorified walk-on and underwent even more surgery during the editing of the film.

But Sophia couldn't do much about ending Ponti's infatuation with Di Lazzaro, whom he promptly cast as leading lady to Giancarlo Giannini and Michael Constantine in *Il bestione* (known in English as *The Eight Wheel Monster*). During the filming of the action thriller, di Lazzaro mentioned in a press interview that she and Ponti were in love, which immediately filled the European scandal sheets with predictions that Sophia would sue for divorce.

That, of course, never happened. The only "divorce" may have been a termination of Di Lazzaro's contract with Ponti's production company, which gossip said that Sophia demanded to make up for all the embarrassment she'd suffered. But the affair continued, and through Ponti's power in the Italian film industry, Di Lazzaro was never at a loss for work. She finally achieved stardom in 1976 in *Oh! Serafina,* directed by Ponti's lifelong friend Alberto Lattuada, who'd been one of the first to recognize Sophia's talent when she played a bit part in his *Anna* back in 1951.

At the completion of *Poopsie* the Pontis returned to Paris, which would be their main home for the foreseeable future. Cipi was enrolled in the Ecole Bilangue and doing so well that they decided to keep him there. "It's a very good school where they speak both English and French," Sophia said at the time. "I want both my children to speak more than one language properly. The schools in Italy are terrible. You should see my nieces. They had to have private English lessons just to learn how to read a menu. Now Cipi speaks better English than I do. He also speaks French like a Parisian, and Italian and German."

In Paris as in Italy, Sophia preferred to stay home with the kids. "Maybe I mother them too much," she once said, "but I suffered so much to have children, and they are gone all too quickly. They belong to their school, then to their wives, then to their jobs. I want to share their lives as long as I can. When I have to leave them for any period of time, I feel mutilated, as though I have lost an arm or a leg."

But there were nights when Sophia liked to take advantage of Paris's rich cultural life and go to the theater, ballet, opera, or concerts. Since Ponti didn't share that interest, she was usually escorted by Jean Barthet, her favorite hat designer as well as a close personal friend.

Scandalmongers started linking Sophia romantically with long-haired pop star Serge Lama after she attended several of his performances at the Olympia Theatre and went nightclubbing with him later. Nine years Sophia's junior, Lama wrote the lyrics (though not the music) to all his material and was considered France's most poetic and romantic *chansonnier* since Charles Aznavour and Gilbert Becaud.

When asked by a reporter to comment on her relationship with Lama, Sophia mischievously replied, "I love his songs, he likes my movies," and left it at that.

Once the Pontis settled in Paris, scarcely a day passed without their being mentioned in the French newspapers, which may have been one of the drawbacks to living directly across the street from the luxurious Hotel George V, a favorite hangout for reporters and photographers on the celebrity trail. Much speculation was raised over the visits to the Ponti residence by handsome film actor Umberto Orsini, which usually occurred at times when Sophia's husband was known to be elsewhere.

In retaliation, Sophia stopped giving press interviews, but before she did she told one journalist why: "If I go out with someone other than Carlo, I'm reported cheating on him. If I stay home with my husband and children, I'm supposed to be trying to save my failing marriage. If I go to the gynecologist, I'm pregnant again. If Carlo hires some other actress for one of his films, I'm crying myself to sleep because he's having a torrid affair behind my back."

On November 13, 1974, in the American Hospital in Paris, Vittorio De Sica finally succumbed to lung cancer at age seventy-three. Ponti, who was in Rome at the time of his death, had to break the news to Sophia by telephone.

"I had no reaction. None at all," she recalled. "I couldn't speak. I felt nothing. My mind was congealed. Actually, my reaction was too big for my senses. My mind could not comprehend that De Sica—Vittorio De Sica—was dead. I did not cry. I felt no need for commiseration. I went to my bedroom and locked the door. I sat down on a chair at the window and looked far across the Paris housetops to the white gleaming towers of Sacre-Coeur. Then in my mind, like a reel of film, a cavalcade of our relationship over the years began. . . . The tears began to come and great sobs rose from within me as we relived our film adventures together and I remembered something that I once read, 'How the years can fly away, and how little one forgets.' "

The next day, Sophia wanted to go to the American Hospital to pay her respects, but De Sica's corpse was being prepared for shipment back to Italy for the funeral and no visitors were allowed. Finally, after umpteen phone calls, someone told her that she could come to the area where the coffin was waiting to be taken to the airport.

When Sophia arrived, she found the sealed coffin in a tiny room where a burning candle was the only light. "It was the saddest place I had ever been in, so unlike De Sica," she recalled. "I put my arms on the coffin and bowed my head on them and meditated about him. A painful sense of loss swept over me, loss of this man I loved, and loss of a part of myself that would be buried with him."

Two days later, Sophia flew to Rome to join Ponti for the funeral. Whether she realized it or not, all the bills were being paid by Ponti, though the arrangements were made by De Sica's widow, the Spanish actress Maria Mercader, their two sons, and his daughter from a previous marriage. Some of the music selected for the service was composed by eldest son Manuel De Sica, who also wrote the score for *The Voyage,* his father's final film.

Since Vittorio De Sica was one of Italy's national heroes, a superstar of stage and screen as well as a master director, the public funeral was Rome's most stupendous since Anna Magnani's the year before. For obvious reasons, Sophia had stayed away from that one, but nothing could keep her from De Sica's, even though she knew it would be pandemonium.

Though part of the cathedral was reserved for family and guests, the remaining places were filled six hours before the service. Tens of thousands more people gathered outside and in the surrounding streets. Sidewalk musicians played favorite songs and themes from De Sica's movies and stage revues. The most reprised was "If I Could Have a Thousand Lire a Month," which he introduced in 1938 and became the theme song of the Depression era.

The crowd applauded when the Pontis arrived, which was what Romans often did at funerals and no doubt signified their appreciation of the movies that the couple had made with De Sica. Once seated inside, however, Sophia became a captive target for the paparazzi.

"During the service, when I started to cry, they pressed near me to get their shots, but I tried to hide my face behind the man in front of me," she recalled. "How awful it is, at times like that, not to be left alone. No respect for grief, or for the Church. No respect even for the dead."

Although it hadn't been planned that way, *The Voyage* entered release in Europe the same week as De Sica's death and all but got buried with him. While critics might have been expected to be more lenient under the circumstances, they savaged De Sica's final movie as the worst of his career and also mocked the romantic teaming of Sophia with Richard Burton.

The dismal European reviews, coming right after the flop of *Brief Encounter* on American television, made it impossible for Ponti to get a distribution deal for *The Voyage* in the United States. *Le Testament* suffered a similar fate, though it opened big in France due to the popularity of Jean Gabin. It took Ponti nearly a year to get American distribution through Avco Embassy (no longer run by Joe Levine), which released it first as *The Verdict* and then switched to *Jury of One,* but with dismal results under either title.

Sophia was starting to look more like a liability than an asset to her husband's production activities, but fortunately some of his other movies were box-office hits. *Andy Warhol's Frankenstein,* shown in 3-D and further helped by an X rating from the MPAA, drew crowds in the United States, with *Variety* predicting a $10 million gross domestically and probably another $10 million in the foreign release.

Ponti was also profiting from his controlling interest in an Italian distribution company, Interfilm, which hit the jackpot locally with imported Kung-Fu actioners and soft-core porno like *A Man Called Karate, Supermen Against the Orient,* and *I Will If You Will.*

In a diversification move, Ponti announced plans to build a huge leisure park similar to Disneyland in southeastern Italy near the booming gulf city of Taranto. Press pundits wondered if it would be called Sophialand, but Ponti seemed to be serious about the project. He'd purchased 250 acres of pine forest for the site and had engaged Tange Kenzo, principal architect of the 1964 Olympic City in Tokyo, as designer.

Ponti attributed the idea to being the father of two young children, which made him realize that Italy had almost nothing in the way of recreational facilities for kids and families. The park would have amusement rides, a wild life preserve, swimming and boating areas, theaters, a sports stadium, and even its own airport. When queried about where he expected to get the financing, Ponti told a reporter, "I'm not worried. The important thing in business is to have ideas. The money can always be found."

For his movie projects, Ponti was now getting funding from tax-shelter groups in Germany, Canada, and the United States. After *La pupa del gangster,* Sophia took a sabbatical while Ponti made two films in Italy, starting with *Brutti, sporchi e cattivi* (later titled in English as *Down and Dirty*). Directed by Ettore Scola, whom many Italian critics regarded as an equal of De Sica, the humanistic comedy starring Nino Manfredi focused on the members of a commune in a shanty town on the outskirts of Rome.

In March 1975, Ponti started the second film in his contract with twenty-two-year-old Maria Schneider, a suspense shocker entitled *The Babysitter,* directed by Réné Clement, a French master who worked frequently in Italy. Since Schneider was reminiscent of the young Sophia Loren and even had a similar pedigree as the illegitimate daughter of a Romanian Gypsy and French film star Daniel Gélin, the European gossip tabloids had a field day insinuating that she had become Ponti's protégée-mistress and was driving his wife insane with jealousy.

If they'd named Dalila Di Lazzaro, the press would have hit the target. But the rumors about Schneider and Ponti seemed improbable when it turned out she was involved in a lesbian affair with twenty-eight-year-old Joan Townsend, a wealthy American playgirl who was staying with her during the filming of *The Babysitter.* After a lover's quarrel, Townsend went berserk and landed in a psychiatric hospital for a month's observation. The repentant Schneider checked in as well to keep her company, which forced Ponti to suspend production of *The Babysitter* until he or someone could persuade her to leave.

"This is the first time I have had to go to see an actress in an asylum," Ponti told reporters. "This affair is very sad—humanly sad."

Ponti tried to collect on the production insurance so that he could restart *The Babysitter* with another star, but that required getting Schneider certified as mentally incompetent. Though she might have been, she was a voluntary paying guest at the hospital and not under its care, so Ponti could only wait until her lover was discharged and hope that Schneider would follow. She did, and the movie was finally finished, but at the insurance company's insistence, Ponti withheld two-thirds of her salary to penalize her.

The elite of Rome, as well as all of Italy, were then under constant threat of kidnapings and terrorist attacks. It seemed only a matter of time before the Pontis bacame targets. In March 1975, the head of the family was singled out while he was driving home alone to Marino after working late at the office. As Ponti's Alfa Romeo approached a lonely patch of the Appia Antica, he was forced to slam on the brakes as he spotted a stalled car blocking the road. Glancing into his rearview mirror, he also saw another car pull up behind him. A masked man carrying a gun jumped out and started running toward Ponti's car.

Crouching down in his seat, Ponti stepped on the gas pedal and tried to drive around the car in front. The masked gunman, meanwhile, started to shoot, shattering the rear window and putting several bullet holes into the car itself before Ponti got away.

When Ponti reported the incident, he was promised a police escort if he phoned them in advance to let them know he would be passing that way late at night. Several months later, Ponti happened to call just as the police were sending a car to his neighborhood to check out an explosion and fire, so they assigned it to follow him. While Ponti was speeding along, another car suddenly pulled out in front of him and tried to force him off the road, but the driver raced away when he saw the police coming up behind Ponti.

As Ponti and his escort arrived at Villa Ponti, they found an unmarked van parked, with its engine running, near the entrance to the estate. Inside the van were rope, tape, and hypodermic needles loaded with drugs, the equipment usually used in kidnaping attempts. Police suspected that the explosion nearby had been detonated to divert them from the kidnap scene. Presumably, Ponti was again the intended victim, though it might just as easily have been Sophia or one of the children.

Around this time, Ponti also had a major health crisis that may have been prostate cancer, though no details were given in a news report that he'd undergone surgery at a clinic in Switzerland. But it's believed that Ponti, now going on sixty-five, had been diagnosed two years earlier, while he was taking Vittorio De Sica to various cancer specialists. According to a Ponti intimate, doctors first tried treating the diseased prostate with hormone medications and radiation therapy, but finally decided to operate to prevent the cancer from spreading to other parts of the body.

That spring of 1975, the Pontis had a happier experience with the successful release of *La pupa del gangster,* which grossed the equivalent of $2 million in its first month of release in Italy and became a hit throughout Europe. Though roasted by the critics, the movie seemed proof that Sophia could still draw crowds if matched with Marcello Mastroianni. It was the public's first chance to see them together in five years.

Still, Ponti couldn't get American distribution, or at least not for the $1 million advance he was asking, so the United States would again be one of the last countries to see Sophia's latest endeavor. That summer, it broke box-office records in Japan, helped in no small measure by a personal appearance tour by Sophia, who'd been the most popular Western actress there since the virtual retirement of Audrey Hepburn.

It was also Sophia's first trip ever to Japan, which she made on her own with secretary Ines while Ponti stayed home with the children. Though Sophia had intended to include some sightseeing, she got not much more than a royal tour of all the movie and television studios. "I did see the insides of three hotels in Tokyo, Kyoto, and Osaka, and they did take me to one temple in Kyoto. But that was mostly for picture taking. I took off my shoes and put on my shoes a dozen times, and kneeled and bowed and saw mostly cameras," she recalled.

In October, Sophia and Ponti flew to Dallas, Texas, for an "Italian Fortnight" sponsored by Neiman Marcus and to host a press preview of *La pupa del gangster,* now titled *Poopsie & Company* for the English-speaking world. Due to a negative reaction, Ponti had no better luck making an American deal. Three years later, he finally gave up and sold *Poopsie* for peanuts to Cougar Pictures, which released it on the exploitation market in a truncated and English-dubbed version.

Before 1975 was over, Ponti had two new movies in the works for Sophia and was also negotiating a $75 million coproduction deal with Mehdi Bouscehri, brother-in-law of the Shah of Iran. Bouscehri reportedly had unlimited funds available through companies that the shah owned abroad. The deal never got done, allegedly because some of the shah's allies reminded him of Mrs. Ponti's place on the Arab boycott list.

After the success of their last movie in Europe and Japan, another teaming of Sophia with Mastroianni seemed mandatory. But Ponti had nothing in mind until Sophia saw his newly completed *Down and Dirty* and was very impressed by the work of director Ettore Scola, who also wrote the script. She asked Scola to create something for her and Mastroianni that would be completely different from anything they had made before for De Sica or other directors. Scola accepted the challenge, but said that he'd need time to come up with an idea.

Ponti agreed to that because he'd already committed Sophia to a new deal he'd made for several movies with Sir Lew Grade, head of ATV, Britain's largest independent television company, which had recently expanded into movie production. Grade had a new spin on Ponti's "up-front" deals, selling the television distribution rights as well as the theatrical in advance to raise the funding. *The Cassandra Crossing,* the first Ponti-Grade coproduction, would eventually get its first television showings on ITV in Britain and NBC in the United States after the theatrical runs.

With Grade taking care of the financing, Ponti provided the production expertise. To *The Cassandra Crossing* Ponti brought director George Pan Cosmatos and writer Robert Katz, who'd worked for him previously on *Massacre in Rome.* This time the material was completely fictional, dealing with an outbreak of deadly plague aboard an express train traveling between Switzerland and Sweden. Detoured by health authorities, the train has to cross over an abandoned bridge that was heavily damaged during World War II and will probably collapse under its weight.

The movie marked Sophia's late entry into the cycle of so-called disaster epics that had started with *The Poseidon Adventure, Earthquake,* and *The Towering Inferno.* Sophia had rarely been part of a large cast of American and European stars, but with her husband as producer she was guaranteed top billing. As in the case of *Operation Crossbow,* she would never share scenes with some of them, thus losing a chance to act with another of Hollywood's great leading men, Burt Lancaster, who played a psychotic American general controlling the train's destiny from a secret military base somewhere in Europe.

Sophia was paired romantically in the movie with Richard Harris, who, coming after Richard Burton, Peter O'Toole, and Peter Finch, gave her the right to claim that she'd worked with all of the boozing wild boys of the British cinema. Harris brought along his new wife, fashion model Ann Turkel, and arranged for her to act a supporting role as one of the train passengers, so Sophia rarely saw either of them away from the set. By the end of production, the Harrises were expectant parents.

The all-star casting scheme found Sophia sharing the spotlight for the first time ever with another female legend, in this case Ava Gardner, typecast as an aging nymphomaniac traveling with her latest boytoy. Since Gardner was twelve years older than Sophia, they weren't really in competition and got along fine in the few scenes they shared. Gardner gave Sophia some advice that she never forgot: "Always shoot your closeups first thing in the morning, honey, 'cause your looks ain't gonna hold out all day."

Sophia made two new friends during the filming of *The Cassandra Crossing,* one through sheer luck when he became a last-minute replacement for James Coburn in the role of a narcotics detective traveling in the guise of a Catholic priest: O. J. Simpson, the football star. Simpson, who was then one of the most admired athletes in the world as running back for the Buffalo Bills, arrived with his wife, Marguerite, and their two kids and immediately captivated everybody. He had a habit of wandering up to Sophia and bursting into his favorite song, "What Are You Doing the Rest of Your Life?" She tried to teach him the lyrics in Italian, but he proved hopeless.

Needless to say, Sophia soon had "The Juice" playing poker and gin rummy with her during the breaks. Sophia moaned and rolled her eyes skyward whenever he won, which was most of the time.

Yet another star of *The Cassandra Crossing* was the father of Method acting, seventy-three-year-old Lee Strasberg, portraying a survivor of the Nazi concentration camps. It was Strasberg's second movie role and his first since his Oscar-nominated debut in *The Godfather: Part II*. The great teacher and head of the Actors Studio didn't try to recruit Sophia or even to advise her, but he fostered one of the most important friendships of her life when he introduced her to his Venezuelan-born wife, Anna.

The third Mrs. Strasberg, the former Anna Mizrahi, was thirty-five years younger than her husband and a onetime actress. Like the Pontis, the couple had two young children, Adam and David. Sophia and Anna quickly discovered that they had much in common and they would become as close as sisters as time went on.

The $6 million *Cassandra Crossing* took four months to shoot, starting in December 1975. The Pontis moved back temporarily to their villa in Marino during the filming of the interior scenes at Rome's Cinecittà. Swiss Railways provided the train that doubled for the Trans-European Express. Exteriors, many shot from helicopters to trace the train's treacherous journey, were filmed in France and Switzerland. The Cassandra bridge, supposedly located in Poland, was actually near Clermont-Ferrand in France.

Carlo Ponti Jr. turned seven during the filming. As one of his birthday presents, his parents promised him a bit role, his first since his cradle appearance in *Sunflower*. This time, Cipi was seen reading a comic book in a crowd scene filmed in the railway terminal at Basel, Switzerland. He earned the equivalent of $8 for his piggy bank.

During the production, Sophia gave an interview that caused surprise and conjecture when it was published in tabloids throughout the world under the title of "The Superstars Who Fell in Love with Me." Written by Henry Gris, a veteran freelancer who was one of the founders of the Hollywood Foreign Press

Association and its Golden Globe Awards, the article amounted to a confession by Sophia that she deliberately flirted with many of her leading men to add sizzle to their romantic scenes.

"It often spilled over into reality," Sophia said. "I liked it. I allowed them to fall in love with me, but never once did I fall in love with them." She made an exception for Cary Grant, who, she claimed, might have won her heart if she hadn't already been in love with Carlo Ponti.

Sophia also singled out Frank Sinatra, Paul Newman, Peter Sellers, and Richard Burton as obviously and definitely smitten with her, and described Clark Gable and John Wayne as "gentlemen too shy to advertise their feelings." A special nod was given to Omar Sharif, whom she called "the most charming of the lot. I loved the way his eyes used to caress me, even when we were playing poker together. I wouldn't say he didn't try to seduce me, but in all fairness to him, he didn't try to take advantage of my liking him. He respected me and Carlo too much."

By the completion of *The Cassandra Crossing,* director Ettore Scola was ready to go with Sophia's rematch with Marcello Mastroianni, which inaugurated a new coproduction deal that Ponti had made with a Canadian tax-shelter group known as Canafox Films. The Pontis stayed on in Italy for the filming, which coincided with the eleventh anniversary of their moving into their villa at Marino.

Sophia had requested something different from Ettore Scola and she got it in *Una giornata particolare* (*A Special Day*), which he wrote in collaboration with Ruggero Maccari and Maurizio Costanzo. Largely a fictitious two-character drama, it was set against one of the most infamous events in Italian history, the May 8, 1938, summit meeting in Rome between Mussolini and Adolf Hitler.

Sofia Scicolone had then been only three and a half years old, but the script gave her a chance to relive her past as a middle-aged housewife with six children. Antonietta's staunch Fascist husband has taken the kids to a parade celebrating Hitler's arrival, but she stays home to do her usual chores. When the family's mynah bird gets loose, she gives chase and finally catches it with the help of a man she doesn't know but who lives in the same apartment building. Gabriele turns out to be a radio announcer who's just been fired for his anti-Fascist opinions. He's considering suicide. They wind up spending the day together, but with a surprising twist when Gabriele confesses to being homosexual. Antonietta takes it upon herself to seduce him to prove that he's a "real" man, but it's obvious that Gabriele submits only out of pity for her and her loveless marriage. Both learn something about passion and themselves before he's carted away by the police and she goes home to fix supper for her returning family.

Scola had made some drastic changes to the standard Loren–Mastroianni formula. "When I devised the story of two people who were confused by and ashamed of their sexuality," the director recalled, "it seemed right to have them played by two actors who had always been used as symbols of triumphant sex. It seemed like another way of celebrating virility and beauty as absolute values, not as commercial commodities."

"I've never played a submissive character before," Sophia said at the time. "I've always reacted. But this woman is a slave. She's been completely humiliated by her husband. She's a dust mop."

The frumpish Antonietta was Sophia's most unglamorous role since *Two Women*. She used no makeup except for some subtle shading to create shadows under her eyes. Her only costume was a shabby cotton housedress, with bits of her underslip drooping below the hemline. Her earrings were cut glass. She had a long run in one stocking and wore cheap ankle-strap shoes. Her hair looked like it hadn't been permed in years.

Sophia's seduction scene with Mastroianni was a radical departure from the tantalizing striptease that she had done for him in *Yesterday, Today and Tomorrow* thirteen years earlier. "I prepared my fantasy for the scene for several weeks prior to shooting it," she recalled. "When the camera finally turned, I was really and truly that housewife making aggressive love to that passive man Marcello was playing. No fakery: In my mind, I was completely that woman having sexual intercourse at that moment."

Happily, Mastroianni had no problems acting a character so different from himself. "People laughed when they heard I was going to play a homosexual," he said later. "I could never figure out why. For me, it was just one more case of doing a job. And fortunately there was Scola as the director—one of those people who is always ready to listen, who creates a wonderful atmosphere on the set, who doesn't consider himself God's gift to the world."

Sophia also responded well to Scola's direction, so much so that some of their coworkers were convinced that they were having an affair. Scola later admitted it to a friend, but said it ended when the production did.

In September 1976, while the filming was still going on, Sophia's sister, Maria, telephoned that their father had just been taken to a hospital in Rome in critical condition. The news came as no shock to Sophia. Riccardo Scicolone had been under treatment for liver cancer for over a year, but that hadn't made any difference to their estrangement. She had seen him just once since the diagnosis and then only at the insistence of Maria, who'd reconciled with Scicolone years ago and enjoyed a pet status that her older sister never experienced.

Yet when a parent is at death's door, one tends to forget past grievances, which is exactly what Sophia did when she rushed to her father's bedside. He seemed more dead than alive when the two sisters arrived, but when he heard their voices, he opened his drugged eyes, looked at them, and sighed *"Sono felice"* ("I'm happy") before nodding off again.

Sophia found herself in a room with three strangers, two of whom turned out to be her half-brothers through Scicolone's marriage to Nella Rivolta. Both men were just a few years younger than Sophia and Maria, and had the same Scicolone nose and full lips. Giuliano Scicolone was a doctor, and brother Giuseppe a bank manager.

Sophia also met her latest stepmother for the first time. German-born Carola Hack was a former fashion model who bore a certain resemblance to Marlene Dietrich and seemed to satisfy Scicolone's taste for movie star lookalikes. His marriage to Nella Rivolta had ended in divorce right after Italy's 1970 law went into effect. Scicolone's common-law wife, the fiftyish Hack was totally devoted to him and had been caring for him at home until it became too much.

Things turned a bit weirder several days later when Sophia returned for another visit and discovered her mother standing vigil alongside Carola Hack. Garbo and Dietrich finally met? In any case, Scicolone was now under an oxygen mask and too far gone to notice.

Romilda Villani had a phobia against hospitals and funerals, so her daughters were stunned to find her holding one limp hand of the man she claimed to hate for ruining her life. But who can tell what feelings, stored up over a period of forty-three years, drove her there?

Later that same day, Riccardo Scicolone breathed his last. A hospital attendant tried to revive him, but failed. Sophia, her mother, and her sister were still in the room at the time, together with Carola Hack and Giuseppe Scicolone.

"I hated my father all my life," Sophia recalled, "but in his final days I forgave him for all the suffering he caused us. As you grow older, marry, and have children of your own, you learn to forgive and forget. I do not forget easily, but I do forgive."

Romilda Villani and Scicolone's ex-wife Nella were conspicuously absent from the funeral, which turned into the expected press circus. Paparazzi stalked Sophia in the church and followed her limousine to the cemetery in cars, on motor bikes, and in a helicopter.

Riccardo Scicolone died less than a month before what would have been his sixty-ninth birthday. News reports were quick to point out that he wasn't much older than his son-in-law, Carlo Ponti, who would turn sixty-six in December. Sophia's response to that can only be guessed at, but as her husband grew older and she still looked like she'd discovered the Fountain of Youth, the age difference between them was becoming an increasingly sensitive matter.

Soon after finishing *A Special Day,* Sophia was back at work again in Ponti's next Canadian-financed coproduction, *Angela.* The script by Charles Israel borrowed from Greek mythology, with the title role based on Queen Jocasta, the mother and later the wife of Oedipus.

The story spanned a period of two decades, from the Korean War to the present. The early scenes required Sophia to portray a woman in her early twenties. As preposterous as that might seem, the plot gets loopier as it rolls along. Angela is a hooker who becomes pregnant by her mobster-lover but doesn't get a chance to tell him before he's drafted into the army. When he returns, he refuses to believe that the baby boy is his. It messes up his mind so badly that he can't concentrate on robbing banks, so the head mobster has the baby abducted. Angela is never able to find her son, but she holds the father responsible and tips off the police about his next heist, which lands him in jail for twenty years. Two decades later, Angela, now the owner of a posh restaurant, is having an affair with a young stud who works in the kitchen. It all ends in a bloodbath when the guy turns out to be her own son and his father, freshly sprung from twenty years in prison, arrives in town seeking revenge.

Due to problems with the Canadian government over the financing for the Italian-based *A Special Day,* Ponti and co-producer Zev Braun were required to film *Angela* in Canada. One of the main reasons that governments grant production subsidies is to create work for their own people. Ponti had dealt with it only minimally in *A Special Day* by hiring one of Canada's top actors, John Vernon, for what was really only a secondary role as Sophia's Fascist husband.

Vernon was again signed for *Angela,* this time for a much juicier part as Sophia's gangster-lover and eventual assassin. A handsome blond newcomer, Steve Railsback, got the role of their son. To add a name that would be more familiar to moviegoers in the United States, John Huston was cast as the sinister ganglord, a role similar to the one that won him acclaim in *Chinatown.*

Shot in Montreal and environs, *Angela* was one of Sophia's unhappiest working experiences, which showed on the screen. Lonely for her two children back in Paris, she also ran into problems with director Boris Sagal, who took the job on short notice when the Canadian Sidney J. Furie got a better offer in Hollywood. Though the Russian-born Sagal was an experienced actor as well, he couldn't fulfill Sophia's need for an "acting" director in the De Sica sense and came closer to being a tyrannical egomaniac like Otto Preminger. Sagal's one saving grace as a director was his training in television, which enabled him to finish the film in five weeks and send Sophia back to her family sooner than expected.

In a horrifying footnote, *Angela* turned out to be Boris Sagal's last theatrical movie. He died four years later when he accidentally walked into a revolving helicopter blade while working on the TV miniseries *World War III*.

By the end of *Angela*, Sophia had an unreleased backlog of three movies, all made within the space of one year, so there were no immediate plans for another. But before she settled back into domesticity, Sophia joined the select group of international superstars who were earning big money for TV commercials that were shown only in Japan. Apparently Japan was far enough removed from the rest of the world that nobody's image would be cheapened by pitching consumer goods and services. On the female side, Sophia was preceded by Audrey Hepburn and Catherine Deneuve.

Sophia had signed a deal with Honda motor scooters for three thirty-second spot commercials for $200,000, which works out to about $2,222 per second. Luckily for Honda, they weren't making a feature-length movie. At that rate, Sophia's compensation would have been at least $12 million! Honda flew a director and camera crew from Tokyo to Rome for the filming. The script required Sophia to motorbike out the front gate of Villa Ponti and cruise around the neighborhood, things she'd never do in real life.

Fortunately, the Honda crew had come and gone by February 8, 1977, when two busloads of police armed with machine guns arrived at Villa Ponti and completely surrounded the estate. Waving a search warrant at the gatekeepers, a deputy from the public prosecutor's office led a group of ten police to the house and pounded on the front door. Servants let them in, but what happened after that is unclear. The Pontis were at home, but apparently too surprised and too frightened to protest.

The police spread around the house, going through every room and making an inventory of furnishings, paintings, sculptures, and whatever other valuables they found. At the same time, another squad of police was searching Ponti's office in Rome, seizing account books and whole filing cabinets of business records.

Although no official explanation was given for the raids, a government insider told Agenzia Italia, Italy's top news wire, that it was the beginning of an investigation into Carlo Ponti's business dealings. He was suspected of income tax evasion, making improper use of government subsidies, and of illegal export of Italian funds.

The next day the Pontis, whose children were already in Paris with their nanny, took off to join them from Rome's Leonardo da Vinci Airport. "I don't want to stay in this country one more minute," Sophia told a reporter.

"It is not possible for me to remain in Italy any longer, much less work here," Ponti chimed in.

A month later, Sophia had to return to Rome to do some soundtrack redubbing for *A Special Day,* which was scheduled to be shown at the Cannes Film Festival in May. Afterwards, when she and secretary Ines Bruscia arrived at the airport for an evening flight back to Paris, a customs officer stopped her and took her to an office for questioning. Although she was not subjected to a body search, all her hand luggage and checked pieces were thoroughly examined. The inspector confiscated several envelopes containing bank deposit receipts and business documents.

Meanwhile, Ines had telephoned Emanuele Golino, Ponti's lawyer in Rome, who rushed there with two of his colleagues. Sophia had refused to be interrogated without them being present. A customs chief also arrived to take charge of the government side.

Sophia had booked her plane ticket under an alias, a common practice for celebrities, but customs claimed it was for shiftier reasons. They wanted a detailed, day-by-day account of her current visit to Rome, what she'd done, whom she'd seen, how much money she'd spent, and so on.

At the end, Sophia was handed back her passport and told she was free to go. Unfortunately, five hours had passed and she'd not only missed her plane, but also the last flight out to Paris. That required waiting until five in the morning, when the next one took off.

Unluckily, someone had tipped off the press about Sophia's ordeal, so the area outside the interrogation room was packed with reporters and paparazzi. To keep them at bay, she got permission from customs to remain there until her flight was announced.

When the time came, the press had been at the airport almost as long as Sophia, so they were in a foul mood as she emerged from the room and headed for the departure lounge. Flanked by her lawyers and secretary, she put on a stone face and bulldozed her way through without saying a word as microphones were thrust at her and flashbulbs exploded.

A similar scene took place when Sophia landed in Paris, where Ponti was waiting for her, but two of the family bodyguards made sure that no one got near them.

Sophia's detention made headlines throughout the world, but nobody but the Pontis and the Italian authorities seemed to know what was going on, and neither side was talking. Meanwhile, gossip tabloids carried tales of Sophia being caught with millions of lire in cash in her handbag and with letters of credit from Italian banks hidden within clothing in her suitcases. Italy was then going through a grave economic crisis. The government had adopted strict regulations to prevent the flight of capital and to strengthen the value of the lire.

Rossano Brazzi, a longtime friend of the Pontis, perhaps said more than he should have when he told the *National Enquirer:* "I don't believe they have done anything wrong. Carlo is a lawyer and a very smart man. He will never do anything that will give the authorities cause to institute valid proceedings against him. There is talk that he has evaded taxes, which is nothing unusual in this country. Many evade taxes in Italy. Sophia feels that the Italian government, which caused them so much trouble over their marriage, is just using them as scapegoats again."

Sophia literally took the heat in Paris a few weeks later, when Ponti happened to be away in Switzerland and a fire broke out in their building on Avenue Georges V in the middle of the night. Earlier that day, Sophia the witch suddenly had another of her eerie premonitions and asked secretary Ines Bruscia if they were insured against fire. "Now that's not one of my everyday questions," Sophia recalled. "In my mind, I clearly saw a fire breaking out, but I couldn't tell when."

Seven hours later, Sophia was awakened by Ines's screams and thought they were being burglarized again. But Ines had smelled something burning, and when they looked out into the hallway opposite the elevator, they could see smoke. They tried to get the concierge on the house phone but couldn't, so Sophia called a friend and asked her to report it to the fire department.

"In my panic, it didn't occur to me that I could call the firemen myself," she remembered. "Then I ran upstairs to where the children sleep. The nurse was already there. We put their blankets over them and each of us carried one. By then, the smoke seemed to be coming from below our apartment, so we had to head for the roof. When we got there, we didn't have the key to the door, so I broke a window with my shoe and we got outside. Already some other residents were there, but nobody had notified us. It was very strange and a little worrisome."

Sophia was wearing only a nightgown. "The temperature was down around freezing, so I went back to the apartment to get something warm to put on and also to leave the front door open in case the firemen had to get in. When I opened the door, I was almost overcome by smoke, so I closed it again. That's what panic can do: a lot of wasted energy and unnecessary danger."

Back on the roof, Sophia could hear the fire trucks wailing, but her friend had given the wrong address and they stopped half a block away. Meanwhile, Sophia and the others watched helplessly from above as the firemen realized the mistake, turned around, and finally started entering the building.

It was another hour before firemen reached the evacuees on the roof with news that everything was under control. The fire had started on the fourth floor and spread to the fifth by the time it was extinguished. The Ponti triplex, which began on the seventh floor, was unaffected except for smoke seepage.

The firemen insisted on taking the two Ponti children down to medicos in the lobby to make sure that the exposure to the cold air and smoke hadn't caused any harm. "They slipped oxygen masks on the boys and disappeared before I could say a word," Sophia said. "They told the rest of us who had apartments above the fifth floor to return and open all the doors and windows to let the smoke out. About six-fifteen in the morning, the children came back up with their nanny. They were both a bit annoyed because the firemen wouldn't let them keep the oxygen masks!"

Sophia felt sick and had a ferocious headache. "I went to the hospital that afternoon and they said I had smoke intoxication," she recalled. "They had me inhale oxygen for an hour and a half and sent me home."

By that spring of 1977, *The Cassandra Crossing* had opened to dismal business in the United States and Europe. Fortunately, no one blamed Sophia for it. Critics compared the movie unfavorably to previous disaster epics and several dubbed its executive producer Sir Low Grade for making an inferior copy.

Grade and coproducer Ponti, however, didn't lose anything in the end. *The Cassandra Crossing* turned out to be a blockbuster hit in Japan, where Sophia's popularity helped it to recoup almost its entire negative cost of $6 million. TV syndication sales later accounted for a profit.

If anything was going to rejuvenate Sophia's career, it seemed to be *A Special Day,* which had turned out so well that Ponti considered it her best chance at an Oscar nomination since *Marriage, Italian Style* thirteen years ago. Entering the film at the Cannes Festival was the first step in the campaign, which would be followed by an Oscar-qualifying release in the United States in the fall.

Ponti preceded Sophia to Cannes, which meant her flying there alone from Paris via Nice on May 19 to attend the gala screening. During the one-hour flight, Sophia had another near-death experience as the Caravelle jet hit air turbulence and plunged several thousand feet before the pilots got it under control. She later said they were the most frightening moments ever as she sat contemplating death and the loss of her children and loved ones.

With both Sophia and Mastroianni in attendance, the Cannes screening of *Una giornata particolare* was rapturously received. Thomas Quinn Curtiss, reporting for the *International Herald Tribune,* said the movie "towers above other contenders" and that "Sophia Loren, daring a nonglamour role as the faded wife, gives what is assuredly her most mature and moving performance."

Yet *A Special Day* won no prizes at Cannes, probably due in part to Carlo Ponti's close friendship with festival director Maurice Bessy. "Everyone was sure that *A Special Day* would get the *Palme d'Or* [best picture award]," public relations executive Simon Mizrahi recalled. "I don't know how many times I heard Bessy saying, 'Carlo, you've got the Palme, no problem,' and 'Carlo, I can assure you it's in the pocket. I'll handle Roberto.' It's simply not done! What contempt for the jury!"

"Roberto" was film director Rossellini, ex-husband of Ingrid Bergman and before that longtime lover of Anna Magnani, who was buried in his family's cemetery plot after she died. President of the 1977 Cannes jury, Rossellini shared Magnani's contempt for the Ponti-Loren alliance, which may have given him a reason for disliking *A Special Day.* But he also had a favorite of his own in another Italian entry, *Padre padrone,* directed by the brothers Vittorio and Paolo Taviani.

"Rossellini wanted to make a statement supporting two estimable but little known directors and glorifying a film coproduced by Italian television, which was becoming the main benefactor of Italian cinema," said Simon Mizrahi. "*Padre padrone* had quite a few supporters on the jury, though not for the *Palme d'Or.* But Rossellini was an incredible fighter and changed their minds one by one. Rossellini fought Bessy through the whole festival, and on closing night Bessy did not go on stage in protest. It was horrendous, shocking and rude. Bessy's behavior really got to Rossellini. He was enormously affected by it, and I am convinced it hastened his death. He had a heart condition and died a few weeks later."

Rossellini's panel of jurors included American film critic Pauline Kael, Swiss actress Marthe Keller, French director Jacques Demy, and Mexican author Carlos Fuentes. *Padre padrone* won the *Palme d'Or*. Whether Sophia and Mastroianni received any votes for the acting awards is unknown, but Best Actress ended in a tie between Shelley Duvall for the American *Three Women* and Monique Mercure for the French-Canadian *J. A. Martin: Photographer*. Fernando Rey won Best Actor for the Spanish *Elisa, vida mía*.

The snub of *A Special Day* brought some outraged comment from the *International Herald Tribune*'s Paris-based Thomas Quinn Curtiss, who knew the Pontis personally and may have been put up to it. "Due to the questionable verdicts of the 1977 Cannes Festival jury—in particular, its neglect of Ettore Scola's *Una Giornata speciale*, generally regarded as the best film to have been shown in competition—future festivals may eliminate the bestowing of awards," Quinn wrote, though time proved him wrong.

Ponti sold the American distribution rights to *A Special Day* to Cinema V, which was one of the few remaining companies in the dwindling foreign import field and had also acquired *Padre padrone*, but for release at a later date. *A Special Day* would be Sophia's first Italian film in thirteen years to open in the United States with English subtitles. Those that followed *Marriage, Italian Style* were not considered of art theater calibre, so they were released only with dubbed English soundtracks and did so poorly at the box office that few people saw them.

Sophia, in fact, hadn't had any significant hits at all in the U.S. for ages, nor had Mastroianni, so Cinema V recommended that Ponti send both of them to the New York premiere for press interviews and TV guest appearances. The public needed to be reminded that they were still in peak condition, and it was essential to positioning the movie as an Academy Award contender.

After eight movies together, Sophia and Mastroianni jokingly called themselves "the Fred Astaire and Ginger Rogers of Italy." During their ten-day visit to New York, staying in separate suites at the Pierre Hotel, they totally charmed the town and did over a hundred interviews, including what turned out to be a highly controversial one with Dick Cavett on his half-hour TV talk show for the Public Broadcasting System.

Cavett got off to a bad start by asking Sophia, "Are you a bastard?" She cringed and told him to change the subject.

In his little boy manner, Cavett later asked Sophia to define the expression "Latin lover." Her immediate answer was, "It's Marcello Mastroianni."

Turning to Mastroianni for comment, Cavett got more than he reckoned for when the actor said with doubt in his voice, "To be a Latin lover, you must be first of all a great fucker."

While Cavett did a shocked double take, Sophia intervened and said, "You must excuse Marcello because he does not know your language very well. I think he means that he's not a love machine."

"That's right," Mastroianni said. "To be a Latin Lover, you have to be infallible. I'm not infallible. I often fall into *fallo*."

Sophia broke out laughing and whispered the meaning of *"fallo"* to Cavett, who promptly and humorously changed the subject by asking, "Do either of you have any hobbies?"

Mastroianni's use of "fucker" was one of the first times that the dreaded "F" word had ever been spoken on the airwaves. It incited angry newspaper editorials and thousands of protests to PBS, which bleeped out the offending word before tapes of the "live" broadcast were sent to stations outside New York.

While staying in New York, Sophia got caught in the middle of a battle between Ponti and Andy Warhol over the *Frankenstein* and *Dracula* movies. Warhol and director Paul Morrissey claimed that Ponti bilked them out of several million dollars in profits, and were getting ready to sue. Warhol's lawyers wanted to send a process server along when he met Sophia at the Pierre for a scheduled interview for his monthly magazine, *Interview*.

Warhol wouldn't tolerate Sophia Loren being slapped with legal papers as she greeted him at the door, but that didn't stop him from disparaging her later in his diary. In his account of their September 22, 1977, encounter at the Pierre, Warhol wrote:

Sophia came out looking beautiful. Then she kept telling us how poor she was, it was so ridiculous. Like we asked her if she wore Valentino clothes and she said oh no, that they were much too expensive for her, and she said she wouldn't be able to stay at a place like the Pierre herself—that the movie people were paying for it. Like she didn't mention that she could have stayed right down the street in her own apartment in the Hampshire House. . . . I'd told Victor [Warhol's sidekick] he couldn't say any dirty words, because when we went to Carlo Ponti's villa in Rome a few years ago they told us that Sophia didn't allow any dirty words in her house and that we'd get kicked out if we said any. Well, the running thing while we were at the Pierre, it turned out, was that Sophia kept saying "fuck." She and Marcello Mastroianni are on the front page of the *Post* for being on the new Dick Cavett interview show on channel 13 and Marcello said, "You have to fuck a lot" when Dick asked him how do you be a Latin Lover. Sophia seemed to think that was so "cute," so she was repeating it.

In a diary entry of two days earlier, Warhol recalled watching Stanley Siegel's daytime talk show:

Brooke Shields didn't show up so he did a live telephone interview with Sophia Loren, who's in town at the Pierre. Her English is good now. But you know, seeing her on TV this morning, she's just . . . trashy. She said she wouldn't let *her* daughter be in a movie like Brooke Shields's *Pretty Baby,* and I mean didn't she just fuck her way to the top? Who's she kidding? She's so pretentious.

A Special Day opened to record-breaking business for an art house release and received generally favorable reviews. Vincent Canby of *The New York Times* called Sophia's performance "magnificent" and said that she and Mastroianni "light up the screen with the kind of radiance you get only from great movie actors who are also great stars." The *Post*'s Judith Crist noted that the movie "reestablishes Sophia Loren as one of the finest of film actresses and places Ettore Scola firmly in the first ranks of film-makers." Kathleen Carroll of the *Daily News* described it as "a tender duet between two performers who, after years of working together, have developed a telepathic ability to understand each other's moods and switches of personality. The electricity between them is of such a high voltage that one never tires of watching them."

Not surprisingly, *The New Yorker*'s Pauline Kael, who'd served on the jury at Cannes, disliked the movie and may have explained why Sophia's work was passed over at the film festival:

Loren wears a drab housedress that is meant to remind you of her unglamorous dishevelment in *Two Women,* for which she won an Academy Award, and you're supposed to applaud her for not being made up. With your husband as the producer and Pasqualino De Santis as the lighting cameraman, who needs makeup? Loren has never looked more richly beautiful or given such a completely controlled great-lady performance.

A Special Day went on to win a Golden Globe as the Best Foreign-Language Film of 1977. The movie also landed a nomination in that category for the 1977 Oscars, along with the Greek *Iphigenia,* the French *Madame Rosa,* the Israeli *Operation Thunderbolt,* and the Spanish *That Obscure Object of Desire. Madame Rosa,* which featured Simone Signoret in a tour-de-force performance, won.

Sophia failed to get nominated for Best Actress, but could content herself with the fact that Signoret didn't either. The all-American nominee list included Anne Bancroft, Jane Fonda, Shirley MacLaine, and Marsha Mason, but Diane Keaton won for *Annie Hall.* Sophia was still the only actor, male or female, ever to win an Oscar for a leading performance in a foreign language.

Mastroianni had better luck and was nominated for Best Actor, helped no doubt by his being one of the first major stars to portray a homosexual. It was his third Oscar nomination, this time in competition with Woody Allen, Richard Burton, John Travolta, and Richard Dreyfuss, who won for *The Goodbye Girl.*

The box-office success of *A Special Day* seemed to give Sophia's career a new lease on life, especially when teamed with Mastroianni, but finding a suitable vehicle for two middle-aged stars wouldn't be easy. For another thing, Carlo Ponti, who could usually be depended upon to help, was up to his eyeballs in financial and legal troubles.

LIVING AND LOVING

J U S T three days after the Oscar disappointment of *A Special Day,* a warrant was issued in Rome for Carlo Ponti's arrest on charges of illegally transferring large sums of money from Italy. Deputy public prosecutor Paolino dell'Anno, who had led the raid on Villa Ponti a year ago, cited Sophia as an accomplice, along with more than twenty other people who worked for or knew the couple. The most surprising on the list were Ava Gardner and Richard Harris, who had allegedly engaged in some hanky-panky with Ponti over their payments for working in *The Cassandra Crossing.*

The government failed to put a figure to Ponti's illegal transfers of lire. But the newspaper *Il Messaggero* reported it as around 20.9 billion lire ($22.5 million) and guessed that most of it had landed in France, Switzerland, and Liechtenstein, where Ponti had been doing business for years through various corporations.

Ponti faced up to six years in jail if convicted. In the meantime, as long as he kept away from Italy, he was a free man. France, of which both Pontis were now citizens, had no extradition treaties with other countries. Italy could, however, try Ponti in absentia. Toward that end, the government started proceedings to seize all of the Pontis' holdings in Italy. That included Villa Ponti and its contents, the ranch near Milan, and considerable revenue-producing properties, such as a resort hotel and several apartment buildings, that Ponti had acquired over the years.

As might be expected, there was slight public comment from the Pontis. "You know as much as we do about the matter," Sophia told a news-wire reporter. "I only know what I read in the papers. Until the trial I know nothing. Of course there will be a trial!"

When reminded of reports that Pope Paul VI had transferred more than $5 billion worth of lire to the United States without being challenged, Sophia said, "Yes, but it is legal for the Church, as it isn't really part of Italy."

Fortunately for the Pontis, the Italian investigation quickly dropped from the headlines due to a concurrent sensation, the kidnaping by the Red Brigades of Aldo Moro, leader of the Christian Democrats. Fifty-five days later, Moro's corpse was found in the trunk of a car in downtown Rome. His murder stunned the nation and had a devastating effect on Italy's tourist trade and the financial markets.

Meanwhile, life seemed to go on as usual for the Pontis. The family's move to Paris two years ago now appeared to have been motivated by more than just a wish to have the children educated under the superior French school system. Sophia may not have even been aware of it, given the secretive ways in which her husband did business.

At the moment, Sophia was working in a new movie, *Brass Target,* which wasn't a Carlo Ponti production but one of several deals that he had negotiated for her while they were in New York the previous autumn for the opening of *A Special Day.* That trip also brought Sophia an offer to star on Broadway in Alan Jay Lerner and Burton Lane's next musical. *Carmelina* was the story of an unmarried Italian mother who's been collecting child support payments for decades from several American GIs she met during the war and later conned into believing that they fathered her daughter.

Though Sophia was immensely flattered that two of America's greatest songwriters considered her talented enough for such an assignment, she'd never acted, sung, or danced on stage in her life. She doubted whether she could do it for even one performance, let alone eight a week for a minimum of eighteen months, which the contract stipulated. Moving to New York also would have been required, so Sophia gave the offer a fast rejection.

Seemingly easier for Sophia would be a "ghosted" autobiography that Ponti sold to William Morrow and Company for a reported $1 million advance. Ponti had several writers in mind, including the couple's longtime confidant Basilio Franchina, but Morrow insisted on A. E. Hotchner, who had coaxed a number one bestseller out of Doris Day in 1975. Hotchner was also a biographer of Ernest Hemingway, as well as a novelist and playwright, so Ponti readily agreed.

After the contracts were signed, Hotchner moved temporarily to Paris to work with Sophia. They met at the Ponti apartment for two hours every morning, five days a week, before the two children came home from school for lunch.

"Sophia was easy to work with in the sense that she responded to questions," Hotchner recalled. "In the beginning she gave me all the answers she'd been programmed to give other journalists. Then, three weeks into it, I dramatically threw the tapes away and said, 'Now we are ready to begin!' Then she did open up. Toward the end, her responses came much faster. At the end she said she felt she'd been psychoanalyzed."

The collaboration took five months, with interruptions for two movie commitments that Ponti had set for Sophia with other producers, starting with *Brass Target* in the late winter of 1978. Sophia was a last-minute addition to the project, spun into a $6 million thriller that had no big names in the cast and needed an international superstar for "boxoffice insurance."

Based on Frederick Nolan's novel *The Algonquin Project, Brass Target* was another in a series of "What if?" movies in the vein of *The Eagle Has Landed* and *Day of the Jackal* that took off from historical fact. Suppose that General Patton wasn't really killed accidentally in a car crash but assassinated by some of his underlings to cover up a robbery of $250 million worth of Nazi gold?

Sophia portrayed Mara Danelo, an adventuress who consorted with both sides during the war to survive and is now the only person who can identify the ex-Nazi assassin being hunted by American military detectives. John Cassavetes, Max Von Sydow, Patrick McGoohan, Robert Vaughn, and John Davidson headed the predominantly male cast, with George Kennedy making a cameo appearance as "Blood and Guts" Patton.

Most of the exterior scenes were photographed at a fortresslike castle that overlooked the medieval town of Burghausen, about fifty miles southeast of Munich near the Austrian frontier. Sophia didn't like Burghausen's only hotel, so producer Arthur Lewis moved her across the border to an inn in picturesque Holzoster Am See and gave her a chauffeured BMW for the fifteen-mile commute between Austria and Germany.

The year 1978 would be a strenuous one for Sophia, with two more movies set to follow *Brass Target*. For the first time in a decade, none carried a producer's credit for Carlo Ponti, though he was still a power behind the scenes as Sophia's negotiator and adviser. Ponti seemed unwilling to commit any funds of his own to production until his problems in Italy were resolved.

Sophia's next film, *Firepower,* was originally part of Ponti's multipicture deal with Lew Grade (by now elevated from Sir to Lord Grade), which had started with *The Cassandra Crossing.* Grade took over as sole producer of *Firepower,* but Sophia stayed on as top-billed star, as had been intended from the start.

The role of Adele Tasca in *Firepower* seemed unlikely to win Sophia another Oscar, but it at least gave her a chance to wear (and keep) a stunning wardrobe by her current favorite designer, a Paris-based Norwegian named Per Spook. Written by Michael Wilson, the action thriller had the newly widowed heroine seeking revenge for her husband's murder, which was an ordered "hit" by an evil American billionaire based beyond U.S. waters on a Caribbean island.

The twisting plot piled on double-crosses, boat and car chases, explosions, and violent killings, and seemed a natural for director Michael Winner, who had had a phenomenal success in 1974 with *Death Wish* and had received instructions from Lord Grade to come up with something equally brutal and fast moving. Of course, Sophia Loren was no Charles Bronson, but the script didn't attempt to turn her into one. All the dirty work was done by her two costars, James Coburn and O. J. Simpson.

Simpson had been a last-minute replacement for Coburn in *The Cassandra Crossing,* but now they would be acting side by side as Sophia's hired guns. The movie was Sophia's second in a row where the only other women in the cast were extras. Heading the supporting cast were Anthony Franciosa, Eli Wallach, George Grizzard, Vincent Gardenia, Victor Mature, and retired boxer Jake La Motta.

Directly from filming *Brass Target* in freezing Bavaria, Sophia flew to the West Indies for seven weeks of locations on sun-drenched Saint Lucia, one of the Windward Islands. Some of Per Spook's outfits would make the heat more tolerable. Sophia went braless beneath sheer crepes and silks. Smart alecks in the technical crew retitled the movie *Nipplepower.* The cameraman kept a bucket of ice water handy to splash on assistants who got carried away by Sophia's charms.

It was twenty-two years since Sophia had done her water-soaked *Boy on a Dolphin,* but men still found her awesome. "I took the job just to be able to say that I once spent seven weeks in the Caribbean with Sophia Loren," George Grizzard quipped to a coworker.

"She's so professional," Michael Winner said in an interview at the time. "The cast has been besieged by bugs, mice, bats, mongeese, and paparazzi, but Sophia never complains. She works six days and sleeps on Sunday. O. J.

screamed like a twelve-year-old when a grasshopper fell on him, but you don't get a peep out of Sophia. The first day we did some filming at sea, the water was very rough and Sophia got violently sick. But half an hour later she was back for her closeups."

Sophia's reunion with O. J. Simpson for a second film started rumors that they were romantically involved, but the thirty-year-old Simpson was another favorite of Lord Grade and the casting seemed solely for box-office reasons.

During the filming of *Firepower,* Sophia's only interest in Simpson seemed to be as a family friend. "My children love O. J. Have you ever seen him run? He's so graceful," she told visiting *New York Post* columnist Diane Judge.

Judge couldn't get Sophia to comment on the Pontis' criminal indictment in Italy, but found her less resistant to talking about her marriage. "My relationship with Carlo is as solid as ever," Sophia said. "We have lived in Paris for six years. Our oldest son, Cipi, is in school there, and loves it, so I wouldn't think of disrupting his life. It is very important for children to be where *they* want to be. Edoardo is too young to go to school. He is blond and beautiful. Yes, I confess they are my only real interest in life. Children, after all, offer the only true continuity to life, no?"

When asked, as delicately as possible, what attracted her to the pudgy and much older Ponti, Sophia said, "I go for brains in men and look beyond the physical. Big, stunning men are just for fun, and I'm not really susceptible to them. I'm not easy to get. When men realize this they have the sense to leave me alone."

Before finishing *Firepower,* Sophia and company traveled to New York and Washington, D.C., for another ten days of outdoor filming. By that time, 1978 was more than half over, but she still had one more movie to make before she could spend much time with her family back in Paris.

While *Brass Target* and *Firepower* may have seemed like desperate choices for an Oscar-winning dramatic actress, Sophia's next was a calculated return to the sort of thing she did best. This time she would be teamed not only with Marcello Mastroianni, but also with the current Italian rage, Giancarlo Giannini, with Lina Wertmuller as the director and scriptwriter.

A former assistant to Federico Fellini (whom she once compared to Jesus Christ), Wertmuller had become one of Italy's most famous filmmakers, acquiring a cult following in the United States with a string of comedy-dramas with Giancarlo Giannini, including *Swept Away* and *Seven Beauties.* In 1976, Warner Brothers decided she was ready for the big leagues and signed her to a deal for three English-speaking productions, all to be made with Giannini as one of the leads.

The first of those, *A Night Full of Rain,* teaming Giannini with Candice Bergen, had already been finished by the time Wertmuller approached Sophia and Mastroianni about appearing in the next. They both accepted on the basis of a sketchy outline, which Wertmuller then developed into a 600-page script with the equally long title of *A Bloody Event at Caminiti Between Two Men Because of a Widow—Political Motivations Are Suspected.* Not surprisingly, the title was boiled down to *Blood Feud* by the time of release.

The story took place in Sicily during the Fascist 1920s. The characteristic Wertmuller conversation piece again expressed her socialist and feminist views, with Sophia as a widow trying to maintain a respectable image while sharing her sexual favors with Mastroianni, the town lawyer, and Giannini, an exiled Italian-American gangster.

Because of the Pontis' legal problems in Italy, Sophia feared going back to work there, so Wertmuller found locations in Greece that could pass for Sicily. But when the Italian labor unions discovered the country was losing a $4 million expenditure and all the jobs that went with it, they raised such a clamor that producer Arrigo Colombo agreed to stay, provided that Sophia wasn't hassled. Authorities said she was free to come and go, or at least until the Ponti case went to trial later in the year.

Sophia welcomed her first chance to work with a female director, not that there were many to choose from. Liliana Cavani was Wertmuller's only competition in Italy, and apart from Agnes Varda in France, there were almost no others of world reputation.

The first woman ever to be nominated for the director's Oscar (for *Seven Beauties*), Wertmuller made a vivid physical impression with her short-cropped hair, white-framed eyeglasses and Fellini-like black outfits and Stetson hats.

"I'm enchanted by the enthusiasm, the strength of this woman who really looks like a man," Sophia said at the time. "The film shows a new me—I'm very excessive, very aggressive, very everything. Even the makeup. It's another face." Some critics would later say it was the face of Anna Magnani on a bad day.

While Sophia had no actual run-ins with officialdom while she was in Italy, she had to contend with public nastiness that seemed to be stirred up from somewhere from within political circles. During the filming of scenes at a studio near Rome, pickets from the Screen Extras Guild, which happened to be on strike at the time, demonstrated outside. Their placards claimed that while

Sophia was receiving $780,000 to play a Sicilian peasant, they earned only a serflike $28 for a ten-hour day. The press could also be counted on for at least one angry story per day about Sophia's luxurious lifestyle and the millions that she and her husband had stashed away tax free in Swiss banks.

Sophia kept silent, but her mother finally complained to a columnist at *Corriere della Sera:* "Thieves, killers, and swindlers are freely able to walk about undisturbed, but the government has it in for Carlo and Sophia, who should instead be thanked for what they've done for their country. My daughter is the most famous Italian actress, the only one who is known and appreciated abroad. And my son-in-law is the greatest movie producer. Now there's talk of putting them on trial like dangerous criminals. It's the price they have to pay for being celebrities. Envy and jealousy are to blame."

Sophia finished working on *Blood Feud* on October 8, 1978, and immediately left for Paris. Several weeks later, the government charged the Pontis with the additional crime of illegal possession of archeological discoveries. Among the artifacts seized at their Marino villa were seventy Etruscan vases that were considered part of Italy's ancient heritage and the property of the state. The Pontis could get up to thirty years in jail for that charge alone.

In January 1979, in Rome, the couple were finally tried in absentia in the case of their alleged violations of the law restricting the export of Italian currency. Carlo Ponti was found guilty, sentenced to four years in prison, and fined 22 billion lire (about $24 million), which supposedly was the sum of his illegal activities. To get that money, the government intended selling Villa Ponti and its art collection, which included hundreds of paintings, drawings, and sculptures.

Sophia was acquitted of charges of conspiring with Ponti, as were all the other defendants in the case, including Ava Gardner and Richard Harris.

The verdict against Ponti was immediately challenged by his lawyers. The case promised to be under appeal indefinitely due to Italy's ongoing political and economic crises.

Once again, Ponti's freedom seemed assured as long as he stayed out of Italy. The seizure of his assets there may have been a steep price to pay, but for the time being the government was still only custodian. There was reason to hope that he would get back his property on appeal.

Meanwhile, after making three movies back to back, Sophia had decided that her only work in 1979 would be promoting her autobiography, which William Morrow was publishing in the United States in April, with the rest of the world to follow right after. Entitled *Sophia: Living and Loving,* the book was subtitled

"Her Own Story" but credited only one author, A. E. Hotchner. Sophia Loren's name didn't even appear in the copyright, which was shared between Hotchner and Victoria Pictures, Ltd., presumably a Ponti-owned enterprise.

Before starting the traditional "book tour" of major cities across America, Sophia took Cipi and Edoardo, now ten and six, on their first trip to Disney World in Orlando, Florida. The boys were still suffering from culture shock when Mamma sent them home to Paris in the company of their nanny.

The autobiography carried few surprises beyond Sophia's revelations of her experiences with Cary Grant, which up to then were known only to them and a privileged few. Grant, who was always ultracircumspect about his private life, complained to columnist-friend Earl Wilson, "I just can't believe that Sophia could exploit our friendship like this."

When Wilson contacted her for comment, Sophia said, "When something as beautiful as that happens to two people, and a great deal of time has gone by, it shouldn't offend anyone." Grant's sensitivity may have been due to a fear that his ex-wife, Dyan Cannon, might use the revelations about his past with their eleven-year-old daughter, Jennifer.

Another protester was Peter Sellers, who complained bitterly about being barely mentioned in the book. Sellers told a reporter in London that Sophia loved him so much that she'd marry him like a shot if Carlo Ponti died.

In rebuttal, Sophia told one of her American interviewers, "Peter and I were never lovers. Look, I wanted to write a book about my life, not about my partners. I have made pictures with Marcello Mastroianni, Clark Gable, William Holden, Alan Ladd—lots of fascinating men—and they will also be in my next book. Peter Sellers would be the lead in that book because he is a great personality and I adored him. Also Alec Guinness; I was flattered by Alec's kindness and attention. But *Sophia* is only about the things that were important to me. And Cary Grant was."

Sophia told a writer for *People* magazine that the most important thing she learned from doing the book was how her estranged relationship with Riccardo Scicolone shaped her choice of men. "Growing up, it was the dream of my life to have a real father like other children. That is why I sought a father everywhere—I made my best films with actors and directors who were old enough to be my father, and I married an older man like him. Carlo and my mother are almost the same age, and when I think about it, it does seem awkward. But I have always been attracted to older men, and I am very happy I married Carlo. He makes me feel protected."

When asked if she was bitter about the Pontis' troubles with the Italian authorities, Sophia replied, "No. These are the laws of Italy, and they were bound to bring charges because we are known—to make an example of us. As for the most recent charges—you realize that I was absolved by the same court that convicted Carlo—we are not unique. You just never hear about the others. Will we ever go back to Italy to live? Maybe one day. I am an incurable dreamer."

After Sophia returned to Paris, with her book nicely established on the American best-seller lists, author A. E. Hotchner gave several interviews about the collaboration. Hotchner intimated that Sophia hadn't been as open with him as he'd hoped. "I wish she had more social warmth, that I could have seen her in more social situations—for the sake of the book and myself," he said. "I would like to see her eating a meal with her children, or in a restaurant. But I never saw her out of that one room of her apartment where we worked."

Hotchner claimed that the hardest part of his job was getting Sophia to talk about her marital relationship. The book contains one brief confession from Carlo Ponti that he'd had extramarital affairs with other women, but doesn't elaborate.

"Carlo chases anything that has ten percent life in it, and everybody knows that," Hotchner told reporter Stephen Rubin. "But in my first go-round with Sophia about Carlo, she acted like she didn't know any of that. Finally I said, 'Sophia, you and I both belong to a grown-up world where people are not going to accept this. I've got to make a statement in here that shows you realize Carlo plays around. You don't have to go into details, especially if you don't get into fights about it.'

"She said, 'We really don't.' So I said, 'You're going to say that you know Carlo isn't as pure as the driven snow, but that there has been no real alliance, which is true. Carlo's never had a mistress stashed away somewhere.' "

Hotchner described Sophia's current life with Ponti: "There's that old regal king/queen sense to it. They sleep in separate bedrooms; still, there's a closeness. They respect each other and talk over everything. If you get involved with a man at sixteen and he becomes the focus of your life, there can't be much vibrancy left in the relationship when you're forty-four, especially if he's that much older."

When another interviewer asked him if he thought Sophia was a happy woman, Hotchner replied, "What is happy? If you equate fun with happiness, no. She says she loves to work and loves her children. But there's a side of her that's unfulfilled. She's gregarious; when she does go to a disco, she can dance all night, but since Ponti hates to go out, she usually stays in. She may not know how to have fun; she didn't have fun as a child.

"She hasn't psychologically overcome her past," he continued. "That's why she works so hard. She's made some unsuccessful pictures just because she feels most alive while working. She says she doesn't let herself be angry about the past because it wouldn't do her any good."

By the summer of 1979, all three of Sophia's backlog of movies had been released, but none enjoyed the success that her book did. *Brass Target* bombed, and its $5 million deficit was later cited as one of many reasons why MGM decided to sell its movie division to concentrate on hotels and gambling casinos. *Firepower,* released by Lew Grade's Associated Film Distribution, did better, but not enough to recover its $8 million cost.

But *Blood Feud* was the worst flop of all. The movie turned out so badly that Warner Brothers refused to release it, which wasn't surprising after their experience with Lina Wertmuller's previous film, *Night Full of Rain,* which was an unmitigated critical and box-office disaster. Titanus took over the Italian release of *Blood Feud,* but it was savaged by the critics and moviegoers stayed away.

As one critic summed it up:

Three improbable characters meet, love each other, despise each other, then go their separate ways: a woman, a socialist, and an Italian-American gangster are symbolically reunited in death. All this is intermingled with postcardlike landscapes, dialogue rendered in an incomprehensible dialect, and with key scenes reminiscent of the worst kind of family melodramas and soap operas.

Another carped that "Sophia Loren is heavy, hawkish and horribly made up like some funny harlot down on her luck."

Lew Grade, whose devotion to Sophia's career seemed second only to Ponti's, acquired the rights for the English-speaking world but had a hard time just getting bookings due to adverse trade reactions. *Blood Feud* finally opened a test run at a New York art theater in 1980, but was quickly withdrawn after brutal reviews and has never surfaced again.

Blood Feud turned out to be Sophia's last Italian movie for years. Perhaps if it had been successful she would have found ways to do more, but its flop, combined with the criminal proceedings against her and her husband, made it impossible for them to operate within the framework of the Italian film industry any longer.

After the dismal returns on *Brass Target* and *Firepower,* Sophia wasn't receiving any international movie offers either, but fortunately the success of her autobiography spawned a mini-industry of its own that more than took up the slack. Like the proverbial chicken and the egg, it's impossible to say which came first, "Sophia" the perfume or *Sophia* the TV biography, but they debuted simultaneously in October 1980, after more than a year of planning and preparation.

The American division of Coty came up with the idea for the perfume, which hopefully would do for fragrances what Gloria Vanderbilt did for jeans. Though movie stars like Audrey Hepburn and Catherine Deneuve had endorsed perfumes before, Sophia was the first to have one actually named for her. Coty claimed that its market research found her to be the only female celebrity about whom nobody anywhere had anything negative to say.

"Sophia Loren has what Italians consider the most desirable quality in a woman, *simpatia,*" a Coty executive said. "She's a woman of great luminous charm, yet a simple down-to-earth type you could chat with over morning coffee."

Sophia's deal with Coty was reportedly worth a minimum of $2.5 million per year against royalties. Besides lending her name to "Sophia," she was expected to participate in the marketing by posing for advertising, appearing in TV commercials, and making promotional tours of department stores and shopping malls.

Coty granted Sophia the right to choose the scent, which after hundreds of testings turned out to be a combination of jasmine and roses, as well as the shape of the bottle and the color of the packaging (scarlet). Unlike her own personal favorite, the luxury-priced "Joy," "Sophia" would be more affordable. The first release would be in two versions, a quarter ounce of perfume retailing at $22.50, and an ounce of spray cologne concentrate at $6.75.

Meanwhile, Carlo Ponti had been trying to sell the movie rights to *Sophia: Living and Loving,* which might have been easy if he'd been willing to let it be turned into a documentary with Sophia as host-narrator. But Ponti wanted a traditional dramatic film with Sophia, of course, as star, which required a tremendous amount of creative thinking to make it work.

With input from several writers, Ponti finally came up with a concept that read well on paper but still posed problems in execution and credibility. Sophia, now going on forty-six, would portray herself from the age of twenty-five onward. Other actresses would take over for scenes of her earlier life, but

Sophia would act in those as well as in the role of her mother. In the latter half, Sophia would portray both herself *and* Romilda Villani, with help from trick photography in shared scenes.

Carlo Ponti was by this time almost seventy, which is probably why he decided to turn over the production reins to his eldest son, Alex, now twenty-nine, who'd been apprenticing in the business for several years. Sophia's stepson had already produced one movie, *Killer Fish* (not surprisingly, for Lew Grade) and had worked for an investment bank in London after finishing his education at Yale University in the United States.

More in tune with current trends in the movie and television industries, Alex Ponti envisioned the by now retitled *Sophia Loren: Her Own Story* as a three-hour TV special and made a coproduction deal with EMI-TV, which then sold the American broadcast rights to NBC. EMI also controlled the foreign release, which could be as a theatrical feature in some countries.

Whether she wanted to or not, Sophia would have to return to Italy for the filming, since there was no way of faking the Roman and Neapolitan backgrounds. Directed by Mel Stuart, the $4 million production would require eight weeks in Italy and another week in Los Angeles for scenes depicting Sophia's contract days at Paramount in the late 1950s.

Joanna Crawford, a novelist and scriptwriter, did the first-draft screenplay, but a lot of new dialogue was written by the Pontis' longtime associate Basilio Franchina and by Sophia herself. A. E. Hotchner was conspicuously absent from the collaboration, reportedly because Sophia was miffed over some of the interviews he gave after publication of their book.

The casting of the principal roles would later cause laughter, especially in the case of the short, pudgy, and balding Carlo Ponti, who was portrayed by tall, handsome, and bushy-haired Rip Torn (and without even a hint of an Italian accent).

Armand Assante, a newcomer who'd just made a strong impression opposite Goldie Hawn in *Private Benjamin,* was signed to play Riccardo Scicolone. Assante happened to be fifteen years younger than Sophia, so he had to be aged considerably to match her impersonation of Romilda Villani. British actor Edmund Purdom, best remembered for singing with the dubbed voice of Mario Lanza in *The Student Prince,* portrayed Vittorio De Sica.

John Gavin, Sophia's costar in *A Breath of Scandal* twenty years before, took the role of Cary Grant. Already outraged by Sophia's revelations in her book, Grant threatened to sue when he learned that he was going to be depicted. The cooler head of his attorney prevailed, however, and they made an out-of-court settlement in which Grant reportedly received script approval of the scenes in which he was portrayed plus $250,000 for the right to use his name.

The hardest casting problem was finding facsimiles of the young Sophia. Three girls aged four, seven, and eleven were hired for the earliest scenes. A twenty-three-year-old Italian-German actress named Ritza Braun, rechristened Ritza Brown, portrayed Sophia from teenage school dropout to the twentyish movie sexpot.

Due to the government's seizure of Villa Ponti, Sophia stayed at the Hotel Excelsior during the Rome locations. Acting out scenes from her past proved a more traumatic experience than describing them in her autobiography. "When I play my mother, I can be detached and reasonably objective," she said at the time. "But when I have to be myself, it is more difficult. It makes me feel naked, exposed, without underwear. My legs tremble. Some of it is from fear. There's no one to tell me if I'm playing myself right."

Romilda Villani, now seventy-one, offered to serve as technical adviser, but Sophia banned her from the set. "Just one glance from my mother is enough to sap my confidence," she said.

Impersonating Romilda Villani, Sophia wore a reddish blond wig, blowsy makeup, and tattered clothes. For dramatic purposes, certain liberties were taken with the character, which later enraged Romilda when she saw the film. "I hate it," she told a reporter-friend. "It's preposterous and quite wrong—at least the way Sophia portrays *me*. I was never a common woman, yet I am portrayed like an ignorant peasant. I was slim and classically beautiful and have the photographs to prove it. I was voted Garbo's lookalike in 1932, so how terrible could I have looked? Perhaps the writers didn't know any better, but Sophia did. I don't know how she could do this to her own mother."

Sophia managed to get through her seven weeks in Italy without being harassed by the authorities, but several months later a new writ was issued that promised to make her a permanent exile. A tax court sentenced her to a month in jail as the end to a long-simmering dispute over her 1966 income tax return.

By the time of the premiere broadcast of *Sophia Loren: Her Own Story* on October 26, 1980, TV viewers had recently been exposed to biopics of two rival sex symbols, Marilyn Monroe and Jayne Mansfield, both now long dead and unable to portray themselves (Cathy Burns and Loni Anderson took over). That may be a reason why Sophia's got the lowest audience rating of the three, though advance reviews didn't help. One critic called Sophia's mother-daughter act "a monumental indulgence. It would have been wiser not to do the film at all." *Variety* sneered that Sophia played herself from age twenty "through the miracles of makeup, minimum lighting and medium-to-long shots."

The broadcast marked the official launching of the "Sophia" perfume. Scenes like those of Sophia as Romilda begging for food for her children during World War II were interrupted by spot commercials of the ultraglamorous Sophia plugging scent. With Christmas just two months away, Coty was determined to put "Sophia" on everybody's shopping lists, but the ads only added to the ludicrousness of the three-hour presentation.

Borrowing from the title of her best-selling autobiography, "Sophia" was being promoted with the slogan "The fragrance of living and loving—wear it with a passion!" In one of her more provocative endorsements, Sophia said, "You should put it on the hot spots. I can tell you a few of those, but others—it's impossible!"

Supported by a $2 million ad campaign and a national publicity tour by its namesake, "Sophia" was an immediate success. By mid-December, many retailers were rationing sales to prevent their Christmas stocks from running out.

In her travels as perfume pitchlady, Sophia became more accessible to the public than she'd ever been as a movie star. In her itinerary of downtown department stores and suburban shopping malls, she signed autographs, kissed babies, and chatted with everybody, often in Italian with her many immigrant fans.

"Women most often ask how I keep myself beautiful," she said at the time, "but something also very nice happens. They greet me like they would their own sister or their mother. And they like to know about my family, how are my children—you know, like when you meet an aunt or cousin."

Accompanied only by a Coty publicist, Sophia traveled light, with just one suitcase, and did her own hair and makeup. But when she arrived at stores garbed in one of her clinging silk dresses by Per Spook, crowds were always so awed that many people applauded.

Sophia's visit to the Cherry Hill Mall near Philadelphia elicited this description in the local newspaper:

She's over six feet tall in her four-inch black stiletto pumps. Her two giant green cats' eyes are outlined in black with little wings at the ends, and the lids are dusted with cypress-green shadow. She has long chestnut hair and a smile that flashes through lips that look like two wedges of cantaloupe. Her huge, beautiful breasts could win a wet T-shirt contest anywhere.

A new component to Sophia's "look" was eyeglasses, which she wore everywhere except, so far, in films or in perfume ads. They started out as a middleaged necessity, since she couldn't see without them and had a sensitivity to contact lenses. When the news got around, she was approached by Zyloware, a major manufacturer of eyeglass frames, about a commercial tie-in.

The result, which gave her a very lucrative reason for wearing them, was the Sophia Loren Eyewear Collection, targeted at women like herself who didn't believe in the old adage that "men rarely make passes at girls who wear glasses." With help from Zyloware technicians, Sophia designed all the frames herself. They were much larger than traditional women's frames. The style that she preferred and wore the most was in gold metal, with intricate cloisonne detailing on the front and outside edges.

"I think wearing glasses is no longer a mere medical necessity as much as a fashion statement," Sophia said at the time. "After all, glasses are like a hairstyle or jewelry, something that people notice about you right away. That's why we should choose them with all the care we devote to other accessories, and think about how they will affect us overall, rather than just the eyes or the face."

Between her work for Coty and the New York–based Zyloware, which also required her to do publicity and to attend sales conventions, Sophia was spending so much time in the United States that having a home there seemed the next logical step for the Ponti family. The couple's two children, now aged twelve and eight, were both attending a Jesuit-run school in Switzerland, which is why Sophia had more freedom to travel these days. She and her husband, meanwhile, were dividing their time between their apartments in Geneva and Paris, unable, of course, to go back to Italy without landing in jail.

Sophia's new best friend, Anna Strasberg, kept urging her to buy a place in Los Angeles, where the Strasbergs lived half the year while Lee conducted actors' workshops. Sophia began looking around with real estate agents and found something she liked near Oxnard, about thirty miles from the Hollywood–Beverly Hills scene. Ponti flew over from Geneva to check it out, and they both agreed it was perfect for their needs.

Situated in rural Hidden Valley, the ranch-estate was considerably larger than Villa Ponti and covered thirty-nine acres of fields and woods. Dubbed "Westhaven" by its most recent owners, comedy star Eve Arden and actor-husband Brooks West, it had originally been the country retreat of one of

Hollywood's legendary heartthrobs, Ronald Colman. And Sophia's former costar, Alan Ladd, had owned the spread next to it until his death in 1964.

The site was in a long valley surrounded by low hills and a mountain known as Old Boney. The security-conscious Pontis were attracted as much by its natural beauty as its fenced-in remoteness from L.A. To get there from the main road, you had to drive through huge gates, cross a bridge over a creek, and then go up a hill through open pastures before reaching the main house. There was also a guest house adjacent to a tennis court, plus a barn, stable, and a windmill that powered the water pump.

Designed with an American family in mind, 'Westhaven" would require some changes to suit an Italian one. But Carlo Ponti liked the surroundings and the southern California climate, which would give him a chance to grow all the flowers and vegetables that he once did at Villa Ponti. A deal was struck, but with all the paperwork and renovations involved, it would be a long time before the Pontis actually moved in.

In June 1981, Coty's "Sophia" won the Perfume of the Year award from the Fragrance Foundation. Sales, however, had turned erratic since the previous Christmas. According to the industry newsletter *The Informationist,* retailers were claiming that it sold well whenever Coty turned on the advertising or sent Sophia on tour, but didn't really move without help.

Sophia began spending more time on the road, which wasn't just to make the perfume a success. With both children in school and no film work in the offing, she needed to keep occupied. "The one thing in life I can't stand is boredom," she said at the time. "I could kill myself if I get bored. I must have things to do, and that I like to do."

She admitted that she even liked doing interviews: "You know why? Because they're not boring for me. Because in each person I meet, I always try to find something special. Of course, if I always met the same person, it would get boring. And even though the questions are more or less always the same, they're phrased differently, so it's like hearing them for the first time. And of course you always answer differently."

In her time away from plugging perfume and eyeglasses, Sophia was reported being romantically involved with Étienne Émile Baulieu, the Paris doctor who developed the controversial "abortion pill," RU486. The gossip started when a French tabloid ran a photograph of Sophia and Baulieu leaving an apartment building in suburban Paris where they allegedly had a love nest.

Eight years older than Sophia, and married with three children, Baulieu seemed to have a remarkably understanding wife. When the story broke, Yvonne Baulieu was reported as saying, "What could he do? He fell in love. After all, Sophia Loren is a superb woman."

The European press reported Sophia getting ready to divorce Carlo Ponti, but changing her mind when he threatened to make sure that she never saw their two children again. A news story claimed that the Pontis were giving up their Paris apartment and settling in Geneva to free Sophia from temptation!

· Evidence seems to point to an affair between Sophia and Baulieu, but when an interviewer once asked her to confirm it, she replied, "No, no. Absolutely not. It was a rumor, but I was never involved with him."

Later in 1981, Sophia received her first good movie offer in several years and decided to grab it. The director would again be Lina Wertmuller, but everybody's entitled to make a mistake now and then, and this time the property wasn't one of her original creations. Based on a critically acclaimed novel by Jorge Amado, *The Miracles, Sins, and Happiness of Tieta* told of a woman from an unspoiled wilderness town in Brazil who moves to the big city to work as a prostitute, eventually buys the brothel, and becomes a confidante of the rich and powerful. The story takes a *China Syndrome* turn when Tieta's hometown is threatened by the building of a chemical plant and she's the only one who can save it from ruin.

Though *Tieta* had Italian financing, it would be shot on location in Brazil. Two formidable actors, José Ferrer and Alain Cuny, were signed as Sophia's costars, with the balance of the cast to be recruited in Brazil.

After Sophia signed the contract, the producers discovered they could shave more than a million dollars off the budget by filming in Italy instead of Brazil. Wertmuller easily accomplished that by shifting the locale of the story to central Italy, which was rich in fertile farmland and had the same problems with chemical pollution as Brazil or anywhere else in the world.

Turning the characters into Italians wasn't hard either, especially in Sophia's case, but a crisis of monumental proportions developed due to her being one of Italy's "most wanted" income tax scofflaws. The moment that she stepped on native soil, she would be arrested and sent to jail for thirty days.

THIRTY DAYS IN JAIL

EVER since she was ordered arrested for income tax evasion in 1980, Sophia had been making public promises like "I intend to accept the decision of the judges of my country. I will return to Italy and hand myself over as soon as I have completed my professional obligations." But she was obviously only stalling for time. Nothing short of Italy dispatching a SWAT team would get her there.

Sophia tried to break her contract for *Tieta,* but producers needed her for box-office insurance and refused. Due to his own legal problems in Italy, Ponti couldn't do much more than counsel Sophia, but they finally decided that it was about time to face the music. Once Sophia served her sentence, she could visit or work in Italy whenever she wanted. Furthermore, her incarceration and the public humiliation that went with it might be enough to appease the authorities and cause them to go easier on Ponti when his own case came up.

Since the start of a $6 million movie depended on the release of its star from prison, all the details of Sophia's arrest had to be worked out in advance by the Ponti lawyers with the Italian authorities. On May 19, she would fly from Geneva to Rome, where detectives would arrest her at the airport and drive her to a women's prison in Caserta, nineteen miles northeast of Naples and her hometown of Pozzuoli.

The schedule was timed to give Sophia a final weekend with her children before she took off. Cipi, thirteen, and Edoardo, nine, were both taking First Communion at their Jesuit school. Though the boys knew nothing about Mama's forthcoming jail term, they must have suspected something was wrong from the number of paparazzi trying to get shots of her last moments as a free woman.

Sophia and her seventy-one-year-old husband looked an unlikely couple when they arrived at the chapel, she glamorously dressed and toting a flash camera, he in a boxy suit and loafers. The boys and their classmates wore white tunics. When they paraded down the aisle, Sophia started to cry. She reached out and patted Edoardo's head as he passed by.

After the service, the Pontis joined the other parents for pastries and hot chocolate, followed by picture-taking in the chapel courtyard. Sophia snapped two rolls of film before gathering up her brood and taking them home for a luncheon celebration.

Three days later, while waiting to board Alitalia flight 411 from Geneva to Rome, Sophia told a TV reporter, "I am going back to serve my sentence, even though it is unjust, because I want to see my mother, my sister, my country, and my friends."

Detectives were waiting for Sophia when she stepped off the plane at Leonardo da Vinci Airport. Her sister, Maria, was there for moral support. She handed Sophia a bouquet of flowers as they made their way to an area reserved for a press conference.

"I have not returned to make a film, but because I love Italy," Sophia told the mob of reporters and photographers. Their questions very quickly sank to the level of what books she planned to read in jail. "This is such a traumatic experience for me that I never thought about it. What do you recommend?" she replied.

Caserta had been the headquarters of all Allied Forces in the Mediterranean area during World War II. The three-story women's prison on via Ianucci was a converted convent and had nuns as well as state penal officers in charge. Sophia's cell on the second floor was actually a thirteen-foot-square room with private bath and color TV. There were only a dozen or so inmates, all doing time for nonviolent crimes like shoplifting or smuggling.

Never in memory had a movie superstar served time in jail. Sophia's life behind bars became a continuing soap opera in the news media. Crowds of her fans camped at the entrance to the prison, chanting Neapolitan songs and dancing the tarantella whenever they spotted her looking out the window of her cell.

Prison director Lilana de Cristofero announced that Sophia was being "treated like other prisoners. We don't believe in uniforms, so she's wearing her own clothes. She's free to walk on the grounds and use the reading room. It's as comfortable as a prison can be. The rooms are pleasant. The food is good. We pride ourselves on having all modern conveniences."

Inevitably, news reports of Sophia listening to music on a Sony Walkman and having an espresso machine in her room caused many Italians to complain that she was enjoying a holiday at taxpayers' expense. Within days, she was transferred to a real "cell" with two other women, where, as the newest arrival, she had to sleep at the top of a triple-decker bunk.

Sophia said later that she was placed under extra surveillance to make sure she didn't get special treatment. She had to take her daily shower with all the other prisoners, and could only have visitors or make phone calls with a guard present.

By week two, the prison director reported Sophia "going through a terrible time. I'm seriously concerned for her psychiatric condition." Prison doctor Rose Caduto told reporters, "We're talking about a bad depressive state that should not be underestimated. She suffers from insomnia and lack of appetite. Her morale is low. She is greatly agitated. I have prescribed tranquilizers to calm her down."

Although Sophia's mother and sister visited daily, she received the most comfort from the prison's elderly mother superior. "A saint! She made me eat, and little by little, she became a sort of a mother to me," Sophia recalled. "Alas, she was very sick, which I didn't find out until I was leaving and she told me, 'I don't feel very well, but I didn't want to worry you while you were here.' She died a few days later. It was as if she'd stayed alive for my liberation."

Sophia's incarceration turned out to be shorter than thirty days. According to Italian law, first offenders were eligible for parole after serving half their term. On June 3, 1982, the Caserta parole board approved her lawyers' request. She was released two days later, having spent seventeen nights as the government's guest.

"What a hell it was," she told reporters gathered outside the prison. "I rarely got any sleep because of the screaming of the other prisoners, some of them trying to slash their wrists."

Looking haggard and hiding behind self-designed Zyloware sunglasses, Sophia said, "It was the ugliest experience of my life. But if you must pay a price in order to see your family and country again, and to get a smile back on your face, than I'm glad I did it."

Asked if she intended writing a book about her ordeal, Sophia said, "Those memories belong only to me. In the beginning, I tried to pretend it was only a film I was making, but it is imbedded in my mind and body like a cancer. I'll never get over it."

An interview several years later seemed to confirm that. "Those days I spent in prison marked me for life," Sophia said. "The most terrible moments were in the night, when they locked you in your room, and you knew that someone else held the key and that you couldn't get out. It wasn't for several days that I truly realized I couldn't leave, couldn't see my children, that I was deprived of my freedom. It's something I would not repeat. I'd run away and go into hiding instead."

Upon her release, Sophia returned to Rome to prepare for *Tieta*, which would be shot at Cinecittà, with exteriors in Florence and the surrounding countryside. But on July 14 she was boarding a plane back to Geneva after the producers failed to deliver her first paycheck. They'd developed a "cash flow problem" over financing they were supposed to receive from Banco Ambrosiana. The bank had been shut down pending an investigation into the mysterious death in London of Roberto Calvi, its chief officer.

Sophia may have cursed herself for taking the job. She could have avoided a lot of anguish and public humiliation if she hadn't, but at least she'd paid her legal penalty and could now visit Italy whenever she wanted. After Sophia's exit, *Tieta* never did get made. Without her name for box-office collateral, the producers couldn't raise financing and finally gave up trying. The biggest loser was director Lina Wertmuller, who had spent more than a year preparing the project.

Before 1982 was over, Carlo Ponti's legal problems in Italy also came nearer to resolution. An appeals court in Rome cleared him of charges of fraud and illegal use of state subsidies, but the government immediately promised to take the case to a higher court.

Ponti was now free to visit Italy whenever he wanted. But to play safe until the outcome of the appeal, he would return only for brief business trips or to escort his wife to film galas or charity functions.

Meanwhile, the Pontis' property remained in government custody. Perhaps just to make Ponti squirm a bit more, two hundred paintings, drawings, and lithographs were "borrowed" from the art collection and "loaned" to various museums around Italy for public exhibition.

After recuperating from her double ordeal in Italy, Sophia took off for the United States for another round of pre-Christmas promotion for her Coty and

Zyloware tie-ins. Ponti and the children later joined her for the holidays at the family's new part-time home in Hidden Valley outside Los Angeles.

The makeover from "Westhaven" to "Rancho Ponti" took nearly two years and a reported $4 million to complete. Reflecting its location and its European owners, the estate blended Spanish-American, Beverly Hills, and Renaissance Italian styles. The cluster of green wooden buildings included a ranch-style main house and two guest cottages (each with its own swimming pool and tennis court). The two stables had been converted into apartments for staff, with two duplexes reserved for Cipi and Edoardo when they got a bit older.

But for the time being, the whole family was based in the main house. Repeating their usual arrangement, Sophia and Ponti had separate bedroom suites, at opposite ends of the building. The interior—a long series of rooms leading off from a huge central living area with two fireplaces—had as many skylights as windows.

Ponti started elaborate rose gardens on both sides of the house, with plans to grow every variety he could find locally or order from a catalog. Neighboring fields were planted with vegetables, herbs, berries, and fruit trees. "We intend to become self-sufficient," Sophia said at the time. "One day, everything on the table, except maybe the wine, will come from here."

After the Pontis took the boys back to school in Switzerland in January 1983, it was starting to look like the couple's movie days were over. Sophia had no offers coming in, while her husband, due to his advancing age and dubious reputation, seemed too much of a risk to get involved with.

Ponti had some ideas for projects with Sophia as star but couldn't find any takers. One was based on the life of Maria Callas, with Sophia's niece, Alessandra Mussolini, filling in for Sophia as the younger Callas and all the singing dubbed from the diva's recordings.

Ponti was also digging into Anna Magnani's repertoire to find a vehicle for Sophia. After being rebuffed by Tennessee Williams for a remake of *The Rose Tattoo,* he settled on *La lupa (The She Wolf),* a famous Sicilian play by Giovanni Virga that had been the basis for a flop Ponti–De Laurentiis film in 1953 with Kerima in the lead. The tragedy about an oversexed woman who torments her son-in-law until he murders her was Magnani's salvation in her last years. She first triumphed in it on the stage in Rome in 1965 with Franco Zeffirelli directing, and revived it several times before she died in 1973.

The death in late January 1983 of George Cukor at age eighty-three terminated another project that Ponti had been discussing with the director since his "comeback" with *Rich and Famous* in 1981. Cukor was the latest to express interest in the Pontis' long planned remake of Tolstoy's *Anna Karenina,* which had previously been a showcase for Greta Garbo (twice) and Vivien Leigh.

Meanwhile, Sophia had enough to keep her busy with her commercial tie-ins. She'd also started working on a new book for William Morrow entitled *Women & Beauty,* which promised to give her something else to promote and also to boost sales of perfume and eyeglasses.

Rumors were circulating that while Sophia was taking time off from movie-making, she had undergone some reconstruction at the nimble hands of Dr. Rodolphe Troques, a plastic surgeon in Paris. Dr. Troques allegedly did some nip-and-tuck on Sophia's matronly breastwork. Syndicated columnist Eugenia Shepherd reported that Dr. Troques was "one of the Pontis' intimate friends, besides being responsible for Sophia's lovely new teenage figure." An article in the German magazine *Weekend* said, "Since the surgical correction of her ample stratosphere, younger men once again cluster around the glamorous film star."

The summer of 1983 found the whole Ponti family back at their California ranch. Sophia had enrolled ten-year-old Edoardo in a special program for young people at the Lee Strasberg Theater Institute, now being run by close friend Anna Strasberg, who took over after her husband's death in 1982.

"Ever since he was a little baby, Edoardo has been making up crazy stories with puppets, saying he wants to be an actor," Sophia explained at the time. "I think that sending him to Anna will be a good experience for him, even if he doesn't continue with it. He doesn't know many American children, so I'm sure he'll make many new friends. He's very extroverted, which is a good quality if you want to be an actor."

Edoardo's older brother, Carlo, who at fourteen had outgrown the nickname of Cipi, aspired to the more serious side of show business. "He's a shy dreamer who plays the piano beautifully and wants to be a classical composer," Sophia said. At Rancho Ponti, Carlo had his own studio, with a baby grand piano and all the latest recording and playback equipment.

That summer, Sophia learned how much she meant to Italian-Americans when she was invited to be grand marshal of the annual Columbus Day Parade in New York City in October. She would be the first woman ever to lead the famous march up Fifth Avenue, which in past years had been marshaled by the likes of Frank Sinatra, Lee Iacocca, Tony Bennett, and Luciano Pavarotti.

The parade's sponsor, the Columbus Citizens Foundation, also voted Sophia its Award of Achievement in the Arts in recognition of her lifetime contribution to international cinema and for uplifting the image of the Italian-American. The award would be presented at a gala dinner at the Waldorf-Astoria Hotel the night before the parade.

Robert Cerasia, executive director of the Columbus Day festivities, flew to Los Angeles to discuss strategy with Sophia. When he told her the parade was likely to include as many as 400,000 marchers and attract 2 million spectators, she said, "I don't want to hear how big it is. What the world doesn't know about me is that I am very emotional. I may look calm and collected, but I'm afraid that I may cry all the way up Fifth Avenue when I see all those people waving and cheering."

Sophia hoped that the parade would be televised in Italy so that her mother could see it. "After all these years, Mammina still refuses to fly, so there's no way I can get her there," she said. "And my children must be back in school in Geneva by that time, but they would want to be there to march with me, oh, yes, especially Edoardo. He loves to sing and dance."

Sophia agreed to make a pre-parade round of press, radio, and TV interviews, which would also enable her to plug perfume and eyeglasses. The latter were a lot easier to hype because she wore them all the time and rarely agreed to be photographed without them. While she might have had a financial motive, the oversize specs also served a cosmetic purpose by making the wrinkles around her eyes less noticeable.

Unfortunately, Grand Marshal Sophia would have to wait a year to strut up Fifth Avenue. Though she did collect her award from the Columbus Citizens Foundation at the Waldorf-Astoria banquet, the parade itself was canceled due to the death of New York's Roman Catholic leader, Cardinal Cooke. She promised to return on October 12, 1984.

A month before her rescheduled appearance, Sophia would turn fifty. In the decade since her fortieth birthday, she'd made only one notable movie, *A Special Day,* and her reign as a cinema queen seemed over. Though she was well preserved for someone at the half-century mark in life, she would have to resign herself to the fact that star roles in a romantic vein were past her and that she'd have to settle for character types or supporting roles if she wanted to continue working as an actress. Judging from the experience of some of her contemporaries, those jobs were mainly in television in weekly series or in feature-length movie "specials."

A regular series was too demanding and also incompatible with Sophia's pitch work for Coty and Zyloware. She'd already nixed an offer to portray the wicked Alexis Carrington in *Dynasty*, a role that finally made a big star of Joan Collins after many years of trying. Then, in January 1984, Sophia was asked to join the cast of the coming fall season of *Falcon Crest* as Francesca Gioberti, half-sister of Angela Channing, the character played by Jane Wyman, star of the series.

Since it amounted to a guest appearance for five episodes only, Sophia figured that she could handle it. But when Ponti demanded $1 million as her fee, Lorimar Productions decided she wasn't worth $200,000 per show and looked elsewhere. Sophia's onetime bosom rival, Gina Lollobrigida, now pushing fifty-seven, took over at a reported $50,000 per show.

An alternative to waiting for offers to arrive is to package your own vehicles, which is exactly what the Pontis were doing at the same time. Ponti's son Alex and Roger Gimbel Productions, who were associated in the TV movie of Sophia's life story, made a similar deal with NBC for *Aurora,* to be shown on *Monday Night at the Movies* in the United States and as a theatrical release elsewhere.

Aurora had a touch of vanity about it. Her youngest son, eleven-year-old Edoardo, was cast in one of the leading roles. The script was specially written for them after Sophia saw how well he did in classes at the Lee Strasberg Institute. Edoardo had become so determined to be an actor that his parents decided to give him a chance to prove what he could do. "Who knows how it will turn out?" Sophia wondered at the time. "He seems to like it very much, and he is quite serious about what he does. Certainly, in terms of talent, he has it all."

Aurora is a taxi driver in Sorrento who, in her younger days, worked as a chambermaid in a hotel and had flings with some of the guests. One of them sired Aurora's son, who was blinded in an accident and needs an expensive operation that can probably restore his sight. To raise the money, she sets out to locate several of her ex-lovers to con each of them into believing he's the father so he'll pay some of the expenses.

With Maurizio Ponzi as director, the filming would mark Sophia's first work in Italy since her jail term and the aborted *Tieta* in 1982. Aurora and son's taxicab search takes them from Sorrento to Rome and finally to the slopes of Mont Blanc in France.

Because *Sophia: Her Own Story* had bombed in the audience ratings, NBC insisted on a top TV star in the cast of *Aurora*. Sophia readily agreed to their recommendation of Daniel J. Travanti, one of the leads of the hit series *Hill Street Blues*. For box-office insurance in the European theatrical release, the other male leads went to Philippe Noiret, long one of France's most revered actors, and Ricky Tognazzi, who was well on the way to matching the popularity of papa Ugo in Italy.

Sophia's close friend Anna Strasberg agreed to take a small role in *Aurora* as Noiret's wife, though her main contribution to the film would be as Edoardo Ponti's dramatic coach. He spent several weeks with Strasberg in Los Angeles before filming began. "I showed Edoardo how a blind person 'sees' with his other senses," she recalled. "One evening, when he was practicing in my home, Sophia slipped into the room. Without looking, he said, 'That's my mother. I can smell her perfume.' "

Carlo Jr. joined Sophia and Edoardo for the production trip to Italy, but Papa Ponti, who still had an arrest warrant hanging over his head, stayed away. Back in her homeland again, Sophia told a reporter that she had no desire to return to Italy to live. "My sons are children of the world," she said.

Though some of the locations took them to Sorrento, only thirty miles from Pozzuoli, Sophia decided not to take her sons on a tour of the places where she grew up. "Not even adults can understand how it was in a village where there was war and hunger," she said. "I don't want my children to see an image of my childhood that is vacant and sad."

Due to his multilingual upbringing, Edoardo spoke almost accentless English, which made him sound less Italian than his mother when they acted together. But apart from that, there were few problems in making a professional adjustment.

"I have to play a double role," Sophia said at the time. "I try to concentrate on my acting, but I can't help watching him like a mother. The first day, especially, there were mixed-up feelings for me. When I'm filming, I like to feel relaxed, not to feel emotions in conflict with the emotions I'm portraying on the screen, so it was difficult to have Edoardo there. He finally relaxed and so did I. Children are wonderful—such sincerity, such spontaneity. Edoardo is easy to work with—he doesn't ask silly questions."

Unhappily, the man partially responsible for Edoardo Ponti's existence, Dr. Hubert de Watteville, died just before filming started and would never see the new acting team in action. "I lost the greatest friend of my entire life," Sophia said. "Without him, I would have been a woman without children and surely, surely the saddest person in the entire world."

NBC scheduled the premiere telecast of *Aurora* for October 22, which would be a month after Sophia's fiftieth birthday. No official tie-in would be made, but her personal milestone would hardly be kept a secret from the world. She chose it as the publication date for her third book, *Women & Beauty*, which was directed at her peers and elders.

"You shouldn't drag yourself down because you turn fifty," Sophia said in an interview. "It doesn't worry me. Every season of life is nice. I think I fit exactly my age, and I don't think I would ever have a face-lift because you can be given a very young face, but they can't change your soul, they can't change your head as you get older. So there's a kind of conflict, isn't there?"

Besides, she said, "My children would not like for me to have a face-lift. They say, 'Oh, Mommy, don't change—you are so beautiful, and you will always be so beautiful. So, I feel very well in my skin."

When asked about her marriage, Sophia said, "Carlo and I have been together for thirty-four years. It's not something provisional anymore. It changes, for everyone changes. Maybe sometimes there are things more important than passion and love and this kind of thing. It grows, and you appreciate the qualities of the person you are with."

She added that "marriage is like a thread. It must go straight or it will ravel. And I think it is always the woman who must keep the thread straight, to save the marriage. That is because women are wise and care about their children. They have to make choices, and they choose for the family—even though sometimes they must sacrifice themselves."

Sophia may have been alluding to recent gossip in the European press about her husband's philandering, which seemed to give her grounds for divorcing him if she really wanted to. Ponti's longtime liaison with Dalila Di Lazzaro, which had gone on for almost ten years, reportedly ended unhappily—for Ponti, anyway—when the now twenty-nine-year-old blonde bombshell dumped her grandfatherly paramour for a muscular hunk eight years her own junior.

Weekend, a German weekly that had been relentlessly stalking both Ponti and Sophia for decades, ran a photograph of him out in public with Di Lazzaro's alleged replacement, twenty-five-year-old Antonella Murgia. The tall, well-stacked brunette, a candidate for stardom since making her movie debut in the Italian *Video Zero,* bore a striking resemblance to Sophia's long-ago rival, Silvana Mangano (by now divorced from Dino De Laurentiis and suffering from serious medical problems that would cause her death in 1989 at age fifty-nine).

The report in *Weekend* described Antonella Murgia as the seventy-three-year-old Ponti's "special cure" for the sexual weaknesses that come with old age.

Murgia was quoted as calling Ponti "tender, sensual, and very generous. . . . He spoils me." The story went on to claim that the lovers intended having a baby together, but an editorial aside raised serious doubt that they would succeed.

As usual, Sophia kept her feelings about the situation to herself. But in October, Ponti was conspicuously missing from her entourage when she flew to New York to make history as the first woman to lead the annual Columbus Day parade up Fifth Avenue.

Wearing a red suit designed by *paisano* Valentino, she set a sprightly pace for the many notables marching right behind her. That year, 1984, happened to be a presidential election year, so they included Vice-President George Bush, who was marching right behind her with wife Barbara, and Democratic presidential candidate Walter Mondale. Organized herds of Mondale supporters had turned out to boo Bush, but they cheered and applauded when they caught sight of Sophia. Officials of the Bush campaign later announced that Sophia's proximity to Bush in the line of march did not constitute a political endorsement. The parade took five hours and had nearly 500,000 participants. "I'm both exhilarated and exhausted," Sophia said at the end. "I've never seen such a big, big parade. The only thing we do like this in Italy is a procession for the saints—a sort of miniparade."

Sophia had returned to Geneva, where the boys were back in school, by the time *Aurora* hit American airwaves. Veteran radio-TV critic Kay Gardella wrote that

Sophia Loren could rise above anything, so it's not surprising that we can overlook the silly plot line and delight in the return of the Italian beauty to TV. . . . The stunning star's most overwhelming asset is her warmth. She's the genuine article, no doubt about it, and this quality illuminates the home screen as she costars with her eleven-year-old son. Understandably, Edoardo Ponti has much to learn about acting, but still he comes across as a likeable youngster with ingratiating qualities.

The trade paper Variety took a negative view:

Not even Sophia Loren's marvelous looks and the stunning Italian scenery can save this piece of self-indulging drivel. . . . The telepic becomes mired in Loren's determination to showcase her son. And that's too bad, because Ponti's performance is acceptable as a supporting character. But this production keeps coming back to the mom and son relationship, and that's just not enough to sustain interest for two hours.

Amusingly, Edoardo wasn't that interested in what the critics had to say about his work. Thoroughly Hollywoodized from living part time in California, he first wanted to know how well *Aurora* had scored in the Nielsen ratings. It did better than *Sophia: Her Own Story,* but got trounced in its time period by ABC's *Monday Night Football.*

Aurora put at least a temporary end to Edoardo's acting career. It brought no outside job offers, and even if it had, his parents were unlikely to accept them. They wanted Edoardo to at least get through secondary school before any further decisions were made about his life's work.

Meanwhile, the fifty-year-old star of the family had no film or TV commitments on deck, but promoting her perfume and eyeware lines was enough to keep her occupied until something came along. Sophia was still turning up in unlikely places like Allentown, Pennsylvania, and Cedar Rapids, Iowa, which once prompted a reporter to ask why she bothered. "You have to," she said. "It would be wrong to give my name to a product and then have nothing to do with it."

Both Sophia and her husband were involved with a new $1 billion resort known as the Williams Island Tennis and Racquet Club. Situated in the intra-coastal waterway between Miami and Fort Lauderdale, the eighty-acre complex was built by Trump Brothers (no relation to Donald) and the Mutual Benefit Life Insurance Company. Besides the expected sports and recreational facilities, it had condominium towers, two luxury hotels, and piers for those who preferred to live aboard their yachts.

The Pontis were listed as "creative consultants" and received the deed to a twenty-fifth-floor penthouse apartment in exchange for their services, which were partly advisory and partly to help to sell memberships.

"I like to do in life beautiful things that interest me," Sophia said at the time. "I hope to bring some of Italy to Florida and to combine it with American comfort." The Mediterranean-style resort was aimed at the increasing numbers of wealthy Europeans who were buying second homes in the area.

Not until 1986 did Sophia get back into acting. For the first time in years, it was in a non-Ponti project. The CBS television movie *Mother Courage,* which had its title shortened to *Courage* to avoid confusion with Bertolt Brecht's stage classic, was produced by Highgate Pictures and based on an acclaimed *New York* magazine article by Michael Daly.

The role of Marianna Miraldo, a Queens, New York, housewife who becomes an undercover agent for the Federal Drug Enforcement Administration, might have seemed specially created for Sophia but was based on a living person, Martha Torres. Her work helped break a $3.5 billion cocaine ring, the biggest arrest since the famous "French Connection" case.

The script by E. Jack Neuman told Marianna's story in a crisp, almost documentary style. Confronted with the hopeless addiction of her eldest son, who's gone from cocaine to mainlining heroin, Marianna is further shocked to discover that a family friend is also dealing in the cocaine trade. Deciding to act, she goes to the DEA, which is at first skeptical, wondering how much she wants for informing. But she convinces them that the only motive is to help her son and to save others from getting hooked. A detective is assigned to work with Marianna and shepherd her through the operation. Before long, she has infiltrated a cocaine ring and is delivering shipments between New York and Miami. Her husband, meanwhile, wants her to quit because of the danger, but she refuses until every member of the gang is caught.

Billy Dee Williams was signed to play Sophia's detective sidekick, with Hector Elizondo as her husband and Dan Hedaya as the drug kingpin. Sophia's two sons in the film, both older than her own children, were played by Michael Galardi and Corey Parker.

Director Jeremy Kagan shot the 150-minute telefilm on a tight thirty-day schedule. "It was nervous breakdown time, a very difficult and emotional role to play," Sophia said in an interview. "Fortunately, Jeremy Kagan works on the same level we do in Italy. He creates that unity needed between director and performer. He has a rare richness of human feeling."

When broadcast on September 24, 1986, *Courage* won Sophia some of her best reviews in years. John J. O'Connor of *The New York Times* wrote that

> Miss Loren can still command attention simply sitting still and letting the light play over those fabulous cheekbones. But after some 30 years as a star, she clearly wants to keep on expanding her employment opportunities. She does just that in *Courage,* with a performance that is beautifully restrained and yet fiercely passionate. . . . She takes an already absorbing story and gives it a distinctive style that is rare in television movies.

O'Connor also noted that "Billy Dee Williams, obviously elated by merely being in Miss Loren's immediate vicinity, gives the most effectively energetic performance he has mustered in years."

Variety, which had blasted Sophia's last two TV movies, raved this time: "Sophia Loren, svelte, more mature, loaded with awesome directness and poise, proves that the star system still works." *Daily News* critic Kay Gardella said, "I've decided to become a self-appointed committee of one to demand more Sophia Loren–starring vehicles on television. I think the actress, who turns in such a substantial job tonight in *Courage,* should head an anthology series where she plays a different part each week, something like Loretta Young once did."

The Pontis were spending more and more time at their ranch in Hidden Valley, California. Carlo Jr., about to turn eighteen in December, was in his last year at private school in Switzerland and hoped to attend college in the United States. Edoardo, four years younger, had similar plans.

Along with their mother, both had become pals with Michael Jackson. The twenty-eight-year-old pop superstar still lived with his family at their compound in Encino in the San Fernando Valley, about fifteen miles from the Ponti homestead.

"My boys called him up and introduced themselves. And we've been wonderful friends since," Sophia said at the time. "Michael's so sweet and nice. He's a wonderful boy. I really love him. His soul is beautiful," she continued. "Sometimes we all go to concerts. He has been to our place for dinner, and we've gone to his home. He's a wonderful human being."

In November 1986, a much older friend of Sophia's, Cary Grant, died suddenly of a stroke at age eighty-two. Just weeks before, she had had an unexpected call from him while she was on a business trip. "Cary phoned my press agent to ask where I was—to contact me. I was in New York and he called me there," she recalled. "He asked how I was, about the children—nothing personal, just always 'Are you happy?' We had a very nice conversation and then we said good-bye. A month later he died. He never called me like that. Sometimes he sent a message through mutual friends, but never a call to Sophia. I felt he wanted to say good-bye."

Sophia later told an interviewer that had she accepted Grant's proposal in 1957, the marriage would have lasted. "I know it," she said with authority. "I know how he felt."

In 1987, Sophia and Ponti would celebrate the thirtieth anniversary of the Mexican proxy wedding; Ponti would also turn seventy-seven that year. The marriage between the two had always seemed incongruous, but the twenty-four-year age difference, which had been manageable when both were younger, had become a serious problem.

Gossipmongers guessed that only their children and joint investments were keeping Sophia and Ponti together. "I wouldn't even call it a marriage of convenience anymore, but a tense, armed truce. They spend as little time together as possible," a family friend told *People* magazine.

But Sophia claimed that their time spent apart was for business reasons, not personal. Ponti refused to comment to the press. "I don't want to answer stupid questions," he said.

Their professional relationship still seemed on solid ground. With his son Alex handling most of the detail work, Ponti had made a deal with Warner Brothers for Sophia's first theatrical movie in eight years. *Saturday, Sunday and Monday* would be another teaming with Marcello Mastroianni in a work by Eduardo De Filippo, whose *Filumena marturano* was the basis for their biggest hit, *Marriage, Italian Style*.

First staged in Rome in 1959, *Saturday, Sunday and Monday* had enjoyed notable success all over the world, most recently in 1973 when Franco Zeffirelli directed it for the National Theatre Company at the Old Vic in London. The comedy depicted the ups and downs of a typical Neapolitan family over the course of a long weekend.

To lift the film out of the art house category, Warner Brothers wanted to make it in the English language and to Americanize it by changing the setting to an Italian immigrant stronghold like Philadelphia or Boston. Peter Bogdanovich was assigned to direct and to select the scriptwriter.

Ponti had also acquired the screen rights to Mario Puzo's novel *The Fortunate Pilgrim*, the story of a widowed Italian immigrant trying to raise five children during the turbulent period in U.S. history between the two World Wars. When Ponti couldn't find a movie studio willing to finance it, he made a coproduction deal for a two-part TV feature with NBC and one of the major Italian networks, Reteitalia.

The choice of Peter Bogdanovich to direct a project that was more suited to the late Vittorio De Sica quickly proved a mistake. Warner Brothers decided to drop *Saturday, Sunday and Monday* when its uniquely Neapolitan humor didn't stand up to Americanization. Ponti agreed and decided to shelve it until he could arrange to produce it properly under Italian auspices.

In the summer of 1987, Sophia started gearing up for *The Fortunate Pilgrim*, though she'd long dreamed of playing the title role. "Mama Lucia is a character that, when I first read Puzo's book fifteen years ago, was somebody I already knew," she said. "She's my grandmother. She's my mother. She's all the people that lived around me in my little hometown. She was not a foreigner to me. I knew every little secret that Puzo was talking about."

Sophia also discovered similarities to her own self: "The whole feeling of starting from nothing and coming to have a better life was very familiar. That kind of determination was within me . . . to try to achieve something and get out of anonymity."

Mario Puzo's first novel, *The Fortunate Pilgrim* was published in 1964, received wonderful reviews, but sold relatively few copies. Its commercial failure inspired the author to write a deliberate bestseller, and though it took him five years, he more than succeeded with *The Godfather*, which was later transformed into one of the highest-grossing movies of all time.

Why Hollywood didn't snap up *The Fortunate Pilgrim* in the wake of the success of *The Godfather* in 1972 is a mystery. It would have made an ideal vehicle for Sophia Loren then, more so than at her present age of nearly fifty-three, which would be a real test of her ability to pass for a considerably younger woman.

Lucia Angeluzzi is only in her twenties when her laborer-husband is killed in a factory explosion, ironically on the same day that she's sworn in as an American citizen. Left to raise three children in a tenement in New York's Hell's Kitchen, she lucks onto a second husband who gives her two more children before he turns out to be a raving lunatic and needs to be permanently institutionalized. Meanwhile, as the decades roll by, Mama Lucia has to cope with a son in the Mafia, another who seems to have inherited his father's madness, a third who goes off to fight in World War II, and a daughter with tuberculosis. Through all her travails, Mama dishes out wisdom with her pasta, keeps her chin up, and dreams of owning a house in the Long Island suburbs.

Edward James Olmos, the Lieutenant Castillo of the top-rated *Miami Vice* television series, got the costarring role of Lucia's loony second husband. A twenty-year-old newcomer named John Turturro played the mobster son. Hal Holbrook was cast as the mature Lucia's love interest. Sophia found a supporting role for her close friend Anna Strasberg, which also provided her with a companion for the nine weeks of filming.

Sophia's stepson, Alex Ponti, now thirty-five, took charge of the day-to-day production, which was more than his father felt able to handle at age seventy-seven. Bizarrely, though *The Fortunate Pilgrim* took place in New York City and environs, the whole movie was being shot in Yugoslavia to take advantage of lower production costs. Though it would be shown on television on two consecutive nights, its running time would be four hours *without* the commercials, which was longer than *Gone With the Wind*.

Director Stuart Cooper, best known for the miniseries *A.D.,* found sites in Belgrade and nearby Pachevco that could pass for Manhattan's pre–World War II tenement districts. Production designer Wolf Kroeger, who'd managed to transform bits of London into the New York of 1906 for *Ragtime,* had an easier task here because background detail tends to be lost on even the largest television screens.

A drawback to filming in Yugoslavia was that the large supporting cast had to be recruited from local actors, many of whom didn't speak English and later had to be dubbed. The looping would give the soundtrack an artificial ring, though at least on television the matching of dialogue to lip movements would be less distracting than on a big theater screen.

The Pontis wanted a stirring musical score comparable to that composed by the late Nino Rota for *The Godfather,* so two of his disciples, Lucio Dallo and Mauro Malvasi, got the job. Sophia's longtime fan Luciano Pavarotti, who once said that her *Aida* inspired him to become a singer, agreed to lend his throbbing voice to the soundtrack to give it a sense of grand opera.

In the last week of March 1988, Sophia and Carlo Ponti made a rare trip to New York together to promote the broadcast premiere of *The Fortunate Pilgrim.* NBC arranged a gala benefit screening of the movie at Lincoln Center to raise funds for the restoration of Ellis Island, the gateway for millions of European immigrants from 1892 to 1954. Prior to the event, Lee Iacocca, chairman of the project, took the Pontis on a guided tour of the island.

Reporters who hadn't seen the couple together in years were startled by their physical incongruity, which had become more pronounced due to Carlo Ponti's advancing age. He seemed to have shrunk by several inches, which made him look like a midget next to Sophia. Though he'd never been a handsome man, Ponti's face was somehow different, perhaps as the result of plastic surgery.

The disparity was reinforced by his wife, who turned up at a press conference dressed in a patent-leather miniskirt and red jacket. Kay Gardella, one of the reporters present, wrote that "Loren is one of the most charming and beautiful women in the world. Although in her fifties, she's still an absolute knockout, with her long, lovely legs extended in front of her, as she demurely responds to questions with her sharp wit and frequent smiles."

Sitting under a bright spotlight to make it easy for the TV cameramen, Sophia charmed the crowd by declaring, "When I saw the light, I said, 'My God, am I going to sit there, and why?' I feel like I'm being examined, like I'm going to have a graduation or something. An actress is very sensitive, so to sit with a light on your face, you feel guilty right away."

By the time of its two-night telecast on April 3 and 4, the movie had been officially retitled *Mario Puzo's The Fortunate Pilgrim* to make sure that everyone knew it was by the author of *The Godfather.* Coming after *Gore Vidal's Lincoln* and *Sidney Sheldon's Windmills of the Gods,* it inspired *New York Post* critic David Bianculli to snipe, "If the title is possessive, the show is repulsive."

Pans predominated, with wisecrackers tending to call it "an unfortunate production," but Sophia escaped relatively unscathed. "With Sophia Loren demonstrating what thesping and presence mean, *Mario Puzo's The Fortunate Pilgrim* is a florid soaper dominated by a world-class actress," said *Variety.* "Mama Lucia's in charge of the proceedings, and Loren's there to command the screen. Her Lucia's a dignified, loving woman whose eyes tell everything—Loren has considerable things to say."

John J. O'Connor of *The New York Times* said that "Miss Loren is terrific, maintaining an innate dignity even while screaming 'Mama Mia!' at regular intervals, and still beautiful, no matter how haggard and worn out she tries to look."

"Sophia Loren stoically endures so many hardships during these five dreary hours that she makes Job look like a Lotto winner. She has worse luck with men than Lana Turner," said Daniel Ruth of the *Chicago Sun-Times.* "Within the limitations of the script, she delivers a solid, albeit dreary, performance. . . . Sitting through the interminable miniseries is far from a pilgrimage. It is a forced march."

What next for Sophia Loren? "I don't have to prove anything any more to anyone. I have to prove always something to myself from now on," she said in an interview. "I've done so many things, and I love so much my profession, but I don't think you can say, 'I've reached everything I wanted to do.' I think you have to always look forward to new goals, new achievements. Sometimes you don't know what they are. But there is a pleasure derived from the drive within you that makes you go forward."

SEXPOT TURNS SIXTY

T H E Fortunate Pilgrim turned out to be the American public's last op-portunity for years to see Sophia Loren in a new work (presumably, they could see her in oldies on TV). The few films that she made afterwards never received theatrical distribution in the United States or, for that matter, in much of the world.

The year 1988 also marked the beginning of the end to "Sophia" the perfume, which had declined sharply in sales since the introduction in 1987 of "Elizabeth Taylor's Passion" by the Parfums International division of Chesebrough-Pond's. Though Taylor's fragrance was a luxury item priced at $200 an ounce, more than twice the $90 per ounce of "Sophia," the marketplace didn't seem to have room for more than one screen goddess at a time. "Sophia" couldn't compete with Taylor's legendary reputation as a mankiller *or* the $10 million promotional campaign that launched "Passion."

Sophia and Coty never disclosed how much she had earned from the tie-in, but industry insiders guessed a minimum of $25 million since the perfume's in-troduction in 1980. Meanwhile, Sophia was still designing frames for Zyloware and endorsing the purchase of condos at Williams Island in Florida.

After Warner Brothers dropped *Saturday, Sunday and Monday,* Carlo Ponti and son Alex made a deal with Reteitalia and Silvio Berlusconi Communications for a telemovie that would be released theatrically outside Italy. Dino Risi, who'd directed Sophia and Marcello Mastroianni before but not as a team, took on the assignment. But problems developed with the script and the project was again postponed.

To fill the gap, Berlusconi, a media magnate who practically ruled Italian showbiz, suggested that Sophia do a remake of her most famous film, *La Ciociara*. Why is anybody's guess, but it would certainly cause millions of curious TV viewers to tune to Berlusconi's Canale 5 to see how Sophia could top her 1961 Oscar-winning performance.

Dino Risi, an admirer if not an imitator of Vittorio De Sica, accepted the directorial assignment in place of *Saturday, Sunday and Monday*. Ironically, Risi had the same problem as De Sica in tailoring *La Ciociara* to fit Sophia, but in reverse due to the passage of nearly thirty years. At fifty-four, Sophia was now even older than Anna Magnani had been when the project was originally conceived for them to portray mother and daughter.

The remake of *La Ciociara* gave Sophia a chance to demonstrate what Magnani might have done with the part. The role of the daughter, also a little older than the adolescent in the earlier version, went to Sydney Penny.

No actor (male or female) in movie history had ever attempted to remake a vehicle that had won them an Oscar, which may explain why the new *La Ciociara* was produced with minimal hoopla. In case it turned out badly, few outside Italy would know it even existed and Sophia would be spared embarrassment, which is what happened. After the telemovie bombed on Canale 5, its chances of being shown elsewhere were slight. It eventually surfaced in the United States as a video cassette in a dubbed English version entitled *Running Away*, which escaped the notice of critics and 99.9 percent of the public as well.

The Pontis were now spending several months a year at their ranch in Hidden Valley, California, except for Carlo Jr., who was living there full time while attending Seaver College, the liberal arts school of Pepperdine University. Determined to become an orchestra conductor, Carlo was majoring in music. He commuted daily to the Pepperdine campus in the Santa Monica Mountains overlooking Malibu and the Pacific Ocean. His onetime nanny, Ruth Bapst, now converted to housekeeper, looked after him when the rest of the family was in Geneva, where Edoardo was in his last year of private school.

"Our life is completely oriented to the children," Sophia said. "We live for them. What makes me happy is when everything goes smoothly for my children and I'm with a man I particularly adore. Then I feel like a teenager. I laugh. I have the sparkle in my eye of fifteen."

In January 1990, Sophia made a surprise appearance at the annual American Cinema Awards ceremony at the Beverly Hilton Hotel in Los Angeles to present the Entertainer of the Year trophy to her friend Michael Jackson. Wearing black military garb, Jackson marched to the podium flanked by six bodyguards.

Sophia had become something of a Jackson groupie. During his last European tour, she attended the concerts in Paris, Geneva, and Rome. While Jackson was in Switzerland, Sophia arranged for him to meet Oona Chaplin, widow of his beloved idol.

Following Jackson's concert in Rome, director Franco Zeffirelli threw a huge celebrity-studded party at which Sophia appeared on a guest list with Gina Lollobrigida. Though the longtime bosom rivals hadn't spoken to each other in years, Michael Jackson persuaded them to pose for a photograph together, with himself, of course, in the middle.

Seven years older than Sophia, La Lollo played occasional character parts in Italian telemovies, but had all but given up acting in favor of a second career as a much-lauded photographer. She'd published several pictorial books and also contributed regularly to leading magazines throughout the world.

Sophia, however, showed no signs of abdicating as a film diva or accepting anything less than star parts. Her commercial tie-ins kept her busy and in public view until the next movie came along, although the gaps between them were likely to lengthen as she got older.

By the time she finally started the much-delayed *Saturday, Sunday and Monday* in 1990, Sophia had been a world star through four decades. It seemed appropriate that she should begin the decade in her most matronly role yet as Rosa Priore, the matriarch of a large Neapolitan family.

Actor-playwright Eduardo De Filippo, who died in 1984 at age eighty-four, had wanted to film *Sabato, Domenica e Lunedi* with Sophia ever since she triumphed in his *Filumena marturano* (*Marriage, Italian Style*), but the Pontis' legal problems in Italy had prevented it. De Filippo had also intended to act in the movie in the showy supporting role of the grandfather, which was performed by Laurence Olivier in England's National Theatre production in 1973.

The title of the play conveys the belief that for ordinary working people, life is really lived in the period from when they start their weekend break until they return to their jobs on Monday morning. Rosa and her husband, Peppino, are going through a fairly common middle-aged marital crisis. Each suspects, wrongly as it turns out, that the other no longer loves him or her, and is having an affair.

Lina Wertmuller, who'd been having a difficult time finding work since the cancellation of Sophia's *Tieta* in 1982, pleaded for the director's assignment and got it. Wertmuller's husband, painter Enrico Job, landed his usual spot as the film's set designer.

By now, Marcello Mastroianni had tired of the production postponements and signed up for other things. Wertmuller wanted to hire her longtime associate, Giancarlo Giannini, but the costarring role of Don Peppino stayed within the author's family through the casting of his actor-son, Luca De Filippo. Luca was fourteen years younger than Sophia, but he passed reasonably well for her husband.

Sophia engaged in some nepotism herself by selecting her niece, Alessandra Mussolini, to play her daughter. Now twenty-six, the plumpish blonde, who acted regularly in TV soap operas, strongly resembled her aunt, with the prominent Scicolone nose and full lips. She'd become one of Italy's top celebrities as a pop singer. The granddaughter of Il Duce was also involved in neofascist politics.

The Pontis and Silvio Berlusconi intended a theatrical release for *Saturday, Sunday and Monday* outside Italy. In the United States at least, they would have a hard time finding a distributor due to the sharp decline in the number of theaters showing subtitled "foreign" films. Dubbing the movie into English made no sense because it would alienate the critics; without favorable reviews, box-office success seemed dim.

By pulling a few strings, Berlusconi's American bureau, RTI-USA, arranged for *Saturday, Sunday and Monday* to have its world premiere showing at the annual Chicago International Film Festival in October, a month before the Italian telecast. The board of governors voted Sophia a Lifetime Achievement Award, which gave her a good reason for coming to Chicago to accept it and would earn much-needed publicity for the festival at the same time.

The entire Ponti family joined Sophia in Chicago for the premiere of *Saturday, Sunday and Monday*. Gene Siskel, the slimmer half of a team of film critics with a syndicated TV show, tried to get Sophia to demonstrate how, during her career, she "handled fame with humor." Hinting at a much-quoted statement she had made years ago, he urged her to repeat it once again for his program's viewers.

"I'm too old," Sophia demurred sweetly. Siskel persisted, pleading even harder. Sophia seemed embarrassed by the unexpected challenge, but held her ground. "No, I'm too old," she repeated. "You say it."

"Everything I have," Siskel ventured, "I owe to spaghetti." Sophia nodded. When an onlooker sitting with Carlo Ponti at the back of the room marveled at Sophia's complaisance, her husband smiled and shrugged: "It's business."

Incredibly, eleven years had passed since the last U.S. theatrical release of one of Sophia's movies (*Firepower*). *Saturday, Sunday and Monday* didn't change her luck. After lackluster reviews at the noncompetitive Chicago Festival, it failed to attract an American distributor and never surfaced again.

Even in its home country, *Sabato, Domenica e Lunedì* failed to stir up much excitement. Telecast on Italy's Canale 5 over two nights in a somewhat longer version than the two-hour theatrical feature, it received a mediocre audience share rating of 18.88 percent.

That disappointment was more than offset by Carlo Ponti's final victory in his long-drawn-out legal problems in Italy. An appeals court ruled in his favor and ordered that all properties seized by the government in 1978, including his villa and art collection, be returned to him. Rumor had it that Ponti's lawyers made a deal with the government in which the villa and its grounds, both of historical significance, would become the property of the state after his death.

The press had a field day guessing how much the Pontis were worth now that their fabulous art collection had been retrieved. If *Paris Match* was correct in evaluating it at $3 billion, Sophia Loren and Carlo Ponti had to be one of the richest couples on the planet. Columnist Liz Smith was more skeptical and dropped a zero off in her appraisal of the 250 paintings, claiming they had a market value of $300 million.

Not surprisingly, the Pontis weren't releasing any exact figures, but Sophia tended to deflate the reports. "Billions, I tell you, it's not true. Absolutely not. I wish it were true," she said in an interview at the time.

Ponti only added to the mystery when he told a reporter, "I have the biggest private collection of Francis Bacon in the world. I don't know exactly how much it's worth—I never made a calculation, because I'm not interested in selling."

Ponti would have plenty of time to get reacquainted with his treasures, since the disappointing *Saturday, Sunday and Monday* seemed to mark the end of his production career. In December 1990 he would turn eighty, an age that was about three times the average of the current power structure in the movie and TV industries. Whatever he did in future would be fronted by his son Alex, who at thirty-nine could still be considered a "player," though he had no major successes to his credit.

In February 1991, Sophia was voted an honorary Oscar for being "one of the genuine treasures of world cinema who, in a career rich with memorable performances, has added permanent luster to our art form."

Given the large number of major stars, directors, producers, and so forth who'd never received Oscars, the announcement of an honorary one to a previous winner seemed unfair and immediately raised protests. The next day, the Board of Governors announced that Myrna Loy, who'd never even been nominated for an Oscar throughout the 125 movies of her fifty-four-year career, would also be presented with an honorary statuette during the annual telecast in March.

Sophia, staying at Williams Island, Florida, at the time, agreed to an interview for the *Entertainment Tonight* TV show, which also provided her with an opportunity to hype resort condos. While taking the camera crew for a cruise on a ninety-foot yacht, she answered a question about the honorary Oscar with "I don't even know if I deserve it."

At the Oscars, Sophia looked as though she'd discovered the Fountain of Youth during her time in Florida. Wearing a gown by Valentino, she received the evening's only standing ovation as she stepped on stage, not much changed from preceding film clips that dated as far back as the 1950s. One of Sophia's costars, Gregory Peck, who'd received his Best Actor award from her during the ceremonies held in 1963, handed over the honorary Oscar.

Trying to hold back tears after the lengthy applause, Sophia reminded the audience of her nomination for *Two Women* back in 1962: "It was so overwhelming for me that the terror of having to face you all made me find so many excuses not to be with you thirty years ago. Tonight, I'm still scared but I'm not alone and I will share this eventful evening with the three men in my life: my husband Carlo Ponti, without whom I wouldn't be the person I am today, and my two sons, Carlo Jr. and Edoardo, who taught me to conjugate the verb 'to love.'

"Words are very difficult to find for me to express it all in this wonderful moment in my life, so I will try to revert to my native language and say simply, '*Grazie, America.*' "

Two months later, Sophia was in Switzerland and decided to fly over to Rome to surprise Romilda. "Two days afterward, my mother died," she recalled. "I was with her. She died in fifteen minutes. She just dropped onto the bed and I could see something was wrong, so I started calling out. 'Come, come!' was all I could say. She had not been ill, but when the concierge came in he told me she was dead. If I hadn't had that sudden impulse to visit her, she would have died all by herself. Incredible. I am so happy I was there."

Sophia had supported her mother in the most lavish style for decades, but there were times when Romilda proved a trial. Not long after Riccardo

Scicolone's death in 1976 and perhaps as a reaction to it, Romilda seemed to go a bit gaga and started frequenting the Rome discotheques, always dressed in the trendiest gear and escorted by men half her age. After a series of embarrassing photo stories in the newspapers, Sophia finally put a stop to it by threatening to cut off Romilda's allowance.

"When Mammina wears skintight jeans, low-cut tops, and boots, she makes not just herself, but the whole family, ridiculous," Sophia was quoted at the time.

Death came to Romilda at age eighty-two. "From the time I started to become a success in movies, she was satisfied enough to live her life through me. She *was* Sophia Loren, my mother. When she died, a great part of me died with her, because she made me feel strong," Sophia remembered.

Only weeks after Romilda's death, Carlo Jr. graduated from Pepperdine's Seaver College. An accomplished pianist like his grandmother, but determined to become an orchestra leader rather than a soloist, he had decided to go for a master's degree in music at the University of California, Los Angeles (UCLA). Younger brother Edoardo, meanwhile, was a freshman cinema major at the University of Southern California (USC).

The family was becoming thoroughly Americanized, though Sophia still refused to wear jeans, or at least to be photographed in them. "At the ranch, it's so nice to wake up in the morning and know that everybody's there," she said in an interview. "After breakfast, Carlo and I do the garden together—maybe that's why my nails are so bad. I concentrate on the trees; we have a lot of bamboo, and I like to cut. Once I start, I am like Attila the Hun."

Whatever marital disharmony existed now seemed to be under control. When asked why the marriage had lasted, Carlo Ponti told a reporter, "Because, in a certain sense, we are two puritans. Real love is something puritan; it is not about money, it is not about sex."

Apparently, the advancing ages of both husband and wife was a contributing factor. "I don't like a man who is all over you all the time," Sophia said. "Emotions are there, you can feel them, it's not important to talk about them all the time."

Sophia hedged on a suggestion that the thirty-four-year relationship had become platonic. "Platonic means to dream, to have another idea, to live in a world of ideas, which is wonderful, too," she said. "It depends on whether you need passion or not. You make choices in life. I'm very passionate with Carlo, in a way. I don't think I could live without Carlo. I need him. I don't need anybody else."

With both children now in college and no longer requiring her everyday attention, Sophia was raring to make more movies, though the demand for fifty-six-year-old leading ladies, which had never been great even in the best of times, was slight. But contemporaries like Sean Connery, Clint Eastwood, and Burt Reynolds fitted easily into the male-oriented action and adventure fare that dominated the studio output of Hollywood and elsewhere.

Despite the handwriting on the wall, she was still depending on her producer-husband to find vehicles for her. "I have to do things with a market in Italy as well as America," she said in 1991. "The only one who really knows both markets is Carlo because he's been working in both for such a long time. He always knew exactly what my character should be in films, what I am really strong in. The pictures where I've been most successful are where I was not a sex bomb, but where I play a really honest and wonderful mother or sister or wife."

In 1992, Sophia found herself receiving more publicity than she desired as the aunt of Alessandra Mussolini, who won a seat in the Italian parliament as a member of the far-right National Alliance, a party closely linked to the neofascist movement. Sophia adored her niece, but she didn't share her political beliefs and tried to distance herself from them to protect her image. Sophia didn't want her name connected with that of Benito Mussolini, for all the obvious professional and personal reasons.

Though she refused to get involved in Italian politics, in the summer of 1992 Sophia became an advocate and fundraiser for a preservation group named after classical historian Theodor Mommsen, which was trying to protect the ancient ruins in the zone around her hometown of Pozzuoli known as the Burning Fields (Campi Flegrei). Rich in Greco-Roman artifacts, the huge area had become a symbol of the devastating effects of neglect and real estate speculation.

In Pozzuoli, the ruins of Anfiteatro Flavio, where Sophia once played as a child and which are only slightly smaller than those of the Rome Colosseum, sat totally abandoned. The grounds of another amphitheater at Cuma housed a lemon grove and a small farm with chicken coops and a pigpen. The ancient sanctuary at Montrusciello had disappeared beneath apartment buildings that were erected without permits. The tomb of Virgil at Fuori Grotta was being used as a public lavatory.

Sophia flew to Naples for a survey tour designed to attract public support and to raise financing. "I will try every method possible to make the Italian authorities take an interest in the problem. And in case that does not happen, I will seek sympathetic assistance from abroad," she told reporters.

Though Sophia rarely visited Pozzuoli these days, she said she returned frequently in her memory: "Since my mother died, my mind has wandered through the early years, just to be able to keep the thought of her alive: what she did for me during the war, and the house we stayed in and which my aunt still lives in. I think of the amphitheater, the Roman monuments around our home. This is your own world. You never give it away. It's a treasure that you carry with you all your life, and if you don't, maybe you are in trouble."

Several months later, in November, Sophia started doing missionary work for the United Nations and flew to Kenya to dramatize the plight of refugees from famine-stricken Somalia and the need for world assistance. Audrey Hepburn had made a similar "goodwill" trip to Somalia for UNICEF during the summer, her last before she died from cancer the following winter. Sophia continued to serve the UN whenever feasible.

In 1993, Sophia received her first good offer for a major theatrical movie in a decade and decided to accept without first reading the script. In this case, it hadn't been written yet, but she admired director Robert Altman so much that she thought his idea for a farcical portrait of the fashion industry could be as successful as his skewering of the movie business in *The Player*. The clincher was Altman's proposal to rematch her with Marcello Mastroianni, which, for one reason or another, hadn't happened since they'd made *Blood Feud* together in 1978.

In typical Altman style, the new movie would flit back and forth between a score of major characters, so Sophia and Mastroianni would join an ensemble of star actors rather than carry the whole show as in the past. It would also mark the first time since the collaboration began in Italy in 1954 that Sophia and Mastroianni acted together in English instead of their native language.

In October 1993, Robert Altman attended all the semiannual *pret-à-porter* (ready-to-wear) shows in Paris to get story ideas and to devise a plan for shooting the whole movie during the next assembly in the spring of 1994. By that time, he'd put together a huge international cast that also included Julia Roberts, Tim Robbins, Lauren Bacall, Kim Basinger, Anouk Aimée, Tracey Ullman, Danny Aiello, Stephen Rea, Forrest Whitaker, Rossy de Palma, Rupert Everett, Sally Kellerman, and Ute Lemper. Such famous designers as Christian Lacroix, Issey Miyake, Gianfranco Ferre, Jean-Paul Gaultier and Sonia Rykiel agreed to appear as themselves.

Since Altman favored improvisation and encouraged his actors to make up their own dialogue and to shape their characters as the filming progressed, the plot was wispy at best but made Sophia the focal point in a police investigation into the sudden death of her husband, the head of the French Fashion Council (played by Jean-Pierre Cassel). The tragedy takes place just as a disparate collection of designers, models, buyers, and newsmongers is converging on Paris for the unveilings of the fall-winter collections.

As the always elegantly turned out Isabella de la Fontaine, Sophia had her most glamorous wardrobe in decades, with all the clothes designed by her friend Gianfranco Ferre, an Italian currently in charge of Christian Dior. Another close friend, the Frenchman Jean Barthet, designed the matching hats, including an astonishing red one with a huge heart-shaped brim that framed Sophia's face to perfection.

Titled *Ready to Wear* for the English-speaking markets and *Pret-à-porter* elsewhere, the $20 million Miramax-backed production took eleven weeks to film, including the fortnight of the actual Paris showings in April. Altman shot everything on location in airports, hotels, museums, restaurants, boutiques, metro stations, on the streets and, of course, at the fashion shows themselves, though some had to be faked when certain designers and influentials decided not to cooperate.

A group including Karl Lagerfeld and Valentino, spurred on by Anna Wintour of *Vogue* and John Fairchild of *Women's Wear Daily,* suspected a hatchet job on the industry. "These people are just paranoid," Altman said at the time. "They don't have any idea what the film is about and would never listen. They're all stupid, self-important people, basically. And they're guilty. Any time anybody says, 'I don't want you talking about me,' that means they've got something to hide. Basically we don't care about them."

Altman's directorial technique included multiple cameras operating at the same time from different perspectives and the "wiring" of the actors with microphones, which meant they were constantly "on" even when he stopped the scene. Often what they said and did *after* he called "cut" ended up in the movie.

Sophia found it a strange but liberating experience. "The film was really like being part of a chorus—many, many people on the set—and everyone had a microphone," she said later. "You were never aware where the camera was—you were, but there were many other cameras that you were not aware of. You really felt free to be able to do what you wanted to do. In the beginning it was a little scary for me because I was accustomed to working to one camera and delivering my lines. Then I got comfortable and thought that every film should be done this way, because the actor is not frozen by the cold eye of the camera because you are not aware of it. It was beautiful! Even as an actress who has been in this business for such a long time, the camera always freezes me because I am aware of it. I thought this way of shooting was absolutely wonderful."

Mastroianni portrayed an ex-husband of Sophia's who suddenly turns up after her current one's death and may have been involved with it. By this time, the two stars had known each other so long that Chiara Mastroianni, his daughter by Catherine Deneuve, was now a grown-up twenty-two and acting a role in the movie.

As part of their screen reunion, Altman wanted Sophia and Mastroianni to recreate a highlight from one of their previous films. "He told us it had to be something that *everyone* in the audience will remember, otherwise it wouldn't mean anything," she said. "So Marcello and I talked and decided the only thing we could do would be the striptease in *Yesterday, Today and Tomorrow,* if I could find the record with the music, which I knew I had at home somewhere."

It turned out to be the same scene, with the same music and the same feeling, but with the passage of thirty years, not the same bodies. Though the eldest of the two at nearly seventy-one, Mastroianni had the easier time of it since he didn't have to remove his clothes. While still physically awesome at almost sixty, Sophia required very subdued lighting, plus a flesh-colored bodystocking.

By the time that her sixtieth birthday rolled around on September 20, 1994, Sophia had finished her role in *Ready to Wear* and seemed on the verge of a "comeback" as she entered her seventh decade of life. "The other night I dreamt it was my hundredth birthday—the celebrations were fantastic, full of friends, flowers, and affection," she said in an interview. "Then there was just my reflection in the mirror, as if I had just had a miraculous face-lift. My two sons, in their fifties, but still with the faces of twenty-year-olds, were watching me with kindness and admiration. These indescribable moments of happiness suddenly vanished and I found myself twisting and turning between the sheets, frightened and gasping for breath. A hundred years, I've made it to a century . . . I started to shout, and at that point I woke up. I tell you, waking up and finding yourself to be forty years younger is a breathtaking experience."

At fifty, she'd published a book on how to stay beautiful. Now she was giving advice on how to keep vital. "My doctor told me, when you get older, don't linger as you get out of a chair, or when you get up out of bed in the morning," she said. "Don't get into the habit of struggling up, one joint after the other. Spring up, even if it hurts a little. Because if you are not careful, you start walking differently, moving differently. Then you start making strange noises—without your even noticing. I know, because my mother used to do it."

In a sixtieth-birthday cover story for *Good Housekeeping* magazine, writer Heather Kirby described Sophia as "143 pounds of female perfection. Her neck is not wrinkled; she has not had plastic surgery. Her nose, described as 'too big' when she first launched herself on a career as a film actress, is neat; her arms are slender and lightly tanned, her legs elegant, and her ankles to kill for. When she walks, she moves like a thoroughbred, hips swaying with a subtly seductive rhythm."

Sophia credited her good looks to heredity. "I am lucky. I had a very beautiful mother," she said. "She had a solid bone structure, which is very important for a face. It is like when you build a house, you have to have a good foundation. Now I see my mother more and more when I look into the mirror. The older you get, the more you begin to look like your own parents."

A week after Sophia's birthday, another cinema goddess, Brigitte Bardot, also turned sixty. Though the coincidence might have been an occasion for an exchange of flowers or champagne, it marked the beginning of a bitter battle over Sophia's latest commercial endorsement—a $1 million deal with Annabella, the famous Italian furrier based in Pavia, near Milan.

Provocative ads featuring an apparently braless Sophia in a mink creation with a plunging neckline had started appearing in top fashion magazines throughout Europe. Bardot, who'd become a crusader for animal rights since retiring from acting twenty-one years earlier, was outraged and sent an open letter of protest to the press that was picked up worldwide.

Bardot branded Sophia "a killer of little animals." Sophia did not respond, but Ponti faxed a comment to his hometown newspaper, *La Stampa:* "It seems to me that Brigitte Bardot has a greater need for money than my wife. Her decision to come out was for publicity. It would have been better for her to keep quiet."

Things went from bad to worse for Sophia as Bardot's supporters joined in. Sophia received so many death threats that the Pontis had to increase security at their various residences in Geneva, Paris, California, and Florida.

Although Sophia was hardly the only major star in the cast of *Ready to Wear,* the fact that it was her first theatrical movie in a dozen years earned her top place in the marketing campaign. As Joe Levine had done over thirty years before with *Two Women*, Miramax decided to push her performance for all the annual awards, though this time it had to be in the supporting actress category because of the size of the role.

Prior to spending the Christmas holidays with her family in Switzerland, Sophia made a trip to New York to do publicity and interviews. Miramax provided her with a suite in the sumptuous Waldorf Towers, where she held court with reporters and photographers while garbed in outfits designed by two of her closest friends, Giorgio Armani and Gianfranco Ferre.

Press accustomed to the casual, unkempt look of younger stars like Julia Roberts and Demi Moore were startled by Sophia's fastidiousness. "Her makeup, hair and cleavage seemed polished to glorious perfection. Though it was only eleven in the morning, she was dressed in a plunging, fire-engine-red suit flashing with rhinestone buttons. Jewels glittered at her throat and wrists," said Mary Talbot of the *Daily News*.

But Sophia claimed to be a woman of simple, routine pleasures. "I like to renew my life every day and have new achievements, but I'm not a workaholic," she told Talbot. "I wake up early, exercise, make phone calls, see friends, maybe go shopping or to a movie. My favorite thing is to curl up in front of the fireplace with a book."

Unfortunately, the majority of reviewers blasted *Ready to Wear* as one of Robert Altman's worst films. Leonard Maltin of TV's *Entertainment Tonight* called the movie "Mind-numbingly awful . . . No plot, no momentum, no point to any of it; a particularly egregious waste of Loren and Mastroianni."

John Fairchild, editor-publisher of *Women's Wear Daily*, was outraged by the movie and started a full-scale war against it, suggesting it should be retitled *Quelle bombe!* Karl Lagerfeld threatened to get an injunction to stop the movie's release. The head designer for Chanel claimed libel over some dialogue that described him as a plagiarist.

Thanks to all its advance publicity and notoriety, *Ready to Wear* opened to big business, but box-office takings plummeted as soon as the bad reviews and word of mouth got around. Still, Miramax had a $20 million investment to protect, so it became more determined to get some award recognition that might help to boost attendance. The New York–based National Board of Review, which had always been kind to Robert Altman's work over the years, voted *Ready to Wear* a previously unheard-of Acting Ensemble Award that honored the entire cast.

Miramax decided to put all its guns behind Sophia for the Oscars and the

Golden Globes. It spent a bundle on full-page "for your consideration" ads in the two daily Hollywood trade papers. Coupled with glamorous shots of Sophia from the film were quotes from whatever favorable reviews could be found, which took some reaching. "Sophia Loren is scintillating. Her mere visual presence in *Ready to Wear* is larger than life," said one from the *Dallas Morning News*. "Witty and outrageous. Sophia Loren, as a *grande dame* of the fashion world, is a highlight in *Ready to Wear*," said another from the *Arizona Republic*.

The Golden Globes, which have long been presented in advance of the Oscars and often influence the choice of nominees for the latter, seemed a shoo-in for an international superstar like Sophia Loren, since the sponsoring organization is the Hollywood Foreign Press Association. She not only got nominated for best supporting actress in a theatrical film (separate Golden Globes are given for television), but also was selected for the honorary Cecil B. DeMille Award for "outstanding contribution to the entertainment field." Cynics said that the second was to make sure that Sophia turned up for the presentation ceremonies, which were being telecast on TBS cable as another of owner Ted Turner's attempts to steal audiences away from the major over-the-air networks.

That night of January 21, 1995, Sophia arrived at the Beverly Hilton banquet for the Golden Globes with two young and handsome escorts, twenty-six-year-old Carlo Ponti Jr. and his twenty-two-year-old brother, Edoardo. Mamma's boys now had ladies of their own, who were also part of the group: Carlo's fiancée, Odile Rodriguez de la Fuentes, and Elizabeth Guber, daughter of producer Peter Guber. Sophia's husband, now a frail eighty-four, stayed home to watch the festivities on television.

The Golden Globe for best supporting actress went to Dianne Wiest for *Bullets Over Broadway*. But Sophia won a standing ovation and fourteen minutes and thirty-six seconds of glorification in the segment devoted to her Cecil B. DeMille Award for her contribution to the entertainment field. Charlton Heston, a onetime DeMille protégé as well as Sophia's costar in *El Cid* over thirty years before, introduced a long array of film clips that had her in tears as she watched them from the audience.

"You get very emotional, you get a little melancholic . . . and then proud of what you've achieved," she said later.

Dressed in a slinky low-cut black gown with a net bodice and sleeves, Sophia accepted the trophy from Heston and her latest director, Robert Altman. In a speech, she called DeMille "a shining star in my universe when I was a child going to the movies in Italy. It's an honor to be associated with this prestigious name."

A month later, despite stepped-up trade paper advertising by Miramax, Sophia failed to get nominated for the Best Supporting Actress Oscar. The eventual winner again turned out to be Dianne Wiest for *Bullets Over Broadway.*

While Sophia didn't win any awards for her performance in *Ready to Wear,* all the hoopla and controversy about the movie put her back in the limelight at sixty plus and set the phones to ringing again with job offers. The most potentially lucrative was for an NBC television series entitled *Daughters of Eve.* Sophia's fee would be $100,000 per episode, or $1.3 million for the initial thirteen-episode season. NBC and the other networks would ultimately reject *Daughters of Eve,* but while the wheeling and dealing was going on, Sophia accepted another movie job, her first with one of the major Hollywood studios in almost thirty-five years. Though the script was still being written, she would team with Jack Lemmon and Walter Matthau in Warner Brothers' sequel to the 1993 comedy hit, *Grumpy Old Men.*

In July, Sophia started work on *Grumpier Old Men,* in which she also joined Ann-Margret from the previous *Grumpy* film. Apart from Sophia's ensemble stint in *Ready to Wear,* it marked the first time in her career that she had to share top billing with another female star. Seven years younger than Sophia, Ann-Margret had been a Hollywood "sex kitten" of the 1960s and later developed into a respected dramatic actress. Now fifty-four to Sophia's near sixty-one, she was an equally well-preserved beauty and would be formidable competition.

In the previous film, Ann-Margret had been courted by the two feuding retirees and ended up marrying the one portrayed by Jack Lemmon. The same scriptwriter, Mark Steven Johnson, created a new character for Sophia named Maria Ragetti, a much-married-and-divorced proprietor of an Italian restaurant that has replaced the bait store where the two avid fishermen always shopped. Furious, the duo try to get Maria's *ristorante* shut down by the health authorities by planting a guinea pig disguised as a gigantic rat in the kitchen. Maria retaliates by dumping a huge pot of marinara sauce over their heads. Amid all the hostilities Maria and Max (played by Walter Matthau) develop a mutual crush and start dating, much to the disapproval of Maria's sourpuss mother. The script was another "first" for Sophia in providing her character with a mamma who played an important role in the story. Ann Guilbert, who filled it, also finds romance with Burgess Meredith, repeating his part as the ninetyish, foul-mouthed and sex-minded Grandpa Gustafson.

Though Sophia had covered a fair share of the United States hyping perfume and eyewear, she never figured on spending two months in Wabasha, Minnesota, the small town of 2,500 population that played itself in the movie.

Given the plot of *Grumpier Old Men,* Sophia had more scenes with Walter Matthau than with Jack Lemmon, two stars who'd also become great pals after nearly thirty years of collaborations that started with Billy Wilder's *The Fortune Cookie* in 1966. On his own, the seventy-five-year-old Matthau had a reputation for being difficult to work with, but Sophia was warned in advance by their mutual friend, Anna Strasberg, and had no problems.

"Sophia made Walter toe the line, and believe me, that's not easy," Jack Lemmon recalled. "She's a great, talented actress, but most of all she's a professional. She adapts very well to the people she's working with."

Lemmon said that "when Walter changed lines and ad-libbed all over the place, Sophia wouldn't act. She'd say, 'What's that? Did we change that? It's okay, I just want to know.' 'No, no, no,' Walter would answer, 'I just wanted to try it.' 'You're not going to do it,' she'd reply. I just loved the way she handled Walter. He could be very naughty."

Director Howard Deutch kept promising Sophia and Matthau a nude love scene, but fortunately he was only joking. "Sophia jumped on me and tried to get into my pants, but that's as far as it went," Matthau remembered. He made Sophia hysterical throughout the filming with help from an assortment of kosher salamis of various dimensions, which kept popping out of his trouser fly when she was least expecting it.

"It was instant sparks, fireworks, between us," Sophia said later. "He's a great man—funny and tender."

One day on the set, Matthau told Sophia, "You know, you're really like a little girl," and she had to agree with him. "It's true," she recalled. "I discover life day by day, and I'm enchanted by things that happen around me. I have a kind of naïveté, and I think it's a pity if you lose that, because when you do, you become bitter, anguished, angry."

Warner Brothers rush-edited *Grumpier Old Men* so it could be released over the Christmas holidays in the United States. Despite generally grumpy reviews, the movie grossed $78 million, which put it ahead of its predecessor. Whether Sophia's addition to the cast made the box-office difference can only be guessed at. But it was the first big winner she'd appeared in since *El Cid* over three decades before.

Not surprisingly, the success of *Grumpier Old Men* set the producers to thinking about a sequel to the sequel, eventually figuring a way to involve Marcello Mastroianni, who accepted instantly just for the chance to work with Sophia again.

That reunion would never take place. While the project was under development, Mastroianni died, at age seventy-two, from pancreatic cancer. He'd kept his illness a secret for years and had been able to continue working in movies and stage plays until the final two months.

He passed away at his home in Paris on December 19, 1996. The next day, Mastroianni's ex-flame Catherine Deneuve and their twenty-four-year-old love child, Chiara, got together with fortyish TV director Anna Maria Tato, his companion for the past two decades, to hold a memorial service at St.-Sulpice Church. Insisting that Mastroianni wasn't religious, Tato wouldn't tolerate a Mass being offered, but she agreed to a demand from Deneuve, a devout Roman Catholic, for a recitation of the church benediction.

Scores of close friends attended, including film stars Gérard Depardieu, Anouk Aimée, and Michel Piccoli, but Sophia Loren was conspicuous by her absence. Press reports cited a longtime rivalry between Sophia and Catherine Deneuve as the reason. A columnist sniped that Sophia wouldn't risk being photographed with the nine-years-younger Deneuve, whose beauty was better preserved and made Sophia look like an old hag by comparison.

But more likely, Sophia stayed away to express her sympathy for Mastroianni's widow, retired actress Flora Carabella, and their forty-four-year-old daughter, Barbara, both of whom were her longtime friends. When Mastroianni's remains were flown to Rome the next day for an official state funeral and burial, Sophia not only attended, but also gave such an emotional performance that she might have been mistaken for the widow herself.

"This is a great grief, like when my mother died," Sophia said after the funeral in Rome. "A chapter in my life has closed. For twenty years, we shared so many films, friendship, life. There was a kind of chemistry between us that could not be compared with anybody else I ever worked with."

Funeral watchers were wondering about the nonattendance of Carlo Ponti, who, besides being Sophia's husband, had employed Marcello Mastroianni more often than any other movie producer and had earned millions from the association. Sophia's escort was her younger son, Edoardo, now nearly twenty-four, and with his slender handsomeness and trendy chin whiskers, not at all the image of his father.

Ponti's frail health and his inability to travel were probably to blame for his absence. Indeed, Ponti, who turned eighty-six just two weeks before Mastroianni's death, hadn't been seen in public for two years. When last sighted in 1994, the perennial shorty had shrunk even more in height, and the sparse hair on his almost bald pate had turned pure white. A studio executive who met him at a film gala in Rome recalls that Ponti's hands trembled and that he seemed a bit dazed and confused, which suggested that he might have Parkinson's disease or some other progressive disorder like Alzheimer's.

The truth sbout Ponti's health is known only to his doctors and his nearest kin, none of whom are talking. But he's reportedly under full-time nursing care at one of several residences that the Pontis own in Switzerland.

Whatever acting jobs she takes in the future, Sophia's legend seems secure. In the autumn of 1996, she made the Time-Life magazine *Entertainment Weekly*'s list of The 100 Greatest Movie Stars of All Time, one of only thirty-seven women in a rather arbitrary selection that tried to be fair to the current generation of stars and had Tom Cruise ahead of Rudolph Valentino and Jodie Foster nosing out Rita Hayworth.

Around the same time, Sophia figured prominently in the Sunday magazine of *The New York Times,* which devoted an entire issue to women who'd had the most impact on the twentieth century. In a full-page black-and-white photograph taken just the month before by Ellen von Unwerth, the recently-turned-sixty-two Sophia looked remarkably youthful, dressed in a very low-cut outfit with a leopard print overjacket and playfully fanning one hand toward the camera like she was trying to hide.

An accompanying prose tribute by feminist author Marjorie Rosen started off with

Forget Venus and Mona Lisa. La Bella Sophia may well be Italy's most breathtaking work of art. First, there's her amazing body—the anatomy of perfect *abbondanza*. Then there's the face—as strong as espresso, and brimming with wondrous contradictions: Neapolitan eyes that flash as much with intelligence as with indignation, too-generous lips that curve as much with humor as with desire.

Rosen observed that whatever the characters Sophia Loren portrayed, she elevated them "by sheer radiance of personality." After recalling some of the "vulgar, silly pictures" that Sophia made abroad for Hollywood studios, Rosen claimed that returning to Italy was her professional salvation:

> Here a string of life-affirming comedies like *Yesterday, Today and Tomorrow* and *Marriage, Italian Style* celebrated her glorious comedic sense and humanity—qualities that help explain her enduring appeal. Even today, at sixty-two, Sophia remains *la forza*—the earth mother of us all.

During the increasingly long breaks between acting assignments, Sophia Loren tends to disappear from public view, but she's rarely idle, dividing her time between Ponti in Switzerland, her sister and nieces in Italy, and especially her two sons, who now live in the United States.

Sophia tries to spend as much time as possible with them at the ranch in Hidden Valley, California, although they often reciprocate with flying visits to Switzerland to see their ailing father. Carlo Jr., who turned twenty-eight in December 1996, was, at the time, studying for a master's degree in music at UCLA, where he was also conductor of the university's orchestra. Carlo aspires to a career in film music similar to that of Vittorio De Sica's son, Manuel, who's regarded as one of Europe's top composers and got his start working on Ponti productions. Though Carlo's *papa* is no longer active, the Ponti–Loren connection will undoubtedly help him to achieve his goals.

Younger brother Edoardo, whose acting career ended in childhood with that one TV movie with his mother, decided to become a director after graduating from USC film school. So far his work has been limited to the stage, where he has directed several plays at regional theaters in the U.S. and at the Spoleto Festival in Italy. Acting a leading role in one of the plays was Edoardo's fiancée, Elizabeth Guber, daughter of one of Hollywood's wealthiest producers. Between them, they should never have to worry about finding "angels" for their productions.

With both sons involved with their own lives now, Sophia also keeps busy with her friend Anna Strasberg, whom she often describes as "my other sister." Although it's not advertised in the prospectus for the Lee Strasberg Theatre Institute, Sophia sometimes gives lectures or does coaching at the school's Los Angeles branch.

Forty years have passed since Sophia became an international star in *The Pride and the Passion*, but her voluptuous figure, huge almond-shaped eyes, and the Neapolitan soul behind them still astonish. Often asked how she stays so beautiful, Sophia claims to have no secret formulas, but recommends getting lots and lots of sleep. In her own case, she has always strived for ten hours. In her younger days, she tried to be in bed by nine. Since turning sixty, she says that she tucks in much earlier, sometimes even in the late afternoon if she's working in a film or has some other stressful activity planned for the next day.

Filming or not, she rises very early every morning, never later than 6:30, revs up on espresso, and does forty minutes of exercise before starting the tasks of the day, which may include gardening or vacuuming the rugs when she stays home. "If I don't keep busy, I have a terrible day, an unbearable guilt complex," she has said.

Sophia stays trim by counting calories, but has never abandoned her daily dish of pasta. "I rarely eat meat, sometimes fish or chicken," she said. "I adore cheese and milk. I don't like alcohol at all. My main meal is lunch because I need time to digest it. You can't sleep soundly with anything heavy on your stomach. It can cause nightmares."

If she continues to take such good care of herself, Sophia Loren should easily make it to the year 2000, which on her personal calendar will mark the fiftieth anniversary of her movie career. Starting out as one of 30,000 extras in *Quo Vadis*, she's had an amazing run that seems far from over.

"When friends remind me that I'm over sixty, I really can't believe it myself," she said not long ago. "I'm really twelve years old—I've *stayed* twelve years old. I am so open to new things, and so open to life. Twelve is the beginning of your adolescence, when you really begin to open your eyes to the world, and I still feel that way. I am so happy for every day and the chance to learn new things. . . . If you're lucky enough to feel like a child, then your life is going to be so much better for you. You can be anything you want to be."

THE FILMS OF
SOPHIA LOREN

*(Year indicates date of production, not release, which often
varies from country to country)*

As Sofia Scicolone, she did background extra or bit parts in *Quo Vadis* (American, MGM), *Cuori sul mare, Il voto, Le sei mogli di Barbablu, Luci del varietà, Toto-Tarzan* and *Io sono il capatz,* all in 1950, and in *Milana miliardaria, Anna, Il mago per forza* and *Il sogno di Zorro,* in 1951.

Under the name of Sofia Lazzaro, she made additional minor appearances in 1951 in *E arrivato l'accordatore, Lebbra bianca* and *Era lui . . . sì sì!*

1. *Africa sotto i mari* (1952) [*Africa Under the Seas,* a.k.a. *Woman of the Red Sea*], her first film under the name of Sophia Loren. Producer: Titanus-Phoenix Film. Director: Giovanni Roccardi. Script: Alessandro di Stefani. Cast: SL, Steve Barclay, Umberto Malnati, Antonio Bardi, Alessandro Fersen. Color, 88 minutes.

2. *La favorita* (1952) [*The Favorite*]. Producer: M.A.S. Film. Director-scriptwriter: Cesare Barlacchi (based on Donizetti's opera). Cast: Gino Sinimberghi, Franca Tamantini, SL, Paolo Silveri. B&W, 76 minutes.

3. *La Tratta della bianche* (1952) [*The White Slave Trade,* aka *Girls Marked Danger*]. Producer: Ponti–De Laurentiis Film. Director: Luigi Comencini. Script: Massimo Patrizi, Ivo Perilli. Cast: Eleanora Rossi Drago, Ettore Manni, Silvana Pampanini, Marc Lawrence, Vittorio Gassman, Enrico Salerno, Tamara Lees, SL, Barbara Florian. B&W, 97 minutes.

4. *Aida* (1953). Producer: Oscar Film. Director: Clemente Fracassi. Script: Adaptation of the opera by Giuseppe Verdi and Antonio Ghizlandoni. Cast: SL (matched with the singing voice of Renata Tebaldi), Lois Maxwell, Luciano Della Marra, Afro Poli, Antonio Cassinelli, Enrico Formichi. Color, 95 minutes.

5. *Carosello Napoletano* (1953) [*Neapolitan Carousel,* aka *Neapolitan Fantasy*]. Producer: Lux Film. Director: Ettore Giannini. Script: Giannini, Giuseppe Marotta, Remigio De Grosso, based on a stage play by Giannini. Cast: Paolo Stoppa, Clelia Matania, Nadia Gray, Leonide Massine, Maria Fiore, Louis Gizzi, SL, Vera Landi, Folco Luilli, the Grand Ballet de Marquis de Cueras, the Ballet Africain de Keita Fodeba, and Joan Baron's French Can-Can Troupe. Color, 124 minutes.

6. *Ci troviamo in galleria* (1953) [*We'll Meet in the Gallery*]. Producer: Athene-Enic Film. Director: Mauro Bolognini. Script: Steno (professional name of Stefano Vanzina), Fede Arnaud, Alessandro Continenza, Lucio Fulci. Cast: Carlo Dapporto, SL, Nilla Pizzi, Gianni Cavalieri, Alberto Sordi, Alberto Talegalli. Color, 90 minutes.

7. *Tempi nostri* (1953) [*Our Times,* aka *Anatomy of Love*]. Producer: Lux/Cines (Rome), Lux du France (Paris). Director: Alessandro Blasetti. Script: Adaptation by Blasetti and Suso Cecchi d'Amico of short stories or sketches by Alberto Moravia, Vasco Paratolini, Giuseppe Marotta, and other noted writers. Cast: Vittorio De Sica, Lea Padovani, Marcello Mastroianni, Toto, SL, Alba Arnova, Eduardo De Filippo, Danielle Delorme, Yves Montand, François Perrier, Dany Robin, Michel Simon, Sylvie. B&W, original six-episode film ran 110 minutes; reduced to five episodes and 92 minutes for belated U.S. release in 1959.

8. *La Domenica della buona genti* (1953) [*Good People's Sunday*]. Producer: Giovanni Adessi. Director: Anton Guilio Majano. Script: Vasco Pratolini, Gian Domenico Ciagni, Massimo Mida. Cast: Maria Fiore, Carlo Romano, SL, Vittorio Sanipoli, Renato Salvatori, Ave Ninchi, Alberto Talegalli. B&W, 99 minutes.

9. *Il paese dei campanelli* (1953) [*The Country of Bells*]. Producer: Luigi De Laurentiis for Valentina Film. Director: Jean Boyer. Script: Adaptation of the popular Italian op- eretta by Lombardo & Ranzato. Cast: Carlo Dapporto, SL, Achille le Togliani, Alda Mangini, Sergio Tofano, Alberto Sorrentino, Billi and Riva, Les Frères Jacques. Color, 100 minutes.

10. *Un giorno in pretura* (1953) [*A Day in Court*]. Producer: Ponti–De Laurentiis Film. Director: Steno. Script: Lucio Fulci, Alberto Sordi, Alessandro Continenza. Cast: Peppino De Filippo, Silvana Pampanini, Alberto Sordi, Tania Weber, Walter Chiari, SL, Leopoldo Trieste, Virgilio Riento. B&W, 92 minutes.

11. *Due notti con Cleopatra* (1953) [*Two Nights with Cleopatra*]. Producer: Excelsa-Rosa Film. Director: Mario Mattoli. Script: Ruggero Maccari. Cast: Alberto Sordi, SL, Ettore Manni, Paul Muller, Alberto Talegalli. Color, 84 minutes.

12. *Pellegrini d' amore* (1953) [*Pilgrims of Love*]. Producer: Tullio Aleardi for Pisorno Film. Director: Andrea Forzano. Cast: SL, Alda Mangini, Enrico Viarisio, Charles Rutherford. B&W, 91 minutes.

13. *Attila, flagello di Dio* (1953) [*Attila, Scourge of God,* aka *Attila the Hun*]. Producer: Giorgio Adriani, for Ponti–De Laurentiis/Lux Film. Director: Pietro Francisci. Script: Ennio de Concini, Primo Zeglo, Ivo Perilli, Frank Gervasi. Cast: Anthony Quinn, SL, Henri Vidal, Irene Papas, Ettore Manni, Claude Laydu, Colette Regis, Eduardo Cianelli. Color, originally 99 minutes, edited to 79 minutes for belated U.S. release in 1958.

14. *Miseria e nobiltà* (1954) [*Poverty and Nobility*]. Producer: Excelsa Film. Director: Mario Mattoli. Script: Mattoli, Ruggero Maccari, based on the play by Eduardo Scarpetta. Cast: Toto, SL, Enzo Turco, Franca Faldini, Dolores Palumbo, Carlo Croccoli, Valeria Moriconi. B&W, 85 minutes.

15. *L'oro di Napoli* (1954) [*Gold of Naples*]. Producer: Ponti–De Laurentiis Film. Director: Vittorio De Sica. Script: De Sica, Cesare Zavattini, Giuseppe Marotta. Cast: De Sica, Silvana Mangano, Toto, SL, Giacomo Furia, Palo Stoppa, Alberto Farnes. B&W, originally

five episodes running 135 minutes, edited to four episodes and 107 minutes for belated U.S. release in 1957.

16. *La donna del fiume* (1954) [*Woman of the River*]. Producer: Basilio Franchina for Ponti–De Laurentiis/Excelsa/Centaur Film. Director: Mario Soldati. Script: Soldati, Franchina, Giorgio Bassani, Per Paolo Passolini, Florestano Vancini, Antonio Altoviti, Ennio Flaiano, Alberto Moravia. Cast: SL, Gerard Oury, Lise Bourdin, Rik Battaglia, Enrico Olivierei. Color, 95 minutes.

17. *Peccato che sia una canaglia* (1954) [*Too Bad She's Bad*]. Producer: Documento Film. Director: Alessandro Blasetti. Script: Alessandro Continenza, Suso Cecchi d'Amico, Ennio Flaiano, based on a story by Alberto Moravia. Cast: Vittorio De Sica, SL, Marcello Mastroianni, Umberto Malmatti, Margherita Bagni, Mario Scaccia, Wanda Benedetti, Mario Passante. B&W, 96 minutes.

18. *Il segno di Venere* (1955) [*The Sign of Venus*]. Producer: Marcello Girosi for Titanus Film. Director: Dino Risi. Script: Luigi Comencini, Franca Valeri, Agenore Incrocci, Ennio Flaiano, Cesare Zavattini, based on a story by Anton Chekhov. Cast: Franca Valeri, Raf Vallone, Vittorio De Sica, Alberto Sordi, SL, Peppino de Filippo, Virgilio Riento, Tina Pica. B&W, 98 minutes.

19. *La bella mugnaia* (1955) [*The Miller's Beautiful Wife*]. Producer: Ponti–De Laurentiis/Titanus Film. Director: Mario Camerini. Script: Camerini, Ennio de Concini, Alessandro Continenza, Ivo Perilli, based on Pedro de Alarcón's play, *The Three-Cornered Hat*. Cast: SL, Vittorio De Sica, Marcello Mastroianni, Paolo Stoppa, Yvonne Sanson, Carletto Sposito, Virgilio Riento. CinemaScope and color, 91 minutes.

20. *Pane, amore e . . .* (1955) [*Bread, Love and . . .*, a.k.a. *Scandal in Sorrento*]. Producer: Marcello Girosi for Titanus/S.G.C. Films. Director: Dino Risi. Script: Ettore Margadonna, Vincenzo Talarico, Risi, Girosi. Cast: Vittorio De Sica, SL, Lea Padovani, Antonio Cifariello, Mario Carotenuto, Joka Berretty, Tina Pica. Color, 85 minutes.

21. *La fortuna di essere donna* (1955) [*Lucky to Be a Woman*]. Producer: Raymond Alexandre for Doumento (Rome)/Le Louvre Films (Paris). Director: Alessandro Blasetti. Script: Suso Cecchi d'Amico, Ennio Flaiano, Alessandro Continenza, Blasetti. Cast: SL, Charles Boyer, Marcello Mastroianni, Nino Bexozzi, Titina De Filippo, Giustino Duran. B&W, 91 minutes.

22. *The Pride and the Passion* (United Artists, 1956). Produced and directed by Stanley Kramer. Script: Edna and Edward Anhalt, based on *The Gun* by C. S. Forester. Cast: Cary Grant, Frank Sinatra, SL, Theodore Bikel, John Wengraf, Jay Novello, Jose Nieto, Philip Van Zandt. VistaVision and color, 130 minutes.

23. *Boy on a Dolphin* (20th Century–Fox, 1956). Producer: Samuel G. Engel. Director: Jean Negulesco. Script: Ivan Moffat, Dwight Taylor, based on the novel by David Divine. Cast: Alan Ladd, Clifton Webb, SL, Alexis Minotis, Jorge Mistral, Laurence Naismith, Gertrude Flynn. CinemaScope and color, 111 minutes.

24. *Legend of the Lost* (United Artists, 1957). Produced and directed by Henry Hathaway for Batjac Productions/Dear Film (Rome), with Robert Haggiag as associate producer. Script: Robert Presnell Jr., Ben Hecht. Cast: John Wayne, SL, Rossano Brazzi, Kurt Kasznar, Ibrahim El Hadish. Technirama and color, 108 minutes.

25. *Desire Under the Elms* (Paramount, 1957). Producer: Don Hartman. Director: Delbert Mann. Script: Irwin Shaw, from the play by Eugene O'Neill. Cast: SL, Anthony Perkins, Burl Ives, Frank Overton, Pernell Roberts, Anne Seymour, Greta Granstedt. VistaVision and B&W, 111 minutes.

26. *Houseboat* (Paramount, 1957). Producers: Melville Shavelson, Jack Rose. Director: Shavelson. Script: Shavelson and Rose, from a story idea by Betsy Drake. Cast: Cary Grant, SL, Martha Hyer, Harry Guardino, Eduardo Ciannelli, Murray Hamilton, Mimi Gibson, Paul Peterson, Charles Herbert. VistaVision and color, 110 minutes.

27. *The Key* (Columbia, 1957). Producer: Aubrey Baring. Director: Carol Reed. Executive producer: Carl Foreman, who also wrote the script, based on the novel *Stella* by Jan de Hartog. Cast: William Holden, SL, Trevor Howard, Oscar Homolka, Kieron Moore, Bernard Lee, Beatrix Lehmann, Bryan Forbes, Irene Handl. CinemaScope and B&W, 134 minutes.

28. *The Black Orchid* (Paramount, 1958). Producers: Carlo Ponti, Marcello Girosi. Director: Martin Ritt. Script: Joseph Stefano. Cast: SL, Anthony Quinn, Ina Balin, Jimmy Baird, Mark Richman, Virginia Stevens, Frank Puglia. VistaVision and B&W, 96 minutes.

29. *That Kind of Woman* (Paramount, 1958). Producers: Carlo Ponti, Marcello Girosi. Director: Sidney Lumet. Script: Walter Bernstein, based on a short story by Robert Lowry. Cast: SL, Tab Hunter, George Sanders, Keenan Wynn, Jack Warden, Barbara Nichols. VistaVision and B&W, 92 minutes.

30. *Heller in Pink Tights* (Paramount, 1959). Producers: Carlo Ponti, Marcello Girosi. Director: George Cukor. Script: Dudley Nichols, Walter Bernstein, based on *Heller with a Gun* by Louis L'Amour. Cast: SL, Anthony Quinn, Steve Forrest, Eileen Heckart, Margaret O'Brien, Edmund Lowe, Ramon Navarro, Frank Cordell. Color, 100 minutes.

31. *A Breath of Scandal* (Paramount, 1959). Producers: Carlo Ponti, Marcello Girosi. Director: Michael Curtiz. Script: Walter Bernstein, based on Sidney Howard's English adaptation of *Olympia,* a play by Ferenc Molnár. Cast: SL, Maurice Chevalier, John Gavin, Angela Lansbury, Isabel Jeans, Frederick Ledebar, Tullio Carminati, Milly Vitale. Color, 98 minutes.

32. *It Started in Naples* (Paramount, 1959). Producers: Melville Shavelson, Jack Rose. Director: Shavelson. Script: Shavelson, Rose, Suso Cecchi D'Amico, from a story idea by Michael Pertwee and Jack Davies. Cast: Clark Gable, SL, Vittorio De Sica, Marietto, Paolo Carlini, Claudio Ermelli, Giovanni Filidoro. VistaVision and color, 100 minutes.

33. *The Millionairess* (20th Century–Fox, 1960). Producers: Dimitri de Grunwald, Pierre

Rouve. Director: Anthony Asquith. Script: Wolf Mankowitz, from Riccardo Aragno's screen adaptation of George Bernard Shaw's stage play. Cast: Peter Sellers, SL, Alastair Sim, Vittorio De Sica, Dennis Price, Gary Raymond, Alfie Bass, Miriam Karlin, Noel Purcell, Diana Coupland, Pauline Jameson, Graham Stark. CinemaScope and color, 90 minutes.

34. *La Ciociara* (1960) [*Two Women*]. Producer: Carlo Ponti (Champion Film, Rome; Les Films Marceau-Cocinor, Paris). Director: Vittorio De Sica. Script: Cesare Zavattini, from the novel by Alberto Moravia. Cast: SL, Eleanora Brown, Raf Vallone, Jean-Paul Belmondo, Renato Salvatori. CinemaScope and B&W, 99 minutes. SL won the 1961 Best Actress Oscar for her performance.

35. *El Cid* (1960). Producers: Samuel Bronston, Robert Haggiag (Dear Film, Rome). Director: Anthony Mann. Script: Philip Yordan, Fredric M. Frank. Cast: Charlton Heston, SL, Raf Vallone, John Fraser, Genevieve Page, Gary Raymond, Herbert Lom, Massimo Serato, Michael Hordern, Hurd Hatfield, Tullio Carminati, Barbara Everest. Super Technirama (70mm) and color, 185 minutes.

36. *Boccaccio '70* (1961). Italian-French coproduction by Carlo Ponti. SL appeared only in the final episode of this three-part anthology by Italy's foremost directors. Preceding SL's were Luchino Visconti's "The Job," featuring Romy Schneider and Thomas Milian, and Federico Fellini's "The Temptation of Dr. Antonio," with Anita Ekberg and Peppino De Filippo. SL's "The Lottery," with Luigi Giuliani and Alfio Vita as coactors, was directed by Vittorio De Sica, from a script by Cesare Zavattini. Color, total running time of 150 minutes.

37. *Madame Sans-Gêne* (1961) [a.k.a. *Madame* in dubbed English version]. Italian-French-Spanish coproduction by Carlo Ponti, with Maleno Malenotti as associate. Director: Christian-Jacque. Script: Henri Jeanson, Ennio de Concini, Jean Ferry, Franco Salinas, Christian-Jacque, based on the play by Victorien Sardou and Emile Moreau. Cast: SL, Robert Hossein, Julien Bertheau, Marina Berti, Carlo Giuffre, Gabriella Pallota, Amalia Gade. Technirama and color, 104 minutes.

38. *Five Miles to Midnight* (1961) [aka *Le couteau dans la plaie*]. American-French-Italian coproduction between United Artists, Filmsonor (Paris), Dear Film (Rome). Producer/director: Anatole Litvak. Script: Peter Viertel, Hugh Wheeler, from a story idea by André Versini. Cast: SL, Anthony Perkins, Gig Young, Jean-Pierre Aumont, Yolande Turner, Tommy Norden, Mathilde Casdesus, with Régine and Guy Laroche as themselves. B&W, 110 minutes.

39. *The Condemned of Altona* (20th Century–Fox, 1962). American-Italian-French coproduction by Carlo Ponti. Director: Vittorio De Sica. Script: Abby Mann, from the play by Jean-Paul Sartre. Cast: SL, Maximilian Schell, Fredric March, Robert Wagner, Françoise Prévost, Alfredo Franchi, Lucia Pelella. CinemaScope and B&W, 113 minutes.

40. *Ieri, oggi e domani* (1962) [*Yesterday, Today and Tomorrow*]. Producers: Carlo Ponti, Joseph E. Levine. Director: Vittorio De Sica. Scripts for the three episodes:

"Adelina/Naples," by Eduardo De Filippo, Isabelle Quanantotti; "Anna/Milan," Cesare Zavattini, Billa Billa, from a story by Alberto Moravia; "Mara/Rome," Cesare Zavattini. Cast: SL, Marcello Mastroianni, Aldo Giuffre, Agostino Salvetti, Armando Trovajoli, Giovanni Ridolfi, Tina Pica, Gennaro di Gregorio. Techniscope and color, 119 minutes. Winner of the 1964 Oscar for Best Foreign Film.

41. *The Fall of the Roman Empire* (1963). Producer: Samuel Bronston, in association with Paramount Pictures, the Rank Organisation, and Roma Film. Director: Anthony Mann. Script: Philip Yordan, Ben Barzman, Basilio Franchina, freely adapted from the writings of historian Edward Gibbon. Cast: SL, Alec Guinness, Stephen Boyd, James Mason, Christopher Plummer, Anthony Quayle, Omar Sharif, John Ireland, Mel Ferrer, Eric Porter, Finlay Currie. Ultra-Panavision (70mm) and color, 187 minutes.

42. *Matrimonio all'italiana* (1964) [*Marriage, Italian Style*]. Producers: Carlo Ponti, Joseph E. Levine. Director: Vittorio De Sica. Script: Eduardo De Filippo, Renato Castellani, Antonio Guerra, Leo Benvenuto, Pier de Barnardi, based on De Filippo's play, *Filumena marturano*. Cast: SL, Marcello Mastroianni, Aldo Puglisi, Tecla Scarano, Marilu Tolo, Giovanni Ridolfi, Vito Moriconi, Generoso Cortini. Color, 102 minutes.

43. *Operation Crossbow* (MGM, 1964). Producer: Carlo Ponti. Director: Michael Anderson. Script: Richard Imrie, Derry Quinn, Ray Rigby, from a story idea by Duilio Coletti and Vittoriano Pettrilli. Cast: SL, George Peppard, Tom Courtenay, Jeremy Kemp, Trevor Howard, John Mills, Richard Johnson, Lilli Palmer, Paul Henreid, Richard Todd, Helmut Dantine, Sylvia Syms, Patrick Wymark, Maurice Denham, Richard Wattis. Panavision and color, 116 minutes.

44. *Judith* (Paramount, 1964). Producer: Kurt Unger. Director: Daniel Mann. Script: John Michael Hayes, from a story by Lawrence Durrell. Cast: SL, Peter Finch, Jack Hawkins, Hans Verner, Zahrira Charifai, Shraga Friedman, Terence Alexander, Zipora Peled, André Morell, Peter Burton. Panavision and color, 109 minutes.

45. *Lady L* (MGM, 1965). Producer: Carlo Ponti. Directed and scripted by Peter Ustinov, from the novel by Romain Gary. Cast: SL, Paul Newman, David Niven, Claude Dauphin, Philippe Noiret, Michel Piccoli, Marcel Dalio, Cecil Parker, Jean Weiner, Tanya Lopert, Catherine Allegret, and with Ustinov in a cameo appearance. Panavision and color, 124 minutes.

46. *Arabesque* (Universal, 1965). Produced and directed by Stanley Donen. Script: Julian Mitchell, Stanley Price, Pierre Martin, based on the novel *The Cipher* by Gordon Cotler. Cast: Gregory Peck, SL, Alan Badel, Kieron Moore, Carl Duering, John Merivale, Duncan Lamont, George Coulouris. Panavision and color, 105 minutes.

47. *A Countess from Hong Kong* (Universal, 1966). Producer: Jerome Epstein. Directed and scripted by Charles Chaplin. Cast: Marlon Brando, SL, Sydney Chaplin, Tippi Hedren, Patrick Cargill, Margaret Rutherford, Angela Scoular, Dilys Laye, Bill Nagy, and with Chaplin in a cameo appearance. Color, originally 120 minutes at British premiere, later cut to 107 for the American release.

48. *C'era una volta* (1966) [literally, "Once upon a time there was . . . ," but titled *Happily Ever After, More Than a Miracle,* and finally *Cinderella, Italian Style* in the English-speaking world]. An Italian-French coproduction by Carlo Ponti for MGM release. Director: Francesco Rosi. Script: Tonino Guerra, Raffaele La Capria, Giuseppe Patroni Griffi, Rosi. Cast: SL, Omar Sharif, Dolores Del Rio, Georges Wilson, Leslie French, Marina Malfatti, Anna Nogara, Rita Forzano, Rosemary Martin, Carlotta Barilli. Color, 103 minutes.

49. *Questi fantasmi* (1967) [literally "those ghosts," but titled in English as *Ghosts, Italian Style*]. An Italian-French coproduction by Carlo Ponti for MGM release. Director: Renato Castellani. Script: Castellani, Adriano Barracco, Leo Benvenuti, Piero de Bernardi, from the play by Eduardo De Filippo. Cast: SL, Vittorio Gassman, Mario Adorf, Margaret Lee, Aldo Giuffre, Francesco Tensi, with a cameo appearance by Marcello Mastroianni.

50. *I girasoli* (1969) [*Sunflower*]. An Italian-French coproduction by Carlo Ponti, in association with Joseph E. Levine and Arthur Cohn. Director: Vittorio De Sica. Script: Antonio Guerra, Cesare Zavattini, Gheorghij Mdivani. Cast: SL, Marcello Mastroianni, Ludmila Savelyeva, Anna Carena, Germano Longo, Galina Andreeva, Nadia Cerednichenko, Marisa Traversi, with a cradle appearance by Carlo Ponti Jr. Color, 107 minutes.

51. *La moglie del prete* (1970) [*The Priest's Wife*]. An Italian-French coproduction by Carlo Ponti for Warner Brothers release. Director: Dino Risi. Script: Ruggero Maccari, Bernardino Zapponi, from a story developed by them and Risi. Cast: SL, Marcello Mastroianni, Venantino Venantini, Jacques Stany, Pippo Starnazza, Augusto Mastrantoni, Miranda Campa, Giuseppe Maffioli. Color, 103 minutes.

52. *La mortadella* (1971) [literally "the salted pork sausage," but titled in English *Lady Liberty*]. An Italian-French coproduction by Carlo Ponti, in association with Warner Brothers and United Artists. Director: Mario Monicelli. Script: Suso Cecchi d'Amico, Leonard Melfi, Don Carlos Dunaway. Cast: SL, Luigi Proietti, William Devane, Beeson Carroll, Bill Deprato, Danny DeVito, David Doyle, Charles Bartlett, Sally DeMay, Edward Herrmann, Susan Sarandon, Dutch Miller, K. Callan, Candy Darling. Color, 95 minutes.

53. *Bianco, rosso e . . .* (1971) [literally, wordplay on the colors of the Italian flag, but titled in English *White Sister*]. An Italian-French-Spanish coproduction by Carlo Ponti, in association with Warner Brothers and Columbia Pictures. Director: Alberto Lattuada. Script: Lattuada, Iaia Fiastri, Tonino Guerra, Ruggerio Maccari, from a story idea by Guerra and Maccari. Cast: SL, Adriano Celentano, Fernando Rey, Juan Luis Galiardo, Luis Marin, Giuseppe Maffioli, Pilar Gomez Ferrer, Teresa Rabal, Tina Aumont, and with niece Alessandra Mussolini portraying SL as a child. Color, 96 minutes.

54. *Man of La Mancha* (United Artists, 1972). Produced and directed by Arthur Hiller. Executive producer: Alberto Grimaldi. Script: Dale Wasserman, based on his play and the *Don Quixote* of Miguel de Cervantes Saavedra. Songs: Mitch Leigh, composer; Joe Darion, lyricist. Cast: Peter O'Toole (singing voice dubbed by Simon Gilbert), SL, James Coco, Harry Andrews, John Castle, Brian Blessed, Ian Richardson, Julie Gregg, Rosalie Crutchley, Gino Conforti. Color, 132 minutes.

55. *The Voyage* (United Artists, 1973). Producer: Carlo Ponti. Executive producer: Turi Vasile. Director: Vittorio De Sica (his last film). Script: Diego Fabbri, Massimo Franciosa, Luisa Montagnana, based on a novel by Luigi Pirandello. Cast: SL, Richard Burton, Ian Bannen, Barbara Pilavin, Annabella Incontrera, Paolo Lena, Renato Pinciroli, Ettore Geri, Olga Romanelli. Color, 95 minutes.

56. *Le Testament* (1974) (literally, "The last will and testament," but titled for the English-speaking world as *The Verdict* and later changed to *Jury of One* for the dubbed version). A French-Italian coproduction by Carlo Ponti. Director: André Cayatte. Script: Cayatte, Henri Coupon, Pierre Dumayet, Paul Andreota. Cast: SL, Jean Gabin, Henri Garcin, Julien Bertheau, Michel Albertini, Gisele Casadessus, Muriel Catala, Jean-Francois Remi, Mario Pilar. Color, 97 minutes.

57. *Brief Encounter* (1974). SL's first television movie, produced for the *Hallmark Hall of Fame* and initially broadcast in the United States by NBC on November 12, 1974. Director: Alan Bridges. Script: John Bowen, adapted from Noel Coward's screenplay for David Lean's 1944 *Brief Encounter,* which in turn was based on Coward's 1935 one-act play *Still Life.* Cast: SL, Richard Burton, Ann Firbank, Jack Hedley. Color, 90 minutes.

58. *La pupa del gangster* (1974) [literally, "gangster's moll," but titled in English *Poopsie,* SL's nickname in the film; a.k.a. *Poopsie & Company* and *Oopsie, Poopsie!* Producer: Carlo Ponti. Director: Giorgio Capitani. Script: Ernesto Gastaldi. Cast: SL, Marcello Mastroianni, Aldo Maccione, Pierre Brice, Dalila di Lazzaro. Color, 91 minutes.

59. *Una giornata particolare* (1975) [*A Special Day*]. An Italian-Canadian coproduction by Carlo Ponti. Director: Ettore Scola. Script: Scola, Ruggero Maccari, Maurizio Costanzo. Cast: SL, Marcello Mastroianni, John Vernon, Francoise Berd, Nicole Magny, Patrizia Basso, Tiziano De Persio, Alessandra Mussolini. Color, 110 minutes.

60. *The Cassandra Crossing* (1976). Producer: Carlo Ponti, in association with Sir Lew Grade. Director: George Pan Cosmatos. Script: Cosmatos, Robert Katz, Tom Mankiewicz. Cast: SL, Richard Harris, Ava Gardner, Burt Lancaster, Martin Sheen, Ingrid Thulin, Lee Strasberg, O. J. Simpson, Lionel Stander, Alida Valli, John Philip Law, Ann Turkel, Lou Castell. Panavision and color, 125 minutes.

61. *Angela* (1977). Italian-Canadian coproduction by Carlo Ponti, in association with Zev Braun, Julian Melzak, Claude Heroux. Director: Boris Sagal. Script: Charles Israel. Cast: SL, John Vernon, Steve Railsback, John Huston, Michelle Rossignol, Luce Guilbault. Color, 91 minutes.

62. *Brass Target* (United Artists, 1978). Producer: Arthur Lewis. Executive Producer: Berle Adams. Director: John Hough. Script: Alvin Boretz, based on the novel *The Algonquin Project* by Frederick Nolan. Cast: SL, John Cassavetes, George Kennedy, Max von Sydow, Robert Vaughn, Patrick McGoohan, Bruce Davison, Edward Herrmann, Lee Montague. Panavision and color, 111 minutes.

63. *Firepower* (1978). Executive Producer: Sir Lew Grade, for Associated Film

Distribution. Producer-director: Michael Winner. Script: Gerald Wilson, from a story idea by Winner and Bill Kerby. Cast: SL, James Coburn, O. J. Simpson, Eli Wallach, Anthony Franciosa, Vincent Gardenia, George Grizzard, Victor Mature, Jake La Motta, Paula Laurence. Color, 104 minutes.

64. *Fatto di sangue fra due uomini per causa di una vedova* (1978) [literally, "bloodshed between two men over a widow," but titled in English *Blood Feud* and later *Revenge* in a dubbed version]. Written, produced, and directed by Lina Wertmuller for Warner Brothers (which later rejected it for release and sold the rights to Associated Film Distribution). Cast: SL, Marcello Mastroianni, Giancarlo Giannini, Turi Ferro. Color, 112 minutes.

65. *Sophia Loren: Her Own Story* (1980). Executive producers: Roger Gimbel and Peter Katz, for EMI-Television. Producer: Alex Ponti. Director: Mel Stuart. Script: Basilio Franchina, Mark Princi, from a first draft by Joanna Crawford. Cast: SL (in double role as herself and Romilda Villani), Rip Torn, John Gavin, Armand Assante, Edmund Purdom, Ritza Brown, Theresa Saldana. Color, approximately 125 minutes (premiere broadcast by NBC-TV in a three-hour time slot on October 28, 1980).

66. *Aurora* (1984) [retitled *Qualcosa di biondo* for Italy]. Executive producer: Tony Converse, for Roger Gimbel Productions. Producer: Alex Ponti. Director: Maurizio Ponzi. Script: Ponzi, John McGreevey, Franco Ferrini, Gianni Mennon. Cast: SL, Daniel J. Travanti, Edoardo Ponti, Angela Goodwin, Philippe Noiret, Ricky Tognazzi, Alessandra Mussolini, Anna Strasberg, David Cameron, Franco Fabrizi. Color, approximately 90 minutes (premiere showing in a two-hour NBC-TV *Monday Night at the Movies* time slot on October 22, 1984).

67. *Courage* (1986) [retitled *Madre coraggio* for Italy]. Producer: Joel B. Michaels, for Highgate Pictures & New World TV. Director: Jeremy Kagan. Script: E. Jack Neuman, based on a magazine article by Michael Daly. Cast: SL, Billy Dee Williams, Hector Elizondo, Val Avery, Ron Rifkin, José Perez, Mary McDonnell, Dan Hedaya, Corey Parker, Richard Portnow. Color, approximately 140 minutes (first broadcast by CBS-TV in a three-hour *Movie Special* time slot on September 24, 1986).

68. *Mario Puzo's The Fortunate Pilgrim* (1987) [retitled *Mamma Lucia* for Italy]. Executive producer: Carlo Ponti, in association with Reteitalia. Producer: Alex Ponti. Coproducers: Norman Brooks, Fern Field. Director: Stuart Cooper. Script: John McGreevey, from the novel by Puzo. Cast: SL, Edward James Olmos, John Turturro, Hal Holbrook, Annabella Sciorra, Ron Marquette, Harold Pruett, Andreina Lairet, Anna Strasberg, Shane Rimmer. Color, approximately 210 minutes (premiere broadcast by NBC-TV in a five-hour time slot spread over two nights in April 1988).

69. *La Ciociara* (1989) [remake of *Two Women,* but this time titled in English *Running Away*]. Producers: Carlo and Alex Ponti, in association with Reteitalia/Silvio Berlusconi Communications. Director: Dino Risi. Script: Risi, Bernardino Zapponi, Lidia Ravera, based on the novel by Alberto Moravia. Cast: SL, Sydney Penny, Frank Loggia, Andrea

Occhipinti, Carla Calo. Color, 101 minutes. [SL made history as the first Oscar winner to ever repeat that performance in a remake. Outside Italy, the TV movie's only exposure has been in the home video market, with dubbed English dialogue written by Diana Gould.]

70. *Sabato, domenica e lunedì* (1990) [*Saturday, Sunday and Monday*]. Producers: Carlo and Alex Ponti, in association with Reteitalia/Silvio Berlusconi Communications. Director: Lina Wertmuller. Script: Wertmuller, Raffaele La Capria, based on the play by Eduardo De Filippo. Cast: SL, Luca De Filippo, Luciano De Crescenzo, Alessandra Mussolini, Pier Luigi Como, Jerome Anger, Enzo Cannavale, Isa Danieli, Mario Scarpetta, Pupella Maggio. Color, originally 200 minutes for two-night premiere broadcast in Italy in November 1990, but edited to 100 minutes for Italian TV syndication and home video (no U.S. release in any form).

71. *Ready to Wear* (Miramax, 1994) [*Pret-à-porter*]. Executive producers: Bob and Harvey Weinstein, Ian Jessel. Producer-director: Robert Altman. Script: Altman, Barbara Shulgasser. Ensemble cast included (alphabetically): Danny Aiello, Anouk Aimée, Lauren Bacall, Kim Basinger, Jean-Pierre Cassel, Richard E. Grant, Linda Hunt, Sally Kellerman, Ute Lemper, SL, Lyle Lovett, Marcello Mastroianni, Stephen Rea, Tim Robbins, Julia Roberts, Tracey Ullman, Forest Whitaker. Color, 132 minutes.

72. *Grumpier Old Men* (Warner Brothers, 1995). Producers: John Davis, Richard C. Berman, in association with George Folsey Jr., John J. Smith. Director: Howard Deutch. Script: Mark Steven Johnson (sequel to his 1993 *Grumpy Old Men*). Cast: Walter Matthau, Jack Lemmon, Ann-Margret, SL, Burgess Meredith, Daryl Hannah, Kevin Pollak, Ann Guilbert, Katie Sagona, James Andelin, Marcus Klemp. Color, 105 minutes.

Some, but far from many, of Sophia Loren's English-language films have been released on video cassette and/or laser disc. Most of her Italian films have not, except for *Two Women* and several of the Mastroianni collaborations. Check stores or mail-order catalogs for current availability.

A unique collectible is the audio compact disc *Sophia Loren: Greatest Hits,* released in Europe in 1995 on the ViViMusica label and distributed in the United States by Qualiton Imports. The thirty-track collection consists of film score themes and fifteen vocal performances, including SL's best-selling "Goodness Gracious Me" duet with Peter Sellers.

BIBLIOGRAPHY

Barzini, Luigi. *From Caesar to the Mafia: Sketches of Italian Life*. London: Hamish Hamilton, 1971.

Basinger, Jeanine. *Anthony Mann*. Boston: Twayne Publishers, 1979.

Battelle, Phyllis. "Sophia Loren: Elegant and Enduring." *Ladies' Home Journal*, July 1984.

Baxter, John. *Fellini*. London: Fourth Estate, Ltd., 1993.

Beauchamp, Cari, and Henri Behar. *Hollywood on the Riviera: the Inside Story of the Cannes Film Festival*. New York: William Morrow, 1992.

Bondanella, Peter. *Italian Cinema: From Neorealism to the Present*, 2nd ed. New York: Continuum, 1990.

Bragg, Melvyn. *Richard Burton: A Life*. Waltham, Mass.: Little, Brown, 1988.

Brownlow, Kevin. *David Lean*. London: Richard Cohen Books, 1996.

Burton, Richard. "My Friend Sophia." *Ladies' Home Journal*, March 1974.

Buss, Robin. *Italian Films*. New York: Holmes & Meier Publishers, 1989.

Canales, Luis. *Imperial Gina*. Boston: Branden Publishing Company, 1990.

Chatman, Seymour. *Antonioni; or, The Surface of the World*. Berkeley and Los Angeles: University of California Press, 1985.

Collier, Richard. *Duce!: The Rise and Fall of Benito Mussolini*. London: Collins, 1971.

Collins, Nancy. "Sophia: The Immaculate Siren." *Vanity Fair,* January 1991.

Crawley, Tony. *The Films of Sophia Loren*. London: LSP Books, 1974.

Cunningham, Frank R. *Sidney Lumet: Film and Literary Vision*. Lexington: University Press of Kentucky, 1991.

De Santi, Pier Marco, and Rossano Vittori. *I film di Ettore Scola*. Rome: Gremese, 1987.

De Sica, Vittorio. *Lettere dal Set: A cura di Emi De Sica e Gioncarlo Governi*. Milan: SugarCo Edizioni, 1987.

De Sica, Vittorio. "De Sica on Sophia Loren." *Vogue*, November 1962.

Dewey, Donald. *Marcello Mastroianni: His Life and Art*. New York: Birch Lane Press, 1993.

Douglas, Kirk. *The Ragman's Son*. New York: Simon & Schuster, 1988.

Dundy, Elaine. *Finch, Bloody Finch: A Biography of Peter Finch*. London: Michael Joseph, 1980.

Eells, George. *Final Gig: The Man Behind the Murder*. New York: Harcourt Brace Jovanovich, 1991.

Epstein, Jerry. *Remembering Charlie: The Story of a Friendship*. London: Bloomsbury Publishing, 1988.

Forman, Milos, and Jan Novak. *Turnaround: A Memoir*. New York: Villard Books, 1994.

Giammusso, Maurizio. *Vita di Eduardo*. Milan: Arnoldo Mondadori Editore, 1993.

Gilbert, Sari. "To Mama with Love." *TV Guide*, October 18, 1980.

Governi, Gioncarlo. *Vittorio De Sica: Parlami d'amore Mariù*. Rome: Gremese Editore, 1993.

Guinness, Alec. *Blessings in Disguise*. New York: Alfred A. Knopf, 1986.

Hackett, Pat (ed.). *The Andy Warhol Diaries*. New York: Warner Books, 1989.

Head, Edith, and Jane Kesner Ardmore. *The Dress Doctor*. Boston: Little, Brown, 1959.

Heston, Charlton. *In the Arena: An Autobiography*. New York: Simon & Schuster, 1995.

Hamblin, Dora Jane. "Carlo & Sophia." *Life*, September 18, 1964.

Hamill, Pete. "Sophia Loren: First I Am a Woman." *Saturday Evening Post*, February 15, 1964.

Hershey, Lenore. "Sophia: Serenely Female." *Ladies' Home Journal*, January 1971.

Hibbert, Christopher. *Benito Mussolini: A Biography*. London: Longmans, 1962.

Hotchner, A. E. *Sophia: Living and Loving (Her Own Story)*. New York: William Morrow, 1979.

Kael, Pauline. *When the Lights Go Down*. New York: Holt, Rinehart and Winston, 1980.

Kaufman, Hank, and Gene Lerner. *Hollywood sul Tevere*. Milan: Sperling & Kupfer, 1982.

Kirby, Heather. "Sophia Loren at Sixty." *Good Housekeeping*, August 1994.

Krantz, Judith. "Joseph E. Levine: Hercules on Sutton Place." *McCall's*, November 1964.

Lanocita, Arturo. *Sofia Loren*. Milan: Longanesi & C., 1966.

Lewis, Norman. *Naples '44*. London: Collins, 1978.

Levy, Alan. *Forever, Sophia: An Intimate Portrait*, rev. ed. New York: St. Martin's Press, 1986.

Liem, Mira. *Passion and Defiance: Film in Italy from 1942 to the Present*. Berkeley and Los Angeles: University of California Press, 1984.

Linet, Beverly. *Ladd: The Life, the Legend, the Legacy of Alan Ladd*. New York: Arbor House, 1979.

Loren, Sophia. *In the Kitchen with Love*. Garden City, N.Y.: Doubleday, 1972.

Loren, Sophia. *Women & Beauty*. New York: William Morrow, 1984.

Loren, Sophia. "Reflections on Turning Sixty." *Hello!*, September 17, 1994.

Lyttle, Richard B. *Il Duce: The Rise and Fall of Benito Mussolini*. New York: Atheneum, 1987.

McGilligan, Patrick. *George Cukor: A Double Life*. New York: St. Martin's Press, 1991.

Mercader, Maria. *La mia vita con Vittorio De Sica*. Milan: Arnoldo Mondadori Editore, 1978.

Minney, R. J. *The Films of Anthony Asquith*. South Brunswick and New York: A. S. Barnes, 1976.

Moravia, Alberto. "This Is Your Life, Sophia Loren." *Show*, September 1962.

Moscati, Italo. *Sophia Loren*. Venice: Marsilio Editori, 1994.

Mussolini, Rachele, with Albert Zarca. *Mussolini: An Intimate Biography by His Widow*. New York: William Morrow, 1974.

Negulesco, Jean. *"Things I Did . . . and Things I Think I Did."* New York: Linden Press/Simon & Schuster, 1984.

Powell, Michael. *Million-Dollar Movie*. London: Heinemann, 1992.

Reed, Rex. "Sophia Loren." *Ladies' Home Journal,* April 1976.

Ross, Lillian, and Helen Ross. *The Player: A Profile of an Art*. New York: Simon & Schuster, 1962.

Seligson, Tom. "Sophia Loren Has a Secret." *Parade,* January 18, 1987.

Sellers, Michael. *P.S. I Love You: Peter Sellers 1925–1980*. London: Collins, 1985.

Shenker, Israel. "The Name Is Ponti, Not Mr. Loren." *The New York Times Sunday Magazine,* June 6, 1965.

Stark, Graham. *Remembering Peter Sellers*. London: Robson Books, 1990.

Stern, Michael. "Carlo Ponti's Work of Art." *Cosmopolitan,* November 1962.

Thomas, Bob. *Golden Boy: The Untold Story of William Holden*. New York: St. Martin's Press, 1983.

Turner, Jim. "Sophia's Choice," *Detour,* December 1994.

Wayne, Pilar, with Alex Thorleifson. *John Wayne: My Life with the Duke*. New York: McGraw-Hill, 1987.

Wapshott, Nicholas. *Carol Reed: A Biography*. New York: Alfred A. Knopf, 1994.

Whitcomb, Jon. "Sophia Loren in America." *Cosmopolitan,* February 1958.

Wiley, Mason, and Damien Bona. *Inside Oscar: The Unofficial History of the Academy Awards,* 4th updated ed. New York: Ballantine Books, 1993.

Winecoff, Charles. *Split Image: The Life of Anthony Perkins*. New York: Dutton, 1996.

Zavattini, Cesare. *Diario Cinematografico,* ed. Valentina Fortichiatri. Milan: Bompiani, 1979.

Zec, Donald. *Sophia: An Intimate Biography*. London: W. H. Allen, 1975.

ACKNOWLEDGMENTS

I am extremely grateful to all the people on both sides of the Atlantic who kindly shared memories and information with me. Listed alphabetically, they include: Robert Altman, Walter Bernstein, Laura Betti, Gloria Carbone, the late Richard Condon, William Devane, Stanley Donen, Eugenio Fata, Marc Ferrara, Norman Flicker, Anthony Franciosa, Joseph Friedman, Massimo Graziosi, Melanie Griffith, Vito Grillo, Henry Gris, Georgina Hale, Mike Hall, Richard Harris, Tippi Hedren, Arthur Hiller, Hy Hollinger, Vittorio Gassman, Robert Hossein, Tab Hunter, Stanley Kramer, Meryl Lauria, the late Rosalie (Mrs. Joseph E.) Levine, Delbert Mann, Chiara Mastroianni, JP Miller, Paul Morrissey, Peter O'Toole, Silvana Pampanini, Anthony Quinn, Martha Rinaldi, Pietro Sasso, Dino Satriani, Ettore Scola, Omar Sharif, Melville Shavelson, Hy Smith, Vicky Tiel, Kurt Unger, John Turturro, Peter Ustinov, Alida Valli, John Vernon, Eli Wallach, Martha Hyer Wallis, Lina Wertmuller, Billy Dee Williams, Shelley Winters, the late Florence Wulach, Franco Zeffirelli. Numerous other friends and professional associates of Sophia Loren and Carlo Ponti also participated, but requested anonymity.

My thanks also go to the staffs of the following research centers for their splendid assistance: the Performing Arts Library at Lincoln Center, New York; the Celeste Bartos International Film Study Center at the Museum of Modern Art, New York; the Italian Cultural Institute, New York; the British Film Institute Library, London; the Cineteca Nazionale of the Centro Sperimentale di Cinematografia, Rome. Paolo Paggetta was of tremendous help in Italy. My multilingual friends Nen Roeterdink, Vladimir Drouz, James Kirkup, and Edith Martorana did the translations of source materials from Europe and Japan.

A special note of gratitude to editor Bob Bender and his assistant, Johanna Li, as well as to Dan Strone, my longtime agent and friend. Last but not least, heartfelt thanks to my family for their moral support: Stella and Russ, Lisa and Brian (and now Kyle!), Marilyn and Phil, and Aunt Ruth and Uncle Steve. And a closing remembrance of some who left an indelible impression on my life: Mildred Bailey, June Christy, Barry Conley, Ella Fitzgerald, Zarah Leander, Barry McGoffin, Jack Nilsson, Evelyn Seeff, Timothy Swallow, Lee Wiley.

INDEX